Yale Studies in English

Benjamin Christie Nangle, Editor

Volume 148

JOHN DAVIDSON
Pastel portrait by Sir William Rothenstein, 1894

JOHN DAVIDSON
Poet of Armageddon

by J. BENJAMIN TOWNSEND

New Haven: Yale University Press, 1961

Published with aid from the foundation
established in memory of Philip Hamilton McMillan
of the class of 1894, Yale College

FOR

WILLIAM CLYDE DE VANE

So, take and use thy work:
Amend what flaws may lurk,
What strain o' the stuff, what warpings
    past the aim!
My times be in thy hand!
Perfect the cup as planned!
Let age approve of youth, and death
    complete the same!

PREFACE

One evening in 1947 listeners to a BBC program called "A Personal Anthology" heard a genteel, modulated voice announce, "Here is a poem . . . which probably very few of you know. John Davidson was a Scottish poet, of the London nineties, who had genius but the incapacity for perfection. This poem is, I think, his one great achievement, and I know nothing quite like it." The voice, which proceeded to read the poem "Thirty Bob a Week," was that of T. S. Eliot. A no less circumspect spokesman for an earlier generation, the late Sir Max Beerbohm, made a similar comment not long afterward. In a review of Martin Secker's anthology, *The Eighteen-Nineties,* Sir Max wrote in the *Observer* for October 3, 1948: "I venture to complain that there should have been much more than there is of John Davidson, who had what I think the other poets had not: genius (and very robust genius)." Genius is a term applied generously by many, but not by these two masters of understatement. If one accepts Herbert Read's definition of genius as "the capacity to focus diversity—the ability to draw into a single burning point of light the discoveries and inventions of a whole generation," no other word describes so aptly the achievement of John Davidson. His genius is not the less because it is focused more distinctly in his personality and in what he stood for than in his art.

There are some writers whose work to be fully appreciated must be read in its entirety. Eliot has said that Poe is such a writer and Allen Tate has seconded him; Davidson is another. This is no more than to say that the personality of some writers is too insistent, protean, or complex to be contained in any one work, that it can be known in all its multiplicity only from studying their entire output. Since his most dedicated follower would not ask this service for Davidson, it is all the more important to have a book about him, now that his place in modern literature can be properly assessed. More than any other figure of his day, he is, to borrow a vintage paradox, uniquely representative.

Although he thought of himself as for all time, no man was ever more of and for his own time than this renegade from Scottish evangelicalism and Victorian compromise. Any study that begins as a portrait of him must end as a portrait of his generation. An aeolian harp—he would have preferred the image of a seismograph—he recorded the shocks and strains that had shaken the guardians of the older order as well as the lesser tremors felt by his con temporaries. An activist like Henley and Stevenson, a pro fessed imperialist like Kipling, for a time an impressionist like Wilde, Symons, Le Gallienne, and other "Rhymers," a social realist like Moore and Gissing, a mystic and sym bolist like Lionel Johnson, Hopkins, and Yeats, Davidson bridged all these movements and yet emerged with a philosophy and style that are his own. Others reflected in dividual fashions more faithfully and achieved a greater discipline of style, but not one, unless it was Yeats, had the consciousness and ambition of this poet's aim: to har monize into something new, satisfying, and permanent the discoveries and aspirations of his age, to reconcile the facts of science and the faith of poetry, to create, as he said, "a new habitation for the imagination of man." We judge him finally by his achievement, but we identify him by his aim.

All periods get stamped in the popular imagination by the character of their most vital, outspoken, or colorful element. Perhaps no period has been more sinned against in this respect than the nineties. With something between worldly indulgence and Philistine disapproval, we speak of the years which closed the last century as "the naughty nineties," "the gay nineties," "the mauve decade," "the *fin de siècle.*" These labels are not merely careless or convenient usage, for we mean to recall the decorative eroticism of Beardsley's drawings, the weekly meetings of a group of self-conscious, exquisite young poets at the Cheshire Cheese, the *succès de scandale of* the *Yellow Book,* and the still larger success and scandal of Oscar Wilde. We mean to recall in short the decadence, preciousness, and extravagance parodied by W. S. Gilbert in *Patience,* Owen Seaman in *The Battle of the Bays,* Robert Hichens in *The Green Carnation,* G. S. Street in *The Autobiography of a Boy,* Max Beerbohm in *Zuleika Dobson,* and John Davidson in *Earl Lavender.* This impression, originating with the *outré,* self-publicized conduct of the decadents and perpetuated by liberally edited memoirs and surveys, constitutes an abuse of the figure: It is mistaking a part for the whole.

Recent biographies and studies of the period have done much to set the record straight. Another might be unnecessary if its subject were not supremely useful. Briefly drawn to the modern Babylon of the feverish sons of Pater, Davidson like Yeats broke away to seek a larger solution, a synthesis that would embrace not only the age-end spirit but the universe. Personal rather than poetic, his synthesis can be understood only in the light of his temperament and life. Hence the biographical framework of this investigation of his thought and its place in the history of the period. Not to know John Davidson or, knowing, to dis-

miss him as an obscure eccentric, a minor poet, an ineffectual Nietzsche, is to throw away a master key: He
opens doors upon his time that others passed by.

Indispensable as he is to an understanding of the turn
of the century with its complex modern sensibilities—
middle-class in origin, aristocratic in pretension; eclectic
and subjective; despairing and visionary—Davidson remains a haunting figure in his own right. He is a living instance of the temperament that assumes the guilt and the
redemption of humanity. His heresy was magnificently
heroic and humanist, if brutally impotent. He demonstrates that the romantic, which is to say also the modern,
artist may portray the tragic experience as much by his
life as by his art, and that he will destroy his art rather than
betray it.

The present study draws upon over five hundred letters,
mostly from Davidson to such correspondents as John
Lane, Grant Richards, Edmund Gosse, William Archer,
Grant Allen, Swinburne, and William S. McCormick.
This hater of history did not preserve the letters that he
received. The correspondence was found in private and
public collections widely scattered between Monte Carlo
and San Marino, California. In addition, twice as many
other documents—original manuscripts, readers' reports,
publisher's contracts, and for certain years complete clipping files—have been examined. I mention this material
simply to preface my grateful acknowledgment of the large
encouragement and help received from many sources in
this quest.

I cannot reiterate too often my sense of abiding gratitude to Menzies Davidson of Flushing, New York, who
gave me unqualified permission to write the life of his
father and to quote ad libitum from the unpublished letters. His unfailing confidence, our many instructive con-

versations, and his delightful company are among the pleasant memories associated with this work.

I am greatly indebted to John Lane the Bodley Head Limited and the Unicorn Press Limited, of London, and the Ball Publishing Company, of Boston, for their permission to make extensive quotation from the works of John Davidson.

Certain portions of this book, although considerably altered, are based upon my dissertation submitted to the Graduate School of Arts and Sciences of Yale University in candidacy for the degree of Doctor of Philosophy.

I hope that it is not a disservice to pay my respects on this occasion to those among my former teachers who directed my researches, assisted in the pursuit of unpublished materials, or read the manuscript in its earliest versions. I speak in particular of William C. DeVane, dean of Yale College, Richard L. Purdy of Yale University, and Willard Thorp of Princeton University. From them I first learned that scholarship need not be divorced from urbanity, wit, and grace.

A number of fellow scholars and pioneers in the period under consideration have furnished information and saved me from pitfalls during various stages of writing the book. I wish to thank especially John L. Bradley of Mount Holyoke College, who introduced me to the works of John Davidson, Jerome H. Buckley of Columbia University, Richard Ellmann of Northwestern University, Bruce Harkness of the University of Illinois, Walter N. King of Montana State University, Cecil Y. Lang of Syracuse University, John A. Lester Jr. of Haverford College, Curtis Page of Drake University, the Rev. Raymond F. Roseliep of Loras College, Walter Swayze of United College, Winnipeg, and Ralph Walker of Aberdeen University.

No biographer can move far without the good will and assistance of the reference librarian and the curator of rare books and manuscripts. For their repeated services ungrudgingly performed I thank Alexander P. Clark, curator of manuscripts in the Princeton University Library; Edward F. Ellis, reference librarian of the Lockwood Memorial Library, the University of Buffalo; Barbara Simison, reference librarian of the Yale University Library; Jean Smith, formerly assistant reference librarian of the same library; and Alexander D. Wainwright, curator of the Morris L. Parish Collection in the Princeton University Library. Donald Gallup, curator of the Carl Van Vechten Collection at Yale University, acquainted me with T. S. Eliot's broadcast cited at the beginning of this preface, and the late Albert E. Gallatin with the comment by Sir Max Beerbohm. Among the earliest to offer assistance was the late J. Harlin O'Connell, an outstanding collector of the nineties.

The inability to complete my researches abroad would have been a crippling handicap had it not been for a number of foreign correspondents who helped me to track down Davidson's letters, ferreted through dusty periodical files unavailable in this country, provided me with firsthand recollections, and permitted me to publish letters in their possession. I thank these many friends of Davidson for their contributions to his biography: Percy J. Dobell of Sevenoaks (Kent), Sarah G. Harvey of Knebworth (Herts), Kenneth Hopkins of London, Mrs. Charles Hill of Alveston (Glos.), Enid Spencer-Brunton Lambart of Locarno, Switzerland, John Logan of Leamington Spa (Warwick), F. E. Lowenstein of Ayot Saint Lawrence (Herts), and Mrs. Grant Richards of Monte Carlo.

The editor of Yale Studies in English, Benjamin C. Nangle, has read in manuscript more versions of this book than either of us cares to recall. It is largely owing to his restraining hand and that of its editor for the Press, Jane

H. Carroll, that the book is not more voluble than it is. I am lastingly grateful to Shirley Duncan Stout, who as much as anyone piloted the ship into port.

The following have kindly granted me permission to quote in this study autograph letters, original manuscripts, and other materials pertaining to John Davidson in the collections which they administer: the Keeper of the Department of Manuscripts, the British Museum; the Head of Special Collections, the Libraries of Columbia University; the Librarian, the Henry E. Huntington Library and Art Gallery, San Marino, California; the Dean of the Library, the University of Illinois; the Keeper of the Brotherton Collection, the University of Leeds Library; the Keeper of the Department of Manuscripts, the National Library of Scotland; the Head of the Department of Rare Books and Special Collections, the Princeton University Library; and the Chief Reference Librarian, the Yale University Library. The particular items in these collections from which I quote are cited in the notes. The notes in the book are separated according to their function. Those that comment on or expand the text will be found at the foot of the page; those that indicate sources only are at the end of the book, numerically by chapters. Where the year in which one of Davidson's works was published differs from the year stated on the title page, I have both in the notes and text given the actual date of publication.

It would be belated and presumptuous to thank, as it were in a codicil, the one person who by personal sacrifice and resoluteness has helped me the most. Under the immunity of a general toast I salute the wives of all scholars.

The University of Buffalo Committee on the Allocation of Research Funds has assisted in the publication of this book by a substantial grant. In thanking them, I should like to think that they may be encouraged to extend similar help to other resident scholars. The Fund for Young Scholars of Yale University has also contributed a generous publication subsidy, for which I am most grateful.

J.B.T.

The University of Buffalo
Buffalo, New York

CONTENTS

CONTENTS

ILLUSTRATIONS

1

PENZANCE, 1909

Whilst thee the shores, and sounding Seas
Wash far away, where'er thy bones are hurl'd,
Whether beyond the stormy *Hebrides,*
Where thou perhaps under the whelming tide
Visit'st the bottom of the monstrous world;
Or whether thou to our moist vows denied,
Sleep'st by the fable of *Bellerus* old,
Where the great vision of the guarded Mount
Looks toward *Namancos* and *Bayona's* hold;
Look homeward Angel now, and melt with ruth . . .
                                        John Milton

Around six-thirty on Tuesday evening,
the twenty-third of March 1909, the poet John Davidson
left the no longer fashionable house that he rented at 6
Coulson's Terrace in Penzance to post a parcel. The parcel
containing manuscripts and reader's reports was addressed
to his London publisher, Grant Richards.[1] Davidson had
been living in the Cornish seaport since May of 1907, having gone there with his wife and younger son, now twenty,
for its reputedly mild climate and low cost of living. A
susceptibility to chronic bronchitis and asthma had induced him to seek out the first; almost complete depend-
ence upon an annual Civil List pension of £100 had
obliged him to leave London for the sake of the second.
Unlike the tourists and resort-seekers, he detested "the

capital of the Cornish Riviera" and always regarded his
residence there as an involuntary exile. He was lonely,
homesick for London, and bitter from repeated failure.
For diversion he had only the two public libraries in
Penzance and long daily walks, which very seldom were en-
livened by the company of a friend down from London.

On the evening in question he told his wife Margaret
that he would be back in time for supper and, in a characteristic gesture, had written out in pencil on a porcelain
menu tablet the "ideal" dinner he expected. He had scribbled down this mock bill of fare in the large hand of a
French maître d'hôtel:

> Crème aux Pommes de Terre
> Boeuf à la Schottische
> Du Pain
> Choufleur au Gratin
> De l'Eau
> Pouding de Riz.

Laughing at his shaky handwriting, he excused it by the
fact that until tea at four-thirty he had been working
steadily on the manuscripts that he regularly read for his
publisher and was about to return.[2] So far as anyone
knows, this wry little joke was the poet's last message.

That he visited the post office and mailed the parcel and
an accompanying letter to Richards was verified the next
day when the publisher received them. These, however,
threw no light on what subsequently happened. The poet
next stopped at the Star Hotel for a single whisky and
cigar, luxuries which in his later years he only rarely allowed himself by setting aside the odd money from the
small monthly stipend paid to him by his publisher. Mr.
Kiddie, the telegraphist at the Western Union Cable offices near by, said on the following day that he had seen
Davidson, smoking a cigar, leave the hotel and turn to-

ward his home. But he did not return to Coulson's Terrace and was apparently never again seen alive. The whisky and cigar were the last refreshment traditionally permitted a condemned man.

When it began to grow late and his father had not returned, Menzies Davidson, the poet's younger son, walked with a friend along the esplanade in the direction of Mousehole, hoping to find him but discovering no trace. Although she suffered an anxious night, Margaret Davidson took no further steps until daybreak. Endowed with the sterling Scottish qualities of devotion and endurance, Mrs. Davidson does not appear to have been a particularly self-reliant woman. For years she had deferred quietly to her husband's strong opinions and sudden caprices; now in a crisis she had no one in Penzance to whom she could turn. It was a mild evening after a bright spring day. For some hours she may have quieted her fears with the thought that her husband had been tempted by the bland weather to continue his evening stroll longer than usual. Davidson had been accustomed throughout his life but especially in recent years to going off on long, solitary walks or tours that sometimes lasted for days. On one occasion he had disappeared without warning for forty-eight hours, only to be found meditating absent-mindedly in Charing Cross Station.

It was natural for Mrs. Davidson to turn first to Grant Richards in London, but there was no way of reaching him that night. The next morning she reported to the publisher and, at his advice, to the police that her husband was missing. The local police authorities were at first confused, the constable in Penzance disclaiming jurisdiction over the case. In spite of initial delays, they subsequently conducted the search with as much efficiency as could have been expected. There were no immediate funds for hiring searching parties, but descriptions of the poet were placed

in railway stations and other public places where he might
be seen. The Coast Guard at Penzance kept a sharp look-
out around Mount's Bay, and the trains to London were
searched. Alexander Davidson, the elder son, then twenty-
two, took leave from his position in London to come down
to help organize the man hunt. After the poet had been
missing for several days it was neither possible nor desirable to keep the event from the newspapers. Both the
local and London press, including the normally reserved
Times, set up a hue and cry, demanding in headlines
"Where Is John Davidson?" "Is He Alive?" and calling
for a more thorough search. Henceforth, until the mystery
was solved, the question of Davidson's fate provided sensational copy for newspapers at home and as far abroad as
Houston and San Francisco.

On April 1, nine days after the poet had disappeared, a
reward of £20 for information leading to his discovery
was offered "by Mr. John Davidson's friends." Up to this
time practically the whole expense of the search had been
borne by the enterprising *Daily Mail* in return for the
first exclusive news story of the disappearance. As both this
newspaper and the *Daily Chronicle* now gave up the case,
Alexander Davidson anticipated that henceforth the family
would have to meet the expenses.[3] The reward, warned
the stern announcement in the press, would not be paid
to anyone who attempted unnecessarily to interfere with
Davidson or to restrict his movements; the poet's relatives
feared that he was mentally deranged and that rough handling would have a disastrous effect. A police poster, widely
circulated in Cornwall, broadcast the reward and described
the missing man:

> Aged 51 years; height about 5 feet 5 ins.; stout
> build; dark complexion; full round pale face; brown
> piercing eyes; dark hair, moustache, and imperial

tinged with grey; bald on top of head; has a varicose vein in left leg, and a mark where a wart has been recently removed from first finger on left hand.

Dressed when he left home in a blue serge suit, dark overcoat, bowler hat, and black buttoned boots.

DAVIDSON always carries one eyeglass, is well known as a literary man, walks very quickly, and has the appearance of a Frenchman.

It is feared that he may be suffering from loss of memory, or some ill may have befallen him.[4]

The poster instructed anyone possessing information to communicate immediately with H. Kenyon, head constable at Penzance. In response to the offer of a reward at least a score of people at various places in Cornwall reported seeing and unmistakably recognizing Davidson. Each report in turn proved unfounded and served only to revive flagging public interest in the mystery, like false clues scattered calculatingly through a detective story.

As the police increasingly resembled a pack of hounds unable to find the scent, conflicting explanations were offered of how the poet had vanished without a trace. Since youth he had suffered from a mild heart condition, but according to Margaret Davidson and the *Times* he had of late enjoyed good health and excellent spirits. Mrs. Davidson herself surmised that, in keeping with his habit of taking an evening walk along the esplanade or elsewhere, he had gone for a stroll, been seized with a sudden illness, and fallen into the sea. Against this conjecture was the fact that since the fatal Tuesday there had been a strong wind from the sea; if Davidson had drowned, his body would almost certainly have been washed ashore. It seemed to others more probable that he had fallen or plunged into one of the many disused mine shafts between Penzance and Morvah. To the end Mrs. Davidson persisted in her belief that her husband had drowned and, as she wrote to Richards, she had "never given the other 'might have beens' a thought." [5]

Grant Richards, who as much as anyone had possessed the confidence of the proud, reticent man, thought differently. He appears to have held the view that Davidson had abandoned his family, perhaps deliberately, but more plausibly in a state of temporary insanity. Richards furthermore expected the poet upon recovery to communicate first with him in London.[6] To support his opinion he recalled that Davidson had spoken to him of a desire to leave home. Regrettably Richards confided this view to the authorities and the press. Quite aside from the pain that it caused the already grieving wife, the evidence against it was overwhelming. Although Davidson periodically had gone off alone on busman's holidays in order to complete contracted work, he had never forsaken his family. Throughout a lifetime of penury and discouragement, when less brave men might have bolted, he had remained a devoted if often withdrawn husband and parent. Again, in spite of recurrent attacks of neurasthenia and the monomaniacal fixations of much of his later work, he had never shown in private life overt signs of mental disorder. Richards' explanation was improbable finally from the practical standpoint because the missing man was known to have had not more than thirty-five shillings on his person when he vanished. Even a man of Davidson's simple needs could not have traveled far or subsisted for long on that sum. Margaret Davidson's reply to the publisher's speculations shows how much more sensible was her understanding of her husband, however incapable she was of sharing his intellectual and spiritual interests. Excerpts from her long letter also illuminate Davidson's dreary life in Penzance:

Have just had your letter read to me.

I don't know what to think of it. I had wild hopes
that you really *had* had news of my husband. . . .

As to his having spoken of going away—it has always been my cry—to get him to go but he would only
say—"WE'VE GOT TO GO ON." He had no money to
spare for that—or in fact for anything.

When the parcels [of manuscripts which Davidson
read for Richards] came pouring in from you I sometimes felt inclined to write and tell you not to send
so many.

One day I threatened to do so, he told me he had
told you "to pile them on"—or something to that effect.

I had hoped he would get a good sum for the song *
and had even said he ought to go to London; but he
had no clothes, no books, &c, &c.

I would have starved to let him go anywhere; but
the poorer he was the prouder he got.

He never would rest, even on Sabbath; I used to
say we might at least get a later breakfast but he told
me it was the quietest time he had all the week. He
was at his desk by nine every morning—until dinner
time doing his own work as he called it and after that
reading or thinking. He always told me he had so
much to do that the days were not long enough. He
used to sum up his cheques, and say in a joking way
—why I can afford a cigar! . . .

Of course we had differences of opinions—but we
had no two ideas in common—that's how we got on so
well—I simply let him do what he liked. I never had
anybody calling even. He used to make me go out and
see some of my neighbours, but I had to tell them they

* "Song for the Twenty-Fourth of May," published in the *Daily Chronicle,* 30 Mar. 1909, and included in *Fleet Street and Other Poems,* 1909.

must not come to see *me*. I was no good to him except
to see that his "creature comforts" were as good as I
could get.

Certainly there was nothing to make him do this
that I can think of on the Tuesday night. I know he
often spoke and wrote wildly about Cornwall. . . .

The awful strain on me has not been lessened by
your letter. I thought 10 o'clock would never *come*. I
shall NEVER see him again.—I'm as certain as that
I'm writing this, that he fell into the sea, which has
not as yet given up its dead.

Sunday Morning

No news, no letters of any importance. If only I got
one scrap. I don't believe in any of the clues. My own
belief is that he is drowned, and has been washed out
to sea where he will never be found. I had rather think
that than what you have tried to make me believe.
Don't think I'm angry—I'm past [it] or anything else.[7]

Sir Arthur Conan Doyle, a fellow Scot and acquaintance
of the family, advanced a more scientific opinion. When
informed by Alexander Davidson that a revolver and two
cartridges had been found missing from the house in Penzance, Doyle offered the conclusion, elementary for anyone,
that Davidson had taken his life. The conclusion was but-
tressed by the poet's lifelong obsession with euthanasia
and suicide. Reluctant to accept this opinion, Alexander
pointed to the unfinished trilogy, *God and Mammon,*
which his father had resolved to complete at all costs.
Doyle conceded, more out of compassion than conviction
perhaps, that it was a strong point in favor of his still being
alive.[8]

In spite of this intervention by the creator of Britain's
most celebrated sleuth, the mystery remained unclarified

until April 15, 1909, twenty-three days after Davidson had last been seen. In making at that time a more thorough search of his father's effects, Menzies found a parcel which contained the manuscript of a last and still unpublished volume of poems with a prefatory note and a covering letter to his London agents, A. P. Watt and Son of Hastings House.[9] The letter, undated but written from 6 Coulson's Terrace, stated that this would be his last book and instructed the agent to arrange its publication on the usual terms with Grant Richards, his literary executor.[10] As if this were not valedictory enough, the prefatory note, also undated, appeared to make his intention even clearer. It read in part: "The time has come to make an end. There are several motives. I find my pension is not enough; I have therefore still to turn aside and attempt things for which people will pay. My health also counts. Asthma and other annoyances I have tolerated for years; but I cannot put up with cancer." [11] The preface also listed five poems featuring renegade heroes—"Cain," "Judas," "Cesare Borgia," "Calvin," and "Cromwell"—under the general title "When God Meant God" which Davidson had intended to comprise the principal contents of the book. "Cain" was the only one written and included. The volume, still according to the preface, was to have concluded with "a second Testament in my own person," * repudiating all religious sects in favor of the universal greatness of man. This open, matter-of-fact farewell left Margaret Davidson prostrate with grief. Menzies at once sent off the contents of the newly discovered parcel to Richards. Judging the mystery solved, wife and son wanted only to know what to do next.[12] No one who had known Davidson in his final years seemed to find it surprising that he should have left a suicide note in the form of a literary preface, so exclusively had he identified himself with his writings.

* In 1908 he had published *The Testament of John Davidson*.

From the beginning the poet's wife had feared that if evidence pointing directly to suicide turned up, she would lose Davidson's life insurance of £200 and his Civil List pension. Since she was without other means of support, her subsequent conduct is pardonable if not strictly ethical. She was also motivated by concern for her husband's reputation. Unwilling to accept the opinion of the police that Davidson had killed himself, soon after his disappearance she had opened the envelope containing his last will to determine how recently it had been drawn up. Reassured by the date, she had not read further. Not until Richards had caused her further anxiety with his speculations did she read the will through and send it on to the publisher.[13] Then came the discovery of the parcel with its grim message. As soon as she was able, she wrote to Richards under stress of great emotion to ask if it would be a felony to hush up the new evidence: "But if you think this is only the ravings of a mad woman just burn it." [14] Apparently the family, on the advice of Richards, decided to withhold the contents of the prefatory note until they could determine what effect it would have upon the widow's claims to the insurance and pension. On April 18 *Lloyd's Weekly* forestalled them by announcing in blue print in the box reserved for the latest news, "Mr. John Davidson the poet has committed suicide." [15]

The poet's will was now made public. Davidson himself had prepared the will in duplicate on August 14 of the previous year and in it had appointed Grant Richards his literary executor. On the following day he had forwarded one copy to Richards in a sealed envelope, with a covering letter urging him to "keep it safely until my death tomorrow or next day, or 20 years hence." [16] The other copy he had sealed and placed in his desk with instructions that it be opened only in the event of his death. Written in his own handwriting and in nonlegal language, the two copies were signed but unwitnessed. In form as well as content the unusual document bespoke its author's persistent and abortive independence. After bequeathing "any money I may have at my death, and my life insurance, and the contents of my hired house" to his wife, if she survived him, or to his two sons, he left some singular instructions: "No word, except of my writing, is ever to appear in any book of mine as long as the copyright endures. No one is to write my life now or at any time; but let all men study and discuss in private and in public my poems and my plays, especially my Testaments and Tragedies." [17] Here was an injunction no less stern than the more famous curse on Shakespeare's tomb. The Testaments and tragedies mentioned by the will were the poet's final works, which proclaimed in bombastic blank verse a defiant message of atheism and scientific materialism. The remainder of the will stated that he had no objections, because "they would be unavailing," to the reissue of any of his published writings, but forbade the publication or production of seven unpublished plays and adaptations or of any other sketch or scenario. The manuscripts of these plays and all other unpublished writings, including his letters, were to be destroyed.* The only exception he allowed was *The Testament of John Davidson*, which Grant Richards published later in 1908. The will concluded:

* Menzies Davidson tells me that these instructions were carried out; his father's papers were destroyed, with the exception of the manuscripts of *Fleet Street and Other Poems* and of three poems found lying on his desk. Davidson himself apparently destroyed the manuscripts of most of his works, once they were prepared for publication, and kept few letters or records. The manuscripts of the following together with those of a few poems have also survived: *A Second Series of Fleet Street Eclogues,* originally in the possession of John Lane and now in a private collection; an adaptation of *Phèdre,* originally in the possession of Mrs. Patrick Campbell and now in the National Library of Scotland; and *The Testament of John Davidson,* originally in the possession of Grant Richards and now in the Princeton University Library.

I hope to live to finish my Testaments and Tragedies; but I may have to die before, and at any moment
now, for reasons that concern myself alone.

I desire this will to be published as soon as I am
dead.

As representative of the family, Richards belatedly announced in the *Times* of April 19 their belief that the poet
had "in a moment of acute depression . . . made an end
of his life." At the same time he denied a persistent rumor
that Davidson had drowned himself and that his body had
been found. The leading newspapers, satisfied with the
evidence of suicide, published his will and a full obituary.
No one has since ever seriously questioned their conclusion. Under the circumstances the curious farewell messages left room for little doubt as to the poet's end. Now
after an interval of half a century it may be time to ask,
"Exactly what did Davidson mean by them?"

The motives for suicide were not so simple or so clear
as the will and preface had seemed to make out. The unequivocating preface itself acknowledged that he had always
known and endured poverty, ill health, and the necessity of
catering to the literary market. "But I cannot put up with
cancer," it added. By advertising in the press for doctors
whom the missing man had recently consulted, the family
determined to their satisfaction that he had been suffering
not from cancer but from a relatively minor indisposition,
hemorrhoids. At no time before his death did he appear to
be experiencing unusual pain. Repeatedly during his life,
moreover, he had shown a capacity to endure pain, and
his writings again and again glorified this capacity.

Three possible explanations exist for the laconic, ambiguous messages which Davidson left behind. The first is
that he anticipated within the near future a waning of his
physical powers and natural death from a wasting disease,

and therefore took steps to bring his writing career efficiently to a close. The second explanation is that, foreseeing the suffering and, for him, physical humiliation of cancer, he resolved upon suicide. Finally, he may have decided to end his life for other reasons, not fully perceived, and have invented the illusion of cancer as a plausible motive. The first is possible in theory because nowhere do the various statements anticipating death explicitly mention suicide. They might be understood to express his intention "to make an end" not of his life but simply of his literary career. Against this theory is the fact that all the statements are more plausible as anticipations of suicide rather than natural death and that strong circumstantial evidence indicates suicide. A person envisaging the misery of cancer might deliberately prepare for taking his own life six to nine months before the event, which would make the second explanation possible. Yet few psychiatrists or brokers of life insurance would regard this as likely in a balanced person, and the only mention of suicide occurs in the preface, believed to be the last of the messages. Davidson was as reticent in private life as he was outspoken in public, so that it is conceivable that he would not tell his family about his having cancer. It still does not make sense that he would mention this as the motive in the preface and not in the will, both of which hint at suicide and both of which he regarded as public statements. At first glance the third possibility seems the least probable since the poet was neither self-evasive nor willfully dishonest. On the other hand, he had always been given to hypochondria, which like his other traits had with the years become intensified to the point of neurosis. In creating a public identity for himself, he was capable of exaggerating a minor personal ailment into a dreaded disease. Extraordinary, complex motives in Davidson's case might well have compelled him to hallucination and self-destruction.

In a very real sense he had been preparing for suicide all his life.

From the messages themselves one can be certain only that their author, expecting an early death when he wrote them, calmly and rationally arranged to leave his affairs in order. No subsequent findings have ever furnished incontrovertible evidence as to his precise meaning in them. Did he commit suicide? If so, did he destroy himself as a defiantly triumphant materialist, a perverted Calvinist, a romantic frustrated by his own imperfections and those of the world, or simply a poet worn out by failure, poverty, and chronic ailments? No one knows. It is possible nevertheless to make some shrewd guesses about the intention of the notes, the nature of the death, and the motivation, but not until the story of his life, personality, and writings, a dark, intricate latticework of Victorian forces and counterforces, of repression and rebellion, has been told.

With the execution of the will and its publication on April 19, 1909, in the principal daily newspapers, the door seemed irrevocably shut against any biography of Davidson or any critical edition of his works. On October 22, 1909, Davidson's executors announced in the *Times* the value of his estate as slightly over £319 and a ruling by the Principal Probate Registry that, since the will had not been witnessed, the deceased had died intestate. In accordance with the law, one-third of the meager proceeds went to the widow and the remainder to the sons. As for the other provisions of the document, no one has ever been bound by them legally or morally, unless he respects as inviolable the aberrations of an exhausted and tormented mind. By his own code of ruthless self-determination Davidson would have scorned any such prohibitions. For the poet's survivors and the readers who had followed so avidly its unfolding in the daily press, the incident was closed. There was no doubt in anyone's mind that the vanished poet had killed himself, although an official verdict of suicide could not be returned. In view of the tragicomedy which followed, it is regrettable perhaps that the seas consented to give up their dead.

2

On the afternoon of Saturday, September 18, 1909, Orlando Humphreys, a fisherman, and James Lawson, a stonemason, were fishing in a punt in Mount's Bay off Mousehole, the village in which they lived, near Penzance. About five o'clock they noticed something floating in the water near Point Spaniard and drifting toward them with the tide. As it came nearer they saw that it was a human body, greatly decomposed but still clothed in a dark grey overcoat and wearing buttoned boots. Gulls hovered above screaming and a single gull was perched on it. The fishermen towed the body ashore, where a group of Mousehole villagers placed it on a stretcher and started off in the direction of a tollhouse above Penlee Point. Certain features of the events which followed recall Shelley's pagan funeral and the procession of Samoans carrying Stevenson's body to the hill above Pago Pago. But Cornwall is not Oceania or the Ligurian coast. Mixed with the primitive simplicity of Davidson's funeral were certain concessions to local Protestant dissent. If the mixture was somewhat ludicrous, it was appropriate to the end of one whose life had been governed by the same contradiction.

As the procession neared the village post office with the remains of England's most clamorous opponent of Christianity, it paused for the bearers to listen to a Salvation Army group singing hymns. With unconscious irony the *Cornishman* later reported that the singing of this evangelical band did not seem out of harmony. In the evening Menzies Davidson arrived at Mousehole from Penzance. Although its features were no longer recognizable, the son positively identified the body of his father from its build, the clothes, and articles which were found in the pockets: a plain straight-stem briar pipe; a packet of Bordman's tobacco, his favorite; a bone paper knife; and a silver matchbox. There were also scraps of paper, no longer decipherable. From this day, the slope above Penlee Point has been known by local inhabitants as Davidson's Hill, and older folk invariably date events from the loss of the lugger *Jane* or the discovery of the poet's body. As any experienced tourist would expect, there is, or was a few years ago, an old cadger in Penzance who for one or more drinks would tell you the story of the discovery in graphic but by no means reliable detail.

Since it was the weekend and Cornish people allow no secular event to violate the Sabbath, the inquest was postponed until the following Monday afternoon. Again with severe disregard for the deceased poet's atheistic principles, the inquest was held in the United Methodist Church. After Menzies Davidson had given evidence of identification and reviewed the circumstances surrounding his father's disappearance, he testified that the dead man had often been absent-minded when in thought. Only three weeks before he vanished he had during an evening's promenade walked over the top of an embankment more than four feet high and fallen.* There was nothing, he added, to suggest that his father had not been perfectly rational or that he had ever been otherwise. The witness stated that he had found a box of cartridges at the time of the disappearance and that two of these together with his

* Menzies Davidson informs me that shortly after his father disappeared footprints leading from a path to the edge of a cliff were found. It was possible to identify the prints by their exceptional breadth and by fitting one of the poet's boots into them. No prints led back from the cliff to the path. Mr. Davidson still regards this, without much foundation, as evidence that his father lost his way and wandered off the cliff by mistake. This evidence was not reported in the press or presumably at the inquest.

father's revolver had been missing; he accounted for the missing shells only by the fact that his father, an accomplished marksman, had fired them during target practice after his removal to Penzance. At the same time he did not conceal the compromising evidence of the prefatory letter bearing on suicide, thought to have been written three months before the event, of the will, and of his father's frequent if jocular references in conversation to doing away with himself.

Further testimony was offered by a physician, Dr. Millar, who presided. Although the body was in an advanced state of decomposition, having been in the sea some six months, Dr. Millar had found a perfectly round cavity in the right temple of the skull and another larger hole exactly opposite that might have been caused by a bullet fired close to the forehead. There was also evidence of a fracture of the skull from a severe blow, but the doctor could not say that this had not been caused by a falling stone or a boat's keel.* Because of the long interval it was impossible to determine if the head injuries had occurred before or after death, and if Davidson had drowned or died before he had got into the sea. The general opinion was that the body had become moored near where it was discovered and therefore had not washed out to sea or drifted ashore. Without leaving the room the jury returned a verdict of "Found dead," not of "Suicide," on the grounds of insufficient evidence. The jury's evasion may have been more of a slight than a kindness to a man who had justified suicide as a heroic and honorable act.

In deference to Davidson's wish that he be committed to the sea rather than interred, steps were taken to bury him

* In Mar. 1950 Wallace Nichols, the Cornish poet, wrote me that he had known Dr. Millar personally and once asked him if, in his opinion, Davidson had shot himself. Millar repeated his original testimony that the body was in such a state that it was quite impossible to have any opinion at all.

off the coast of Mousehole between that village and Newlyn. The body was enclosed in a plain pitch pine coffin
with brass mountings and a breastplate bearing the simple
inscription, "John Davidson, died March 23, 1909, aged
52." Those in charge proposed to take the coffin from the
hut where it lay, transfer it to a ship's lifeboat, tow it some
miles out to sea, and commit it to the water. Feeling against
this plan ran so high among the residents of Mousehole
that it was necessary to delay the burial. It is possible that
the opposition of this strongly evangelical community was
prompted by the unusual character of the funeral, but an
equally strong Celtic heritage might have been expected
to condone its pagan features. The principal objection
among the fishermen was the practical one that if the coffin
were deposited off shore the trawls would bring it up again
and the situation would be unhappily repeated. In view of
this objection the harbor master and a representative of
the County Council sent urgent telegrams to Gladstone,*
the home secretary, for permission to go ahead with the
burial. Around midnight came his solemn judgment: "I
cannot reply on legal point, but am unable to approve of
any course other than burial in ordinary way, or cremation
in accordance with law." The miracle is that Davidson,
arch iconoclast, did not rise from his coffin to defy the
orthodoxy vested in the Home Office. At this point Alexander Davidson wired for and received permission to bury
the body seven miles out to sea.

Mousehole remained firm, however, and thereby lost the
distinction of being the point of embarkation. On Tuesday morning, September 21, the body of almost the last of
the later generation of English romantics was placed in an
open hearse and taken to Penzance harbor. A carriage containing Davidson's two sons and a friend completed the

* Herbert John Gladstone (1854–1930), youngest son of William Ewart
Gladstone, the prime minister.

procession. When they reached the harbor the body was transferred to a large ship's boat and was towed out to sea by the steam launch *Nora*. On board were the two sons, the Reverend J. S. Patrick Fagan, vicar of Newlyn, and five others. A representative of the *Cornishman* furnished an eyewitness account:

> Shortly before noon the Nora steamed slowly out of the harbour, with the flag lowered to half-mast, and as she passed the pier-head all those who had gathered there reverently stood bareheaded till the launch and her grim charge had passed. When steaming down the bay, fishermen paused in their occupation and lifted their caps.
>
> The sea was remarkably calm even for summer, and it was lit by brilliant sunshine. As the grim procession was leaving the land, the boom of an explosion from the then distant quarries sounded strangely like a funeral salute.
>
> Ten miles down the Bay the steamer was stopped, and four men stood by the coffin . . .

As the body was committed to the sea, Mr. Fagan read the burial service and a brief tribute of his own to the deceased poet's life work. Only George Foote, belligerent leader of free thought in England, seemed aware that even these "maim'd rites" would have outraged a poet who had denied God and the immortality of the soul. Commenting on this "display of religious bigotry," Foote noted in the *Free-thinker,* of which he was editor, "The religious outrage perpetrated at the burials of Swinburne and Meredith has been repeated at the burial of John Davidson. Not even Freethinkers are safe against their nearest relations." [18]

Throughout his life Davidson had been jealous of his dignity, but especially in later years had been too quick to defend it against attack. In "The Last Journey," the epi-

taph written for himself as an epilogue to *The Testament
of John Davidson* (1908), he momentarily rises above this
self-awareness to state with real dignity a Lucretian stoicism in the face of death. The first and last stanzas of this
valedictory are:

> I felt the world a-spinning on its nave,
>   I felt it sheering blindly round the sun;
> I felt the time had come to find a grave:
>   I knew it in my heart my days were done.
> I took my staff in hand; I took the road,
> And wandered out to seek my last abode.
>   Hearts of gold and hearts of lead
>   Sing it yet in sun and rain,
>   "Heel and toe from dawn to dusk,
>   Round the world and home again."

>   .   .   .   .   .

> Farewell the hope that mocked, farewell despair
>   That went before me still and made the pace.
> The earth is full of graves, and mine was there
>   Before my life began, my resting-place;
> And I shall find it out and with the dead
> Lie down for ever, all my sayings said—
>   Deeds all done and songs all sung
>   While others chant in sun and rain,
>   "Heel and toe from dawn to dusk,
>   Round the world and home again."

The last journey of the chief prophet of materialism in
English literature took place fittingly at Land's End as the
sun was sinking. Although his miscarried funeral and the
intemperate controversy waged after his death belonged
not to him but to the living, they too befitted a harassed,
disputatious spirit that would not easily be laid.

3

For a brief time after the poet's disappearance and death
a flurry of excitement arose in the literary world. A number of his fellow writers, who with few exceptions had
played the Levite in his decline, now hastened with the
best intentions to prove themselves Samaritans. Mrs.
Davidson was without funds; as she had feared, the poet's
pension had been automatically suspended and until death
was established she had been unable to collect from the
insurance policy. J. M. Barrie generously sent her £100,
and the Royal Literary Fund voted her a sum of £200.
Bernard Shaw suggested, in the event that the pension was
not renewed, a benefit performance of a play which he had
commissioned Davidson to write but which had never been
produced: "It was not popular enough for a popular theatre; and it was not advanced enough for a coterie theatre." [19] Offers of help came from other sources, including
John Lane who during the nineties had published the
writer's more successful volumes of lyrics and plays. When
Mrs. Davidson's attempts to have her husband's pension renewed for her benefit had failed, James Douglas and Sir W.
Robertson Nicoll urged in the press its continuation. The
signatures to a petition got up for this purpose read like a
Who's Who of contemporary authors. The names included
J. M. Barrie, Hilaire Belloc, Robert Bridges, Arthur Christopher Benson, Austin Dobson, R. Donald, A. L. Gardner,
G. L. Groves, Thomas Hardy, E. V. Hodge, Andrew Lang,
W. L. Locke, H. W. Massingham, Sir W. R. Nicoll, Bernard Shaw, and William Watson. The pension was resumed in April 1910 and ultimately Margaret Davidson
received her husband's insurance.[20]

Perhaps the most ardent, and certainly the most voluble,
expression of sympathy came from Marie Corelli. After
Davidson had disappeared but before his suicide had been

confirmed, the popular novelist wrote a letter of condo-
lence to Mrs. Davidson, but she reserved the full force of
her feeling for an extended correspondence with Grant
Richards.[21] In these letters she is the voice of outraged
womanhood. Complaining about the extraordinary apathy
of the press in the affair, she exclaimed, "They could write
reams about that fraudulent humbug Miss Charlesworth,
and concerning the loss of this fine poet and truly gifted
man, they seem indifferent." * And she added, "If I were a
man I would never rest till I had found him!" Two days
later she wrote in the same clamorous vein, stating that she
had written *"at once"* to Lord Burnham of the *Daily Telegraph* but excusing herself from making a public appeal
on the grounds that the "gutter-press" would accuse her
of doing it " 'to advertise myself.' " "It was so in the case
of poor unhappy 'Ouida,' " she continued, "who I *knew*
(from private information) was almost STARVING—and I
wrote a letter to the Daily Mail proposing a 'testimonial to
her *genius*'—(not a *relief* works!) and for that I got insulted, and the press said I had 'outraged' the suffering
Ouida to the last possible extent!!—Yet the poor woman
died in *want*. So *never again* must I plead for my brother
and sister authors, however much I love and admire their
works. For I never was jealous of any one of them knowing
how hard the fight is—and I have room in my heart for
them all." When on April 19 the newspapers announced
Davidson's presumed suicide and published his will, she
persisted in her refusal to believe that he had killed himself or was dead. She was persuaded that he had either "met
with some foul play" or gone off to " 'rest' by taking some

---

* Miss Charlesworth was a young woman whose recent "disappearance"
to elude her creditors had been widely publicized in the newspapers.
Others noted the disproportionate space devoted to her undeserving case
as compared to Davidson's, although the large number of clippings dealing
with Davidson's disappearance, in the Princeton University Library collection, indicate that he was not slighted.

other occupation." She recognized from his will, however, the symptoms of "that fatal malady, a *morbid* egotism, which persuaded him that he was 'too uplifted and great' for the 'common' public." Perhaps wisely, the author of *The Sorrows of Satan* and *The Mighty Atom* had never despised the common public. Sniffing at suicide as *"cowardly,"* she "had imagined Davidson to be of finer mould than to shrink from either disaster or disease" or from the "divine *battle*" of life, "in which all the forces of heaven are on the side of *faith* and *courage*." Having fashioned Davidson's character and fate according to her familiar formula, Marie Corelli volunteered to contribute to any subscription fund got up to aid Mrs. Davidson.

William Watson, who resembled Davidson only in his fervent devotion to lost causes, shared Marie Corelli's indignation at the general indifference to his fellow poet's end. He was even more concerned with the larger issue of public responsibility for the welfare of the artist; nor did he hesitate like her to communicate his views to the press, although he could have been forgiven for regretting it later. In a letter to the *Times* of April 26, 1909, Watson excoriated the press and the public alike for neglecting the poet and driving him to a violent end. He conceded that Davidson's later poetry was crude, hoarse, and strained and that the best of his work could be gathered up in a few pages. The blame for this he placed squarely upon the shoulders of the public and critics for "perpetually demanding from a poet an output . . . such as no artist can produce without doing murderous violence to his powers and his artistic conscience." "For let there be no mistake about it," he charged, "John Davidson died because he could not make a living . . . his blood is upon us, as surely as if we had slain him with our own hands." [22]

Watson's attack upon the public conscience provoked a considerable stream of comment. Most of it was impartial

and just, a small part of it approving, but some of it
sounded, as Watson later commented, "a note of coarse
and callous indifference." [23] In the discussion which followed, responsibility for the welfare of the artist was placed
variously upon fate, society, and the artist himself. Filson
Young, a young novelist and a staunch friend of Davidson
in his last years, now came to his defense as he had during
his lifetime. In an article entitled "The Truth about John
Davidson," he revealed that the poet had become an "essentially lonely man of an uncouth, ill-accommodating spirit,
who had learned not to depend on his affections as a source
of strength" and to whom his work had been literally everything. To an even greater extent than most artists, therefore, he had depended almost entirely on public recognition of his writings for emotional and spiritual sustenance.
Young placed responsibility for his friend's death at the
door of the critics for refusing to distinguish between the
frankly commercial writer and the artist who has a serious
artistic goal. It was not the neglect of the general public
nor the miseries of poverty which hounded Davidson out
of life, he reported, but "a conspiracy of silence" among his
fellows.[24]

The *Academy* fanned the dispute with a series of abusive
articles attacking Watson's position and denouncing him as
"something of a poet," " a great deal of a journalist," and
"a pensioner of the Liberal party." [25] Piqued that the author of *The Testament of John Davidson,* "this dangerous
and impious work," should have received any recognition
at all, much less a pension of £100, the review denounced
Grant Richards for having published the work, James
Douglas and H. W. Massingham for having forced it down
the throats of their unsuspecting readers in the liberal
Star and *Nation,* and Watson in particular for insisting
that public support of the poet had been inadequate. With
an airiness worthy of Marie Antoinette the *Academy* ob-

served, "To a man of Mr. Davidson's birth, parentage and
surroundings a hundred a year was a very useful addition
to the income which he was enabled to earn as a journalist
and a man of letters." "Your true poet," it added in a shaft
directed as much at Watson as at Davidson, "would rather
write a perfectly beautiful poem and die of starvation in
the gutter immediately afterwards than receive a cheque
for a thousand guineas from the editor of a hapenny paper
for writing a series of sonnets devoted to the abuse of the
sovereign of a foreign country." It testifies to Watson's
forbearance or sobriety that he refrained from remarking
to this fatuity that the true poet would obviously prefer
both to write the perfect poem and to receive promptly a
check for a thousand guineas.

Few poets in Davidson's time were able to earn a living
by poetry, fewer a fortune as Browning had. Since it
scarcely would have occurred to a self-respecting Edwardian man of letters to turn his hand to banking, medicine,
insurance, or teaching school, this left only journalism.
Until the last few years of his life Davidson attempted to
supplement his meager income by writing for the periodicals. His journalistic output was considerable during the
nineties but not large by the measure of that time; its frequent merit and significance have not been fully recognized. He failed in journalism as in other undertakings
and for the same reasons: He could not sustain invention,
and he refused to sacrifice his principles to popular taste.

The insensibility with which the *Academy* commented
upon Davidson's death is understandable only in the light
of earlier events. Toward the end of his career the messiah
of materialism had come to take his gospel with deadly
earnestness. He identified himself so inseparably with this
message that criticism which he should have overlooked
or regarded as an academic skirmish provoked bitter exchanges of personal insult. One of these feuds had been

with Lord Alfred Douglas, the friend of Wilde, who for
a number of years had controlled the *Academy*. As a
snapping, yawping watchdog of ultra-Tory opinion, the
Academy under Douglas took the extreme conservative
position on all matters, political, artistic, and moral. Short-
sightedly it regarded Davidson, who preached the rule of
an elite, who deplored socialism and communism, and
whose radicalism was aristocratic and intellectual, as a
dangerous threat to the establishment. There is no question that Douglas or, if not he, his toady Frank Harris
wrote the articles in the spirit of an old grudge.

The controversy by this time had reached such propor-
tions that the *Times,* which ordinarily declined to lend its
columns as arenas for journalistic bouts, felt compelled to
arbitrate. Its editorialist adopted the impartial and safely
fatalistic position that the contemporary artist, unlike
Homer or Michelangelo, was working in a commercial age
where there was no general demand for beauty or agreement on what was beautiful; he could therefore only determine for himself the nature of beauty, strive to create it,
and take his chances on popular approval.[26] It was a pretty
cold grate to offer the artist. William Watson, who had
started the debate, was allowed to shoot the Parthian arrow.
In a second letter to the *Times,* which its editor firmly
headed "A Last Word on John Davidson," Watson again
made no attempt to defend Davidson's supremacy as a poet
but stated that his fellow writer was a greater poet than
Otway or Chatterton, and predicted that one day his case
would be ranked with theirs as instances of English dullness and inhumanity.[27] It was evident to all but the least
rational participants in the debate that no more remained
to be said on the subject. The personal tragedy which had
precipitated the controversy was in its violence unusual if
not unprecedented. And the larger problem of society's

debt to the artist had led as always to inconclusive generalization.

While Watson, Young, and James Douglas were gallantly breaking lances in Davidson's behalf, most of the periodicals and newspapers were content to note his death with conventional obituaries that reviewed his career and endeavored to assess his place in English letters. Almost as if startled to learn that he had survived so long, virtually all agreed that he had been in his earlier eclogues and ballads of the nineties a poet of considerable promise, even achievement. Yet the most sympathetic of these critics observed that in his final decade the poet had sacrificed the fulfillment of his lyric powers to expound a materialistic creed patched together from Darwin, Nietzsche, and other revolutionary nineteenth-century thinkers—"a new gospel which," as the *Nation* pointed out, "indeed, is suspiciously like many old gospels with scientific jargon added." [28] The results, the critics lamented, were turgidity, crudity, and incoherence which resentment of individual failure had increased with every new volume. It was again left to the *Times* to sum up. Although all of Davidson's later works were as far removed from the fine indignation as from the serenity that marks good poetry, it ventured to hope that the selection of his poetry published a few years before his death,* "where his power is kept in control and beauty is not sacrificed to sociology," would guarantee him an enduring place among his contemporaries.[29] This arbitrary division of a poet's work into an early "happy, romantic" period and a later one of "bitterness, disillusionment, and withdrawal" is a familiar over-simplification among *pseudodoxia epidemica*. Applied to Davidson it is irreconcilable with the facts.

Consistently Davidson sought in his writings a synthesis

* *Selected Poems,* London and New York, John Lane, 1905.

which would reconcile conflicting elements in his personality and justify it not merely to others but to himself. For this reason all his writings—poems, plays, essays, stories, and novels—are intensely autobiographical and of a piece. Rarely do they crash through the aesthetic sound barrier from the subjective to the universal. As personal records and as documents in the history of modern ideas, however, they are unsurpassed in the interest and consistency of what they reveal. Only now with the interval of time, the re-examination of his forgotten juvenile writings, the recovery of much of his private correspondence, and the new sympathy for the Victorian's dilemma, is it possible to understand the Scottish renegade as he was never able to understand himself or to make himself understood. The clues to the riddle of his unhappy life and tragic death lie in the influences which shaped his earliest years. "In my beginning is my end," with its corollary, "In my end is my beginning," of T. S. Eliot's Christian psalm is nowhere more strikingly illustrated than in the self-inflicted martyrdom of John Davidson, materialist and antichrist. To his contemporaries he seemed at the last a bizarre anomaly, his words crude and unintelligible; to us his life appears outwardly uneventful, his work understandable enough but of little interest. A spate of recent studies of Victorian figures makes it clear that Davidson was no freak and that the spiritual disease which took in him so peculiarly violent and fatal a course was endemic to a whole generation of middle-class Victorian intellectuals.

2

SCOTLAND, 1857-90

Whoso would be a man, must be a
nonconformist.
                    Ralph Waldo Emerson

John Davidson was born on April 11,
1857, in the small manufacturing town of Barrhead in
Renfrewshire, Scotland.[1] Barrhead is situated about six
miles south of Glasgow. If you take the express north from
Dumfries to Barrhead, you pass through the heart of Ayrshire familiar to tourists as "the Burns Country." Your
guidebook will point out the white farmhouse of Ellisland
in which Burns composed "Tam o' Shanter"; Craigenput-
tock, Carlyle's home, where *Sartor Resartus* was written;
Auchinleck with the mansion of the Boswell family; and
Kilmarnock, made famous by a single book. It was in Ayrshire that Wallace first defied the English, from here that
Bruce set out for Bannockburn, and on its wild moorlands
gathered the Covenanters who in the seventeenth century
renounced allegiance to the Stuarts. Here were distilled the
traditional Scottish traits of hard courage, vigor, and independence. Rich, then, in history, literature, and natural
scenery, this country was as much a part of Davidson's
heritage as his father's religion which he soon rejected or
the new science upon which he built a faith no less austere.

29

Determined to be original, to acknowledge no ties with the past, he nevertheless remained unmistakably Scottish until the end of his life. His character was stern, proud, perfervid, and completely uncompromising, relieved only in his earlier years by a pawky imagination and a mordant humor.

Davidson's Scotland was not limited to the country south of Glasgow but included the entire south bank of the Firth of Clyde and extended from Ballantrae northeast to Stirling and the Ochils. Alexander Davidson, the poet's father, came from an Ayrshire family who for more than a century had held the farm of Glenhead at Girvan, a small coaling town far out on the south bank of the Clyde below Ayr. Starting out as a commercial traveler, Alexander Davidson studied for the ministry and in the course of time became a minister in the Evangelical Union, one of the many dissenting offshoots of the United Secession and next to the "Auld Lichts" the strictest. He married Helen Crockett, daughter of Alexander Crockett, the parish schoolmaster at Elgin in northern Scotland. By her he had three children: John, George, and Euphemia. The poet's parents apparently shared the same background: They were middle class, evangelical, moderately well educated, and extremely modest in circumstances.

In several places in his ballads and eclogues Davidson has left portraits of his parents as dour, impoverished, and devout Scots. He invariably depicts the father as a single-purposed religious zealot:

> His father, woman-hearted, great of soul,
> Wilful and proud, save for one little shrine
> That held a pinch-beck cross, had closed and barred
> The many mansions of his intellect.[2]

Elsewhere he is "our evangelist, whose little purse/Opened to all save us; who squandered smiles/On wily proselytes, and gloomed at home." [3] In "The Wastrel," a poem which appeared in the miscellany, *A Rosary*, of 1903, a puritanical pastor preaches on the subject of the prodigal son and by indirection cites his own son in the family pew as a modern instance.[4] The shame of the pastor's wife and daughter are balanced by the rebellious son's determination to return to London:

> Oho, for London Town again, where folk in
> peace can die,
> And the thunder-and-lightning devil of a train
> that takes me there!

Several ballads of the nineties portray his mother as a long-suffering, pious woman, subservient to her bigoted husband. "A Woman and Her Son," for example, describes dramatically the slow death of a devout, careworn woman while her son cruelly recalls her "fifty wretched years" as orphan, wife of "a crude evangelist," and penniless widow. Mouthing blasphemies, he in vain urges his mother to renounce her faith for his unbelief. In the conclusion to the poem Davidson expresses his ironic attitude toward all theological differences and his belief that only love and hope matter. When the mother is three days dead, she rises in mockery of Christ to confirm her son's conviction that there is no heaven or afterlife; whereupon he goes mad.

Although there may have been some resemblance to the originals in these family portraits, they are clearly and grotesquely exaggerated. To take a more positive view, Davidson probably acquired from his mother a gentleness, a kind and loyal nature, a wry sense of humor, and a love of music, literature, and the out-of-doors. From his father largely came the other side of his character, its pride amounting to *hubris,* its severity, fervor, and obstinacy. The important fact is that the poems which describe his father and mother and which were written a decade or

more after Davidson had reached maturity preserve images
of his childhood that rankled in his memory for the rest
of his life. Why did he draw these melodramatic caricatures of his parents? They are not living; they lack the
flesh and blood, the redeeming features, and the complexity of all human beings. It is as if the son in his anxiety
to justify his revolt against parental authority had reduced
his father and mother to their religious principles, as he
was later to sublimate his own personality in principles
equally rigid and abstract. Both the savagery and the sentimentality of his recollections suggest that mixed with his
personal righteousness was a sense of guilt and remorse.

When John was still in his second year his family moved
from Barrhead to Glasgow, where his father had been appointed pastor in the Evangelical Union Church in Mont-
rose Street. The only memories of his birthplace which the
poet retained in later life were possibly the only happy
ones, the garden of the Evangelical Union manse and an
adjoining field with sheep and cows.[5] In Glasgow his father
served for two years as a colleague to the Reverend Dr.
James Morison, founder of the Evangelical Union. Morison, a zealous evangelist, had been one of the ablest of the
younger ministers in the United Secession Church in Scotland. In 1841 he had been expelled from this denomina-
tion for advocating the heretical doctrine of universal
atonement in place of the harsher Calvinistic dogma of the
Westminster Confession, which made salvation dependent
upon divine grace.[6] Thus Morison anticipated the liberal
departure in 1853 of Frederick Denison Maurice, who proclaimed his disbelief in everlasting damnation and of
whom Bishop Pusey declared that they "worshipped different gods."[7] As less restrained dissenters joined the Evangelical Union and enlarged its liberal doctrines, the Union
veered further and further away from the Presbyterian tradition and closer to evangelicalism and Arminianism. At

no time rapid, its growth was steady, until by 1853 it included fifty congregations in the larger industrial cities
and western counties around Glasgow. Still, the sect never
prospered widely, which may account for the reduced and
narrow circumstances of Davidson's formative years.[8] A
Theological Academy was eventually established with a
program that featured ardent revivalism and absolute tee-
totalism, including the advocacy of the cold-water cure.[9]

A strict teetotaler himself, Alexander Davidson received
from his congregation a handsome watch in recognition of
his work in behalf of temperance, a subject on which he
frequently lectured. Years later, after his son had inherited
the watch, it was often pawned to pay the rent and only
somewhat less often to supply the owner with his occasional
glass of whisky. The atmosphere of self-denial which Davidson breathed at home determined the nature and extent
of his subsequent revolt. In "Lammas," from the *Second
Series of Fleet Street Eclogues,* Ninian, a London journalist, describes his own childhood training:

> It was engraven deeply on my mind
> In daily lessons from my infancy
> Until I left my father's house, that not
> Ability and knowledge, beauty and strength,
> But goodness only can avail.[10]

Endowed with unquenchable vitality and power of the
senses, which as with Henley and Stevenson increased
rather than diminished with physical infirmities, the young
Davidson must have chafed against the restrictions of his
background. Under these restrictions he developed a lifelong aversion to hymns, sermons, conversions, revivalism,
and pledges.

If Alexander Davidson was a staunch evangelical, by
joining forces with James Morison he set an example for
courageous nonconformity which his son was to follow.

The same indomitable will and dedication to an ironclad
ideal are found in father and son. Gradually their conflicting religious views opened a gulf which similar temperaments only widened. The theme of a son's conflict with his
father in several of Davidson's autobiographical ballads is
one that is familiar from the novels of Samuel Butler,
D. H. Lawrence, and James Joyce; from *Father and Son,*
Edmund Gosse's memoir of his youth; and from recent
studies of the period.

The clash of personalities and generations is always
cruel, but when strong filial love and religious conviction
are added, the antagonism becomes intolerable. In "A
Ballad in Blank Verse of the Making of a Poet," a poem
written by Davidson in his early thirties, a dying father
curses his impious son:

> The city of gold,
> The jasper walls thereof, the gates of pearl,
> The bright foundation-stones of emerald,
> Of sapphire, chrysoprase, of every gem,
> And the high triumph of unending day
> Shall be but wildfire on a summer eve
> Beside the exceeding glory of delight,
> That shall entrance me with the constant thought
> Of how in Hell through all eternity
> My son performs the perfect will of God.[11]

A struggle between open defiance and deeply buried guilt
plagued Davidson for the rest of his life. It is reflected in
all his works in which he tries to justify rebellion, heresy,
and finally patricide, in the name of self-fulfillment. Always he translated personal conflict into intellectual principle. His preoccupation in his writings with the antagonism of parent and child, his romantic isolation, and his
ultimate acceptance of a code in which the dilemma of love
and hatred at odds is resolved take their origin in this early,

persistent conflict. As he came in time to identify himself with both sides of the conflict, with the disobedience of the son and the supreme authority of the father, he sought simultaneously to glorify sin and expiate it.

Precisely how long the Davidsons lived in Glasgow is not known, but they next moved to Greenock where they put their son to school at the Highlander's Academy. There or at home the boy began to discover those English classics which shaped his first works. At six he was by his own claim a daily reader of *Pilgrim's Progress*. In his tender, whimsical story, "The Pilgrimage of Strongsoul" (1890), he was to record the impact of this book upon the imagination of a sensitive, fanciful boy. At seven he discovered Scott, whom he read voraciously, and by twelve he was absorbed in Shakespeare and *Sartor Resartus*. It was at this time, in his twelfth year, that the eager and aspirant youth made his debut as an author. When questioned in later years about this early piece, Davidson recalled it as "a sturdy ballad on the defeat of the Moors by Ramiro, King of Spain, when under the celestial sword of St. Jago twice thirty thousand heathen fell," a sanguinary chronicle which he "willingly let die." Although he eventually wrote ballads presenting a detached, ironic vision of life, there was nothing equivocal or halfhearted about these juvenilia.

In 1870, when he was only thirteen, his parents may have suffered financial reverses, for they removed their son from school and put him to work. From this time on he was never to know respite from the dreary task of earning a living. Greenock, on the south side of the Firth of Clyde, had already developed into a flourishing and teeming seaport with sugar refineries, shipbuilding yards, iron foundries, and engineering works. Young Davidson first found work in the chemical laboratory of Walker's, one of Greenock's great sugarhouses. After the Food Adulteration Act was passed in 1871, he put this apprenticeship to good advantage by becoming assistant to the Public Analyst in Greenock, a fairly responsible post for a lad of fourteen. Among his tasks was to weigh portions of 16.6 grams of beet for precipitation with acetate of lead in the polariscopic analysis of sugar—a mechanical operation, no doubt, but one which should have taught him a respect for the exactness of practical science.

His tedious work as laboratory assistant did more to kill than kindle an early enthusiasm for science. Although he had no more liking for this work than he had shown for that in the sugar refinery, he was scrupulously attentive to his duties. A more patient, even-tempered youth would have accepted cheerfully the monotony of this post in place of the marvels of chemistry. No such temperance could be expected of Davidson, who developed early a repugnance for the prosaic facts of science along with an enthusiasm for its romance and mystery. In the opinion of his friends of the time, "literature already had him in thrall." It was on the wings of romance and imaginative speculation that he approached science; he would have preferred the high adventure of the *Argo* to the painstaking researches of the *Beagle*. With literature science offered him freedom from the narrow confines of an evangelical minister's house and the drudgery of a sugar-beet factory.

In 1872, therefore, he resumed his schooling, again at the Highlander's Academy where for four years he did double duty as pupil and teacher. Once more he was able to devote much time to the insatiable search for knowledge and escape furnished by literature. He not only read further in his native classics, committing to memory the whole of Shakespeare's *Sonnets* and Milton's *Comus,* if we are to believe his own recollections, but also "alighted on literature at large like a locust-swarm, devouring with a special and somewhat singular avidity everything in the way of a translation." Judging from his later interests, by works in

translation he meant those of the German and French romantics. It is hard to believe that he found their works in
his own home or at the academy, where they would not
have been thought suitable for impressionable young
minds. Somehow he managed to borrow them. Carlyle had
led him to Goethe, Herder, Lessing, and Schiller, whose
mark upon his early efforts, especially the narrative ballads, is as evident as Shakespeare's and Scott's. Years later
Davidson tried his own hand at translating plays of Hugo
and Coppée, and the *Lettres persanes* of Montesquieu,
with a command of French that was largely self-taught.

Among other early influences that Davidson mentions
during a rare interview in later life was the natural setting
of Scotland in the vicinity of Greenock. He speaks of the
image of the great tidal water which swept up and down
past Greenock, the firth bearing its varied traffic of steam-
ers and pleasure boats, its business emphasizing by contrast
the large, serene mountain ranges and quiet hamlets that
framed it. "When I am alone and not pre-occupied," he
reflects, "the sweep of the coast between Helensburgh * and
the entrance of Loch Ling comes before me, and however
far I may travel in the future, no other coast can be so
deeply graven on my memory." Not even the rocky cliffs
of Penzance, along which he strolled alone in his seclusion
and from which he was believed to have leapt to his death,
were more familiar to him than these scenes of his childhood. During his school holidays Davidson roamed among
the Ochils with their green slopes, rocky gorges, and waterfalls, developing a taste for solitary rambles which constituted his principal recreation for the rest of his life. Along
with the western firth, these misty, pastoral hills appear
in much of the young writer's work: the prose fiction of
Perfervid and "The Pilgrimage of Strongsoul," the play
Smith, and many of his nature lyrics.

* An eighteenth-century resort town opposite Greenock on the Clyde.

At this time two inevitable events occurred. He began to write seriously plays and verse; he also seems to have fallen in love with a young girl whom he calls Annie Smith and whom he introduces into his second play, *A Romantic Farce,* written in 1878. Nothing is known of this youthful attachment which may have been invented and which was certainly idealized. The juvenile verses celebrating it, however, appear with minor changes in *A Romantic Farce.* Although they possess a tenderness and fresh evocation of the natural scene, the conventional sentiments, frequent flatness, and technical lapses of the six stanzas give little promise of the poet to come. Three other plays which he also wrote in this period he "mercifully put to the match." A fourth, *An Unhistorical Pastoral,* began to engage his attention when he was seventeen but it was not actually written for another three years.

2

In 1876 Davidson left Greenock to attend Edinburgh University for a single session, the only formal advanced education he received. Since he does not appear to have had close relatives in Edinburgh with whom he might have lived, he probably took cheap lodgings in a narrow, congested street near the university. At Edinburgh University there was little of what is commonly thought of as undergraduate life. A student matriculated by paying his fee and was thereby entitled to attend the lectures of illustrious men, whom he seldom met socially without a special introduction. Robert Louis Stevenson has left us a sharp picture of the life of a Scottish student at this time:

> The English lad goes to Oxford or Cambridge; there, in an ideal world of gardens, to lead a semi-scenic life, costumed, disciplined, and drilled by proctors. . . .

At an earlier age the Scottish lad begins his greatly different experience of crowded class-rooms, of a gaunt quadrangle, of a bell hourly booming over the traffic of the city to recall him from the public-house where he has been lunching, or the streets where he has been wandering fancy-free. His college life has little of restraint, and nothing of necessary gentility. He will find no quiet clique of the exclusive, studious and cultured; no rotten borough of the arts. All classes rub shoulders on the greasy benches. . . . At five o'clock you may see the last of us hiving from the college gates, in the glare of the shop windows, under the green glimmer of the winter sunset. The frost tingles in our blood; no proctor lies in wait to intercept us; till the bell sounds again, we are the masters of the world; and some portion of our lives is always Saturday, *la trêve de Dieu*.[12]

How Stevenson employed the liberty which he celebrates is a familiar story. Davidson with less ready funds was probably not so wild or irresponsible. With his fondness for walking he missed the long tramps in the Ochils, for there were no such attractions in the vicinity of Edinburgh. Instead he contented himself with walking in busy Princes' Street, the Canonsgate, and up and down the steep incline of Arthur's Seat. At the same time he too must have played the sedulous ape to the old masters and new prophets and felt for a time an exciting sense of freedom. Perhaps it enabled him to declare his independence from family and orthodoxy as Stevenson declared his.

Then as now the university was noted for its scientific minds and medical school, where Lister had taught in the fifties and Darwin had attended lectures in the twenties. There is no record of what courses Davidson took there or what associations he made. He entered too late to meet

Stevenson who left the university prematurely without a
degree in 1873 and too early for James M. Barrie who
matriculated in the year following Davidson's attendance.[13]
A. Conan Doyle entered Edinburgh to study medicine at
the same time as Davidson and their similar interests in
science may have brought them together, but there is no
history of any meeting. Nevertheless he moved to some
extent in the same circle of young literati as Stevenson
had.* Later in London he knew both Doyle and Barrie,
and Henley as well, but it seems that it was not until the
nineties that similar interests and possibly the common
Edinburgh background brought them together.

Revolution was in the air at Edinburgh. Among a certain cynical group of students there was much laughter at
the old theology and great reverence for Professor Huxley.[14] Many illustrious professors were associated with the
university at this time, and Davidson undoubtedly attended some of their lectures. David Masson, Carlyle's
close friend and the biographer of Milton, was professor
of rhetoric and English. The piety and austerity of this
celebrated lecturer were balanced by the humor and pic-
turesqueness of the Greek professor, John Stuart Blackie,
who was as likely to lecture on Egyptian crocodiles as on
Homer and who habitually appeared in Princes' Street in
the incongruous garb of a wide slouch hat and tartan.
In addition there were Campbell Fraser, who taught logic;
Henry Calderwood, moral philosophy; Philip Kelland,
mathematics; and William Young Sellar, Latin.[15] Whether,
as Barrie said of Stevenson, Davidson looked in on his

* Writing Grant Richards shortly after Davidson's death, a former
Edinburgh friend of the poet recalled, "I knew him well many years ago
when I was attending classes in Edinburgh. We had many friendly discus-
sions together and not infrequently had to agree to differ. I met him first
at the house of a common friend, where I sometimes met also R. L. Stevenson." A.L.S., from Evan Maclean, dated 29 Apr. 1909, from Drumnadrochit,
Inverness, P.U.L.

classes when he happened to be passing that way [16] or, more like the young Barrie himself, was a dutiful and attentive student, it is impossible to say. He was, we know, unusually observant, quick, and equipped with a prodigious memory. In time he taught himself to play the piano creditably and learned unaided some German and considerable French, so that to amuse his children he was able to write simultaneously French and English verses, French with the right hand, English with the left.

An explanation of his departure after a single term is not hard to find. Even one session must have made heavy inroads upon his or his family's meager savings, and funds for further education were probably unavailable. Still, other young men without capital but with good minds and a determination to train them have managed to secure a university education. Ungovernably romantic, restless, and anarchic, Davidson must have been something of a young Hotspur at this age. It is easy to picture him impatient with the slow and cautious methods of classroom procedure, eager "to pluck bright honour from the pale-faced moon"; and with honor, the final answer to the riddle of life. Edinburgh failed to furnish a ready-made answer.

There is good reason to believe that in his early years he viewed the world in much the same manner as in later life, when he repudiated all past culture and much of the present. As an apprentice poet he was conventionally romantic, seeking in pastoral utopias of Shakespeare's and his own invention escape from the world which puzzled, repelled, hurt, or worst of all ignored him. Gradually, out of a smattering of scientific knowledge to which the year in Edinburgh may have contributed, he was to invent a new, materialistic cosmos, but it was only Illyria or Arcadia in another form. If Davidson had remained in Edinburgh to complete his education, to round out his training in science, natural philosophy, and literature—but why speculate? The spirit which drove him may have deprived his work of intellectual and formal order, but it gave the same work a fire and vigor that are not to be found in equal measure among his contemporaries.

Whether he left Edinburgh out of impecuniousness or impatience with academic thought and routine, Davidson seems to have leapt from the frying pan into the fire. For the next twelve years, with the exception of one, he devoted himself to an occupation which he came to loathe and which in his most penurious state he afterward shunned, teaching school. In this he followed the time-worn course of other aspirant writers who, to support themselves and find leisure for writing, have turned hopefully to the stepmother of the arts.

His first position after leaving the university in 1877 was at Alexander's Endowed School in Glasgow, which with characteristic candor he always called "Alexander's Charity." Although he detested the drudgery, confinement, and narrowness of the place, Glasgow was not without its compensations for the restless young man who had already begun to write verses and who by this time had finished four poetic dramas. Among his literary friends were William Freeland, William Canton, and others of the Ballad Club or the *Glasgow Herald*.[17] The city had its own ancient and distinguished university with a considerable library, renowned professors, and a reputation for liberalism induced by the teaching of John Nichol and the Caird brothers.[18] In the latter nineteenth century the hiatus between the academic and artistic worlds was not so great as it had been or later became. In all probability Davidson's first contact with the literary great came through Nichol, professor of English at Glasgow University. Just when Davidson made Nichol's acquaintance is not known, but all indications point to the fall of 1877. Both were in Glasgow at that time, Davidson as usher at Alexander's

Charity and Nichol as lecturer at the university. Davidson was twenty and Nichol forty-four. Although the young writer left Glasgow in the following year and did not return there to live until 1889, he preserved a deep and lasting regard for his early mentor.

Nichol, son of the celebrated astronomer and Glasgow professor, John Pringle Nichol, was an accomplished scholar,* a skillful, popular lecturer, and a kind if candid, often brilliant critic. He was already the friend of several outstanding poets, among them Alexander Smith, Sydney Dobell, and Swinburne.[19] It now seems curious that the author of the historical drama *Hannibal,* and of verse that is academic, uninspired, and marked by classical restraint, should have been the friend and guide of such flamboyant and revolutionary poets as Smith, Swinburne, and Davidson. The explanation is to be found not in his pedestrian verse but in his liberal sympathies and independence of mind.

A true Scot, Nichol was a great hater of shams; he abhorred all "unrealities" and "unveracities." [20] Again, he had to a marked degree the metaphysical bent, and his conversation like his lectures was grounded in philosophy. A friend said of him, "He was loyal to his ideals and his obligations, loyal to truth, loyal to his friends, and he was so always and unmistakably. He was full of prejudices and vehemences, and these he wore not 'lightly as a flower,' but as badge and blazonry, which called on you to rank yourself alongside of him, or to attack him. But underneath the excesses which were so potent was a deep and reverent candour." [21] Here is the perfervid Scottish character as seen in Carlyle and in Davidson himself. With such a man the young poet could have had only a sympathetic and

* His scholarly works include full-length studies of Byron in the *English Men of Letters,* Francis Bacon, Burns, and Carlyle; a history of American literature; and articles on the Scottish poets in the *Encyclopedia Britannica.*

strengthening relationship. His early association with so constructive a critic may partly explain his bitterness toward later detractors.

The atmosphere in the Nichols' home at 14 Montgomerie Crescent in Glasgow was one Davidson found congenial. The elder Nichol, John Pringle, an ardent liberal and friend of Kossuth and Mazzini, had publicly supported the movements for freedom in Austria, Hungary, France, and Italy, had endorsed the cause of antislavery in the United States, and had countenanced free thought in religion. His son too had started out as an advanced thinker, refusing to take his Master of Arts degree at Oxford as long as religious tests were required. Although in later life he recanted, becoming an admirer of Lord Balfour and Dr. Martineau, the tradition in the Nichol family was a progressive one that appealed to the rebellious students. Always interested more in the philosophical side of religion and theology than in the ecclesiastical, and never more orthodox than a nonpracticing Unitarian, John Nichol by example, if not by actual counsel, encouraged Davidson in his defiance of religious orthodoxy and helped him on his way toward atheism and scientific monism.[22]

In January 1878, the year in which the second series of his *Poems and Ballads* appeared, Swinburne visited his old friend Nichol in Glasgow. They had been undergraduates together at Balliol and fellow members of the "Old Mortality" society, founded by Nichol for the writing and reading of essays. Its members, lifelong friends, had included also G. R. Luke, A. V. Dicey, T. H. Green, and, in later years, Walter Pater. Professor Jowett and Newman were their gods; Arnold, whom they despised as reactionary and partial, their chief grievance. Often while at Balliol and after, Nichol and Swinburne had spent vacations together. Something of their relationship, cherished

through the years, is suggested by a cryptic entry in
Nichol's journal for June 7, 1860: "To Cumnor with
Swinburne. Edgar Poe, and green leaves. Chaucer in the
evening. Jowett sends for me, to his inner room; rest on the
sofa . . . Must to London to hear 'Don Giovanni' and
visit and make love and dance." [23] The youthful friendship had been sustained by periodic reunions and by a distinctly uninhibited correspondence.* Nichol's advanced
ideas, aired in conversation and letters, may have helped
Swinburne to rationalize his libertine inclinations. Although only four years his senior, the Glasgow professor
exercised on his friend as on much younger poets an intellectual, critical, and quasi-paternal influence.

The reunion at Glasgow in the winter of 1878 was a
joyful and boisterous one, although Nichol must have been
pained by his friend's physical condition. "The pleasant
voice remained, but all the traits of fairyland were gone,"
recalled another companion of Balliol days who had not
seen Swinburne since they were undergraduates and who
met him now in Glasgow. But to the students at the university he seemed a marvel, all that was urbane, sophisticated, daring—in a word, modern—as he marched about
the Quadrangle "very fashionably dressed, in a close-fitting
long Melton coat of dark blue, and the neatest of little
shoes, his top hat balanced on his great mop of hair."
Adopting him as university "laureate," they published
some of his political sonnets in a college magazine.[24] Here
was a latter-day Byron, the initiator of a new romantic re-

---

* Professor Ralph Walker of Aberdeen University informs me that
John Nichol's papers, including correspondence from Swinburne, were
destroyed by his heir. Although Nichol's letters to Swinburne also no
longer exist in the original, Professor Cecil Lang, editor of the collected
letters of Swinburne, states that copies of some of them in Edmund Gosse's
hand are in the Brotherton Collection of the University of Leeds Library.
Professors Walker and Lang believe that both sides of the correspondence
were destroyed in the interest of propriety.

volt which, often among its principal exponents and always among its imitators, expressed itself in dandyism and decadence but which ideally was made of nobler stuff.

One evening during this visit, Professor and Mrs. Nichol invited Davidson, still teaching at Alexander's Endowed School, to meet the brilliant and distinguished guest at their home. In a letter to his clergyman-friend, John Service of Inch, dated January 26, Nichol playfully urged the latter also to come meet Swinburne, in the hope that the blasphemer might yet be "plucked from the burning," and suggested the following Thursday, "as some ingenuous souls, named students, are to meet 'the poet,' commonly supposed of mischief, on the evening of that date." [25] One wonders if it was on this occasion that the meeting so momentous to the young poet took place. Davidson had already sent some of his unpublished verses to the celebrated visitor, who, according to Edmund Gosse, Swinburne's biographer, later received him with great cordiality, "laying his hand upon Davidson's head in a sort of benediction, and addressing him as 'Poet.' " [26] It is not difficult to imagine the delight which the younger man took in the unconventional and irreverent observations of the elder, who was described at this time by another of Nichol's friends as "one of the finest talkers of sense, and certainly the best talker of nonsense, I have ever met with." [27] As "the little, silver hatchet-face, the Silenus of his time," Swinburne was conscious of a reputation to maintain. Imagine, moreover, Davidson's rapture when this demon god proceeded to chant aloud in the professor's study the verses which the younger man had sent him.[28] It may have been at this moment that Davidson resolved to go eventually to London, the Pandaemonium of rebel poets.

In any event, shortly after this visit he wrote to Swinburne from his lodginghouse, enclosing some further verses and asking for assistance:

Mrs. Stephen's
51 Whitevale St.
Glasgow.
28. 3. 78

To the nightingale of poets, these, with every good wish from a singing bird of some description, and probable quality.

The drama which you looked at in Professor Nichol's and which I left with McLehose,* that Barabas has not yet made any sign concerning. Meanwhile I have left my hellish drudgery in Alexander's Charity, and applied myself to the rubbing up of some short pieces and the writing of a number of sonnets which were ready to flow. These with the concurrence of Professor Nichol I send to you with the plain and outspoken request that if you think them worthy you will endeavour to find them in a publisher.

I think them deserving, otherwise I would not trouble you with them. If I am what I take myself to be, my opinion carries great weight.

If I can make no money in two months by my verses, then shall I become an actor.† If the theatre doors remain barred, the gate of heaven is open; and by means of a pistol or laudanum I will regain that inheritance which you and I and all poets have lost, and which our writings are a vain attempt to realize.

* James MacLehose, a Glasgow publisher and a friend of Professor Nichol, who may have introduced Davidson to him. In quoting Davidson's letters I have retained all errors in spelling, grammar, and punctuation except where they obscure the sense; in this event I have taken the liberty of correcting the error without making mention of it.

† In his novel, *Laura Ruthven's Widowhood* (1892), Davidson leaves what may be a self-portrait in the character of a young Scotsman, Alexander Murdoch, alias Leonard Brandon, who found himself at the beginning of an acting career handicapped by his Scottish name and accent. Davidson, who had a fine speaking voice and read aloud well, may have suffered the same experience.

[Written vertically in a large hand, which appears to be Davidson's, across these last three lines is the word "Perhaps."]

I suppose a volume of short pieces will find a readier market than a drama, though I believe my comedy to be a more artistic production.

These pieces range from my fourteenth year.*

I send them to you because I have seen you, because you did not patronize me, because I can trust you, because I take you to be not only the greatest poet since Shakespere, but also the greatest writer as he was likewise before you. Your writings overpower me and overawe me.

You will probably wonder that there is next to no echo—at least I think so—of your style in any verses of mine that may deserve the name of poetry. The reason is that on account of the Philistinism in which I have been brought up, and which is both the nitrogen and oxygen of the murky atmosphere of Greenock— within the veil of which I thank God I did not live, but by the shore—such a volume of ozone as your poetry is regarded as the subtlest poison, and I possessed no golden lightning-rod to attract it to me, so that it is just a year since I began to revel in that divine ether.

Into your hands I commend my verses.

                                        JOHN DAVIDSON.

Swinburne.

P.S. I know you will *suddenly pity my impatience.*

P.S. Were I a member of Parliament I would bring in a bill to establish a new order of merit, to consist of four members only and always: the title would be

---

* Some of these poems are probably included in Davidson's first volume of verse, *In a Music Hall and Other Poems,* 1891.

the absence of all title, and the first four members.
Swinburne, Tennyson, Browning (*Pervervidum Sco-
torum*) Carlyle.

J. D.[29]

Even if one discounts its youthful extravagance and self-
consciousness, this letter, the earliest that has survived, reflects an emotional contradiction that was lifelong. On the
one hand are candor, enthusiasm, shrewdness, and a bravura approaching egoism; on the other, the premonition
of failure, the despair and threat of suicide found in his
later writings, private and literary. Of considerable interest are this early mention of suicide and the preoccupation
with scientific phenomena and jargon. The single word
"Perhaps" more than anything else reveals a fundamental
insecurity. Aside from the date and the reference to his
early works, this letter might have been written as plausibly in the last year of his life. Embarrassed by it or a similar foolish outburst, Davidson again wrote to Swinburne
from Glasgow in May of the same year:

> . . . I am miserable about the letter I sent you—it
> was the child of misery itself, a wretched weakling. I
> do not wish to unsay a word of admiration. I am
> ready, and have been any day since I began to read
> your works, to lay my neck beneath your feet and call
> you King. It is that unveracious confession of realities
> which torments me: though perfectly safe with you it
> never should have been written. If it is not burned,
> please burn it; for supposing you were to die—may
> you live as long as you desire!—and some Bozzy were
> to lay hands on it! [30]

Little seems to have come of this early encounter; but
Swinburne's impress is found in the originality and nonconformity of Davidson's thought especially in matters of

religion and sex, if not extensively in the formal patterns
of his verse. These, as the younger poet notes, had already
begun to take shape before he knew the other's work.
Davidson found an opportunity to repay Swinburne's early
kindness when eleven years later he reviewed for the
Academy his benefactor's *Study of Ben Jonson*.[31] Concerned more with his own views on the function of criticism than with Swinburne's on Jonson, and more with
Swinburne's style than critical judgment, he did praise
ecstatically those qualities in the older writer that to him
were the noblest in literature: originality, spontaneity,
and sincerity. As late as 1895 when invited to name his candidates for the Laureateship, Davidson replied that Swinburne was the only possible choice.[32]

3

"That Barabas," the publisher to whom Davidson refers
in his first letter to Swinburne, evidently never made any
sign concerning the young poet's play. The play must have
been *An Unhistorical Pastoral,* completed in 1877 while
Davidson was still teaching at Alexander's Charity. Its rejection was scarcely an auspicious beginning for a stage-
struck youth who had proposed to besiege the theater in
the double capacity of actor and playwright. In the mean-
time, while he struggled to win attention in the theatrical
and literary world, he was obliged to support himself. He
therefore continued reluctantly and with even less promise
a career as schoolteacher. His retirement in the early spring
before the end of term from his position at Alexander's
Charity, in order to "rub up" some short pieces and write
a series of sonnets, was somewhat premature. He remained
a schoolmaster for the next eleven years until 1888, the list
of places in which he served reading like a register of public schools in southern Scotland.

After leaving Glasgow in 1878 he was for three years

English master at Perth Academy, and while there he may have met the young woman whom he was to marry a number of years later. An unsigned article appearing in the *European Mail* in 1945 leaves a picture of the reluctant and rebellious schoolmaster of Perth.[33] The writer, who claims to have known Davidson in that period, recalls that the poet already had a reputation for holding unorthodox views and that the local people did not quite know what to make of him. Having some talent as an elocutionist, he used to recite "Tam o' Shanter," "King Robert of Sicily," and similar set pieces at local concerts and entertainments until the rector of the academy intimated that this conduct did not accord with the dignity of an English master. In protest Davidson resigned his post. If the rector had known the blasphemies in blank verse which Davidson was soon to write and which, one guesses, were already seething in his mind instead of these familiar platform exercises and the football song reputedly composed for the academy boys, he would not have waited for his English master's resignation. After this strategic withdrawal Davidson repeated the now familiar pattern of irresolution by spending the next year, 1881–82, at Kelvinside Academy in Glasgow and still another, 1883–84, at the Hutchinson Charity School in the neighboring city of Paisley. Like Alexander's Endowed School, Hutchinson Charity provided education for children of families too poor to pay even the nominal "wages" or fees. Unless it is preserved in the annals of some obscure public school, there is no record of the intervening year. These *Lehrundwanderjahre* were briefly interrupted when in 1884 he took a position as clerk in a Glasgow thread firm.

On October 23, 1884, he married Margaret Cameron MacArthur,* two years his junior and one of a large, prosperous family living in Perth. Her mother, Menzies

* Died 11 Oct. 1944.

Cameron, in gratitude for a secure and prominent social position in Perth, stolidly bore her husband fifteen children. John MacArthur, Davidson's father-in-law, was owner of a bobbin factory that manufactured reels for jute mills in India and, presumably in recognition of this commercial achievement, was elected mayor by the citizens of Perth. Little else is known of this family. When he died in 1916 John MacArthur left £650 to each of his surviving children, including Margaret Davidson, but her share came too late to help the poet. Unless it was he who provided the clerkship in the thread factory, MacArthur gave his daughter's husband little material assistance. Nevertheless he had the businessman's reverence for his son-in-law's profession. During a visit to the Davidsons in London in later years, he took one of their children to see Westminster Abbey and proudly remarked, "One day your father will be buried here!" The Scots are proud and independent; it is doubtful that Davidson would have accepted help at any time from his wife's family or even allowed her to mention their distress. Few of Davidson's closest friends, probably only John Lane and Edmund Gosse, knew until too late the full extent of his poverty. Before John Davidson left Scotland, two sons were born, Alexander in 1887 and Menzies in 1889.*

The work in the thread factory at Glasgow held too little future for a man with family responsibilities. More importantly it left the aspirant poet scant time or inclination for writing. One indirect consequence of this interval was the section "In a Music-Hall" in the volume of that title. In prefatory verses to this series of realistic music-hall vignettes, the poet dully recalls his work as junior clerk. From ten in the morning till six at night he wrote "memo-

---

* Alexander Davidson died in 1940; Menzies was still living in November, 1954, when I consulted him about the material in this chapter, but I have since lost touch.

randums and things" or indexed letter books when the office boy was not about;

> And nothing could please me at night—
> No novels, no poems, no plays,
> Hardly the talk of my friends,
> Hardly my hopes, my ambition.

> I did as my desk-fellows did;
> With a pipe and a tankard of beer,
> In a music-hall, rancid and hot,
> I lost my soul night after night.

> It is better to lose one's soul,
> Than never to stake it at all.[34]

Marriage rescued him from the loneliness and futility of this life only to oblige him to resume the frustrations of teaching. Henceforth he had obligations as a husband and father which he could never satisfactorily meet but from which he could not escape. For three years after his marriage, from 1885 to 1888, he taught at Morrison's Academy in Crieff, and for a fourth year, 1888–89, at a small public school in his home town of Greenock.

There is no further record of these years as schoolmaster, but the facts speak for themselves. Six different teaching posts in twelve years: a terse history of fruitless toil, restlessness, and near poverty reflects the eternal antipathy of the creative spirit to pedagogy. Responsible too were the young man's hatred of the older religion and his dedication to the heretical principles of the new science. These drove him to continue singlehandedly the struggle long after a truce had been declared between the opposing sides. There never was a Scot, not even Carlyle, who could bear a grudge so long and bitterly. Even in middle age he could not recall these half-wasted years without risking a tirade. In rejecting Arnold's high seriousness as a *sine qua non* of the best poetry, Davidson, whose work was frequently marked by a high and humorless seriousness of its own, could think of nothing more damning to say than that "a pedantic frowsiness hangs about it; it is redolent of classroom and lecture—precinct and atmosphere alien to the genius of poetry." [35]

Meanwhile he stole time from earning a livelihood to write more poems and plays and to seek a publisher for them. He had finally succeeded in interesting the Glasgow house of Wilson and McCormick in several of his early efforts. In 1885, while he was still clerking in the thread factory, this firm had issued *The North Wall,* a highly original, farcical shilling novel, and the verse drama, *Diabolus Amans.* In the following year the same concern published *Bruce: A Drama in Five Acts,* a chronicle play in blank verse. *Diabolus Amans,* a sensational melodrama featuring a hero who both preaches and practices unorthodox views on religion and sexual behavior, alone of these works was published anonomously.[36] Davidson may have been prompted to this secrecy by regard for his parents' feelings or by so practical a consideration as his own reputation as a teacher. Is it venturing too far to feel the pressure of Professor Nichol's firm hand in this anonymity? In his later works he did not hesitate to express openly the same views. More probably the anonymity reflects the conflict between a desire to defy and an abiding sense of guilt which in subsequent works persisted in a different form.

His next work was published in 1888 by the former senior partner of Wilson and McCormick, Frederick W. Wilson. Davidson himself describes the circumstances in a postscript to a letter that he wrote to the publisher John Lane in the fall of 1893.[37] The enterprising young writer persuaded Frederick W. Wilson and Brother of Glasgow to accept a dramatic piece in three acts entitled *Smith: A*

Tragedy in place of a story which they would have preferred and which he promised to furnish later. Although
it is somewhat more restrained than *Diabolus Amans,
Smith* is in the same melodramatic, rhetorical, extravagantly romantic tradition of the Spasmodic poets, Alexander Smith and Sydney Dobell. The play was published in
a small edition of three hundred copies at two and six; the
author never received a shilling from the book. When as
he had agreed Davidson later offered the Glasgow firm the
story "The Pilgrimage of Strongsoul," the offer was ignored. Writing Lane again in the early nineties, he recalled
his early publisher with a malevolence that might well
have given the later publisher pause: "Frederick W. Wilson—very small, squints abominally [*sic*], legs misshapen.
You can't mistake him . . . Remember you have one of
the worst types of Scotchmen to deal with." [38]

By 1889 the energetic tyro had ready three more plays
but in a markedly different vein. Wholesome, lighthearted
fantasies, they were *An Unhistorical Pastoral,* shelved
eleven years earlier; *A Romantic Farce,* which he assigned
to Edinburgh, 1878; * and the more finished, mature extravaganza, *Scaramouch in Naxos,* composed at Crieff in
1888. Thus the first two of these romantic comedies had
been written before the publication of the more boldly unconventional *Diabolus Amans* and *Smith.* All three were
on the surface innocuous pastiches of Elizabethan pastoral
comedy, Scottish whimsy, and contemporary message. In
1899, unable to find a publisher for the trio, the author
had them privately printed at Greenock in a collected edition with the unassuming title, *Plays.* There was no indica-

* Davidson's memory may not be serving him rightly here. In 1878 he
was teaching at Glasgow and Perth. Unless he completed *A Romantic
Farce* during a visit to Edinburgh in that year, the place or date he gives
is incorrect. It is possible that he postdated the play in order to place it
in date of composition after *An Unhistorical Pastoral.*

tion of authorship beyond the publisher's imprint which read simply "John Davidson, 12 Brisbane Street," the address at which he lived.

Davidson sent a number of copies, wryly inscribed "With the publisher's compliments," to editors and critics who he hoped without much foundation would call attention to them. One of the first copies went to George Meredith at Box Hill, who acknowledged the gift tardily but apologetically:

> I wish I had written you, after reading your volume
> of Plays. I did better perhaps in speaking of them to
> friends, but that does not warm the author; unless the
> friends grow laudatory, & a public is found for him. In
> truth I have to shun the duty of writing letters; I can
> hardly get on with my work. Your vol of Plays ap-
> peared to me full of promise, mark the word. But full:
> remarkable for literary skill, ease in the run of lines,
> & a fantastical humour good in youth. I trust that you
> may succeed.[39]

Although there is no evidence that Meredith's sponsorship extended beyond this courteous if cautious gesture, Davidson was greatly heartened by it.* Read carefully, the letter implies reservations to what appears wholehearted approval, for there is no mention of any dramatic merit in the plays. No collector himself and scarcely tolerant of collectors,† Davidson three months later sent Meredith's let-

---

* Meredith did in 1906 endorse Davidson's nomination for a pension, stating in a letter to Mrs. J. G. Butcher that Davidson was "a worthy writer" and regretting deeply that he was in need of it. *Letters of George Meredith*, W. M. Meredith, ed. (2 vols., New York, 1912), 2, 577.

† To one solicitor of an inscription he replied, "Although I hate and abominate the 'collector' of anything at all, I have a notion of what the collector values." He accordingly returned unaltered her copy of his *Plays* with the comment, "Now this copy of 'Plays' is one of those I sent out for review—'With the publisher's compliments' on the title-page is in my

ter to a friend, Allen Park Paton of Greenock, in fulfillment of a promise and with the observation, "I am glad on
the whole to get it out of my hands, as I am tempted to
show it to people who shouldn't see it." [40]

Additional copies went to Mackenzie Bell,* Theodore
Watts,† and A. H. Japp.‡ In a letter dated October 28,
1889, which accompanied the copy to Mackenzie Bell, the
author wrote:

> The book is reviewed in last week's *Academy,* by
> Mr. Cotterell.§ As there is no publisher's name on the
> title-page the press is taking little notice of it. It is
> important for me—apart from the egotistical desire to
> see one's book attended to—to have some authoritative
> reviews. I sent a copy to the *Athenaeum* in May, but it
> has not been noticed. May I ask you to forward a sec-
> ond copy of my "Plays" to Mr. Theodore Watts with
> the enclosed note which is open for your perusal?
> Perhaps if he should glance at them, he might think
> it worth while giving them a small space in the
> *Athenaeum.* If you object to do this pardon my trou-
> bling you, and dispose of the second copy as you
> choose. In any case I must beg you to pardon the
> liberty I take.[41]

own writing: to add anything more would be to lessen rather than enhance
its value. The copy is in a sad condition: I hope you got it for a shilling."
A.L.S., to Miss Everson, dated 26 Apr. 1902, from Streatham, in the Yale
University Library.

* Henry Thomas Mackenzie Bell (1856–1930), poet and critic, author of
works on Charles Whitehead, Christina Rossetti, and A. C. Swinburne.

† Theodore Watts, subsequently Watts-Dunton (1832–1914), author of
Aylwin, friend of the Pre-Raphaelites, confidant and literary executor of
Swinburne.

‡ Alexander Hay Japp (1839–1905), poet but chiefly critic and scholar of
De Quincey, Stevenson, and Thoreau; author of *Three Great Teachers of
Our Own Time . . . Carlyle, Tennyson and Ruskin.*

§ George Cotterell, poet and journalist, apparently of Scottish birth;
author of *The Banquet* (Edinburgh, 1884), a political satire, and two
volumes of verse (London, 1890 and 1894). His dates are unavailable.

The author of the initial letter to Swinburne, written eleven years before, is scarcely recognizable in this chastened plea. Although Mackenzie Bell obliged by sending the book to Watts,[42] it was at no time reviewed in the *Athenaeum*. With the exception of *Bruce,* which received encouraging reviews in both the *Athenaeum* and the *Academy,*[43] the early plays were virtually unheralded. Only George Cotterell, of the critics who mattered, called attention to the collection, expressing his qualified approval that "good as they are, the final impression left by these plays is that Mr. Davidson is equal to better work still." [44] For further and still far from enthusiastic notices of these romantic comedies, the playwright had to wait until the collected edition of *Plays* appeared in London in 1894.

If this debut as a playwright was unpromising, Davidson had even less success with his early poems. His first volume of lyrics, *In a Music Hall and Other Poems,* did not appear until late in 1891 after the removal to London, when it was published by Ward and Downey.* Writing to John Lane about that time, Davidson described his difficulties in getting these poems into print:

> With the exception of three short pieces the poems were all written in Scotland. None of them are comic, although one or two are humorous. In 1884 a number of them including "In a Music-Hall" were announced for publication by a Glasgow firm, but they put them aside in favour of an historical play "Bruce"—not included in the volume of plays Elkin Mathews has. Again in 1888 another Glasgow firm thought of pub-

* On 25 Feb. 1892, Davidson wrote to Edmund Gosse, to whom he had sent a copy of the volume, "It seems about to die alike unchristened, and undamned. The Title 'In a Music-Hall and Other Verse,' [sic] is, I am told, against it; and being dated 1891 it is apt to be ignored." *The Library of Edmund Gosse,* Ewan H. M. Cox, comp. (London, 1924), p. 86.

lishing "In a Music-Hall &c"; but it was again set
aside in favour of a blank verse tragedy entitled
"Smith"—not in my volume of "Plays." * The Scotch
publishers were afraid of a certain breadth to be
found in some passages. I have included one poem
written in my fifteenth year; the rest were written between the ages of nineteen and thirty.[45]

Which poems were guilty "of a certain breadth" it is hard
to imagine. Certainly there are frank, controversial sentiments throughout and poems like "The Rev. Habakkuk
McGruder of Cape Wrath, in 1879," a satire upon the
Robertson Smith incident,[46] which were calculated to dis-
please the not so very "Free" and "United" Kirk. On the
other hand there is nothing as shocking as some of Burns'
poems or exhibiting as much latitude as *Smith,* which
the publisher accepted, and other plays by Davidson published before he left Scotland.

In spite of these discouragements the poet had been
doggedly edging his way into the literary world for some
time. He had by now published several books, corresponded with noted literati, and written reviews for the
Glasgow Herald, the *Academy,* and other journals. Although he himself sought the notice of the critics and was
deeply sensitive to their reception of his works, he regarded the reviews that he wrote as no more than a meal
ticket or a form of self-advertisement. In a comment on
one of these reviews he wrote to his friend Dr. Japp, "The
book you happily call an 'odd medley,' got, the better portions of it, scant justice from me I am afraid; but it was
very difficult to feel anything but amazement and disgust
at the bulk of it; and this affected the general judgment.
But at the bottom of all my reviews I write—on the rough

* The three short pieces are undoubtedly the three lyrics entitled
"From Grub Street." The Glasgow firms referred to are Wilson and
McCormick, and Frederick W. Wilson and Brother respectively.

copy I mean—'What the deuce does it matter?' " [47] And he
once told W. Robertson Nicoll "that the work of reviewing
was simply intolerable, and that it was a humiliation for
a poet to have to review the new verse books as they came
out." [48] He could never understand why people "whose
bread and butter is found" succumbed to the infatuation
of reviewing.[49] For the rest of his life he had more or less
regularly to practice journalism to keep the pot and the
poet boiling. As in his purely literary ventures, he made
only sporadic efforts to supply the public with what it
wanted or fancied it wanted, as every successful journalist
must do. More often he used a review to air his own irrelevant and unwelcome opinions. Either he did not take
his journalistic work earnestly or he took it too earnestly.
Writing Gosse after Davidson's death, William Watson
observed, "Poor Davidson, he was not much of a journalist
—I believe I myself had much more of a journalistic ap-
titude than he—and when his poems didn't pay it was a
horrible fate to have to eke out a livelihood by the exercise
of a faculty which he hadn't got." [50]

More tardily than most writers, Davidson perceived that
he could not afford to wait longer to commit himself entirely to a hazardous profession. For seventeen years he
had attempted without success to combine schoolmaster-
ing and writing. The drudgery of teaching obstreperous,
hidebound boys deprived him more and more of the time,
energy, and freedom necessary to any writer. To a young
writer in revolt a choice was inescapable. In *Smith* the
character Hallowes, by no coincidence a schoolteacher
turned poet, denounces his former occupation in a mouth-
cramming outburst:

> I'm done with it . . . These squalid years
> Of mental boot-blacking are ended now—
> The shameful pedagogy. . . .

Shameful! a devil's compact! I for food
Have made myself a grindstone, edging souls
Meant most for flying . . .
Intolerance in religion never dreamt
Such fell machinery of Acts and Codes
As now we use for nipping thought in bud,
And turning children out like nine-pins, each
As doleful and as wooden. Never more
Shall I put hand to such inhuman work! [51]

The long series of appointments at obscure, narrow
schools, which had provided food and shelter, had starved
the poet's soul. He at last decided to reverse the regimen.
In 1889, at the end of term, he shook the dust of school-
rooms from his feet forever, although he can never be said
to have put down the ferule.

At the age of fifteen John Davidson had begun the serious composition of verse, yet he was thirty-two before he
finally turned to writing as a sole livelihood. The intervening years, although not entirely lost to authorship, were
a bitter, repressive purgatory. Absent from them were two
staple ingredients that go into the making of a writer, personal freedom and literary discipline. Without question
the man's personality and the tragedy of his life took shape
in this period. Why did he not make the break sooner?
One can only conjecture. The literary capital of Great
Britain was of course London, and if it was difficult to attract the public's notice from the provinces it was equally
difficult to peddle one's wares in the glutted metropolis.
David Gray furnishes an example of the young Scot coming to London full of talent and high hopes, then starving and sleeping in parks, only to return home to die. The
one open gate into literary London was still through Fleet
Street, as Henley, Stevenson, Shaw, and others discovered.
To succeed in journalism required a certain flair, if only

an imitative one, a readiness to swallow pride, and connections. Davidson lacked the last two and the capacity to develop the first.

He was not alone in getting off to a slow start. Of his more or less exact contemporaries, Shaw, Conrad, Kenneth Grahame, Francis Thompson, William Watson, A. E. Housman, and James Barrie did not establish a firm literary foothold until the nineties, many not until after Davidson's initial success in 1893 with the first volume of *Fleet Street Eclogues*. Even Oscar Wilde, George Moore, William Sharp, all older, and the considerably older Henley published their best or most familiar work in the nineties. With a few exceptions, notably Aubrey Beardsley and Max Beerbohm, both artists before writers, there were none of the fledgling-geniuses of the earlier romantic movement. Davidson's contemporaries, however, had preceded him to London by a number of years and had already adapted themselves to the urbanity and club-like intimacy that have always characterized the London literary and journalistic world. Arriving late, the Scot found himself associated and competing with a younger generation: Richard Le Gallienne, Lionel Johnson, Ernest Dowson, William Butler Yeats, Rudyard Kipling, and Stephen Phillips. Beyond this he retained a rigidity and naïveté of spirit which, in spite of a distinguished air, betrayed his underlying provincialism. To the retarding influence of circumstances and origin must be added that of a strong puritan streak and a devotion to duty almost penitential. These qualities, more than any other, testify to his persistent Scottishness.

3

SOMETHING OLD, SOMETHING NEW ...

> We Poets in our youth begin in gladness;
> But thereof come in the end despondency and madness.
> *William Wordsworth*

Three common romantic themes recur in Davidson's early writings: escape, revolt, and the worship of nature. The order in which they appear or at least the emphasis which they receive describes a pattern matching roughly that of his life before he left Scotland. Works reflecting a desire to escape from uncongenial surroundings at home correspond to the youthful excursions into the Ochils and into Elizabethan literature. Lyly, Spenser, and Shakespeare were favorite reading at this time. In somewhat later plays revolt and satire predominate. These show a growing revulsion from the harsh Protestantism and vulgar commercialism of contemporary Scotland supported by an independence more courageous than disciplined. Since a man with a metaphysical bent is never satisfied simply to flee or to fight, Davidson by degrees worked out a stopgap philosophy based largely on nature worship. He derived this early faith partly from the comfort offered by his native landscape to a gnawing sense of isolation, partly from his reading of the older nineteenth-century singing masters, and finally from a sampling of the new science to which Darwin had given authority and impetus. It would be cramping truth to insist upon a strict classification of his Scottish output according to these romantic themes since in most of it all three appear. In spite of this overlapping, a development can be discerned.

Like Shakespeare, whom the young romantic most desired to emulate at this time, he turned first for a lovelier or more heroic projection of life to pastoral comedy and the chronicle play. Davidson was not, of course, the first nineteenth-century author to discover in Shakespeare a playwright's handbook. Shelley, Tennyson, Browning, Swinburne, and others less notable attempted ambitious chronicle plays and tragedies in what they chose to regard as the Elizabethan vein. Although the Scottish schoolteacher may have been encouraged by their example to try his own apprentice hand, his romantic comedies and single history play are the result of a close and reverent reading—more reverent than close—of their Shakespearian models. They are a labor of puppy love, an attempt to recapture subjectively rather than artistically the idyllic world of eternal youth, imperishable love, and the ultimate triumph of innocence. In Illyria, the Forest of Arden, and Prospero's island he found what he was looking for and most needed at this time, escape. At first he only half perceived that Shakespeare's comedies do not overlook the evil and folly of man and are, within their pleasant convention, a microscopic satire upon society. Not until the last of these early comedies, *Scaramouch in Naxos,* did the maturing playwright show a fuller understanding of his master in irony.

It is not surprising that the beginner should have launched himself by imitating first one model, then another. Art begins by imitating itself, says Malraux, and the history of nineteenth-century English drama before Shaw is almost entirely one of imitation or adaptation. It is not surprising either that, like most imitators, Davidson in his first two plays, *An Unhistorical Pastoral*, written in 1877, and *A Romantic Farce*, in 1878, should have copied only the superficial characteristics of their originals. The lack of restraint which later characterizes the poet's own style is foreshadowed in his exaggeration of Elizabethan romantic convention. Emphasizing plot to the neglect of character portrayal, conflict, and clarity of message, the plays abound in stock situations while the long arm of coincidence is repeatedly stretched out of joint.

The virtually unknown author of *An Unhistorical Pastoral* acknowledged in a foreword that his plot came from Allan Ramsay's *The Gentle Shepherd*, "a Scotch Pastoral" as its subtitle defined it, of the early eighteenth century. Universally popular in the nineteenth, Ramsay's pretty, sententious play had gone through innumerable editions and been "attempted" several times in colloquial English before Davidson undertook his still bolder version. *The Gentle Shepherd*, itself a pastiche of Elizabethan pastoral romance, concerns the love of a young shepherd and a humble lass of the Restoration period, who after a series of complications discover in turn that they are both of noble birth and therefore free to marry. Not merely the uninterrupted popularity of this agrarian idyl appealed to the resourceful young Scot looking about him for a peg on which to hang his own bonnet. During these salad years physical vigor was feeding his impatience with the pious morality and snobbery of the average Scottish household. The themes of natural love and democratic freedom which he imagined Ramsay's work to contain strongly attracted him. Into the patently commonplace story of *A Gentle Shepherd* he read the daring message that the course of true love, if never smooth, surmounts all social barriers. His liberties with an earlier work sacred to many Scottish households speak for his defiant independence.

It is less easy to conjecture why Davidson, in refurbishing the eighteenth-century period piece, substituted an Elizabethan for Ramsay's Scottish setting. This essay at "restoration" showed as little judgment as if a collector of fine furniture were to turn a Chippendale chair into a Chinese palanquin. What had redeemed a stale, implausible story in *A Gentle Shepherd* had not been any hidden revolutionary message but the skill with which Ramsay had adapted it to a Scottish setting. The characters, the dialect, the imagery, and the humor were genuinely Scottish and rustic. In using the plot of the earlier play, Davidson undertook to repay Ramsay's debt to Shakespeare by making of the Lowlands pastoral with all its quaint but fresh charm a faint Elizabethan facsimile. To accomplish this he dipped liberally for situations and comedy into *Twelfth Night, The Tempest,* and *The Winter's Tale,* borrowing as well Oberon, Titania, and Puck for an extraneous interlude in the last act. Only the cynical thought that radical changes were necessary to justify still another version of Ramsay's play would seem to justify such a hodgepodge.

There is a further explanation. With the perversity of an unreconstructed Scot Davidson wished above all things to avoid being taken for a provincial. He scorned in literature the use of homely Scottish subject matter and dialect. Admiring Burns as a passionate liberal and a great lover, he took special pains not to imitate him or other dialect writers. Except for a few episodes in its history, its magnificent scenery, and the fertile imagination of its inhabitants, Scotland represented to him moral enslavement and the worship of trade. These prejudices were so deeply and bitterly rooted in his upbringing that he could not write dispassionately of his native country while he lived there or, except rarely, return to it in his works once he had left. Proudly he was a man without a country as, he always protested, he was a man without a creed. Seeking a universally acceptable synthesis, he strove to cut himself off from his national heritage. Precisely because it was far removed from contemporary Scotland and closer to actual nature, because it was Edenic and therefore more real to him, he chose a world of make-believe in which to re-create an unfallen man. The theme is a worthy one; the pity of it is that in his impatience with literary form he did not trouble to treat it more inventively and confidently.

Only a willful, immature mind that would rather startle than please can be responsible for the glaring technical flaws of *An Unhistorical Pastoral*. There is no pretense to plausibility in the action, no respect for verisimilitude of character, only a wanton formlessness. Coincidence and improbability are, to be sure, part of the stock in trade of romantic comedy; the reader who has made a willing suspension of disbelief might not be troubled by the departure from normalcy if he did not sense that the author himself is embarrassed to be caught at these children's games. His attitude toward his medium, sometimes serious, sometimes facetious, too often comes close to a snicker. When a father finally identifies his son in the play, he does so by not one but three of the conventional signs: a crescent mole beneath his left breast, a birthmark on his cheek, and around his neck a "gold chain quaintly wrought." Carried away in an ecstasy of extravagance, Davidson in the final scene has the heroine's reputed mother reveal the girl's true identity "By names, dates, papers, birth-marks, jewellery." [1] The trouble is not that the parody is so outrageous but that the outrageousness is not sustained or its purpose always clear.

W. S. Gilbert and Oscar Wilde were to employ the recognition scene, aside, soliloquy, and similar romantic

68 SOMETHING OLD, SOMETHING NEW . . .

clichés with great comic success because in their works a deliberately artificial style and a satiric purpose are consistently combined and artfully preserved. In the Davidson of these early comedies there is evidence of a split artistic personality, of a condescension to romantic conventions which secretly attracted him, of a sensitive and sentimental nature that intellectually humored itself. His is the self-conscious pose of the romantic malcontent, the melancholy Jaques who finds relief from mockery in tears, from tears in mockery. Halfway between Byron and Shaw, he turned to Elizabethan pastoral comedy for the pagan freedom that he could not find in Scottish evangelicalism. But he retained enough of his congenital practicality and humor to be uncomfortable in this artificial atmosphere. His search for a personal compromise, a *modus vivendi* of the spirit, came like a curtain between him and full artistic responsibility.

Flagrant violation of the laws of probability and possibility is not the only imperfection in the youthful comedies. Often labored, they suggest a not very deft rubbing from the antique. The reader is subjected to periodic lapses in taste; clumsy pseudo-Shakespearian punning and clowning are an excuse for humor, the comic subplots are forced, and much intended pathos declines into bathos. In a misguided attempt to create a fresh, synthetic language the too anxious, too fertile writer mixes with modern colloquial speech archaic words, Scotticisms, and coinages, or goes to earlier romantics for picturesque words like "krakens," "cuttle-sea," "carkanet," and "tinchel-wares." He exercises equal license in syntax with the result that a language which is meant to be liberated and authentic is often merely mannered and polyglot.

With all its borrowed finery *An Unhistorical Pastoral* has redeeming qualities. It possesses a youthful vitality and gaiety that are entirely its own. Commenting upon this

work in 1902, William Archer noted that it had been
written "when Mr. Davidson must have been very young";
but added, "nevertheless he proves himself indubitably a
poet in the very force and freedom with which he reproduces the vices, and some of the minor virtues, of his
model." [2] Although the reader searches in vain for lines
to remember, the total effect of the play is engaging. At
least once in this debut the poetry anticipates the Miltonic
surge and preoccupation with the cosmic associated with
Davidson's later blank verse works:

> Three lustres has this orb in heaven rung,
> Swinging around its vast and vaulted bell
> Of measured space, striking its own deep knell
> From side to side, a huge and pendulous tongue.[3]

And elsewhere in an eloquent denunciation of the commercialism of modern England, distant rumblings of the
prophet's voice that thunders forth in the mature works
are heard. If these initial plays are largely a summer holiday of pleasant landscapes, pastoral love, and lyric song,
the rose in them sometimes pricks and the bee stings. The
young poet's satirical bent, which emerges more strongly
with each new work, shows itself most clearly in this first
play in the character of Guido. A caricature of the puritan,
or more precisely of the Calvinist with worldly motives, he
is a hypocrite in the tradition of Jonson's Tribulation
Wholesome and Ananias in *The Alchemist,* an advocate
of self-abnegation who is secretly avaricious.

Conscious of its immaturity and of an ambiguity of purpose that left it open to misinterpretation, Davidson near
the end of his career offered a defense of his first play that
is not entirely rationalization after the fact:

> Any one who reads with attention my *Unhistorical
> Pastoral,* the pleasure of my twentieth year, will per-

ceive already a fresh departure. It is true the matter
and manner of that masque are old, although the
understanding of it is new; but there is no fault in its
antiquity: a poet, especially in his youth, will celebrate the obsequies of the past—and in his old age
also, if it be his mood. And it will be his mood; for as
long as life continues youth dies not in the poet's
blood and brain whatever else may be destroyed.[4]

There is, then, some method in the madness of the play.
At times the method seems no more than that of mockery,
an important if far from explicit element in its imitativeness. Always impatient with form as such, Davidson in his
earlier *jeux d'esprit* appropriated whatever vehicle at
hand, traditional or at the moment fashionable, fitted his
need. It is not always clear in these five-finger exercises
whether he is attempting a serious copy or, conscious of
his own lack of invention and the limitations of his model,
an impudent parody.

At other times, to give him his due, he employs the venerable romantic formulas for a purpose and with an understanding that are genuinely new. He recognized that the
time-honored conventions of romance were not so much
outmoded as corrupted by an ancestor worship which
could not see their matter for their manner. In the lusty
spirit of Elizabethan literature he recognized his own robust, joyous love of life. In its comic technique he saw a
serviceable medium that need not be taken seriously for
his serious comments upon contemporary society. This is
what he meant when he wrote thirty years later of the "new
understanding" motivating his Elizabethan comedies. As
yet, his ironic stratagem was not fully worked out because
his view of life remained inchoate, as his understanding of
Shakespearian comedy was incomplete. Only in time did
he see in nature neither a setting for bucolic masquerades
nor a last resort of absolute innocence, but a realm in

which the paradoxes and contradictions that exist everywhere declare themselves with unabashed honesty. When in the nineties he came to use the traditional ballad, the pastoral eclogue, and the Elizabethan song as vehicles for this cosmic irony and amorality, the greater strictness of these lyric forms enabled him to achieve an ironic impact that is often more than a tour de force.

2

A Romantic Farce, his next play, although set in contemporary Scotland, is nonetheless another mock-Elizabethan tissue of farfetched absurdities and puerilities. In a wild contagion of matrimony at the play's end, designed to demonstrate that love is a universal leveler, four sets of lovers, representing four estates of society, are joined in marriage; a fifth, already married, is reunited. Again the borrowings are apparent: in the main pair of lovers, Rosalind and Orlando; in another, which provides a comic parallel, Benedick and Beatrice. All the lovers appear two by two in a grand finale which, together with stock situations and lyrics like

> You jest at me, you mock my heartfelt love;
> You put me off and on even as a glove,

convinces one that, after Gay and Gilbert, Davidson deserves credit for fathering the modern musical comedy.

Containing only a few less archaisms and bizarre coinages than his first play, *A Romantic Farce* is written in much the same style. Amid all the vacuous artificiality, however, there is some merit and much promise. Homely images are grace notes in otherwise cloying lines:

> In midnight watches I have often wept
> To hear the waves with melancholy tongues
> Lapping my ship, to see the crowded stars
> Rejoicing like a family in heaven.

Davidson's prose also contains vigorous, if mixed and uneven, imagery: "But these clear-starched opinions, which
young men collar themselves with in the first moon of
manhood, will soon soil, and be washed and wrung to a
rag." [5] How soiled and shapeless "the first moon of manhood" is next to this other freshly laundered metaphor.

The verbal experimentation and ingenuity, the abortive
return to Elizabethan English, the desire for linguistic
purity reflect a romantic longing for a golden age which
goes hand in hand in these comedies with direct attacks
upon Victorian shibboleths. Through his love for a vir-
ginal maid the Elizabethan hero of the play is able to
throw off his nineteenth-century ennui and recapture the
pristine innocence of life:

> Eden, indeed! Adam I envy not
> His grand originality; for when
> I say to you, "Sweet May Montgomery,
> I love you," I speak words I seem to make.
> As sweet and strange they are as when first said
> By Adam when he first beheld his Eve.
> I feel within, about me, and above
> The freshness of creation. Everything
> Is new, and every word a white-hot poem:
> I am a poet, too, as great as Adam;
> To speak, as in his time, is to invent.[6]

Having taken upon himself the corruption of the aged
world, the last Adam begins his search for a rebirth. In
these lines Davidson hints at the ironic heresy which he
makes more explicit in later works; namely, that passionate physical experience—here young love, later torture
and murder—is redemptive and vitalizing. Genesis 1 and
2 are retold with Prometheus as hero: Man's first step toward self-realization was the heroic act of original sin;
guilt and remorse constituted his fall. Davidson's hero is

no less sincere and no less autobiographical because he voices a longing common to many young poets and to the best poets of his time, a longing for man's unfallen identity. So unpredictable, however, were his fellow poets of the nineties—at their best paradoxical, at their worst perverse—that what recommended his youthful plays to them was not his genuine yearning for the elemental in experience and the clean in expression but his apparent decadence of style.

Promethean impiety, at this time scarcely adumbrated, is not the chief heresy in *A Romantic Farce*. More unequivocating are its related observations on love and marriage. The sophisticated Clown has the task in the play of redefining these shopworn conventions. A mouthpiece for the author, he advises one of the young lovers not to addle his brain by imagining that he loves a particular lady any more than a particular lady would admire him if it were not for the fictions of novels and poetry. "It is womankind you love," he declares. "The world's a mere expansion of Adam and Eve: I look upon it as one man and one woman —as manhood and womanhood: and I believe, if you sounded the thought of the world, you would find that is how it regards itself." When his pupil questions the apparent cynicism of this, Clown rejoins, "There is not a maid, a wife, a widow, whose fancy any man, if he set himself to it, could not conquer; not any man whom any woman could not subdue if she chose." Passages like this make one think less highly of Shaw's originality of thought if all the more highly of his wit. Regarding the poet as the universal experiencer, Clown pronounces that the poet's love for his mistress is shared

> By every beauty he may see or hear;
> Whether it be of seas, of flowers, of skies,
> A wind, a woman, or a music note.[7]

This view of the poet anticipates Nietzsche's "free spirit" and Shaw's "artist-philosopher," among other neoromantic concepts of the artist. Retrospectively it is a decadent form of Wordsworth's concept of the poet's higher moral calling and pantheistic identification with nature filtered through the rhapsodies of the Spasmodic poets.

The conclusion to *A Romantic Farce* introduces a final challenge to conformity in marriage. A convention of romantic comedy and the Scottish custom of common-law marriage may prompt the principal lover to recommend

> A further deviation from the path
> Beaten by ages, dusty with the trade
> Of thronging use and want.[8]

Accordingly the several couples are united in a ceremony unsanctioned by justice or priest, with the exception of two innocent rustics. Their union belongs so intimately to the world of nature that the author is loathe to desecrate it even with this informal service. If Ferdinand and Miranda are discernible in the young lovers of these comedies, so are Juan and Haidée. Davidson's view of love and his antipathy to the institution of marriage are merely an extension of Shelley's iconoclastic idealism and Byron's naturalism to which Darwinian thought and the excesses of the industrial revolution gave a new lease on life without much altering their character. Intoxicated by his discovery of ideas already familiar to others, this third-generation romantic is as yet saying little more than the second generation of Whitman, Swinburne, and Meredith had implied or stated as plainly. Clown in *A Romantic Farce* poses as spokesman in the sphere of love for a "new realism." This is a misnomer for a later manifestation of the romantic search for the ultimate in human experience, divorced in this instance from Victorian sham, evasion, and complacency. Utopian in aim, the "new realism" might better be regarded as the old paganism or naturalism rejuvenated by the doctrine of evolutionary progress.

If sincere convictions occasionally crop out like new grass among all the paper flowers of this second comedy, there is again much posturing and self-mockery. Davidson is altogether aware of the foolishness as well as the prettiness of this nonsense. With the self-conscious sophistication that made Edna St. Vincent Millay so exciting to the flapper and her boy friend of the twenties, the least innocent of the women in the play gives vent to a nostalgic longing for youth:

> My beauty—ay,
> Half of my beauty for the dewy dawn,
> The fragrance, and the shadow of heaven, the blood
> That knows not what it would, bathing the thought
> With odorous tides, the rapture of life, the swoon
> Of innocence, the infinite longing,
> The sweet pain, and a pure, brave boy to love me!

As anyone who has written his own adolescent sonnet knows, these sentiments do not derive from first-hand experience; their author had been reading Edward Fitzgerald, the Pre-Raphaelites, and probably, since he met him about the time that they were written, Swinburne. Conscious of their absurdity but unable to control it, Davidson undercuts it in the practical comment of another character:

> My love, you are happier in this fantasy
> Than when you were the thing and knew it not.[9]

In these early plays Davidson is forever playing Mercutio to his own Romeo.

Many romantics, and Davidson is no exception, recognize, now playfully, now painfully, a reality that seldom lives up to the ideal, the elusiveness of the human dream. With them he also feels that this is no reason to give up the pursuit of the ideal. The roguish extravagance or seeming indifference with which he continues to employ the conventions of Elizabethan pastoral comedy indicate that he sees in them a ready-made, outworn tradition, but one more faithful to nature and his own ideals than that of Victorian morals and most Victorian literature. In this year of his coming of age irony is more of a protective device against taking himself and others too seriously than, as it becomes later, the cornerstone of his philosophical system.

For all its lighthearted escapism *A Romantic Farce* reveals an increasing satirical power and rebellious spirit. Its hero, another Elizabethan wooer, more than once puts aside his courtly manners to voice in rough verse and unmistakable terms the sentiments of nineteenth-century revolt—a revolt, in Davidson's case, that is social and moral rather than political. He speaks indignantly of "Fashion, propriety, convention" and of "all dogmas false and fashionable." In a scornful denunciation of the fatalism of another character, the romantic hero proffers a religion of self-reliance that may recall Carlyle and Emerson but also looks forward to Davidson's more mature works:

Face fate and stare it down. Why, this is fate,
This only: other slave we cannot have
Than those same hands and feet of circumstance.
Master it, master it; or fire and flood
Are drowned and scorched like moths and drops of dew![10]

This exhortation shatters the bucolic illusion of the piece, if it can be said ever to have existed. Henceforth in the play the poet can talk convincingly of love and fate only in the key of the "new understanding." The thought of *A Romantic Farce* is distinctly mid-century as its scene, carpeted with heather, thistle, and furze, is unmistakably that of the Scottish hills. It was with some justice that the author, in writing about these plays to John Lane in 1893, protested,

"I wonder, however, why I am still accused of being an Elizabethan. I never was an Elizabethan . . . always a Davidsonian." [11] When Lane brought out in 1894 the collected edition of his plays, Davidson took the opportunity to stress the modern sources of his first two romantic comedies. This, he explained to the publisher, would prevent the charge of derivativeness which greeted the first appearance of these plays: "Some Reviewer reading a passage here and a passage there said 'Oh: a mere pastiche of mere Elizabethanism' as if I had sat down my head buzzing with Shakespeare and Beaumont and Fletcher and written at Random. The plots of these two juvenile plays were carefully studied, elaborated, and simplified . . ." * [12] Be that as it may, the history of his early development as a writer of verse plays is that of his gradual emancipation from his Elizabethan leading strings and his emergence as a Davidsonian. In his second play the "runnable stag" of his later and best-known lyric, so transparently a symbol of himself, has already turned in flight to gore the leading hounds.

The defiant outburst of Davidson's hero was written just three years after William Ernest Henley, tormented by tuberculosis of the foot, had scribbled from his cot in an Edinburgh hospital ward his remarkably detached impressions of human suffering and his will to rise above them. Henley embraces the fullness of life:

> Carry me out
> Into the wind and the sunshine,
> Into the beautiful world. . . .
>
> Free . . . !
> Dizzy, hysterical, faint,
> I sit, and the carriage rolls on with me
> Into the wonderful world.

* See Appendix A.

His well-known "Invictus," published in 1888, voiced more somberly and didactically the spirit of assent, in answer to the decadent ennui and pessimism of the early Swinburne:

> Out of the night that covers me,
>   Black as the pit from pole to pole,
> I thank whatever gods may be
>   For my unconquerable soul.* [13]

The heroes of *A Romantic Farce, Smith,* and of the much later Testaments and Mammon plays, like the poet of Henley's *In Hospital* and "Invictus," stand completely alone, unsupported by faith in any force external and superior to the individual will. They are Promethean in their unbelief, exultant in their supremacy. At the very outset of his career Davidson, like Henley, adopted heroic vitalism as an essential ingredient in his philosophy.

Ample precedent existed in the century for the creed of self-reliance and self-determination. A hardy wild flower, it cropped up in many places under different names. As so often, Wordsworth was the grandsire of them all; but Byron, Tennyson, Matthew Arnold, Browning, Carlyle, and other giants of preceding generations mixed it with their own peculiar solvents until it became a universal panacea for the spiritual ills of the age.[14] Part of the tradition of "sturdy manliness" and "rugged optimism" inculcated by

---

* Contrast Swinburne in "The Garden of Proserpine":

> From too much love of living,
>   From hope and fear set free,
> We thank with brief Thanksgiving
>   Whatever gods may be
> That no life lives for ever;
> That dead men rise up never;
> That even the weariest river
>   Winds somewhere safe to sea.

Poems and Ballads, I, in *The Complete Works of Algernon Charles Swinburne* (Bonchurch), Sir Edmund Gosse and Thomas J. Wise, eds. (20 vols., London, William Heinemann, Ltd.; New York, Gabriel Wells, 1925), vol. *1* of "Poetical Works," p. 301.

Dr. Thomas Arnold of Rugby School, self-reliance was as central to nineteenth-century ethics as honor to that of the sixteenth, conscience the seventeenth, and decorum the eighteenth. So important was this stern individualism that under its impress Darwinian thought, fundamentally deterministic and pessimistic, became the basis for a new optimism and humanism preached by Herbert Spencer, William Clifford, and Thomas Huxley.

Man's moral strength had been for the older Victorians a sufficient emblem of the superiority of the spiritual to the material. With the American transcendentalists and Whitman, the triumph of the individual soul was ensured because it alone had permanent existence, the physical world merely reflecting the spiritual. Although the elder statesmen of Victorian letters continued to find comfort in these solutions, Swinburne and Meredith among later liberated spirits could accept only a naturalistic universe consistent with more recent findings in the natural sciences. Retaining the ethical ideals of work, struggle, and independence advocated by their elders and often the same spiritualistic terminology, they made man by virtue of his mind the highest form of physical being, earth become conscious of its purpose. Joseph Warren Beach summarizes Meredith's understanding of this relationship in such poems as "Earth and Man":

> Earth owes to man whatever is attainable through conscious thought. But man has no thought save from earth; from her he has the very laws which his thought enables him to formulate; from her, the emotional reactions that underlie his religion, wrong or right. Even when he is at odds with her, it is her essence in him that provokes him to this reaction.

From earth, and not from any transcendental source, man derives both his physical and moral being.[15] Davidson joins

forces with Meredith and Swinburne to challenge the
dualism of Tennyson and Browning.

It is this curious alliance of Victorian ethics and Victorian science that Davidson was preserving in his apprentice plays and which he codified in many of his remaining
works. Fortunately for their own serenity Wordsworth and
Dr. Arnold did not live to see their chickens come home to
roost in the barbaric feathers of Henleyan activism and
Davidsonian materialism. The distinction of Davidson,
England's leading materialist writer, lay not in originating
or importing a new philosophy; it lay in carrying the
metaphysics of Meredith and Swinburne and the ethics of
Henley and R. L. Stevenson to their inevitable conclusion.
Unlike Meredith and Swinburne he came to feel the need
to discard the old terminology of spiritual idealism along
with the myths and concepts of Greece and Christian Europe. Unlike Henley and Stevenson he did not recant in
later life, returning as they did to the comfort and re-
spectability of theism.

Up to the present point Davidson, still a probationer,
would seem to have been repeating by rote the catechism
available to him in the writings of older thinkers. If this
were the whole story he would have expressed their ideas
with greater clarity and positiveness, as he would have
faithfully imitated their styles. His need to construct a new
faith was more deeply subjective and urgent. With Blake
he might have said:

I must Create a System, or be enslav'd by another Man's:
I will not Reason & Compare: my business is to Create.[16]

Since he was in a desperate hurry to get on with his system,
he appropriated, not always with discrimination or complete assimilation, whatever lay at hand that would serve
his purpose. This system, which was to be his monument

and his tomb, was therefore highly derivative, but its spirit was vital and unique.

The century was ripe for John Davidson; it had sown dragon seeds and should not have been surprised to see a giant spring up from the furrow. That he evolved a creed which was at once a logical synthesis of previous thought and a subjective extension of it speaks at once for his intellectual sensitivity and independence. Scratch a Scot and you find a paradox. He may have cursed his paternal religion with his first breath and damned it with his last, he may have left his native country to become an English man of letters, but he was at heart incurably Celtic. Only a faith with paradox at its core would satisfy him. He required on the one hand a conception of man and the universe that would contradict the pessimism of Calvin and the self-abnegation of the evangelicals. In their place he would substitute joy, action, tenderness, and love. He sought on the other hand a new creed that would offer in equal measure the tough strength and passionate intensity of the rejected faith. The apostate's sense of guilt, in his case nourished by repeated failure, finally made him stress austerity to the exclusion of joy. Although he enjoyed an early period of carefree hedonism and in his darkest days moments of saving humor, his spiritual pride fed fires that at their quietest were only banked.

3

In his first two plays Davidson had used an established dramatic convention as an excuse for a free play of fancy and a latitude of thought that were more often puzzling than piquant. The levity and artificiality of pastoral romantic comedy had got in the way of a deeper, as yet half-admitted purpose—to air serious views. Clarity comes with certainty, and the ambiguity of the youthful works results from a divided mind. Before he could discipline an inclination to caprice and paradox, he must work out more fully his intellectual synthesis and a personal style to go with it. For his next dramatic work, *Bruce: A Drama in Five Acts,* written in 1884, he chose another sixteenth-century vehicle, the chronicle play. A prefatory note to the 1894 edition of the *Plays* stated that *Bruce* was "now called more correctly 'A Chronicle Play,' " adding that although it had been issued in Glasgow in 1886, it was "now actually published for the first time." * Because of its essential seriousness and emphasis upon character in action, this genre was more suited to Davidson's need to explore his advancing convictions.

By now a journeyman playwright, he proceeded with greater care in preparing his third play. A study of Shakespeare's histories taught him the advantage of telescoping or omitting unessential historical events. Like most Elizabethan chronicles, including Shakespeare's early history plays, *Bruce* is episodic in structure. What gives Shakespeare's chronicles their unity, however, is a clear political theme and their portrayal of the effect of character upon history. *Bruce* lacks this kind of unity. The play depends for its shape and interest upon a series of vividly presented but unrelated scenes and upon certain personal revelations. *Richard II, Henry IV, Richard III,* and the rest are relatively detached, consistent comments upon history, the nature of the state, and the origin of authority in human affairs, written, to be sure, from a recognizable Tudor bias.

---

* Davidson also stated in this preface that *Bruce* had undergone revision since it originally appeared in 1886. A comparison of the two versions shows that, while a few superficial changes were made, the two editions are substantially the same. An extensive correspondence with John Lane, now in the Princeton University Library, suggests an ulterior motive for implying extensive revision: Wilson and McCormick, the original publishers of *Bruce,* were contesting the title to the play. By establishing that this was a completely new, revised edition, Davidson and Lane hoped to weaken the case of the Scots firm.

Bruce is a subjective, lyrical, at times rhapsodic arrangement of emotions, impressions, and views whose only coherence is that given by the author's romantic temperament. In this respect it is closer perhaps to Marlowe than to Shakespeare, and to the Spasmodic poets than to Marlowe. The talent which emerges impressively in Davidson's one venture into drama with a factual background is more lyrical than dramatic.

Subtlety of characterization is also absent from the play. Wallace, Bruce, and Edward, the principal male characters, are forcefully drawn but barely distinguishable. Although uncomplex and unindividualized, each has a morbid interest in self-analysis. The introspective author has clearly drawn in the several heroic figures of the drama nearly identical idealizations of himself. This predominating interest in examining his own inner conflicts and creating a heroic persona of himself is not confined to the men. Although Isabella, the heroine of *Bruce,* affected William Archer as a living woman and struck him as possessing something of the eternal feminine as well,[17] another critic reached a more considered judgment of Davidson's characters. He found them without exception very much alike: "All are men and women in misfortune, strength supported by tenderness, but in life, misfortune develops latent differences of character instead of toning them away." [18] Abstractions rather than individuals, the heroes of Davidson's plays are invariably strong-willed, solitary, robustly masculine men, whose softer side is revealed in tender love affairs and stout friendships. Similarly the heroines are tiresomely alike in their unswerving gentleness, loyalty, and courage. With their inevitable black hair and low foreheads they remind the reader of other nineteenth-century feminine ideals: the sloe-eyed, olive-skinned Eastern beauties of Byron and Moore; the intensely long-suffering Griseldas of the Spasmodics; the Pre-Raphaelite "stunners," their languorous lids, full lips, and arched necks inviting illicit but spirtualized love; and the garrulous, aggressive "new women" of the end of the century. Davidson's heroines, neither chaste nor fallen but unimpeachably pure, are only remotely related to the Pre-Raphaelite Jenny, Faustine, and "Dolores, the world's delight"; or to such new women as Paula Tanqueray and Mrs. Erlynne. While they owe much of their character and lineaments to the Spasmodic heroines, they are essentially a subjective ideal. Together Davidson's heroes and heroines reflect the precarious balance of masculine and feminine qualities in the personality of their creator. The continual introspection which obstructs *Bruce's* action and results in stereotyped characters only enhances its autobiographical interest.

Weakness of dramatic structure and character portrayal may not be too heavy a price to pay for the remarkable improvement of the blank verse in *Bruce* over the poetry of the previous plays. As if its ethical themes of human liberty and courage in the face of numbing adversity required more stalwart language, the verse begins at once to flow evenly and vigorously. It is still literary, still derivative, especially in some of the descriptive passages, but there are many more instances where fancy supports rather than trips up sense. Throughout, a manly style complements manly sentiments, as in Bruce's desire to substitute action for conscience:

> I would to God that I might ever hear
> The trump of doom pealing along the sky,
> And know that every common neighbour day
> Is the last day, and so live on and fight
> In presence of the judgment.[19]

In these verses as elsewhere Davidson has not yet freed himself from the yoke of Shakespeare and Tennyson, but in this play he bears it more gracefully. For the first time his blank verse conveys ideas and emotions in a style no longer self-consciously playful and imitative but charged with deep convictions. The poet has found the courage to be himself.

Davidson is nowhere more successful as a writer of blank verse in this play than in passages that are descriptive but intensely lyrical. He ransacks nature for imagery with which to convey the extremes of human emotion and action. Among the most vivid poetry is a series of eye-witness accounts of the Battle of Bannockburn. A young friar speaks:

"St. Andrew and St. George! Fight on! fight on!"
A whole year's storms let loose on one small lake
Prisoned among the mountains, rioting
Between the heathery slopes and rugged cliffs,
Dragging the water from its deepest lair,
Shaking it out like feathers on the blast;
With shock on shock of thunder; shower on shower
Of jagged and sultry lightning; banners, crests,
Of rainbows torn and streaming, tossed and flung
From panting surge to surge; where one strong sound,
Enduring with continuous piercing shriek
Whose pitch is ever heightened, still escapes
Wroth from the roaring war of elements;
Where mass and motion, flash and colour spin
Wrapped and confounded in their blent array:
And this all raving on a summer's morn,
With unseen larks beside the golden sun,
And merest blue above; with not a breeze
To fan the burdened rose-trees, or incense
With mimic rage the foamless rivulet,
That like a little child goes whispering
Along the woodland ways its happy thought . . .

Rhetoric to be sure, this ingeniously sustained verse paragraph, but rhetoric of the most robust kind and in its verbosity not unsuited to the bookish friar. It is deliberately
offset by the terse, homely image of an old woman:

> The battle's lost before it's well begun.
> Our men fall down in ranks like barley-rigs
> Before a dense wet blast.[20]

In nature's violently contrasting moods and in the richly
varied notes of blank verse the young poet finds a convenient, not to say sympathetic, reflection of man's infinite
diversity. *Bruce* is the first of the plays in which the future
ironist squarely faces life on its own terms. For images with
which to describe the contradictions of life as he has experienced them he turns to the scene which he knows best,
the rugged Scottish landscape. When he turns to a subject
that he knows less well, the motives for men's actions, to
illustrate these contradictions, he oversimplifies. He is
never more a nature poet than in these dramas.

When Davidson's early plays with the exception of the
anonymous *Diabolus Amans* were republished in a single
volume in 1894, *Bruce* was singled out by several critics as
the least perplexing of the collection and the only one
likely to succeed in dramatic presentation. Archer suggested that it be the opening play in a Scottish literary
theater or "with a little trimming . . . justly claim a place
in the repertory of a national theatre." [21] This may have
been one word for Davidson's verse play and two for a
national theater, for which Archer, Henry Arthur Jones,
Shaw, and Harley Granville-Barker were at the time determined agitators. It nevertheless speaks for the poet's originality that in *Bruce* he invested the superannuated costume piece of the nineteenth-century theater with a stirring message, some exciting scenes, and considerable poetry
of merit. In spite of its eloquence and strength *Bruce* is

marred by the unevenness, a mixture of the trite and a
fresh, vital talent, evident in his other plays of this period;
but it is less marred. He was to try his hand repeatedly at
historical romantic drama, but he never recovered the authenticity of this youthful play.

4

Scaramouch in Naxos, completed in 1888, is the last of
the plays written in Scotland. Although it follows in date
of composition the melodramas *Diabolus Amans* and
Smith, still to be considered, it is closer in style and spirit
to the romantic comedies. Subtitled "A Pantomime," this
work is a frank experiment in recruiting still another
dramatic tradition for his purposes. Writing it a decade
later than the other comedies, Davidson is more conscious
of the need to concoct a new medium that combines entertainment, satirical message, and artistic form. A prose prologue introduces Silenus, a character in the play, who
affably and modestly addresses the "gentle readers":
". . . I would fain say, hearers, but I am afraid I shall
never fool it on the stage." He proceeds to define the "True
Pantomime," a kind of secular offspring of the medieval
Feast of Fools. Pantomime by this definition is "a good-
natured nightmare" in which the established authorities
are overthrown:

> . . . Our sense of humour is titillated and strummed,
> and kicked and oiled, and fustigated and stroked, and
> exalted and bedevilled, and, on the whole, severely
> handled by this self-same harmless incubus; and our
> intellects are scoffed at. The audience, in fact, is, in-
> tellectually, a pantaloon, on whom the Harlequin-
> pantomime has no mercy. It is frivolity whipping its
> schoolmaster, common-sense; the drama on its apex;
> art, unsexed, and without a conscience; the reflection
> of the world in a green, knotted glass.[22]

More simply, the world of the pantomime is a topsy-turvy Wonderland of apparent nonsense and slapstick, which in the semblance of a prank reverses and ridicules the usual values; it is, in short, a comic version of an ironical, unmoral universe. Behind the false face of farce, garbed in the parti-colored tights of Harlequin, the author of *Scaramouch in Naxos* can pirouette around the idols of the temple and market place, toppling them over one by one.

Intoxicated as he is by the possibilities of adapting the pantomime, Davidson is aware of excesses in his experiment. The play is "too pretentious . . . too anxious to be more than a Pantomime," he concedes without sham modesty in the prologue.[23] To justify the ambitiousness of his scheme he predicts that from pantomime will spring a new poetical comedy, just as he hopes that from his sensational dramas, *Diabolus Amans* and *Smith,* will emerge some new development in poetic tragedy. Good as *Scaramouch in Naxos* is, the prologue is more brilliantly oracular than the comedy designed to illustrate it. Davidson's conception of the *"True Pantomime"* is a minor critical landmark in the development of classical English comedy from Jonson and Marston to Gilbert and Shaw. William Archer owned fourteen years later that he had repeatedly expressed the same view in very nearly the same words, forgetting that Davidson had been beforehand with him. He added that while he still agreed wholeheartedly in principle with his predecessor, he did not find it put to practice anywhere in the play.[24] The experimental aim of the play and its introduction of stock comedy figures as automatons for ideas—a device carried over into Davidson's later serious plays—may be said to anticipate the "Über-marionettes" of Gordon Craig and the *petits drames pour marionettes* of Maeterlinck. At the same time let it be confessed that Craig's and Maeterlinck's innovation proved a sterile one. The whimsy and fancifulness of *Scaramouch* likewise look ahead to the same strain in G. K. Chesterton and James Barrie, but Davidson lacks the urbanity, poise, and humanity of these dramatists. In his anxiety to create a new comedy he does not so much fall short of their mark as overshoot it.

The presence of Scaramouch, Harlequin, and Columbine in the play suggests a superficial debt to Italian *commedia dell' arte;* the reliance upon slapstick and supernatural machinery belong to English low comedy, notably the traditional Christmas pantomime. For other features the author is more directly indebted to the English masque and the Jacobean comedy of humours. These miscellaneous borrowings do not obscure the fact that this play is a further, more successful attempt at adapting English romantic comedy to contemporary satire and message. Its romantic interest is supplied by a pair of young lovers: Ione, a mortal, and Sarmion, a handsome god who renounces immortality and his home on a distant star to remain with his earth-bound sweetheart. Although Davidson confines this interest to a subplot and gives allegory a wide berth, the romance of Ione and Sarmion expresses a major theme of the play, the sanctity of natural, pagan love. In preferring physical love and death to spiritual immortality, they like their counterparts in the first two comedies condone the fatal choice of Adam and Eve. This turnabout tale is characteristic of Davidson's ironic treatment of traditional myth elsewhere in his writings. The situation of Ione and Sarmion and the playful tone of the play remind one of *Iolanthe* (1882), to which it may also be indebted.

Contrasting with the innocent love of Sarmion and Ione and obstructing its happy fruition are the materialistic motives of the major characters. The principal object of *Scaramouch in Naxos,* its disarming author is at no pains to conceal, is to satirize modern trade and enterprise. Heretofore he had denounced this Victorian bugbear in isolated passages of heavy invective. In this play he chose to pillory the profit motive lightly and throughout. Scaramouch, an unscrupulous impresario modeled on the American showman, P. T. Barnum, is the epitome of Philistine opportunism as it might affect interstellar commerce. When a visitor from Earth seeks to buy the wine of the gods and protests at the outrageous price, Scaramouch cynically observes:

> The old story, sir—
>
> East and west, and north and south,
>   Under the crescent, or under the cross,
> One song you hear in every mouth,
>   "Profit and loss, profit and loss." [25]

This engaging entrepreneur operates in simple accordance with the principle of supply and demand. If it were not for the public with its vulgar demands he would not exist. Yet Davidson does little more than skirt the problem; he offers no extended criticism, proposes no solution. There is none of the righteous anger and heavy handling of the earlier or later dramatic works. When at the conclusion of the play Scaramouch is changed into an ape and sentenced to tour on national exhibition for a year, one feels that the punishment does not fit the crime or the proper criminal, society.

Likewise, ideas which Davidson in other works treats seriously, even ponderously, are here held in abeyance or caper off into a jest. Silenus, one of the mythical figures in the play, explains genius:

> What is genius? This:
> Perception of our bent and tireless zeal
> To track it out against the wind of fate.
> Have we not followed with a quenchless thirst
> Deep drinking?

Or the nature of divinity is briefly debated:

> *Silenus.* It matters not: if you feel confident that
> you are a god you must be one.
> *Glaucus.* But any one might be a god at that rate.
> *Silenus.* Surely, surely; confidence makes gods and
> goddesses of the merest mortality.
> *Scaramouch.* Mars and martyrdom! I shall be a god
> too.
> *Silenus.* Do good Scrub, do: be a god: be the god of
> gulls.[26]

These exchanges are not, it must be confessed, much fun-
nier in context than here. It is verbal wit crudely employed
for self-mockery and not sufficiently supported by comedy
of character and situation. Davidson's effort to undercut
his natural sobriety deserves mention. The fact that he is
often content to pull his own leg does not mean that he
takes his ideas any less seriously. But in this play he is
studiously preserving the pose or defense of the romantic
ironist. "The romantic ironist," says Irving Babbitt, "is
often morbidly sensitive about himself, but is ready to
mock at his own convictions." [27] There is in Davidson's self-
parody a great deal of the romantic's *amour-propre* as well
as his diffidence.

Glaucus, the father of Ione and a pantaloon who aspires
to divinity, completes the unmasking of Victorian commercialism and snobbery by Jonsonian comedy. A Jacobean humour character in modern dress, this dupe is a
prototype of the ambitious father who would marry his
daughter to a stranger if it would procure him a higher
social position. Watching Sarmion caress Ione, he muses:

> Suppose, now, my daughter were to marry a god: she
> would become a goddess; and I, the father of a goddess
> and the father-in-law of a god, would perforce, be
> made a god also—a minor god. I would have been

contented to be a baronet; in my dreams I have sometimes beheld myself a lord; but to be a god!—[to Ione
and Sarmion] Ha! you are getting on together.

When Ione asks her father what god he could possibly be,
he modestly replies, "Probably just a god. Doubtless there
are gods of nothing in particular, merely decorative." [28]
But his castle in the air soon towers as high as the top of
Olympus. Speculating further that Juno must be getting
old, he plans to become Jove's father-in-law. Thus Glaucus
is at once a parody of that Victorian cliché, the *arriviste*
tycoon, and the butt of serious social satire. The fluent
epigrammatic wit of this play, now recalling Gilbert, now
anticipating Wilde, marks an advance over the pseudo-
Shakespearian fooling which clogs the early comedies.

Scaramouch in Naxos illustrates the extravagant humor
which Davidson was developing at this time and employing
with gusto in verse, drama, and the maddest of fiction, *The
North Wall* (1885) and *The Great Men* (1891). At its best
it is good-natured, lively, and incisive. Carrying the ironic
implications of the play over into its style, the maturing
satirist almost succeeds in preserving the illusion of complete detachment. With exceptional forbearance he re-
frains from invective and preaching to puncture by swift,
sharp thrusts and to argue by comic illustration. Again,
the slavish imitation and reckless indifference of the early
plays have been chastened into a personalized, sophisticated technique. The echoes of Shakespeare, Jonson, Keats,
Shelley, Tennyson, and others that persist are no longer
surreptitious or solemn but slyly impudent.

For all this, the originality of *Scaramouch in Naxos*,
which the London wits of the nineties most admired
among Davidson's Scottish plays, does not derive from any
real novelty of idea or form. It goes little beyond a refinement of that irreverent and frequently irresponsible

playfulness which from his first writing flickered over the familiar and unquestioned. As a style it was a possible port of call but not one at which a serious young author could permanently debark. Granting him a well-earned niche among late Victorian jesters, one cannot overlook the absence of artistic restraint and decorum in this whimsical drama and fiction. Davidson does not so much nod as overgenerate; he sins by excess of comic virtue. Drollery, whimsy, buffoonery, irony, and paradox which respect nothing beyond man's simple, natural impulses become virtually an end in themselves. With a mind more willful than willed, and more critical than creative, the playwright does not spare even himself the whip. He parodies not only Shakespeare but himself parodying Shakespeare. When Scaramouch is asked why he speaks in explosive, staccato fashion, it is Davidson who with tongue in cheek replies:

> What am I to do? The world is old; it has been satiated with originality, and in its dotage cries bitterly for entertainment. A public man must therefore be extravagant in order to distinguish himself. My felicitous alliteration and prompt non-blasphemous oaths constitute my note, which is the literary term for trade-mark—a species of catch-word, in fact.[29]

The ready cynicism, ennui, and self-mockery of the young romantic sigh or grin forth from these confessions. Exploiting the vice of imitation, the early Davidson has made an exaggerated Shakespearianism his "note" or, to borrow the music-hall jargon he uses elsewhere, his "biz."

Satire and irony require some touchstone, either in the real or the ideal world, from which they depart and to which they return. Davidson's first two comedies reveal that he is all the more a satirist for being a romantic idealist. The world of innocence for which he yearns through-

out this period is that of a nature uncorrupted by civilization, and specifically that of young love. In place of the
false ideal of Mammon to which Glaucus and Scaramouch
do homage, he offers that of Bacchus. Bacchus in this play
is not the "pampered and audacious old mountain-rover"
that the world conceives he must be "after a supposed
debauch extending from end to end of the Christian era";
but "the big, beardless boy," the god of nature, liberty,
and love. He symbolizes the joyful, unrepressed life of
natural man as Silenus, his foster father, symbolizes the
world's opinion of this life. Oddly enough it is Silenus
who describes the approach of Bacchus and Ariadne in
their Titianesque voluptuousness and grandeur:

> He comes in all his state: the chariot-wheels
> Like silent billows roll; from side to side
> The tigers' heads between their velvet paws
> Like lilies eyed with flame, sway noiselessly,
> Or, poised on high, breathe odours to the moon.
> Taller than Ariadne by a head
> He stands with her upon the chariot-floor:
> They have been lovers since he found her here:
> His arm is round her neck; one loyal hand
> Droops on her shoulder, and the other holds
> A careless rein: her face lifts up to his
> The deep, sweet melancholy of desire;
> And he looks down, high mystery in his eyes—
> The passionate love of these sweet centuries;
> Unstaunched, uncloyed.[30]

The sensuous, melodic language of this play continues to
recall the Elizabethans and the lyric verse of Tennyson;
but the absence in it of Elizabethan or Victorian morality
and the substitution of a pagan naturalism suggest the
dyer's hand of Blake, Byron, Fitzgerald, and Swinburne.

   Scaramouch in Naxos provides an insight into the poet's

state of mind at this crossroads in his career and the artistic predicament which he faced. Torn between a fierce alienation from his native culture and a gentle, naïve idealism, he sought an understanding of life that would serve both. By his own verdict he came closer in this play than before or for some time after to achieving a personal and stylistic synthesis. Writing to H. T. Mackenzie Bell from Greenock in November 1889, he stated at the head of the letter, "Of my three 'Plays,' I have most faith in 'Scaramouch in Naxos.'" [31] Although he still vacillated between revolt against the actual world and escape to one that matched his ideals, no work of the Scottish years anticipates as clearly his later ironic acceptance of all that life can offer, be it dark or bright so that it be real.

4

THE DEVIL'S DISCIPLE

Go to the Fiends of Righteousness
Tell them to obey their Humanities, and
not pretend Holiness.
William Blake

During the interval between the romantic comedies of his coming of age and the satiric melodramas of his late twenties, Davidson's disputatious spirit had accumulated a force and articulateness that he could neither suppress nor temper. He renounced withdrawal and guerrilla tactics for frontal assault. The melodramas, *Diabolus Amans* and *Smith,* openly attack established religion of whatever creed and offer a passionate brief for the mystic worship of nature. Even more than the early experimental comedies, these verse dramas seek to treat the familiar, not to say trite, with a "new understanding."

Since Davidson never acknowledged authorship of *Diabolus Amans,* published anonymously in 1885, or for that matter never so much as mentioned it, there is no way of knowing exactly when he wrote the play. In its flamboyant style and candor it resembles *Smith* more closely than the comedies, but the message of both plays appears implicitly in *A Romantic Farce.* The stock characters and plot of *Diabolus Amans* do not preclude the possibility that the work is a theatrical rationalization of the author's own marriage to Margaret MacArthur in 1884, a reasonable date for its completion. Totally devoid of dramatic structure and credibility, the uninhibited melodrama is still the most significant of Davidson's Scottish works. It contains the frankest expression of his thought up to this time and furnishes indisputable evidence that he hewed out the general form of his later philosophic system much earlier and more independently than up to now has been believed.

The action of *Diabolus Amans* is laid in contemporary Scotland and France. Nine episodic scenes trace the struggle in the protagonist, ironically named Angelus, of Diabolus or the force of evil with what might be called the antidevil or the force of good. During a convivial stag party given by Angelus at the outset of the play, he and his friends debate the question:

> What if the Devil were a man in love,
> And loved a woman good as women be
> Who are not wicked:—what's the sequel, say? [1]

As the rakehell-poet Angelus is in love with the chaste and devout Donna, whose name is the feminine equivalent of "lord" or "master," the play attempts to answer this academic question and to define the exact nature of good and evil. In the ironic answer which it gives lies the seed of Davidson's mature thought.

Pursued by remorse for his profligacy and feeling unworthy of the pure Donna, Angelus is soon troubled by visions of his "spectral self," a variation on the *Doppelgänger* or "double" of earlier German romantics. In the case of Angelus, who is Davidson, these visions are prompted by a vestigial Calvinistic conscience and an involuntary yearning of the body for its sloughed–off soul:

> The self I do not love, and could not love,
> The self which I would slay if it were flesh. (p. 14)

Davidson is not merely declaring intellectual war on the concept of a spiritual life centered in the soul; he is also recognizing the two sides of his own divided nature which he has not yet satisfactorily reconciled. Like Blake, Byron, James Thomson, Meredith, and Swinburne before him, he will find, before this play is finished, in irony and moral relativism a refuge from the classic dichotomy of matter and spirit.

Scorn for all religion not immediately derived from nature and fear that he is too corrupt for Donna drive Angelus into exile. After a lengthy sojourn in France, during which he subjects himself in turn to the disciplines of Notre Dame and the evangelical Huguenots, an unrepentant Angelus rejoins Donna in England. Although she continues to love "the public prayer and anthem" and he remains the resolute apostate, they are finally united by the simple device of mutual consent. Donna vows with an unmaidenly eagerness that promises a quick conversion to her lover's naturalism:

> Thy ship shall never rot in port for me,
> So help me God! (p. 140)

The play thus ends in a convenient compromise: Love, which speaks a common but in Davidson by no means mute language, supersedes all faiths and resolves all differences, "so long as each shall call / Good good, and evil evil" (p. 140). This may be a satisfactory solution in theory; in dramatic practice as in life it is less than convincing. The problem of the lovers' religious and moral differences in *Diabolus Amans* never descends from the rarefied regions of hypothesis and allegory to the terra firma of everyday reality. The heroine comes off a hypocritical, priggish chippie, a Victorian Pamela Andrews; the hero, a superannuated Byronic adventurer.

The purpose of Davidson's startling morality play is not

dramatic, however, but frankly doctrinal and didactic. It rejects by turn the doctrines of original sin and divine election, Roman ritual and authority, and the too easy salvation of the evangelical. In their place it offers the supreme sanction of natural impulse, individual experience, and inner vision. No less dogmatic than the canons which it refutes, the play seeks to demonstrate by means of melodrama and rhapsodic assertion the truth of Hawthorne's dictum which Davidson quotes from *The Scarlet Letter* as an epigraph to his work: "A man can transform himself into an angel, if he will only, for a reasonable period of time, undertake an angel's office." As Davidson understands this, man is self-redeemed; God does not exist in any institution, dogma, or supernatural being but only in individual man who by good deeds and fidelity to his beloved discovers divinity within himself. *Diabolus Amans* is an intriguing mixture of heresy and puritanism, of nineteenth-century science, free thought, and Scotch Protestantism.

2

By virtue of its theme this sensational verse drama belongs to the romantic tradition of diabolism. The tradition had been popularized in the second half of the eighteenth century by the vogue for Gothic romances and made notorious by the philosophic libertinism of de Sade and the Medmenham Abbey orgies associated with John Wilkes and Charles Churchill. Consorting frequently with the occult, diabolism ran its scarlet course through nineteenth-century literature, until its final flare-up in the excesses of the decadents and the witty heresies of Bernard Shaw. To recall a few works of which it is the central theme is to point out some of the literary landmarks of more than a century: Blake's "Prophetic Books," Coleridge's "Rime of the Ancient Mariner" and "Christabel,"

Keats' "Lamia" and "La Belle Dame sans Merci," *The Scarlet Letter,* to mention but the most obvious of many instances in Hawthorne, Melville's *Moby Dick* and *Billy Budd,* the poems and tales of Poe, Swinburne's lyrics, Stevenson's *Dr. Jekyll and Mr. Hyde,* James' "Turn of the Screw," and Shaw's *Devil's Disciple* and *Man and Super-man.* In spite of its prevalence there is little uniformity in the treatment of the theme. Each author adapted it to his particular moral outlook and interest, whether introspective, didactic, scientific, political, philosophical, or psychological. Few by the end of the century were unaffected by the vogue for diabolism; but in Swinburne, Davidson, Frederick Rolfe, Oscar Wilde, and Aubrey Beardsley, whom Roger Fry called "the Fra Angelico of Satanism," it achieved the distinction of a cult.

A *Bildungsroman* in dramatic blank verse, *Diabolus Amans* descends indirectly from earlier portraits of the impious hero: Blake's Job, Shelley's Prometheus, Byron's Manfred, Goethe's Faust, but most immediately from the defiant outcasts of the Spasmodic dramas. These verse plays include among others Philip Bailey's *Festus* (1839), Sydney Dobell's *The Roman* (1850) and *Balder* (1853), and Alexander Smith's *A Life-Drama* (1852). The epithet "Spasmodic," which Carlyle had originally applied to Byron, was appropriately borrowed by Professor William Edmonstoune Aytoun of Edinburgh to designate this younger school of poets, who were among the victims of the Byronic plague that threatened to eradicate literature from Western civilization. Shelley, Keats, Goethe, and the German romantics were other influences. The Spasmodics, several of whom were born or lived in Scotland, had been discovered and "puffed" by the Reverend George Gilfillan of Dundee, like the earlier Samuel Rogers a literary arbiter of some influence. Inspired by a passionate devotion to the revolutionary principles of 1848 and a hatred of Scottish materialism and religious intolerance, the Spasmodic school was in certain respects a regional movement. Although related through Byron, Moore, and Campbell to the tradition of the romantic outlaw stemming from the Continent, it developed under peculiar conditions and, properly regarded, is a trunk line of the romantic movement. *Diabolus Amans* and *Smith* perpetuated a strain that had apparently died out from inbreeding and its own extravagance. By combining it with other romantic strains, these plays gave the Spasmodic tradition new vigor and amplitude, if little refinement.

The Spasmodic plays, written in extravagant, involuted blank verse, depict the flamboyant careers of their satanic heroes. Almost unreadable, the ponderously romantic and didactic dramas or dramatic poems contain isolated passages of splendid rhetoric. Aside from their overwrought style, their distinguishing features are a metaphysical interest in the divine and cosmic, a preoccupation with sin, a pathological emphasis upon physical and mental suffering, and a celebration of the grander phenomena of nature. They call frequently upon the sun, stars, moon, day and night, mountains, waterfalls, and the sea for imagery and symbolism. The Spasmodic hero, always a Titanic egoist, unabashedly commits the most monstrous crimes; rape, murder, kidnaping, blasphemy, and incest are everyday occurrences. Ultimately tortured by remorse, he is saved through love for a pure woman, generally one of those whom he has betrayed. *Diabolus Amans* and *Smith*, as well as the blank-verse poems and plays of Davidson's final years, possess in generous measure all these characteristics.

At their very best the Spasmodic dramas of Davidson's predecessors are extremely uneven, vivid language giving way to dull verbiage, poignancy to bathos, striking realism to the grossest improbability. Byron alive would have shuddered at the excesses committed in his name by these devotees. Arriving late in the provinces, the Byronic vogue made up for its tardiness by intensity and persistence. The principal works of the Spasmodics coincide in date almost exactly with the novels of the Brontës. Where the sentiments of *Childe Harold* and the *Giaour* poems became transmuted into something rich and strange by the gray phantom gloom of Haworth parsonage, Byronism reached in the ravings of the Spasmodic poets its point of greatest deterioration. A swift and terrible retribution was at hand.

Credit for delivering a death sentence to the preposterous, frenzied drama is generally given to the same exasperated critic who had dubbed its authors "Spasmodic," Professor Aytoun.[2] In 1854 this brilliant satirist with several scalps already swinging from his belt published *Firmilian; or, the Student of Badajoz*, a "Spasmodic drama" by "T. Percy Jones," who represented Alexander Smith. An anonymous sham notice by Aytoun in *Blackwood's Magazine* for May 1854 had announced the work and pommeled the Spasmodics lustily, thereby making *Firmilian* even before publication a *cause célèbre*. Accomplishing the considerable feat of exaggerating the already exaggerated, Aytoun's parody is one of the most successful and delightful travesties of a period that includes no lesser parodists than W. S. Gilbert, Robert Hichens, Owen Seaman, and Max Beerbohm.

In a mock preface signed by Jones, the author of *Firmilian* states, "My object in Firmilian has been to typify 'Intellect without Principle' "; and he concludes with a modest admission which is no exaggeration of the Spasmodics' theory of writing or their conceit:

> I am perfectly aware that this poem is unequal, and that some passages of it are inferior in interest to others. Such was my object, for I am convinced that

there can be no beauty without freaks and undula-
tion.

I am not arrogant enough to assert that this is the
finest poem which the age has produced, but I shall
feel very much obliged to any gentleman who can
make me acquainted with a better.[3]

From the outset *Firmilian* overlooks none of the excesses
of the poets whose works were already half-conscious parodies of themselves. The language of the play is ludicrously
fustian and strange, full of puns and such verbal curiosities as "usufruct," "imposthume," "depone," "gibbous,"
and "bedral." Of such were the pebbles which Demosthe-
nes crammed into his mouth to cure himself of stammer-
ing. Other earmarks of the Spasmodics which Aytoun
burlesqued were their antipapistry and blasphemy, their
clumsy clowning and punning in the supposed manner of
Elizabethan comedy, and their pedantic but uninformed
obsession with the physical sciences and metaphysics. The
same stylistic faults and preoccupations mark Davidson's
sensational dramas, both early and late, where they are
treated with alternate levity and seriousness.

A Spasmodic's Spasmodic, Firmilian, the hero of the play,
is incorrigibly immoral and arrogant, conscious only of his
transcendent calling as a poet. This calling permits him to
seek with impunity the most lurid criminal experiences. He
poisons three friends during a drinking bout. Later he
blows up a cathedral, a deed solemnly repeated by Davidson's Mammon in a play written in 1907, fifty-three years
afterward. Prompted by a belated desire to know the pangs
of remorse, Firmilian hurls his dearest friend and benefactor from the top of the Pillar of St. Simeon Stylites. As
amorous as he is destructive, this irrepressible lover is always ready to "wile away an hour" with Lilian, Mariana,
Indiana, or some other all too willing maid. His slothful

conscience finally overtakes him in the persons of a "Chorus of Ignes Fatui" who address him in the deservedly classic chant:

> Firmilian! Firmilian!
> What have you done to Lilian?
> There's a cry from the grotto, a sob by the stream,
> A woman's loud wailing, a little babe's scream!
> How fared it with Lilian
> In the pavilion,
> Firmilian, Firmilian? [4]

These lines were enough in themselves to blight the careers of the Spasmodics.

Aytoun may have spearheaded the reaction against the movement, but there are signs that it would have come in any event, possibly from within the ranks. Their uninhibited anarchism had already begun to spend itself, and by 1856 at least one of their supporters was prepared to call a halt. In a review for the *Oxford and Cambridge Magazine* of Dobell's *England in Time of War* and George Macdonald's *Within and Without,* another "Dramatic Poem," Professor John Nichol took the Spasmodics severely to task. Nichol deplored the desire of authors to attempt works alien to their genius:

> There is nothing in which the result of such a mistaken tendency is more manifest than in the flood of Dramas we have had poured upon us during the last six years, by writers who, with various degrees of excellence, have shown themselves to be anything rather than dramatists. Those poets are, for the most part, either didactic or lyrical, and the freest and best expressions of their thought are, with few exceptions, as far as possible removed from that which is dramatic. They paint scenery with a pencil dipped in all the

hues of nature; they describe feeling, often with exquisite truth; but there is little or no action in the
writings of what we may call our last generation of
singers. Their works will live rather for the beautiful
they contain than as being beautiful or true themselves.

Nichol goes on to describe in greater detail and with less
charity these poetic dramas, "plays of the new order, where
some one talked about his feelings and fate, through scores
of dreary pages, with 'a pause,' 'a long pause,' and 'a very
long pause'; or held parley with the most patient of
beauties, in most interminable dialogues, broken up by
most unmeaning ditties." [5]
    Aytoun's hoax had been so elaborately conceived and
ingeniously executed that it nearly misfired. Several critics
overlooked the irony, taking it for a serious imitation of
the writings of the Spasmodic school. Aytoun himself confessed to a friend that he had been surprised when he sat
down to write it "to find how very closely some of the
passages approximate to good poetry." [6] This may be the
one flaw in *Firmilian* for it is often indistinguishable
from that which it satirizes. This seeming ambiguity, however, calls attention to a very real ambiguity in the Spasmodic dramas themselves and in Davidson's plays which
derive from them. Their naïveté, eccentricity, and formlessness were not altogether uncalculated. In their swash-
buckling attack on the evils of the industrial revolution
and their quixotic fight for freedom in every sphere, poets
like Dobell, Smith, and Davidson often winked at their
own excesses.[7]
    Earlier romantics had found escape, adventure, or self-
fulfillment by carrying imitation to the point of fabrication: James Macpherson (1736–96) had forged manuscripts in Gaelic by a legendary third-century Celtic bard,

Ossian; Thomas Chatterton (1752–70) had discovered a
medieval monk of Bristol, Thomas Rowley, whose works
had been entirely of Chatterton's own making. Similarly
the Spasmodics sought compensation for narrowness of
environment and conscience through their romanticized,
sensation-loving heroes, cruder, less sophisticated predecessors of the devotees of Pater who also cherished each
moment for its own sake. The invention of alternative
and dual personalities is characteristic of the romantic
spirit wherever found. In the Spasmodic poets imitation
took the form not of fabrication or projection into figures
of the dim past but of deliberate self-caricature and hyper-
bole, contrived, parodic, Byronic. Self-mockery is one form
of self-destruction or self-atonement. The supreme romantic may transcend the limitations of life and self through
aesthetic idealism like Keats, personal idealism like Shelley, or political idealism like Byron. The romantic of
smaller endowment will attempt to overcome these limitations by inventing for himself an alternative personality
or by destroying in himself the norms of art and society.*
The Spasmodics furnish an analogy in the nineteenth century to the antiaesthetic, antisocial pranks of the Dadaists
in the twentieth, and to that paradoxical impulse in James
Joyce, Ezra Pound, and Gertrude Stein which risked, some

* The forgeries of first and rare editions of Tennyson, Browning, Swinburne, Ruskin, and others by Thomas J. Wise, the disinterment of the
skull of a Piltdown man, the Cardiff Giant, the Kensington Stone, and
other later hoaxes may have been partly motivated by a similar romantic
impulse. In a period when bibliography and research were less accurate
and less thoroughly checked, it was a temptation, not always resisted, to
manipulate or improve on prosaic truth and at the same time to show
one's superiority to Philistine society by hoodwinking it. In some instances these hoaxes were perpetrated by knowledgeable amateurs who
sought to discredit or embarrass to their own satisfaction the encroaching scientist and scholar. Often the scholar or scientist became an unwitting accomplice. The social psychology governing these deceptions has
not, to this writer's knowledge, been fully explored.

say cultivated, unintelligibility in order to begin with a clean slate.

Clever as it is, Aytoun's parody merely exploited the element of self-parody present in the Spasmodic style. By helping to laugh sensational melodrama out of countenance as the Spasmodics had already laughed themselves out of court, *Firmilian* signed its own death warrant with that of its principal victims. Smith and Dobell went on to write more disciplined lyric poetry superior to their dramatic poems, but their spirit and reputation had been irreparably injured. Only within a small, closely knit circle, at the center of which presided John Nichol, did their prestige and influence continue undiminished. In one of two sonnets addressed to Nichol in May 1881, Swinburne wrote:

> More even than praise of one unseen of me
> And loved—the starry spirit of Dobell,
>   To mine by light and music only known.[8]

In spite of his harsh judgment of their dramas, Nichol by correspondence or personal friendship linked the earlier generation of Spasmodics with Swinburne and Davidson who perpetuated their romantic dynamism.

Never widely known in less parochial literary circles, *Firmilian* had all but vanished into obscurity by the time that Davidson came to write his plays; but there is no question that he knew it. Aytoun's farce, delivered as a *coup de grâce* to Spasmodic drama, now reads like a prophetic satire upon Davidson's philosophical melodramas, *Diabolus Amans* and *Smith,* and his much later *Godfrida, The Theatrocrat,* and *Mammon* plays. Instead of preventing Davidson from imitating Spasmodic verse drama, *Firmilian,* it seems more than likely, called his attention to its possibilities as a vehicle for satire, irony, and self-mockery. It thus confirmed the ambivalent attitude toward literary convention which he had already adopted in the romantic comedies, whose lyric effusions and Elizabethanism also reveal a Spasmodic influence.

It would be wrong to leave the impression that Davidson wrote in the Spasmodic vein by default, out of poverty of invention or impatience with literary form. These played a part certainly, prompting him to copy carelessly the surface characteristics of whatever literary tradition came to hand. Beyond this, one side of his nature had an innate sympathy with their rhapsodic emotionalism. The stronger, more enduring qualities of the Spasmodics as well as their mannerisms appear throughout his career in many of his works. None of their ability to paint impressionistically in glowing colors or their psychological realism is lost in Davidson. To a greater extent than Shakespeare's comedies, their monodramas lent themselves to his worship of nature, his celebration of natural man, and his fascination with science. To the interest of the earliest romantics in astronomy and psychology and that of the Spasmodics in the "practical" sciences of geology and biology, Davidson added the introduction of chemistry and electricity into poetry. He took a further cue from his immediate forerunners by glorifying the individual and his right to determine his own destiny. Like them he was interested in man's more passionate, subjective experiences, and with them insisted upon spontaneity, irregularity, and the non-artificial in art. Like them he perceived with sensitivity the grander beauties of nature. And like them he was highly moral in his fervent immorality. The Spasmodics furnish with Davidson and Swinburne a vein connecting the more familiar outcrops of romanticism at the beginning and end of the century.

Of all the Spasmodics who might have served him as a model, Alexander Smith (1830–67) most resembles Davidson. Dobell's Christian piety, strong sentimentality, and physical frailty would not have recommended him as a guide. And Davidson shared with Bailey only those traits common to all Spasmodics. Aside from these general characteristics of style and theme, he derived specific suggestions from Smith. Before Davidson, Smith wrote of trains and telegraph wires in *A Life-Drama,* where they symbolize middle-class faith in material progress, and in *City Poems* (1857) where they are celebrated for their own sake. Glasgow's foundries, black river, and stone walls inspired Smith's songs as the sooty bricks of Fleet Street and the oily Thames later inspired Davidson's. The impressionistic essays comprising description of country scenes, local legends and allusion, and fresh, ironical observations found in Smith's *Dreamthorp* (1863) and *A Summer in Skye* (1865) prompted the younger Scot's *Sentences and Paragraphs* and *A Random Itinerary,* although neither writer had a monopoly on this sort of thing. Smith himself characterizes the "ideal essayist" in phrases that prophetically describe Davidson's prose style:

> The essayist is a kind of poet in prose . . . [who] plays with his subject, now in whimsical, now in grave, now in melancholy mood. He lies upon the idle grassy bank, like Jacques, letting the world flow past him, and from this thing and the other he extracts his mirth and his moralities. . . . The essayist who feeds his thoughts upon the segment of the world which surrounds him cannot avoid being an egotist; but then his egotism is not unpleasing. . . . And it is this egotism, this perpetual reference to self, in which the charm of the essayist resides.[9]

Comparing Smith to other partisans of the Spasmodic movement, John Nichol found that he had "the fullest melody, the most concise expression," and the greatest mastery "in the portraiture of nature and passion alike"; and

that "with less perhaps of reflective power, [he] more
rarely offends against the rules of taste than his com-
peers." [10] Disposed by circumstance and temperament to
ape the Spasmodics, Davidson had sufficient judgment to
pattern himself on the best of them and to appropriate
what was strongest and most vital in his work.

As the youngest Spasmodic, Davidson was no mere imi-
tator or poetaster; Spasmodic enthusiasm is only one ingredient of many in the synthetic compound that he finally
prescribed. In certain respects he departed markedly from
their more characteristic failings. Like Smith and Dobell
in their less familiar lyrics, he reined in his imagination to
write simple ballads, delicate villanelles, and unpreten-
tious songs. Their penchant for irony and self-parody is
more fully developed in Davidson, whose deeper sense of
humor enabled him in youthful extravaganzas to see the
folly of everything and in the nineties to arrive at a comprehensive philosophy of irony. *The North Wall,* his first
novel, published in the same year as *Diabolus Amans,*
matches *Firmilian* in satirizing the Spasmodic's inane
stress upon extraordinary, shocking experience as the sole
basis of art. At the beginning and again at the end of his
literary career, Davidson was strongly influenced by the
Spasmodics, yet he surpassed by a wide margin their best
efforts. His talent and output were superior because his
philosophic vision was larger; but his indifference to artistic perfection, a matter of temperament which like them
he rationalized as aesthetic theory, blinded him to the
danger of employing their tricks.

Smith, Bailey, and Dobell looked back to the earlier
romantics, to their espousal of the cause of liberty and
their love of humanity and the larger interests of life.
Davidson, who was conscious only of looking ahead, received from them the baton to run a final lap and win a
victory that they scarcely anticipated. He did not share

their fierce hatred of political oppression, their democratic
leanings, their fanatic love of the land north of the Tweed;
or, if he did, only briefly and imitatively. Instead he
evolved an aristocratic radicalism and imperialism altogether alien to their principles. Works like *Festus, Balder,*
and *A Life-Drama,* moreover, contained religious doctrines that were already anathema to the author of *Diabolus Amans* and *Smith.* Although fascinated by immorality,
blasphemy, and doubt as expressions of revolt, the Spasmodic poets never espoused atheism. They were on the
contrary extremely religious with distinct evangelical leanings. To exorcise the mid-century specter of doubt they
offered a fervent, personal, but essentially orthodox Protestantism. Some of their works uphold all the important
ecclesiastical dogmas: the immortality of the soul, universal salvation, and the trinitarian principle. No matter
how iconoclastic the heroes of Smith, Dobell, and Bailey
may be, they ultimately repent and through pure, unfailing love are led to the altar and the baptismal font. The
way of revolt for them is the way to renewed piety and
humility. The bower is no antechamber to the chapel for
Davidson's heroes, for whom revolt is the way to heroic isolation or death. In *Diabolus Amans,* of the early plays the
closest to the Spasmodic tradition, Angelus wrestles in one
of the longest matches on record with the dark angels of
Christianity but, lucky in war as in love, emerges victorious. Even with the formidable Donna on their side,
the forces of Christianity are routed. In appropriating
their aesthetic ideals of spontaneity and sincerity, Davidson briefly accepted the Spasmodics' notion of divine inspiration, only to change it to one that might be called
"automatism," an automatic writing that is self-inspired
and instinctual.* In spite of several major differences,

* Unfamiliar with Freud and the modern understanding of myth,
Davidson in various pronouncements on art anticipates only in a general

many of the same personal traits and cultural influences
come to bear on Davidson as on the Spasmodics. His writings furnish an enrichment of the Spasmodic impulse,
halted by its own limitations, *Firmilian,* and changing
public taste.

3

Alexander Smith, Sydney Dobell, and their immediate
followers, although seeking greater spiritual freedom for
the individual, belonged to an earlier generation of dissenters who wished to liberalize and revitalize established
religion not destroy it. Often mistaken for revolutionaries,
they were theologically as well as politically ameliorists.
Retaining their religiosity, pretensions to mystical experience, and metaphysical mannerisms, Davidson found that
they had built pagan fires only to heap ashes on their
heads. *Diabolus Amans* invites no compromise with formal,
orthodox religion. Its unflinching antiecclesiasticism is
nevertheless a logical extension of the Spasmodic crusade
for a subjective religion and belief in the poet's direct inspiration from God. Once again the renegade Scot carries
an earlier doctrine to its inevitable if unwelcome conclusion: Evangelicalism, stressing personal communion with
God, leads readily enough to the worship of man as God.

Angelus does not make the reader wait long to learn
what religion he would substitute for the obsequious worship of "Milton's god" and unscientific faith in "the manufactured wafer." The nature of his divinity is protean, however, as Angelus runs the gamut from transcendentalism to
naturalism, from evangelical Protestantism to scientific
humanism. At the beginning of the play God for this devil's
disciple is still that of the theist, at once transcendental, the

---

way the theories of André Breton. Nevertheless the germ of *surréalisme*
and automatism, as of other modern art movements, can be found in his
work.

"Greater Being," but, more importantly, immanent and perceptible in nature:

> Whate'er offends the taste and shocks the sense,
> And quarrels with the tints of Earth and Sky,—
> Whate'er is prose and is not poetry,
> Father of Lies, I relegate to thee,
> And I will none of it. . . .
> —I am a poet! and the soul of all
> Hath sacraments more fitting; Sea and Sky,
> These are the symbols of the Infinite;
> These are the letters of the Everlasting. (pp. 78–80)

The idea that the phenomena of nature objectify the spiritual and moral was central to the Spasmodic theory of poetry.[11] In Davidson's expression of this idea, Coleridge and Shelley join in mixed company with Dobell, Whitman, Swinburne, and Meredith. *Diabolus Amans* offers a miscellany of nineteenth-century religious belief.

For the transcendentalist a mystical experience is always within the realm of possibility, and Angelus is soon telling Donna of his:

> My heart was beating outwards into space
> I felt it pulsing at the furthest sphere
> With ever-widening waves of consciousness,
> I swept all space, I tenanted all time,
> For I was God, I was Eternity. (p. 64)

The expression of this is once again Spasmodic, as is the assertion of the poet's spiritual self-sufficiency, but its implications go far beyond Bailey's Arminianism, Smith's deism, and Dobell's pietistic Christianity. There is more of self-absorption than self-transcendence in the experience recorded here, and it is not very far from the deification of the individual upon which all of Davidson's later thought rests.

When Davidson wrote these lines and those that follow in *Diabolus Amans,* he conceivably knew in addition to the Spasmodic poets the work of the German idealists, Kant, Fichte, Schelling, and Hegel, not in the original nor perhaps in translation, but through the expositions of Coleridge, Carlyle, and others. In addition he probably had some knowledge of "Novalis" (Friedrich von Hardenberg) and certainly of Emerson and Thoreau, who is the subject of an early poem. Finally, he must have had an indirect acquaintance with the teachings of all through Walt Whitman's *Leaves of Grass,* which at the very time that *Diabolus Amans* appeared was being prepared for Scottish publication in the offices of Davidson's own publisher, Wilson and McCormick.[12] From Whitman he could have derived the notion of a monistic universe in which the spiritual and material are essentially one. From him could have come also the concepts of universal harmony and order, the centrality of the individual soul, and the democracy of being. The fact that some years later he dismissed with a contemptuous shrug Whitman's "amorphous" and "overrated rhapsodies" [13] would not indicate, in Davidson's case, that he owed him nothing—on the contrary Davidson frequently imitated the traits of other poets whom he later disavowed. This sponge-like eclecticism may detract from his originality but it adds immeasurably to his interest.

The religion that Angelus builds is deeply subjective. Even when it seeks not to be, *Diabolus Amans* is intimate and confessional. Again and again in this first manifesto in the development of the poet's materialist gospel, the proof of a divinity rests upon immediate personal apprehension. Angelus believes in God simply because he is a poet: The poet is dependent upon divine inspiration and perforce is a believer. The poet is also invariably the lover and "No lover lives and not believes in God." Love and the goodness that it promotes suffice to sanctify Angelus' religion and justify it on ethical grounds:

> Love shall be co-extensive with the life,
> And e'en Diabolus an angel be. (p. 70)

These notions Davidson had directly from the Spasmodics, who in turn had borrowed them without restraint or much assimilation from Blake and the early Shelley. God and Godwin, Shelley's libertarian father-in-law, share honors about equally in the dramas of the Spasmodics.

For Davidson at this point love is the solvent which holds in harmonious suspension all life's contradictions:

> What if the Devil were a God in love!
> Away with it, your fond antithesis,
> Your sharp division into good and bad. (p. 10)

According to this moral relativism, which Davidson in later works justified as inseparable from "cosmic irony," everything has its place in the universal harmony. The physical and spiritual are part of one continuum; all is resolved by human and divine love which are the same; moral and spiritual choice are waived altogether or become wholly empirical; sin and virtue are synonymous. Angelus' hallucinations in which he beholds his "spectral self" or conscience symbolize his initial reluctance to accept a wholly relativistic universe. They reflect as well Davidson's own struggle to come to terms with a divided personality and foreshadow the doctrines of "irony" and "immorality" which he devised as philosophical splints to mend a fracture largely psychological.

Angelus' free-wheeling thoughts on good and evil are an echo of the moral relativism found throughout the century where it operates as an antidote to an equally powerful moral positivism. In Blake, Shelley, and Byron this moral juggling takes the form of a reversal of good and evil, as it

does in Samuel Butler and Shaw among later ironists. By
this turnabout, Christian humility and Philistine conformity are synonymous with evil, the liberty of nature and love
with good. Others, including Whitman, Swinburne, and
Meredith, set out later to destroy all moral dichotomies by
a doctrine of universal purity and acceptance, which held
that there are no failures or contradictions in the universe,
no real conflict of good and evil. In "Dolores" Swinburne,
still content with the first phase of the revolution, switches
labels:

> I have passed from the outermost portal
> To the shrine where a sin is a prayer;
> What care though the service be mortal?
> O our Lady of Torture, what care? [14]

Meredith, whom Davidson thought "the foremost man of
letters in England," [15] rejects moral distinctions altogether
in commenting on human responsibility in *Modern Love:*

> . . . I see no sin:
> The wrong is mixed. In tragic life, God wot,
> No villain need be! Passions spin the plot:
> We are betrayed by what is false within.[16]

Both the idea of good and evil reversed and the idea of
good and evil interchangeable find a place in *Diabolus
Amans*. Regarded as a problem in moral mathematics, the
play begins with the hypothesis that conventional good
and evil should be transposed, only to advance rapidly to
the proof that good and evil are indistinguishable.

Davidson's own conception of moral responsibility in his
tragic dramas does not go much beyond Meredith's: Human motivation and conduct derive from nature which is
essentially mutable, amoral, strenuous, highhearted, and
antithetical. In *A Rosary,* the younger ironist penetratingly
analyzed Meredith's position:

In Mr. Meredith's poetry Nature is always intellect. Even when he writes of "Woodland Peace," it is the peace of faculty, not absorbed in contemplation, but employed in strenuous thought. Nature with him is above suffering; she understands and rejoices in her agonies as in her triumphs. . . . [She is] a restless and untiring experimenter . . . terror and mystery to the coward, to the merely emotional animal; love and mystery unveiled to strength and talent.[17]

Swinburne, advancing to this second phase of the revolution, also viewed nature as all-inclusive, paradoxical, neither created nor creating but "self-existent":

> One forceful nature uncreate
> That feeds itself with death and fate,
>   Evil and good, and change and time,
> That within all men lies at wait
>   Till the hour shall bid them climb
>   And live sublime.[18]

Davidson shared with Swinburne and Meredith this quasi-mystical view of nature as the universal matrix. At the same time he shared, if at all, only temporarily and superficially the former's sensual hedonism, passionate devotion to political freedom, and refurbished paganism or the latter's tough intellectuality, evolutionary optimism, and ethical utilitarianism. He picked the minds of these naturalistic thinkers and sometimes echoed their ideas without apology or acknowledgment. It is not always clear, at least to this reader, when in *Diabolus Amans* he is echoing Swinburne and Meredith and when with them earlier oracles available to all. In any event, nineteenth-century hedonism and notions of perfectibility furnished him with the scaffolding rather than the beams and girders of his final system.

It is likewise impossible to say exactly where Angelus parts company with the earlier romantics and with Emerson, Whitman, and the transcendentalists in order to adopt the earth-and-man worship of Swinburne's "Hertha" and Meredith's "Earth and Man." From the blurred edges of Angelus' thinking one gathers that Davidson was unaware of fundamental distinctions among his predecessors. But as the play progresses it becomes clear that the religion which Angelus is painfully shaping not merely repudiates the supernatural and clerical but departs radically from the idealist's, pantheist's, and transcendentalist's conceptions of the deity. For Davidson's hero God does not exist outside of man, "the doer and the deed," in whom alone exist the strength, purity, and power of redemption commonly attributed to divinity:

> Wouldst thou believe in God, thou must be good.
> Outside of goodness shalt thou find no God,
> Although thou look for Him in His own House,
> His palace—emerald Earth and azure Heaven. (p. 109)

Likewise in Swinburne's "On the Downs" mother nature replies to the poet, "There is no God, O son, / If thou be none"; and in "Hymn of Man" Swinburne proffered a new unitarianism of man and God:

> Thou and I and he are not gods made men for a span,
> But God, if a God there be, is the substance of men which
>   is man. . . .
> Not each man of all men is God, but God is the fruit of the
>   whole;
> Indivisible spirit and blood, indiscernible body from
>   soul.[19]

Davidson, on the other hand, was to assert that each man of all men *is* God. The gospel adumbrated by *Diabolus Amans* is as humanistic as it is naturalistic, but as yet it does

not go much beyond Swinburne's pseudomystical mouth-
ings. Angelus' love for Donna may lead him, en route,
to Swinburne's Pan and Meredith's Comic Spirit rather
than to an eighteenth-century Platonic ideal or the Christian God, but in the end it leads him back to the individual
self. Love for him comes perilously close to self-love, divine
worship to self-worship.

The boundaries that separate the various creeds of the
theist are not inflexibly drawn. It is therefore an easy heresy
to progress from finding God in man, as earlier romantics
and the Spasmodics had done, to finding that man is God.
Whitman by asserting the divinity of man, Swinburne the
humanity of God, and Meredith the natural mutability and
mortality of all being had left Davidson no alternative but
to state unequivocally that apart from man there is no
God, apart from physical life there is no being. He concludes *Diabolus Amans* with his own version of the Beati-
tudes:

> The pure in heart, the true in word and deed,
> The strong to suffer and renounce, the great
> In loving, as they live the Blessed Life,
> May come to know the else unknowable,
> Best known unto the best. Thou must be God
> To see Him, know Him and believe in Him. (p. 110)

Out of context Davidson's sentiments and the style in
which he couched them are often indistinguishable from
those of the evangelical pulpit, where as a boy he had ample
opportunity to learn them. One of the more successful
passages in the play is a Protestant hymn that could be
inserted without fear of detection into any nonconformist
hymnal:

> Hadst thou a desert earth tenanted lonely,
>   Hadst thou rebelled against goodness all-tender,

Then had He died for thee, died for thee only,
    For so dire the offence, and so dear the offender,
    He had died for thee only.

Leaving the Fair of Earth's Folly, my Brother,
    Go on a pilgrimage passionate, lonely;
Weep by the River of Tears as if other
    Never had sinned, and as if for thee only
    He had died, O my Brother. (pp. 71–2)

The devil quoting Scripture often surpasses his independent efforts.

The elevation of man to divinity, like the descent of the Christian God to man, is based not only upon his capacity for love and goodness but also upon his indomitable will in the face of adversity. By Davidson's time the comparison of man's struggle to a battle had become a Victorian cliché,* as had the gospel of work to which this play subscribes:

In my worst days, I thought not at the end,
What pleasure have I had, but, what work done! (p. 134)

The significance of Carlyle's countryman and disciple lies not so much in the anthology of these clichés worn smooth and thin, which his writings provide, but in his readiness to live and die by what others had only professed. *Diabolus*

---

* Compare Davidson in *Diabolus Amans:*

>   The soul of man, the Mansoul that we know,
>   Suffers a siege and lifelong, which demands
>   Protracted heroism, and the strength
>   That beaten, baffled, crushed and left for dead,
>   Always recovers and repairs the breach
>   As fast as it is made, and from the walls
>   Shouts "no surrender!" to the foe beneath:
>   Till Death, our good ally, with succour sure
>   Cuts through the sharp fire and relieves the town,
>   And rolling clouds of dust retreating show
>   The enemy retires, the siege is raised. (pp. 101–2)

Amans, moreover, goes beyond the nineteenth-century tonic of pride in struggle and suffering to anticipate a theory made explicit in later poems and plays. By this theory pain and pleasure are not opposite poles of sensation but equivalent states of being at its most intense and desirable. Their identicalness is analogous to that of sin and virtue, God and man. Pain soon becomes a potion in Davidson's medicine kit as sex is in Swinburne's and laughter in Meredith's. In the glorification of pain as one of the privileges of conscious matter, he provides a philosophical buttress for the morbid fascination with pain of the decadents. Those who would attribute to Nietzsche this celebration of the human will as it rises above suffering and defeat have only to turn, for earlier, readily available precedents, to much of Victorian literature and to the poet's own youthful efforts, written at a time when the German's work was not yet known in England.

Striking as are the parallels between Davidson and his immediate intellectual forebears, their influence is of secondary importance. It was not exposure to agnostic poets so much as his desire to cast off the emotional moorings of his childhood in order to steer his own free course that led him just about this time to discard a transcendental, mystical God for the divinity of man. Meanwhile, he was not averse to using the charts of earlier navigators in these spiritual waters, but in sailing beyond known regions to reach the true El Dorado he meant to rely on science. His early faith in science to furnish a more valid cosmogony and metaphysics is touchingly naïve:

> I rather listen to the scientist
> —Inspired interpreter of the holy writ,
> Why then the mountain burns with fire and smoke,
> Till all I see and all I touch is God,
> And science seems the true theology. (p. 138)

Among the current scientific ideas which Davidson duti-
fully echoes in *Diabolus Amans* is the post-Darwinian belief in ameliorist evolution. In rhymes that jingle when
they do not jangle, the poet finds "in Nature's plan / Platform for a perfect man," for "Call him Christ or call him
Buddh, / God is for us,—God is good" (p. 136). When
Angelus makes a final appeal to Donna to unite on their
nuptial bed in what he vaguely calls a "passion for the
Highest," he proposes a faith that is a blend of mid-century
doubt, evolutionary theory, and eroticism:

> But charged each with other's consciousness
> Deepening and doubling individual life,
> Let us with stronger pinion make for Heaven,
> Though it were but the future of mankind.
> Only as we are loyal to the light
> Within us, shall we love each other. (pp. 139–40)

There is a suggestion here of the *élan vital* or Life Force of
Shaw and of Shaw's and Davidson's predecessor, Samuel
Butler. In time, however, Davidson vehemently repudiated the idea both of spiritual or intellectual evolution and
of natural or eugenically controlled evolution. Outdistanc-
ing his contemporaries, he ultimately declared his belief
that in man the material universe had already achieved the
fullest perfection possible. Only a timidity bred by Christian meekness, he stated once his philosophy had gelled,
prevented man from recognizing his own divinity. One may
still safely say that without Darwinism the Scottish materialist would never have conceived his "new poetry" or his
"new understanding" of man as the highest achievement
attainable by matter. In his atheist's progress, Darwinian
evolution served as a pontoon bridge by which the pilgrim
retreated from the Celestial City back across the River of
Faith, and which he then blew up as expendable.

Davidson's originality lay in refuting, extending, or syn-

thesizing the original discoveries of others. *Diabolus Amans*
is a potpourri of contemporary advanced thought, gathered by an impressionable and as yet unfocused sensibility.
If this early play lacks form and centrality, it is because
Davidson's own personality and thought are still inchoate.
No great perception is needed to realize that Angelus, like
all of Davidson's heroes, is an idealized self-portrait.
Through his protagonist's anguished quest, the author
has traced his own rebellion against Calvinist and evangelical orthodoxy and his search for a substitute faith. A
crude outline of naturalistic thought from Wordsworth
through Butler is available in Angelus' self-centered speculations. Although Davidson like Swinburne and Meredith
retains in this play the terminology of theism and idealism—"God," "soul," "spirit," "Being"—the metaphysics
which he roughs in is clearly agnostic, if not atheistic. Implied if not yet fully stated is the scientific humanism of
his later jeremiac plays and Testaments. By "consciousness" he already means a refined form of sensation; Heaven
no longer exists for him outside of man's sense experience;
God, if not rejected in name, is virtually synonymous with
man. The problem for this last of the vociferous Victorian
protestants is a common one, to state heresies in a language
haunted by orthodox meanings. In searching for a "new
language" with which to state a "new poetry," he at times
solved the problem resourcefully by giving to traditional
myth a new interpretation or by creating a new myth out
of the facts of science. Too often, as in *Diabolus Amans,*
he impatiently resorted to didactic assertion, clumsy allegory, and angry bombast. More a lyric poet than he was a
dramatist, and a synthetic philosopher than he was a poet,
Davidson was intent on reiterating his own beliefs. With
the ordinary requirements of good theater or enduring
poetry he was much less concerned.

4

Smith, written in 1885, the year in which *Diabolus Amans* appeared, but not published until 1888, is a tragedy in three acts. Like *Diabolus Amans* and other Spasmodic dramas it is chiefly in blank verse, with interspersed songs. In naming his hero Smith, Davidson is celebrating the uncommonness of the common man. Yet it is no coincidence perhaps that the principal character bears the name of the leading Spasmodic poet or that the play is dedicated to Alexander Smith's close friend and adviser, John Nichol. *Smith* possesses all the attributes of Spasmodic verse drama: a Byronic hero, solitary, courageous, and iconoclastic; a poet-friend as sensitive and despairing as the protagonist is self-assured and defiant; a wholly spontaneous and ardent love for a noble, understanding, chaste woman; extravagance of sentiment and language; and violence of action. Even so, in *Smith,* as compared to *Diabolus Amans* and other examples of the tradition, Davidson has ridden his high horse with curb and bit.

The central situation, which supplies all that there is of plot, is simple enough. Smith, a vigorous man physically and intellectually and a primitive prototype of the Hemingway hero, is "the kind of man that healthy girls / Yield to at once." [20] At the beginning of the play he is planning a vacation in the mountains with his delicate friend Hallowes, a schoolteacher turned poet. Their excursion is forestalled when Smith meets Magdalen, lovely daughter of the jealous Graham and fiancée of the craven Brown. Falling instantly in love, the two elope. In their flight they reach the top of a high mountain where they find the body of Hallowes, who in romantic despair and weariness has committed suicide. When Graham, Brown, and others overtake them at this spot, Smith and Magdalen leap together to death rather than deny themselves and their love.

Once again the playwright is fully conscious of the absurdity of his plot, although this does not deter him from using claptrap as a vehicle for his most serious ideas. On the other hand he gives his scenes greater contemporary feeling and satirical bite than in the previous plays, and when the situation threatens to get out of hand and plunge into nonsense, he turns it into farce. Halfway between the Elizabethan buffoonery of the comedies and the unrelieved solemnity of *Diabolus Amans,* the comedy in *Smith* is inseparable from its seriousness. Bidding her lover a final good-by, Magdalen asks him for a first and last kiss that is not wholly undesigning:

> [*He folds her in his arms and kisses her.*
> Smith.   You are faint, my love.
> *Magdalen.*   Oh, have pity, sir!
> Smith.   I will have pity.
> [*Goes out carrying her.*] (p. 237)

Davidson is well aware that such histrionics and posturing belong to the tradition of *Firmilian* as much as to that of *Festus* and *A Life-Drama.* He also recognizes that the rhetoric in which he expresses his ideas is unmistakably Spasmodic. Hallowes speaks of giving up his post as schoolteacher and denounces the sterile profession

> With lips that shook and molten eyes, his voice
> Hushing and sparkling as his passion tore
> A ragged way through wordy wildernesses,
> Or spread, where image failed, in shallows vague,
> The margin lost in rushy verbiage . . . (p. 223)

It takes a Spasmodic to describe one. Knowing that our sweetest music is often too bad for tears, that our most sincere actions are not without their clumsiness, Davidson employs the Spasmodic style, first with unabashed earnestness, then with facetious bravura. His own comment on the ironic intention in the play is helpful. When *Smith* was first published it carried the subtitle, "A Tragedy"; when it reappeared in the 1894 collection of plays the drama was "called, as originally intended, 'A Tragic Farce.' " [21]

The author's conscious purpose in *Smith* as in *Diabolus Amans* is to express unequivocally certain revolutionary ideas. The violence of these ideas and his own vehemence predisposed him to romantic melodrama. For this he had found a model in the blank-verse dramas of the Spasmodics. Too impatient or unsure to improve on their ready-made formulas, he smiles at stale contrivances which support ideas he wishes to be taken seriously. He is again the jaded romantic resigned to dressing truth in the tawdry trappings of platitude and rhetoric. The result is a fundamental contradiction of design which invalidates both the ideas and the comedy. In *Smith* the Spasmodic features are not so unmistakably and continuously funny that they provide, as in *Firmilian,* a sustained travesty. Nor is the play any more convincing as serious tragedy, although its central situation is implicitly tragic in the manner of Ibsen's problem dramas; that is to say, individuals suffer and die not because they violate a higher moral order but because in their strength or weakness they violate a false social order. Behind the willful extravagance of this drama is more than artful evasion, however. Davidson wishes to demonstrate a thesis, the contradictoriness of existence; but he demonstrates it halfheartedly and unconvincingly. He lacks the humanity to animate the thesis and the inventiveness to create for it an appropriate and individual style. The style of *Smith* and *Diabolus Amans* illustrates by way of metaphor rather than expresses through absorbing drama their central idea. The action in Davidson's early plays as in his late ones has no plausibility and the characters no identity beyond their function as allegorical embodiments of ideas and the author's personal problems.

5

Behind the ironic mask of *Smith,* the poet is intensely earnest and subjective. In the single figure of Angelus, the hero of *Diabolus Amans,* Davidson had attempted often with confusing results to portray his own complex ambitions, doubts, and compulsions. In his next play by simple parthenogenesis he portions out his personality between two characters, the poet Hallowes and the thinker Smith. This device bears the earmarks of psychological conflict as well as of artistic expediency. Hallowes, the renegade schoolteacher and thwarted poet, represents the visible surface, the hypersensitive, gentle, romantic young man yearning for the approval of his fellows:

Give me to dream dreams all would love to dream;
To tell the world's truth; hear the world tramp time
With satin slippers and with hob-nailed shoes
To my true singing: fame is worth its cost,
Blood-sweats, and tears, and haggard, homeless lives.
How dare a man, appealing to the world,
Content himself with ten! (p. 228)

All the humiliations of the young Davidson crush Hallowes: the "squalid years of mental boot-blacking" as schoolteacher, the "daily packets" of manuscripts returned by publishers, the frustrated desire for friendship and recognition, and the thoughts of suicide. Faced by the prospect of grudging charity, estranged friends, and the sneers which success grants to unfulfilled genius and mediocrity, Hallowes takes his life. Although the theme of suicide had already appeared in his correspondence and was to amount to an obsession in his writings, it appears here for the first time in his work.

Smith represents all that Davidson aspired to be, both the unattained heights and the unfathomed depths. He is a stalwart, intrepid, articulate rebel. Departing from the

Spasmodic norm, he knows neither guilt nor remorse. Since we are all one part Walter Mitty, the henpecked husband, and another part Walter Mitty, "the Undefeated, inscrutable to the last," Smith is as much a self-portrait as Hallowes. Unlike his friend, the retiring poet, he is a man of virile strength and resolute action. When Hallowes proposes that they collaborate on a message to rock the world, Smith delivers a curtain speech that is a terse summary of the will to power:

So soon! But you are right: one must become
Fanatic—be a wedge—a thunder-bolt,
To smite a passage through the close-grained world. (p. 230)

Here as elsewhere Davidson's imagery, if only unconsciously, is sexual. Like Whitman, Swinburne, and Meredith before him and D. H. Lawrence after, Davidson celebrates the sexual drive as the basic, energizing force in man. Similarly, the lovers' leap with which the play concludes, like the suicide of Hallowes, is as much an act of heroism and triumph as of defeat. In *Smith* Davidson endeavors to give equal and simultaneous stress to the positive and negative sides of life, but as his thought hardened he was to accentuate the positive. The sexual act and suicide are ideally a defiance of respectable society and a means of virtually mystical self-fulfillment. Sexual potency and prowess, treated with romantic gusto and some humor in the early works but with ponderousness in those of his final period, are among the distinguishing features of the Davidsonian hero.

To make closer the identification of himself with Smith, Davidson assigns to his hero still other characteristics that he possesses or would like to possess. A powerful thinker, the title character of this prophetic play is no effete individual. An effeminate, snobbish, " 'versity man" says of him, "He lacks the college stamp." He is close to earth and to humanity: The barmaids understand him when he "talks philosophy." Davidson attempts no more seriously in his portrayal of Smith than in his other dramatic personages to create a unique, plausible personality; he wishes to suggest only an elemental, telluric force that he felt within himself but that was not confined to himself. Taken together, Hallowes and Smith, the David and Jonathan of this play, are a composite self-portrait of opposite but not mutually exclusive *personae* in which Davidson saw himself. The psychological phenomenon of a dual or multiple personality characterizes many of the figures of the turn of the century, including Yeats ("the man and the masks"), Frederick Rolfe ("Baron Corvo" among other aliases), William Sharp ("Fiona Macleod"), Mrs. Golding Bright ("George Egerton"), and Oscar Wilde, in whom Edmund Wilson sees a tragically divided temperament willing its own destruction.[22] The androgynous figures in the work of Aubrey Beardsley and early drawings of Paul Klee reflect the same romantic yearning for synthesis, personal and artistic. Significant is the aspiration in these figures to an epicene or Tiresias-like identity embracing the dualism of sex, an aspiration which in at least two instances became tragically diverted into active homosexuality and hermaphroditism. Like literary fabrication and self-parody, narcissism, the multiple personality, and bisexuality are manifestations of a romantic irony which pervades the past century; they are symptoms of its quest for a solution to the conflicts which haunt it.

6

Davidson had pretty thoroughly demolished orthodox religion, both Protestant and Catholic, in *Diabolus Amans*. With an ambition characteristic of his entire output, he proceeded in *Smith* to attack all tradition and to establish millennial substitutes. The revolution which *Smith* exu-

berantly calls for is more cataclysmic than any envisaged
by Alexander Smith or Sydney Dobell. It includes in its
destructive wake all "the hydra-headed creeds," the sciences, literature and much of language, commerce, and
society as now constituted. Standing superbly aloof, proud,
superior, self-willed, yet lonely, the heroic individual finds
solace in two sources, love or companionship and nature.
The two are closely allied in Davidson's thought.

Civilization, he feels, has obscured and corrupted the
essential meaning of love by attaching to it connotations
which it does not properly possess; and language has become too decadent to redefine it. As a consequence love is
for society prurient, impure, and unnatural. Love is for
Smith pure, wholesome, and completely natural. He
preaches first love, single love, free love, and, a Spasmodic
to the last, this is what he practises. To redress the balance
upset by Victorian hypocrisy and repression, Swinburne
and Meredith had accepted unabashedly physical, sensual
love. Swinburne extolled and Meredith wrote with casual-
ness of the body and its procreative function, so long a
source of shame. The poet with them accepts or celebrates
the fact that, in Yeats' words,

> Love has pitched his mansion
> In the place of excrement.[23]

Davidson's eroticism, only less sensual than Swinburne's,
less cerebral than Meredith's, is equally a staple item in
his metaphysics. This shift in emphasis from the spiritual
nature of man to the physical is one turning point in the
nineteenth century from an outlook that is transcendentalist to one that is naturalistic. For Davidson love, at once
physical and mystical, is an expression and a part of the
universal order. As irony becomes the unifying principle
of his universe, love is irony's agent. This kind of love has
nothing to do with religious sanction or social institutions,

except insofar as it consciously defies them. With the gradual acceptance of this new meaning of love, Davidson predicts, other worn-out concepts, such as sin and virtue, will
vanish; there will be a universal house cleaning, a "Dooms-
day of nicknames."

Davidson recognizes that, however essential, love and
the enjoyment of nature are subject to an inescapable if
purposeful flux. This notion is so common in the nineteenth century that he probably derived it from no one
source, but he may have known about its ultimate origin
in Lucretius. Davidson's worship of the natural world contains none of the personal comfort and spiritual instruc-
tion, none of the certainty, of Wordsworth's faith. About
to plunge to his death, Smith finds life no more than a
miser's gold, a cultured man's impressions, or lust's delight;
it is a mere moment of immortality, he asserts with bittersweet resignation. His only comfort is that beneath this
flux, this fleetingness, he perceives the permanent, continuous order of nature. The author of *Smith* is not yet wholly
certain of what this permanent and ordered stuff is made.
At this point his position is reservedly agnostic and monistic, but he cannot be content to stand still. He can only
retreat as others had done and were to do, or go on to that
of the thoroughgoing atheist and materialist.

7

Smith's ambiguous subtitle, "A Tragic Farce," contains
more than an uneasy apology made long after the offense.
Still not completely organic to his work, paradox and irony
have become too large a part of Davidson's total view of
things to be dismissed as a mere stylistic conceit. More far-
reaching than would at first appear, the poet's irony in this
play looks toward an irony of outlook as much as of
method, a philosophical irony that embraces not merely
the work and the author himself but the entire universe.

With larger understanding and resourcefulness, he transformed a youthful cynicism and sense of personal inadequacy into a positive metaphysics. *Smith* comes close to this intellectual solution, but an artistic solution is still absent. When he confuses parody with philosophic irony, the still awkward playwright is betrayed into unforgivable lapses.

The philosophical position (the unsympathetic think it a pose) toward which Davidson is moving in *Smith* is one which Irving Babbitt has labeled "romantic irony." Babbitt describes this kind of irony as a centrifugal outlook which forever seeks to escape a moral or spiritual center, to deny all commitment and therefore all responsibility, and to enjoy complete license. It produces what he calls the "disintegrated and multiple personality." Consciously avoiding the narrows of rationalism and Philistinism, the romanticist, he says, pretends not to take himself or his ideals seriously and conceals his sympathies behind a mask of self-parody.[24] Babbitt's account, limited to a study of the earlier romantics, is clearly hostile. Although some might regard it as stirring cold ashes to reply to Babbitt now, it will do no harm to let an early partisan define and defend this view of reality.

Friedrich Schlegel is writing about what he calls Socratic irony, although it is clearly the romantic relativism deplored by Babbitt:

> Socratic Irony is a unique form of conscious dissimulation. It is equally impossible to imitate it or to make it clear. For him who has it not, it will remain, according to his own obvious confession, a riddle. It is not meant to deceive anyone, except those who consider it a deception and who either rejoice in the splendid sport of making fun of everybody or else get angry when they suspect that they also are the objects

of the sport. In it is to be included all jest, all earnest, everything transparently open and everything deeply concealed. It springs from a union of the feeling of life as an art with the scientific spirit, from the conjunction of a complete nature-philosophy and a complete philosophy of art. It introduces and arouses a sense of the insoluble conflict between the finite and the absolute, between the impossibility and yet the necessity of a complete communication between the two. It is the freest of all licenses for through it one is enabled to rise above himself; and yet it is the most lawful, for it is absolute necessity. It is a very good sign if smug commonplace people do not know how they are to record this constant self-parody of taking jest for earnest and earnest for jest.[25]

The principal attribute of irony, as here defined, is its comprehensiveness, what Hegel terms "ensemblism." It rejects nothing, includes and reconciles everything: science and art, metaphysics and aesthetics, determinism and free will. It does not deny the presence of conflict in the universe; it finds in conflict the elastic tension that produces harmony; it reduces reality to a paradox. Romantic irony has had an enduring and deceptive attraction for modern man. Other nineteenth-century poets had been or were to be ironists—Blake, Byron, Clough, Swinburne, Meredith, Hardy, and Yeats—but Davidson was the only one to take upon himself the task of formulating in verse a complete philosophical system with cosmic irony at its core. By their uncritical reflection of much that was current, their acceptance of a nature at once pastoral and "red in fang and claw," and their ironic ambivalence, his earliest poems and plays foreshadow this system.

Confronted by the ever-changing face of nature and of

love, the romantic is overcome with insecurity, with what
Kierkegaard has described as "a sense of Helplessness." *
He often adopts in this extremity an ironic attitude as a
defense against despair. This suspension of belief is at
best time-serving. Taking his cue largely from the earth
worship of Swinburne and Meredith and his manner from
the Spasmodics, Davidson in youthful works contracted to
transform an essentially verbal and negative irony, reflecting personal disillusionment, revolt, and uncertainty, into
a constructive synthetic philosophy. The mid-century ideas
of naturalism and ameliorist evolution, like the Spasmodic
technique, he adopted tentatively and out of expediency.
Like the tattoos commissioned by a young sailor, impru-
dent and adrift, they were trademarks that did not go very
deep but were indelible, and they can be found, only
slightly blurred, in his later writings. In the lyrics, novels,
and essays of the nineties, his middle period, irony is even
more fundamental to his thought and the basis for an individual style. In a final period irony as a principle of cosmic
order and unity led him to an unqualified acceptance of
scientific materialism. Thus a principle, which began as a
rationalization of personal conflict and of a mutable, complex, inexhaustibly varied world, petrified into a glamorous
synonym for the bleak stasis and terror of a despiritualized
universe. Like many a revolutionary, Davidson ended in
counterrevolution. This was for him the greatest, most
tragic irony of all.

* Considered in retrospect and in the context of general European
thought to which he belongs, Davidson is perhaps the chief English pro-
genitor of twentieth-century existentialism. His works and his life make
a significant contribution to the history of modern subjectivism from neo-
Kantian idealism to the anarchistic humanism of the school of Paris
existentialists.

5

LONDON, 1890-98

We were the last romantics—chose for theme
Traditional sanctity and loveliness;
Whatever's written in what poets name
The book of the people; whatever most can bless
The mind of man or elevate a rhyme;
But all is changed, that high horse riderless,
Though mounted in that saddle Homer rode
Where the swan drifts upon a darkening flood.

William Butler Yeats

The young Davidson is a blurred figure, half fact and half self-created legend. For an impression of him as he was at this time, the biographer must rely almost entirely upon the portraits of the schoolteacher turned poet contained in his works. It takes no great discernment to see that these are often distorted. With his arrival in London early in 1890 there emerges a clearer image. The legend gathers accretions, but there are also reliable recollections by people who knew him. The image remains, nevertheless, a double one of a sharply divided personality seeking spiritual and emotional cohesion. Through one lens appears a dutiful husband and father, an impecunious penny-scribbler, squat, bald, and undistinguished, living a prosaic existence in suburban villas and third-story flats; a reticent, sensitive, tenderhearted recluse, nursing thwarted ambitions. Viewed through the other, he is a

135

dignified, nattily attired man of letters, more a bank manager than a Bohemian in appearance, with a Vandyke beard and a skillfully contrived toupee; a Rhymer and the friend of Rhymers, playwrights, and actors; a member of a fashionable club; one of the more promising younger poets; and in his own estimation a proud challenger for the laureateship. Together the two images add up to a life of high dedication and great disappointment; to an attempt to meet the world on its own terms and, failing in this, to make the world meet him on his, resulting in the world's scorn and mockery. Meanwhile, amid hard work and sacrifice there was hope, some success, and friendship.

The story of Davidson's bid to win a foothold in literary London is not an unfamiliar one. Like Samuel Johnson he arrived with little money and few connections; * he was obliged to take modest lodgings and to eke out a meager living by hack work. Unlike Johnson he was accompanied by no merry David Garrick but a family of three dependents. Settling first at 20 Park Ridings, Hornsey, Davidson soon learned all the inconveniences of living in a removed, inexpensive suburb of North London. Shortly after, he was put to the added expense of placing his two sons on a farm in Sussex because of the ill health of Sandy, the elder.

For a considerable time after his arrival in London, he tried every conceivable kind of potboiling but was unable to earn an adequate income. He may even have returned temporarily to Greenock.† Reviews, he recalled later, were

---

* Scottish associates soon followed him to London. Professor John Nichol took residence in South Kensington in the autumn of 1890, and William Canton, a former subeditor of the *Glasgow Herald,* arrived in 1891 to accept the general managership of the publishing house of Isbister and then editorship of *Good Words.*

† "His first experience of life in London was disheartening. In three months he wrote a solitary review for the 'Academy' and an article for the 'Spectator.' He returned to Greenock for a space, and his second attempt in London proved more successful." The London *Evening Gazette,* 19 Apr. 1909.

his mainstay.[1] He contributed these to the *Glasgow Herald,*
the *Academy,* in which he is listed as a contributor as early
as January 1890, the *Illustrated London News,* and most
frequently to the *Speaker.* For the last he also edited "The
Week," a column of literary events and comment.[2] T.
Wemys Reid was the founding editor of the *Speaker* and
A. T. Quiller-Couch, known to his readers as "Q," its
assistant editor.[3] Published weekly by Cassells, this organ
of left-wing liberalism conducted for a number of years a
warm but friendly rivalry with the *National Observer*
(earlier the *Scots Observer*), a militant Conservative journal
edited by W. E. Henley.[4] Among the *Speaker's* other contributing poets were Richard Le Gallienne, William Watson, W. B. Yeats, and of course "Q"; its staff also included
at various times J. M. Barrie, A. B. Walkley, George Moore,
H. W. Massingham, L. F. Austin, Barry O'Brien, and Au-
gustine Birrell. Although Davidson was not a heavy contributor of signed poems and sketches until 1894, he later
stated that Sir Wemyss Reid had given him his first chance
in London.[5]

Besides his connection with the *Speaker,* Davidson was
subsequently literary critic of the *Star,* founded in 1888
and credited with being "the first newspaper [in England]
to give labor expression in the press." [6] It also had the distinction of launching several outstanding writers, for Bernard Shaw was its music critic, A. B. Walkley, its drama
critic, and Richard Le Gallienne, Davidson's successor. By
his association with the *Speaker* and the *Star,* Davidson
became known early in his London career as a champion
of the working class, a label which stuck but which was
largely misapplied. Throughout his life he found it necessary with many contemporaries to fall back upon journalism of one sort or another to keep the wolf from the door.
He contributed most frequently to the *Speaker* until 1899,
but he appeared also in the *Daily Chronicle, Spectator,
Saturday Review, Living Age, Outlook, Athenaeum, Pall*

Mall Gazette, Fortnightly Review, and *Illustrated London News,* while during half of the decade he served as a kind of London correspondent to the *Glasgow Herald.* After the turn of the century his work appeared in still other periodicals. With a resourcefulness bred of poverty and a recalcitrant muse, he compiled several later collections of verse and prose from his journalistic writings.

Able to write prose only with the greatest difficulty although often with wit and originality, and loath to sacrifice his principles to public taste, the poet whose first success was as the journalist's bard never succeeded in the cutthroat competition of Fleet Street. Writing Grant Richards after Davidson's death, Sir John Hammerton recalled an attempt of the poet to get a start as leader writer on the old *Daily News.* On his first night at the job he worked from nine P.M. until after midnight producing seven hundred and fifty words on Napoleon, a lifelong idol of his. When E. T. Cook, the editor, regretted that he could not use this copy, Davidson at once resigned, refusing any pay for his turn at the desk but taking with him the manuscript with the idea that he might "work it into a book some day." [7] Until the end of his life he planned but never completed the work on Napoleon.

The parallels between his career and that of Gissing's hero, Edwin Reardon in *New Grub Street,* are numerous and striking; they testify all too sadly to Gissing's intimate knowledge of literature as a trade. Davidson has left his own observations on journalism in prose and verse but is nowhere more explicit than in an early essay in the *Speaker:*

> The ever-increasing numbers, ambitious of literary distinction, who flock to London yearly, to become hacks and journalists, regard the work by which they gain a livelihood as a mere industry, a stepping-stone

to higher things—alas! a stepping-stone on which the
great majority of them have to maintain a precarious
footing all their lives. But they do not choose the inferior work that pays: they offer, or think they offer,
the public, through the publishers, bread; but the
public—still the thought of the hack—wants stones,
and these they are forced sorrowfully to supply. What
wonder if they sometimes take to laying about them
with scorpions! And what wonder if they often accept
their fate and become fat and flourishing! [8]

Quixotic Davidson yielded more often to the temptation of
laying about him with scorpions than to that of becoming
fat and flourishing.

Such candor and independence, characteristic of the
Scot, may account for his first great fiasco. In 1891 he undertook to subedit a gallant but short-lived periodical that survived just long enough to be christened the *Weekly Review*. Little is known of this abortive venture, which among
so many more established journals probably died of suffo-
cation. A letter from Davidson to Ernest Rhys, one of the
contributors, is all that remains by way of a *memento mori:*

Dear Rhys,
     Did you not know that the Weekly Review died a
natural death three weeks ago? Mr. Fleming * announced on a Saturday afternoon that he had determined to face his loss and in half an hour I left The
Weekly Review for ever. I don't know whether Fleming means 'to face the loss' of his contributors. You
should write him. I shall infallibly turn up on Friday
to wish you God speed.[9]

Behind the cavalier air of this brief letter, Rhys has commented, "a Fleet Street tragedy is revealed." Unlucky in

* I have been unable to identify Mr. Fleming.

his first journalistic exploit as in so many others, Davidson
did not in reality take such defeats lightheartedly. "Humour he had in plenty," said Rhys, "but it was a grim
humour when it came to questions of bread-and-butter,"
as it generally did for him.[10] The last sentence of the note
refers to a send-off supper given by the Rhymers' Club on
the eve of Rhys' wedding.

2

Exactly when Davidson first encountered the Rhymers
is not known. And it is not known for certain when and
under what circumstances the club was founded, although
it began before October 1891 and continued to hold meetings until the summer of 1894.* The Rhymers convened
every Friday evening at the Cheshire Cheese, the restaurant
in Fleet Street where the even more renowned club of
Johnson, Goldsmith, Garrick, and other eighteenth-century
celebrities had met. Literary clubs were numerous at the
turn of the century and included such once famous but
now largely forgotten groups as the Fitzroy Settlement, the
Odd Volumes Club, the Omar Khayyám Club, and the
"Henley Regatta" as Beerbohm dubbed it. With Henley
presiding, the last regarded itself as a rival faction to the
Rhymers.†

Opinion differs as to whether or not Davidson was a
full-fledged member, since he contributed to neither of the
club's anthologies, *The Book of the Rhymers' Club* (1892)

---

* Rhys recalls that the club was conceived one night at the Cheshire
Cheese by T. W. Rolleston, W. B. Yeats, and himself and that it was
agreed to limit the group to ten, a rule that proved elastic. (E. Rhys,
Everyman Remembers, p. 105.) In a less probable account Victor Plarr
appears to confuse the Rhymers with the Fitzroy Settlement. (V. Plarr,
Ernest Dowson, 1888–1897, pp. 63–4.)

† Charles Whibley, Rudyard Kipling, George Wyndham, George
Steevens, Wilfrid Pollock, Vernon Blackburn, W. B. Yeats (also a Rhymer),
G. S. Street, and H. B. Marriott-Watson were among the members of the
Regatta. (Buckley, *Henley*, p. 152.)

and *The Second Book of the Rhymers' Club* (1894), nor is he listed among the members given at the beginning of each book. It is unlikely that he was one of the charter members, but Dr. George A. Greene, who acted as honorary secretary to a club without rules or officers, lists him among the official members; W. B. Yeats and Victor Plarr, also members, concur.[11] Rhys, alone dissenting, states that Davidson, while a frequent attendant at the Cheshire Cheese, "refused to become an out-and-out member, saying he did not care to be ranked as one of a coterie." Rhys attributes his refusal to an angry pride resulting from a hard life and want of recognition as well as to an artistic jealousy and temperamental incompatibility that made him take a dislike to several members, notably Yeats.[12] This explanation is premature for Davidson had not yet become embittered and the Rhymers included some of his closest associates, among them E. J. Ellis, who had illustrated his volume of short stories, *The Great Men* (1891), Lionel Johnson, and Richard Le Gallienne. The last was an early London acquaintance and sponsor who may have introduced Davidson to this company. With his customary independence the member for Scotland chose to remain aloof from any cause or group. Officially enrolled or not, he attended regularly the weekly meetings of the club, and it was undoubtedly through the connections established there that he became affiliated with the Bodley Head press and the *Yellow Book*. Other Rhymers not yet named were Ernest Dowson, Ernest Radford, Arthur Symons, John Todhunter, and Arthur Cecil Hillier.*

---

* In addition Yeats lists Selwyn Image, Herbert Horne who attended less constantly, and William Watson who joined but never came. Francis Thompson, he remembers, came once but never joined; and Oscar Wilde sometimes attended if they met in a private house, as the club occasionally did. Wilde's hatred for Bohemia prevented his joining the club at the Cheshire Cheese. (W. B. Yeats, *Autobiography*, p. 144.) According to Guy Harrison who quotes from Dr. Greene's list, the following were at one time

Gathering first for supper, embellished by old ale or venerable liquors, in the little coffeehouse boxes downstairs, the group later retired to a smoking room with a sanded floor on the top story. In this sanctum they smoked churchwarden pipes and read aloud the verses which all were expected to bring to each meeting. Criticism of these verses seldom extended beyond occasional grunts, supercilious smiles, or raised eyebrows. By far the best reader, says Rhys, was Yeats, who "intoned his verse with a musical voice and very haunting cadence," while Johnson had "a demure, gentle voice . . . a mouse's recitative," and Rolleston "the plain military voice." [13] Of Davidson, who had a splendid, deep bass and a nearly infallible memory, who read well but infrequently, and who had thought of going on the stage, Rhys says nothing.

A composite group of different ages and nationalities, with varied interests and poetic aims, the Rhymers' Club was little more than a social gathering or at the most an instinctive herding together for the sake of mutual appreciation and protection. In the two anthologies, containing poems extremely disparate in quality and style, the conscious or subconscious influence of Swinburne, Rossetti, and Pater is evident; [14] and in the contributions of Symons, Le Gallienne, and Dowson, that of Verlaine and the French symbolists.[15] Although the aesthetes and impressionists were the most productive, articulate members, they were only one among several elements. The absence of a common cause beyond providing a vehicle for minor verse suggests that the books, like the club, were a *liaison de convenance*. To be sure, the Rhymers were all rebelling consciously against mid-Victorian standards and taste, but they were unable to unite on a constructive program. Only

affiliated with the club as permanent guests: John Gray, Edward Rose, J. T. Nettleship, Morley Roberts, A. B. Chamberlain, Edward Garnett, and William Theodore Peters. (Plarr, p. 133.)

Yeats, who liked to make speeches and recite, and Davidson, who expressed protest by stern silence or, occasionally,
explosive remarks, ruffled this languid atmosphere.

The robust, forthright Scot could not have felt at home
in so precious an element. Scornful of the self-conscious
artificiality that prevailed in the upper room, yet hungry
for companionship, he seldom participated actively in the
meetings. He could not have expected to shine in a company where Yeats was accepted as the presiding spirit and
Dowson as the most promising poet.[16] His role was that of
a solitary, self-appointed devil's advocate. For a man of
Davidson's independence there was more satisfaction in
constituting a loyal opposition of one than in sitting with
other combatants of decadence at the feet of Henley, the
Prospero of Solferino's Restaurant in Soho.

In his autobiography Yeats writes that Davidson "saw in
delicate, laborious, discriminating taste, an effeminate
pedantry, and would, when that mood was on him, delight
in all that seemed healthy, popular, and bustling." [17] The
poem most commonly associated with decadence, its surfeit
of passion and cult of desolation, remains Dowson's "Non
sum qualis eram bonae sub regno Cynarae":

> I cried for madder music and for stronger wine,
> But when the feast is finished and the lamps expire,
> Then falls thy shadow, Cynara! the night is thine;
> And I am desolate and sick of an old passion,
>   Yea, hungry for the lips of my desire:
> I have been faithful to thee, Cynara! in my fashion.[18]

Commenting on Dowson's lyric Davidson remarked, "I say
this poem is not a fine poem, it is not even a good poem." [19]
And when Yeats praised Herbert Horne for his knowledge
and exquisite taste, Davidson was moved to exclaim indignantly, "If a man must be a connoisseur, let him be a connoisseur in women." It was to offset the febrility and effete-

ness of his fellow poets that Davidson admired the quality which he found lacking in them, "blood and guts."

For all his own pose of stalwart masculinity Davidson was true to the Rhymers in his fashion. Quite probably in the hope of supplying them with more "blood and guts," he introduced at one meeting four burly Scotsmen, who to the more delicate poets present seemed uncouth barbarians. After one Scot had read a long poem on the lifeboat, another had described his violent and colorful adventures in Australia, and the remaining two had indulged in heated argument, Davidson insisted that all four be put up as members. Whether it was from complacency bred of good manners, as Yeats suggests, or because they were cowed into submission, the Rhymers consented, resolving privately never to meet again. By means of considerable campaigning and a special meeting, Yeats succeeded in having the four Scots voted out. When he met Davidson a few days after this counteraction, he found the representative from Scotland excessively amiable. On parting Davidson shook his hand and declared enthusiastically that the Irishman had "blood and guts." [20]

Another friend whom Davidson attempted to introduce at a gathering of the Rhymers was Morley Roberts. Both Davidson and he read pieces designed to offset the calculated refinement of their audience. After they had left, those remaining passed a resolution to admit no more members and to preserve the club as "a sacred and forbidden place of resort and consolation for pure poets." When this was reported to him Davidson took refuge in laughter and "the conviction that all of the Rhymers together would not make a man of his worth." Another evening, after his sponsor had declined to accompany him to a small get-together of some Rhymers, Roberts arrived at the rooms of one of them to find four of the strange young men sitting hand in hand before the fire. Astonished, he asked, "What

the hell are you fellows holding hands for?" At the conclusion of the evening, during which they had taught Roberts
to drink deep, Ernest Dowson and Lionel Johnson embraced each other on the landing and then fell downstairs
locked in each other's arms and "emitting sparks like a
Catherine wheel, but luckily landing unharmed." Upon
hearing of the event Davidson replied that it was what he
had sent Roberts to see. "His contempt for them was vast
and explicable," observes Roberts, who adds his own
comment upon the consistency behind the contradictions
of the poet's character: "Davidson, for all of his savage
self-assertion, his denial of religion and accepted morality,
was a sober and clean-living man. Oddly enough for a
poet he loved his wife. So did Browning, and like Browning he was sober. The peculiar Bohemian life of the minor
poet of those days disgusted him. He was proud and
haughty and grew daily in a desire for dignity." [21]

To illustrate his friend's natural combativeness and
equally strong instinct to preserve dignity, Roberts recalls
a quarrel late one night at the Café Royal, then a fashionable gathering place of London cosmopolites. When a
Frenchman, who fancied himself or his wife insulted by
Roberts, precipitated a brawl, Davidson rose "and with
flashing eyes and much action shouted, 'My friend will
fight you all—my friend will fight you all!'" Roberts es-
caped the consequences of "this general and very generous
challenge" when the two opposing parties were herded to
separate exits in Glasshouse and Regent Streets.[22] Although
he was courageous and sturdy, it is difficult to imagine
Davidson jeopardizing his wig and poise in an actual fight.
He reserved his rebelliousness for the larger issues of life,
refusing to dissipate them in what seemed to him the vain
skirmishes and empty peccadilloes of the decadents.* In

* Davidson's public manner was divided at this time between a natural
reserve and masculinity, and an acquired desire to appear abreast of Con-

his whimsical novel *Baptist Lake* (1894) he alternately satirizes and copies to perfection their extravagant gestures and epigrams. And in the story, "Banderole's Aesthetic Bill," first printed in the *Speaker,* he treats mockseriously aestheticism, and specifically Ruskin's proposal that trains be manufactured to look like dragons, by having a booby introduce into Parliament a bill calling for railroad tracks of damascened steel and stations designed as castles, kiosks, and pavilions. In his own earnest dedication to beauty Davidson did not overlook the inertia of reality and the absurdities to which all partisans go.

3

Ernest Rhys and Frank Harris, admittedly a reproachable historian, have testified to a hostility both personal and professional between Davidson and Yeats.[23] Rhys and Grant Richards attribute to the Scot a strong prejudice against the Irish as well as against Yeats, but neither makes clear which came first.[24] Some antipathy there may have been between the two men, but it can scarcely be attributed to professional jealousy at this time. Not until Yeats had begun to outdistance all his contemporaries did his fellow Celt resent him as a more successful rival. Rhys recalls encountering Davidson a year or two after the Rhymers had ceased to meet and speaking of some books of poems by former members that had recently enjoyed a considerable vogue, among them Yeats' *Secret Rose.* "With that," relates Rhys, "he turned upon me and said with an angry laugh: 'I hate the Irish nation.'" Rhys uxoriously replied, "But, you know, my wife is an Irish-

tinental fashion, as a carefree invitation to William Canton reveals: "We shall take a little cup of tea somewhere, dine in the St James's Restaurant, every man Jack of us courageously and quietly at his own expense. I forgot the absinthe: you must take tea earlier than five. At that hour we shall take the absinthe—the proper time as a whet for dinner." A.L.S., dated 30 Apr. 1893, from 20 Park Ridings, Hornsey, N., P.U.L.

woman." Recovering himself with "a delightful reverse," Davidson said, "Ah, your wife is a nation in herself." In the early days, however, each regarded the other's debut as lyric poet with cautious respect and approval.* Morley Roberts, who had met Yeats at supper in Davidson's house on one of the rare occasions that the poet entertained at home, was reluctant to admit that during this time Yeats showed greater promise than Davidson. He perceived that Yeats did not become too easily despondent and endured for a long time on little appreciation. Davidson, on the other hand, either because he had a family to support or because his spirit was more vulnerable, yielded to the Giant Despair.[25]

Although Yeats testifies that he saw much of Davidson in the days of the Rhymers, he "never got behind [his] Scottish roughness and exasperation." [26] Both were provincials, to be sure, and shared the provincial's prejudices, notably an impatience with the detachment, apathy, and cosmopolitanism of the cultured university men who largely made up the membership of the club; but they do not seem to have been drawn together by this common bias. Yeats explains with inverted snobbishness that, whereas the provincialism of Le Gallienne, Symons, and even Davidson was curable, his was not.[27] This is not exactly true: Yeats' provincialism was cultivated, Davidson's largely unconscious and more enduring. While Yeats openly scorned the cosmopolitanism of certain Rhymers but privately envied and admired it, Davidson on the surface imitated their cosmopolitanism but deep within scorned it.

Beyond their common Celtic background, both poets

* In his review of Yeats' *The Wind among the Reeds* Davidson described Yeats as "an original poet of note" and declared that "he has attained a knowledge and insight into the way and beings of the twilight, unseconded in our time." (O'Brien, ed., *The Man Forbid*, p. 92.) For Yeats' opinion of Davidson's *In a Music Hall* . . . , see below, ch. 6, p. 216.

were moreover individualists, agitators, and controversialists. But Davidson was reserved, ironical, dignified, and with very few exceptions completely conventional in his sober dress of the gentleman and in his manners. If he subsequently became wilder in speech and conduct, it was because the world did not recognize him as a poet or heed his message. Yeats, on the other hand, was a thoroughgoing Bohemian. With his verbosity, aestheticism, passionate dedication to Celtic lore and irrelevant causes, and outré costume of brown velveteen coat, loose tie, and ancient Inverness cloak that his father had discarded twenty years previously, he no doubt exasperated the reserved Scot. Moreover the young Yeats was in his attitude toward society neither affectedly indifferent nor proudly aloof; he was a fighter, a campaigner, and an organizer; he would as soon address a meeting, sooner in the early days, as write a poem. To Davidson, who inherited Carlyle's contempt for externals, artificiality, and caprice, Yeats must have seemed precious, effeminate, cocky, and lacking in poise. It should not be forgotten that, if both were at bottom proud spirits, mystics, and fervent crusaders, Yeats was Davidson's junior by eight years. His youthful zest, indifference to the feelings of others, and bumptiousness could easily have antagonized the older man.

There were, finally, more fundamental differences. Yeats in many of his views must have clashed with Davidson: in his hatred of Ibsen; his severe judgment of journalism; his repudiation of life as a subject for the artist, a prejudice inherited from Villiers de L'Isle-Adam; his anti-realism; his aristocratic bias; his hatred of progress and science, which he called "the religion of the suburbs"— in short, in his comprehensive intellectual snobbishness.[28] Unquestionably such views alienated Davidson who at this time was a recognized liberal. Later the Scottish materialist's belief in the supremacy of an élite and the evolution of Yeats' thought into something sterner than the aestheticism of the eighties and the decadence of the nineties might have produced a greater intellectual tolerance between them. If the one eventually emerged as an aristocrat of the material and the other as an aristocrat of the creative spirit, they had in common their aristocracy and their desire to fashion a new poetry out of a hierarchic view of man and the cosmos. But whereas Yeats learned to subordinate his historical and metaphysical system to craftsmanship and sympathy with humanity, Davidson like Blake in the Prophetic Books made his later poetry the servant of metaphysics and personal anger. In comparing the late work of the two Rhymers, it is more just to place Davidson's Testaments and tragedies alongside of Yeats' prose statement of his philosophy in *A Vision*.

Their mature verse shows that Davidson and Yeats were at opposite poles in their conception of poetry and the function of the poet. Although he attempted to drift with the currents of impressionism and realism, to write the "pure poetry" for which Yeats clamored, Davidson during most of his career adhered to the nineteenth-century thesis that the poet should be a great teacher and an interpreter of the age. His message may have been revolutionary but his purpose was traditionally polemic, just as his style was a synthesis of that of his predecessors and contemporaries. In early encounters with the Rhymers, Yeats sensed their essential conservatism and fought to purge them of it. Looking back at this period, he recalled, "I saw—now ashamed that I saw 'like a man of letters,' now exasperated at the indifference of these poets to the fashion of their own river-bed—that Swinburne in one way, Browning in another, and Tennyson in a third, had filled their work with what I called 'impurities,' curiosities about politics, about science, about history, about religion, and that we must create once more the pure work." [29] It was not Davidson but Yeats who, with his use of a fresh symbolism and his recognition of the imagistic value of myth, history, nature, and allusion, looked ahead to a genuine "new poetry." Davidson, the last of the Victorians, and Yeats, almost the first of the moderns, quite literally spoke different languages. In a retrospective judgment that is completely devoid of rancor but without sympathy Yeats felt that had Davidson also gone to school to Dowson or Johnson, or Horne or Symons, and learned from them conscious, deliberate craft and the value of scholarship, he might not have been consumed by his own violent energy and nervous vitality.* Yeats sums up his final impression of his contemporary: "With enough passion to make a great poet, through meeting no man of culture in early life, he lacked intellectual receptivity, and, anarchic and indefinite, lacked pose and gesture, and now no verse of his clings to my memory." [30]

4

Another of the Rhymers and Davidson were on closer terms, although it is difficult now to explain fully the affinity between the willowy, long-haired, mannered Le Gallienne, who affected a sage-green velvet jacket and flowing tie and who was called Dick, Ricky, and other pet names, and the proud, burly Scot, who abhorred exhibitionism in any form and was indignant when addressed by

* Yeats did not include any of Davidson's poems in *The Oxford Book of Modern Verse* which he edited. This may be because he felt that Davidson had written his best poetry before the turn of the century and had been fittingly represented in *The Oxford Book of Victorian Verse,* edited by Quiller-Couch. In all probability he made the common mistake of linking Davidson with the decadents, whom he dismissed with remarkable failure of feeling and memory: "Then in 1900 everybody got down off his stilts; henceforth nobody drank absinthe with his black coffee; nobody went mad; nobody committed suicide; nobody joined the Catholic church; or if they did I have forgotten." Introduction, *The Oxford Book of Modern Verse* (New York, Oxford University Press, 1936), pp. xi–xii.

a nickname.* A passionate devotion to letters sometimes produced strange bedfellows in the nineties. Certainly no more varied or vital group of personalities will be found than those that gathered at the Cheshire Cheese or were later associated with the Bodley Head and the *Yellow Book.* In the case of Davidson and Le Gallienne, a mutual devotion to literature may have been strengthened by a strain of sentimentality and sensuousness and a romantic libertarianism common to both. Yet Davidson, whose romantic impulses were held in check by stern self-discipline, was as discreet in conduct as the other was sometimes scandalous. Their friendship illustrates once again the acceptance and cultivation of paradox by these romantics.

The friendship originated on Davidson's side in a feeling of gratitude for professional assistance. Although remembered as a prolific writer of lyrics and prose fantasies, Le Gallienne was even more active and influential as a journalist. Literary critic of the *Star* and reader for the Bodley Head press, he was in a position to give many poets their first start.[31] Le Gallienne accepted for John Lane and Elkin Mathews of the Bodley Head the manuscript of Davidson's *Fleet Street Eclogues* which they published in April 1893.[32] Never one to make a stinting gesture, Le Gallienne also praised the lyrics in the press. Writing his publishers shortly after the volume's appearance, Davidson asked, "Is Le Gallienne responsible for both these exceedingly generous notices in *Star* and *Chronicle?* He has my very heartiest thanks; but I shall tell him so myself." [33] Within three months the first volume of *Fleet Street Eclogues* had gone into a second edition. It was through this book that Le Gallienne came to know Davidson, and he recalled later that Davidson's rec-

* Writing Lane in 1898, he said, "I don't like you to say 'Dear J. D.' If I were called Jebediah Dolittle, it would be merciful to use initials, but Davidson is a capital name." A.L.S., dated 29 Nov. 1898, from Streatham, N.L.S.

ognition of this and other services was always generous
and wholehearted.[34]

Le Gallienne was dubious of the poet's next work, a
series of impressionistic, discursive travel sketches in prose,
based on walks near London, entitled *A Random Itinerary*. Nevertheless it was on his recommendation, lest the
new discovery take his work elsewhere, that Lane published the book in 1893 in a small edition with a frontispiece by Laurence Housman, the brother of the poet.[35]
With Davidson's successive volumes of verse his champion
continued to puff him in critical reviews. Surveying his
fellow Rhymer's output to date in June 1894, he applied
to him the poet's own definition of a personality as "a man
whose presence is power." The source of this power, Le
Gallienne was among the first to recognize, lay in Davidson's dual nature:

> There is a burliness of constitution underlying his
> most delicate fanciful work. Its beauty is that best
> quality which is the blossom of robust deep-rooted
> health; and its sweetness is that sweetness which is
> hived in the hearts of strong men. This background of
> manhood gives Mr. Davidson a unique significance
> among the younger men. There is not another among
> them of whom it can be said . . . they suggest no
> such liberal strength as Mr. Davidson's least perfect
> work suggests . . . I may be wrong, but at any rate,
> speaking for myself, Mr. Davidson is one of the few
> living writers whom one can allow to nod occasionally
> with untroubled faith.[36]

Extravagant as this praise is, it is not unqualified. Le Gallienne accepted the imperfectness of his friend's work as
the necessary price of his greatness. The "whimsical association of incongruities" which he discerningly noted in
the lyrics was symptomatic of an ambivalent personality

for which the cure was ultimately to prove deadlier than
the disease. Meanwhile in a handful of the lyrics of the
nineties Davidson achieved a harmonious fusion of sweet-
ness and strength. Le Gallienne's recognition of his aim
in these lyrics encouraged Davidson as much as adverse
criticism later defeated him, and bound him to his benefactor with hoops of steel.

Briefly he toyed with the idea of dedicating his second
volume of lyrics (*Ballads and Songs*, 1894) to Le Gallienne.
Whether his hesitancy derived from pride or principle is
not clear. Pride for him very early became principle. In
any event he wrote to Lane of his decision not to have a
personal dedication on the grounds that this would spoil
his intention in the other dedications and in the two little
poems at the end of the volume, which he pointed out
were "full of acknowledgment of interest and pleasure
in Le Gallienne." With growing self-reliance that comes
close to querulousness, he added:

> I made up my mind five years ago never to dedicate
> a book to anybody, and the prejudice against dedica-
> tions is still strong. I never see one without loathing—
> I actually hate temporarily a dedicator and a dedi-
> catee. Call it morbid callousness or whatever you
> like, I would sooner not publish a book than dedi-
> cate it to anybody. My mind of course may change
> as to dedications, but I don't think it will ever change
> as to the inadvisability of dedicating a book to a man
> who has praised one. If the praise was genuine he re-
> quires no thanks, if it was not genuine he doesn't de-
> serve any. Appreciation can be repaid in kind,* and

* Actually Davidson was still in Le Gallienne's debt because he had
apparently written only the one notice of the latter's *Prose Fancies*. On
the strength of this Le Gallienne denied logrolling for Davidson. See
The New Fiction and Other Papers (London, Westminster Gazette Library,
1895), 3, 44.

I have not been backward in doing so when the opportunity offered.[37]

Accordingly, *Ballads and Songs,* like all Davidson's works with the exception of *Smith,* carries no personal dedication. The volume is introduced, however, by the other dedications which he mentions in the letter to Lane:

TO MY FRIEND

WHAT is between us two, we know:
Shake hands and let the whole world go.

TO MY ENEMY

UNWILLING friend, let not your spite abate:
Help me with scorn, and strengthen me with hate.

The first of these couplets was originally sent in a personal letter to Le Gallienne; its reappearance in the volume seems to imply a tacit understanding that the book is for his friend. Together these open letters convey something of the poet's increasing sense of isolation and persecution.

At the end of the volume are found the two little poems, "For H.[esper] J.[oyce] LE G.[allienne]" and "In Memoriam M.[ildred] LE G.[allienne]," appropriate tributes to his friend's first child and his deceased wife. Both reveal unashamedly the tender, sentimental side of Davidson which Le Gallienne had remarked. The one had been sent to the proud father when his daughter was born.[38] On the death of Le Gallienne's first wife, Davidson wrote the second of the lyrics, a poignant epitaph. The last stanza and the best, which alone is printed in *Ballads and Songs,* is:

Our songs are sweeter far;
The flowers about our feet
Sweet and more sweet;
And every star
Is starrier,
Because of her.[39]

Both poems greatly moved the recipient. On Davidson's side, when a critic ended a review with the slur that the poet was currying Le Gallienne's favor in the volume, he wrote to William Archer, "If my book is to be damned because I wanted to please Le Gallienne I don't care. He is a boy, much younger than his years, walks in the world with a wooden sword in one hand and a rose-water sprinkler in the other, but will yet take to himself a weapon worth handling, cut his hair, and behave himself according." [40]

One event in particular brings out Davidson's character and the nature of his friendship with Le Gallienne. At a meeting of the Playgoers' Club on Sunday evening, December 9, 1894, soon after his wife's death, Le Gallienne delivered a lecture entitled "The World, the Flesh, and— the Puritan," defending free love and extolling the virtues of the "new hedonism." This subject, the *Speaker* reported, "proved too strong even for the stomach of a by no means squeamish institution." [41] While daring, the topic was far from taboo in artistic circles, for the "fallen woman," the "society woman," and the "new woman," as she was variously known, was a fashionable and controversial personage of the time. She had been the chief attraction in Arthur Wing Pinero's *The Second Mrs. Tanqueray* (1893), Oscar Wilde's *Lady Windermere's Fan* (1893), and Henry Arthur Jones' *The Masqueraders* (1894); she had brought instantaneous and unlimited success to an unknown woman writer, "George Egerton," whose volume of stories, *Keynotes* (1894), excited attention on both sides of the Atlantic; and in the role of a kept woman reclaimed by love she was the heroine of a sensational play by C. Haddon Chambers, *John-a-Dreams,* which Beerbohm Tree was at the very moment producing at the Haymarket and stoutly defending against a score of outraged theatergoers in the columns of the *Times.*[42]

Le Gallienne had ventured too far, even in the opinion

of his closest friends, by abandoning the immunity and the anonymity of the artist to endorse personally a way of life that threatened the standard British household. The *Speaker,* to which the prodigal son had been a frequent contributor, undertook to chasten and chastize him. It attributed a conduct that was otherwise unprecedented and unaccountable to "the vice of the literary temperament . . . when there is no judicious friend to pump cold water on it, to rush out of doors and blacken the marketplace." As if this were insufficient explanation, the *Speaker* further attributed the outrageous performance to "the spoiling that generally comes for a while from a too facile success," and to the corrupting fumes of Grant Allen's new hedonism.[43] All were stunned at what seemed an obscene act by a darling boy who had been known indulgently as mischievous and romantic but who now appeared a salacious satyr. Other journals and newspapers for the most part expressed disapproval by ignoring the event or declining to quote the lecturer *verbatim.*

If Le Gallienne's imprudence was in character, so was Davidson's reaction to it. Although he himself had addressed a poem "To the New Women" and written playfully on the subject in *Baptist Lake, Earl Lavender,* and other fiction, he felt that perhaps Le Gallienne had exceeded the bounds of good taste and sound judgment. Writing Lane shortly after the lecture, he expressed concern tempered with caution:

> This is distressing about Le Gallienne. I cannot imagine however that his lecture was other than ironical. He seems to have applied my idea of a Harlot's Trades Union to a general Trades Union of Sinners. Surely it was all irony. I had written him on Monday. If I write him now he will know that I have been advised; he will scent a plot. Besides so headstrong a man

must be talked with rather than written to. Who is to do it? [44]

The publisher, who had begun his career with the discovery of Le Gallienne and who was now apprehensive for that poet's and his own reputation, must have replied at once, proposing that Davidson be the elder mouse to bell the young tom. On the Sunday following the lecture Davidson again wrote to Lane, reluctant to interfere:

> Where would be the good of my talking to Le Gallienne? To begin with I don't know the nature, in its extremity at any rate, of the enormity he has, or may have, committed. Secondly, Le Gallienne is as "dour" and "thrawn" as a Scotchman is fit to be. He would probably, as a Scotchman certainly would, listen to admonition and even appear to be admonished out of friendship; and then go straight away and harbour seven other devils worse than the first.
>
> We shall see. I certainly can't start the subject: if he refers to it, it's a different matter. I am inclined to think, however, that the real thing that sticks in people's throats is not so much what Le Gallienne said, as that he said [it] across his wife's grave, as it were: she is hardly six months dead. And can one talk of that? [45]

Whether or not the incident ended here is unimportant; the fragments suffice to give an insight into one of Davidson's few close associations. Characteristic is the mixture of loyalty with detachment and reserve. Characteristic too is the attribution to Le Gallienne and the public of feelings that are really his own. Outspoken and unorthodox in his own writings, he was reticent and exaggeratedly attentive to decorum in private affairs. Like many men who display great courage in public, he feared the lowering of defenses and the ready exchange of confidences required by intimate friendship. At the same time that he shied away from the close relationship that existed among certain Rhymers because it seemed to him unmanly, he envied their easygoing camaraderie.

Reluctant as Davidson was to intrude in Le Gallienne's personal affairs, he remained after his own way a staunch friend and was eager enough to defend him in public. In 1894 the *Westminster Gazette* published a series of articles and letters on the subject of literary logrolling with specific reference to Le Gallienne who signed his reviews "Log-roller." [46] Davidson came to Le Gallienne's defense against this "concerted attack" in a letter that testifies eloquently to a deep regard for his friend. He attacked savagely "these impotent and inept scribblers, who, having nothing in them deserving praise, are utterly unable to comprehend the laudable in others." Grateful for an opportunity to repay many kindnesses, he took special pains to avoid offending Le Gallienne with an expression of undue sympathy. The letter concludes:

> It hardly becomes me to say even this much, because until Narcissus * struck the flint there was no welcoming fire anywhere for me, and yet even for that reason it more than becomes me to say how much I admire him and the lonely appreciative height where he stands barked at by scavenging dogs of depreciation.

A postscript adds that he is sending the gist of the letter to the *Westminster* for publication.[47] Davidson could love as fiercely as he could hate, but he found increasingly less occasion for the first as he did more for the second. During the last decade of his life his energies were largely consumed in waging his own wars with "scavenging dogs of depreciation."

* Le Gallienne had written *The Book-bills of Narcissus* (1891) and used this pen name.

The friendship between Davidson and Le Gallienne came abruptly to a close when the latter emigrated to America in 1895. As Le Gallienne pointed out, his association with the older writer belonged to the years of transient brightness and, when the dark years came, his comrade no longer had a gallant squire to attend him in the lists of Fleet Street. Recollecting the nineties almost three decades later and from another country, he remembered still vividly Davidson's rocky, stubborn personality, "full of Scotch fight, with no little of Scotch pig-headedness." He once more recalled as vividly the other side of the Scot's twofold character which only his few intimates were permitted to see:

> But with him, as with the lion in Holy Writ, within whose jaws the wild bees built their honey-combs, it was a case of *ex forte dulcedo;* for beneath his proud, rather pragmatic exterior, and that Highland manner which brings a suggestion of always going armed against offence, his nature was full of human kindness and repressed tenderness.[48]

5

Sobriety, obstinacy, and pride were always present in Davidson's character. They were held in check for a time by a resilient irony and a few minor professional triumphs, as they were subsequently nurtured by disappointment. Eventually he withdrew, a modern Timon, into misanthropy and exile. His initial promise as a London poet is closely linked with the publishing firm of Elkin Mathews and John Lane. This distinguished partnership had begun in the summer of 1887 when Lane and Mathews opened in Vigo Street a small book shop called the Bodley Head. With its publication of Le Gallienne's *Volumes in Folio* in 1889, the Bodley Head henceforth dedicated itself to bringing out minor verse and fiction in limited, tastefully designed editions.[49] Although sometime in the summer of 1894 the Rhymers' Club disbanded as casually as it had formed, many of its members continued to meet and discuss their work during informal smoking parties at the small office in Vigo Street. In October 1894 the partnership of Mathews and Lane was dissolved. Lane took over the Bodley Head and moved its premises across the street to his own apartment, No. G-1, on the ground floor of Albany,* where a small bay window for displaying books and a shop door opening on the street had been constructed.

From these elegant surroundings Davidson's sturdy volumes of verse with their unassuming titles and format appeared regularly for six years. Mathews and Lane boasted of being "Publishers, and Vendors of Choice and Rare Editions in Belles Lettres," producing such collector's jewels as John Gray's *Silverpoints,* Oscar Wilde's *The Sphinx,* and John Addington Symonds' *In the Key of Blue* with exquisite designs by Charles Ricketts. A lone advocate of severity, Davidson laid down the law that "there was to be nothing fanciful for him—plain, honest dark blue buckram was what he wanted"; and that is what he always got.[50] Yet few books published by Lane are more simply satisfying to the eye than Davidson's *Ballads and Songs* in its "honest dark blue buckram," with a chastely executed line

* A famous and still fashionable block of chambers fronting Piccadilly and backing on Vigo Street, between Regent and Bond Streets. Among its residents have been Byron, Bulwer-Lytton, Gladstone, Disraeli, Macaulay, Arnold Bennett, and, since the admission in recent years of women residents, G. B. Stern. It has also figured prominently in literature as the residence of Dickens' foppish usurer, Fledgeby, in *Our Mutual Acquaintance;* Aubrey Tanqueray in Pinero's *The Second Mrs. Tanqueray;* Ernest Worthing in Wilde's *The Importance of Being Earnest;* any number of Ouida's guards-officer heroes; and the young aristocrat turned sailor in Terence Rattigan's *While the Sun Shines.* See John Prebble, "Albany, Piccadilly," *Town and Country,* June 1955, pp. 68, 85, 88–90.

drawing of lilies and birds by Walter West in gilt on the cover and in black and white on the title page.

Elkin Mathews and John Lane were not Davidson's first London sponsors. When they published the first volume of *Fleet Street Eclogues* in 1893, he had already been represented by three novels, a collection of short stories, and his initial volume of verse, *In a Music Hall and Other Poems* (1891). All these had been published by the London firm of Ward and Downey. *Perfervid: the Career of Ninian Jamieson,* illustrated by Harry Furniss and containing also the delightful study of a child's imagination, "The Pilgrimage of Strongsoul and Saunders Elshander," had appeared in 1890; *The Great Men,* a collection of ten short stories and the early novelette, "A Practical Novelist" (previously published in Scotland as *The North Wall*), with illustrations by E. J. Ellis, in 1891; and *Laura Ruthven's Widowhood,* in collaboration with C. J. Wills, in 1892.

The adventures of capricious, madcap heroes each with an *idée fixe,* these comic extravaganzas are an attempt to create a new fiction by combining incongruously elements from the picaresque novel, Scott's romances, Dickensian caricature, and the whimsy of Thomas Love Peacock for the sake of spoofing contemporary mores. Davidson treats in turn and with mock seriousness literary society, modern journalism, and such high-brow cults as Darwinism, the aestheticism of Pater's devotees, flagellation, spiritualism and Madame Blavatsky. Although perversely guilty of the very excesses that they burlesque, the urbane novels are written in reaction to the sentimental, didactic Victorian novel in parts, and particularly to the products of the Kailyard School. The latter was the name given to a group of Scottish novelists headed by J. M. Barrie, who poured out regional novels featuring Scottish dialect, lore, and quaintness.

Davidson's novels for the most part are clever, entertaining pastiches with the virtues and vices of most *fin de siècle* fiction. On the one hand they are witty, satirical, adroit, revealing a fine objectivity and humor. On the other, they exhibit excessive carelessness or excessive artificiality. Deficient characterization, absence of plot and structure, preposterous scenes, and pleasant but incongruous sentimentality occur side by side with a precious style relying heavily on paradox and epigram. While their chief object appears to be mockery, they feature at the same time strong-willed, egoistic, Carlylean heroes, and the purity and imperishability of the love bestowed upon them by the heroines. They manifest the same combination of serious purpose and impudent method as the early plays. Portioning out equally charity and malice, these whimsical tales attempt with imperfect success to preserve the ironic impartiality of Davidson's other writings of this time. The trend in fiction which they did much to advance was nevertheless a healthy one; it is not going too far to list them with the picaresque extravagances of Richard Le Gallienne, Robert Hichens, G. S. Street, Max Beerbohm, H. G. Wells, and G. K. Chesterton, which they just precede in time, in the evolution of the modern English satirical novel. The satirical novels of Evelyn Waugh, Aldous Huxley, and George Orwell are also indebted to them, if less directly. Davidson followed this fiction with still more of the same kind: *Baptist Lake* in 1894; *Earl Lavender,* with a frontispiece by Beardsley depicting flagellants, in 1895; and *Miss Armstrong's and Other Circumstances,* mostly reprints of short stories and prose sketches, in 1896.

It was the extravagant humor and undeniable originality of this early fiction as well as of *Scaramouch in Naxos* and the other comedies which brought Davidson to the attention of the Rhymers and in turn persuaded John

Lane to publish his verse. With Mathews or under the
imprint of the Bodley Head, Lane published all Davidson's volumes of verse during the nineties. Following one
another in rapid succession, too rapid for a poet who was
also writing short stories, travel sketches, reviews, "têtes-à-
têtes," and causeries in addition to at least one play, the
small but chunky volumes of poetry appeared, five in six
years. *Fleet Street Eclogues,* which inaugurated this substantial output in 1893, was followed by *Ballads and Songs*
in November 1894 and *A Second Series of Fleet Street
Eclogues* in December 1895. Davidson's poetry by this time
had begun to lack the spontaneity and originality of the
early volumes. Even so, Lane faithfully produced two further collections, *New Ballads* in October 1896 and *The
Last Ballad and Other Poems* in December 1898. After
this the poet abandoned all hope of making a livelihood
or attracting favorable notice by his lyrics. No further volume of shorter poems appeared until July 1906 when
Grant Richards published *Holiday and Other Poems* containing several of his better known lyrics.*

As he was clearing out some old papers one day after
working on a new story, Davidson came across the remains
of the original manuscript of *Fleet Street Eclogues.* His
immediate impulse was to burn the manuscript but on a
second impulse he sent it to the man who had taken the
risk of publishing the poems and to whom he now wrote,
"If that is merely putting *you* to the trouble of burning it,
pray excuse it." To explain the manuscript's condition, he
added, "The book in which F. -S. E. were written was an
old note-book of my father's which came into my hands
in the beginning of 1892. I took out my father's notes,
which were theological, and so loosened the stitching, that

---

* *Selected Poems* (London, John Lane, The Bodley Head, 1905) contained no new poems.

many of the leaves on which I wrote have been lost." [51]
More than Scotch parsimony is reflected in this use of his
father's notebook; it symbolizes the precarious balance of
open defiance and subconscious respect which he bore his
antecedents. In sending the manuscript to his publisher,
Davidson knew that the ironic circumstance of its composition would not escape him. The laconic nature of the
letter typifies the somewhat constrained friendship between them.

Davidson's difficulties with the early publishers of his
plays had the happy effect of uniting him and Lane in a
common cause. In 1890 the author had transferred rights
to the 1889 edition of *Plays,* which he himself had published, to T. Fisher Unwin, who brought out a second
issue. Much to Davidson's indignation, Unwin canceled
the original title page and without authorization issued
the volume with the new title of *Scaramouch in Naxos.*
Elkin Mathews and John Lane obtained the rights from
Unwin and in 1893 brought out a third issue with the
original title page restored. When in the same year these
publishers, wishing to capitalize on Davidson's success as a
lyric poet, sought to bring out a new and de luxe edition
of the early plays, the original editions turned up like a
fistful of bad pennies. Frederick W. Wilson, the Glasgow
publisher of *Bruce* and *Smith,* and Unwin were reluctant
to give up the copyright to the early volumes.[52] Accounting
for Unwin's motives, Davidson wrote to Lane, "Spleen
can drive an effeminate man to extraordinary depths of
stupidity"; and he approved Lane's action of restoring the
original title page of *Plays* as "not only legal, but righteous . . ." [53] Unwin threatened Davidson that if he issued
a further edition of *Scaramouch in Naxos* and its companion plays, he did so at his own risk.[54] Humoring his own
spleen, Davidson retaliated by proposing that Lane publish in the form of a fable his correspondence with Unwin;

THE FABLE.

There was once a husbandman who found a vine growing by the wayside. He uprooted it, and planted it in his cellar. After a time, on visiting it, he found that the grapes were sour; whereupon he sold it to another husbandman, who set it in the sunlight. When the grapes were ripe the first husbandman wished to gather them, but was forbidden to do so.

THE MORAL.

The entire correspondence and not a word more.

The *Author* would be happy to reprint the fable, Davidson predicted, and Lane's firm "would be hailed as the champion of the author, having thrown down the gauntlet against all the old traditions—the colleague, not the adversary, of the author." [55] Not relishing the role of participant in a lawsuit, both Lane and the Author's Society declined to publish " 'Scaramouch' in Paternoster Row: a Fable for Publishers." [56] Only after protracted negotiation with Wilson and Unwin and the accumulation of much bitterness for Davidson did Mathews and Lane proceed to publish the new edition of *Plays* in 1894.

Of all the writers and designers whom Lane introduced to a discriminating public, and they included such *enfants terribles* as Ernest Dowson, Aubrey Beardsley, Oscar Wilde, Lionel Johnson, G. S. Street, Richard Le Gallienne, and later Gertrude Stein, none could have been more baffling and at times exasperating to him than Davidson. Taking his profession as poet solemnly, he habitually declined to mix business with pleasure or friendship. A printer's error or a delayed royalty loomed as large as a rejected manuscript. He accepted no favors in getting his works published or publicized, and he gave none, for he

could ill afford it. When Lane offered to pay for American copyrights, he politely insisted that the cost be de-
ducted from his virtually nonexistent royalties. His letters
to Lane show him continually pressing for "the sum now
due me!" Lane was "a man of business and not a man of
sentiment," as he once confided to Esmé Wingfield-Stratford, who describes him as "one of the hardest drivers of
a bargain that ever printed contract, but also a passionate
art-lover with a *flair* for producing beautiful books and
attracting the pink of young authors." [57] If Davidson insisted on prompt payment for his manuscripts, he may well
have been motivated by a knowledge of his publisher's
close-fistedness, as Lane respected him for his own.

Seldom did the poet descend from his quiet, sensitive
aloofness to the sociable atmosphere and ready collaboration that prevailed at the Bodley Head. Yet Lane, anxious to promote his author's reputation, seems to have
been determined to penetrate the wall of reserve. In letter
after letter Davidson declines invitations to dine with the
Lanes and to meet celebrities. At first he excuses himself
pleasantly if firmly, pleading the embarrassment of previous social commitments, lack of funds and "the ordinary
garb of civilisation," or "a piece of frightful drudgery"
which he cannot put aside:

> I don't see how I can possibly come on Thursday.
> I am out tomorrow night, on Friday afternoon, and on
> Saturday night. I find that it is quite impossible to go
> one where without going another where: one has no
> excuse. "You went there, sir? Come, now, you went
> there! Very well then, you must come here." And I,
> the most goodnatured of all poets, past, present, and to
> come, yield. The result is that I have no income for
> January. I can work like a nigger, and I can play like
> a kitten, but I can't do both together. And going

about costs money! I am worse off economically than I was two years ago; and editors take me aside gravely and warn me not to put up my prices! That is what drives men into the hands of agents.

Then he adds, "Even in the best of moods, in the most uninterrupted times, I wander about for days, blind, deaf, dumb, and moping: then I write a line or a stanza, and then—*da capo!*" [58] As he became less successful and more impoverished his refusals assume a brusqueness that betrays the wound they gave to his ego. Without doubt one of his greatest handicaps was his incapacity to be gregarious in a profession and a decade that were, above all else, sociable. At the same time it is a sign of his genius, for the genius either has no public life or his public life is identical with his private life.

Not that he was a recluse; he enjoyed the close and loyal friendship of several fellow writers and, in the early days at least, periodically went out in company. Margaret Davidson seldom accompanied him on evening excursions. She was a loyal wife and devoted mother but did not share her husband's intellectual interests or principles. Moreover there was no money for party frocks, for servants to look after the children, or for entertaining in return. Although convivial, Davidson was so proud that he would accept few kindnesses that he could not repay with interest. He entertained male friends, as royalties or later his pension infrequently permitted, at his club, the Grosvenor, until impecuniousness and the withdrawal to Penzance obliged him to give up his membership.

Ernest Rhys recalls meeting Davidson occasionally at literary parties. The first time was at the home of Mrs. William Sharp, the wife of "Fiona Macleod," in Greencroft Gardens shortly after *Fleet Street Eclogues* had enjoyed a small success among the cognoscenti. At one point

in the evening Davidson, who on occasion was as full of irrepressible mirth and a desire to shock as he was generally
dignified, snatched off what appeared to be a fine head of
black, glossy hair but was in reality a wig.[59] He wore the
wig only to appear younger in a profession that catered
to youth and often doffed it in private company as if it
were a hat.* Although his attitude toward his baldness, at
once self-conscious and cavalier, is redeemingly human, the
frequency with which references to this stunt occur is
curious. It suggests that he was often exasperated and suf-
focated by polite literary society and felt a boyish impulse
to startle it. It also suggests that there may have been very
little else about the man colorful or memorable enough
for acquaintances to record. Few would have sensed that a
split attitude even toward the trifling, which nearly everyone shares, was in Davidson particularly acute and persistent.

Another "at home" took place years later at the Rhyses'
own villa in Hermitage Lane. It included among the
guests Ford Madox Ford, who Rhys remembers was then
editing the *English Review*,† Yeats, Ezra Pound, Winifred
Emery, Ernest Radford, Davidson, and a strange, gloomy
young man, D. H. Lawrence. Yeats, as usual, dominated
the "rich, bizarre and varied entertainment," chanting or

* Frank Harris also recalls his performing this stunt and his explanation, "I was prematurely bald and a little ashamed of looking so old;
now I'm thinking of leaving my head as it is; but the flies annoy me,
and so I put off the decision." "A few years later," Harris continues, "he
doffed the disguise finally and I think his appearance was improved
thereby, for his forehead was remarkable—domed like Swinburne's and
Shakespeare's" (*Contemporary Portraits*, p. 125). Menzies Davidson tells
of an incident at the Grosvenor Club when his father, growing warm
before the fire, asked if there was anyone in the room under thirty. When
no one replied in the affirmative he exclaimed "Thank Heaven for that!",
removed his wig, and tossed it into the fire.

† As the first number of the *English Review* did not appear until Dec.
1908, this soiree must have taken place in the last few months of Davidson's life.

having chanted in a "haunting wail" his own verses. In a pique at being shut out, Pound munched on red tulips, devouring in the course of the meal the entire center-piece. When asked to recite, Lawrence with his back to the guests read inaudibly and interminably from a little black book until his host invited him to rest. Davidson, arriving unexpectedly and very late, refused point-blank to con-tribute to the entertainment until finally persuaded to read "In Romney Marsh" with its lilting rhythm and great ring. When the company next grew restive at the recitation of Yeats' "The Man Who Dreamed of Faeryland," their flagging interest was revived with "a special form of claret cup with a little tarragon and pomegranate juice inter-fused." [60] This must have been a unique occasion, con-sidering the figures who were there and the generations represented. It is not difficult to imagine Davidson's dis-comfort in the "arty" atmosphere that prevailed in this and other suburban homes of those who practised the arts. He was never more at ease in this atmosphere than Lawrence and for much the same reason. If he frequented it inter-mittently, always existed on its fringe, and briefly imitated its fashions in his writings, neither he nor his poetry ever belonged wholeheartedly to a snobbish intellectual coterie.

From these and similar accounts one can glean some-thing of the figure which the émigré poet from Greenock cut in literary society. In spite of the toupee, fashionably cut beard, monocle, and conservative dress, adopted to lend either dignity or youth to his appearance, he must have seemed like some gnome out of Andersen or the brothers Grimm. Only five feet, four inches tall, he was extremely broad, with great shoulders, thick strong hands, and short spatulated fingers, "the mark of a ploughman," he said defensively. He weighed nearly two hundred pounds. In spite of his sturdy build he had a delicate con-stitution, indicated, he was likely to point out, by a com-

paratively thin neck.[61] During this London period he
often took excursions into the country on a bicycle built
especially low to the ground to accommodate his short
legs. When he suffered a heart attack after one such trip he
was obliged to abandon the diversion.

In spite of Davidson's self-esteem, readiness to take offense, and reserve, among other crotchets, the business
relationship with Lane continued until 1899, after the
poet had turned almost entirely to the theater as an occupation. There are no signs of an abrupt, unfriendly
rupture. Although sorely tried, Lane seems to have preserved for his protégé a strong liking and patience long
after a less astute publisher would have grown weary of
humoring him. This was his tribute to genius. For his part
Davidson always felt that he owed Lane deep gratitude.
It might be for the gift of a hamper of fresh oysters which
the publisher sent him and which he acknowledged in a
mood of sportive fantasy.[62] It might be for the opportunity which Lane gave him of eking out a precarious existence by reading manuscripts submitted for publication.
He was most grateful of course for Lane's having made his
work known and for continuing to publish his successive
volumes of lyrics after their initial success had waned. "To
discover or create a buying public for minor and other
poetry must always be a great feat," he once said; and
added, "to have achieved it nowadays, and in the manner
in which it has been done at *The Bodley Head,* is to have
established a record." [63] And he wrote to Lane after reading a favorable review:

> It is something, it is great, and high even, in a certain
> measure and kind, as Cromwell—who was the great-
> est man that ever lived—would have said, to know
> that one's work, such as it is, is not altogether despised.
> You have made men know of me; that is a great part

of my ambition; and for that I shall always be much
beholden to you. Knowing that when I die I cease for
ever, I should like the memory of me to last a little.[64]

If in later years he was more grudging in his expression
of indebtedness to Lane, it was because he knew and re-
sented that all Lane's efforts on his behalf had not com-
pensated for his own lack of staying power.

6

Through his affiliation with the Rhymers Club and the
Bodley Head, Davidson inevitably became a contributor
to the celebrated *Yellow Book.* The birth of the *Yellow
Book* like that of the Rhymers is surrounded by contradictory legend, although there is general agreement that it
took place in January or February 1894. Credit for originating the idea has been variously attributed to Aubrey
Beardsley, George Moore, and Frank Harris; to D. S.
MacColl who claimed that he gave the idea to Henry
Harland; and to Harland himself and John Lane.[65] Whatever its origin, Lane agreed to be publisher and appointed
the young American novelist, Henry Harland, literary editor and the still younger, brilliant black-and-white artist,
Aubrey Beardsley, art editor. It was to be a quarterly and
the first of thirteen numbers appeared in April 1894. The
founders envisaged a magazine devoted to belles-lettres
that would present "the oldest school and the newest side
by side, with no hall-mark except that of excellence and
no prejudice against anything but dullness and incapacity." [66] The list of contributors to the first issue is impressive in range and stature. Representing literature are
Henry James, George Saintsbury, and Edmund Gosse
among the more established men of letters, with Richard
Le Gallienne, Max Beerbohm, Arthur Symons, Arthur

Christopher Benson, George Egerton, George Moore, Hubert Crackanthorpe, and Arthur Waugh among the younger writers. In artists there is as great a variety, ranging from Joseph Pennell, J. T. Nettleship, and Frederic Lord Leighton, R.A., in the more conservative, realistic tradition, to Beardsley, Walter Sickert, Laurence Housman, and Will Rothenstein, among the modern aesthetes and impressionists.

Rising with an almost unprecedented éclat on the spring morning that it shone bright and dazzling from the shop window in Vigo Street, the *Yellow Book* in its debut made the mistake of many reviews: It promised a quality which it could not hope to keep up. Nevertheless it offered to the discriminating reader a rich and catholic talent surpassed only by the short-lived *Savoy* among the journals of the time. Few important writers and graphic artists of the day —whether aesthete or vitalist, *vers de société* poet or harsh realist, academy painter or impressionist—did not at some time appear in its pages. If its editors and contributors can be said to have had any concerted purpose, it was to overthrow the Victorian tabernacles and erect golden calves in their place. More practically it provided a useful outlet for the minor verse and stories of writers whose work had more literary merit than journalistic appeal. The *Yellow Book* was the first of a long succession of reviews that have refused to cater to middle-class interests and have signaled bravely the rich heterogeneity of modern art. By reason of its cover and drawings by Beardsley and the reputation for Bohemianism or dandyism of certain contributors the magazine achieved from the outset a popular but largely undeserved reputation for decadence. An examination today of its contents, occasionally brilliant and daring but more often merely respectable, makes it hard to believe that it ever enjoyed an immense *succès de scandale.* The *Yellow Book* gave to the decade it adorned its own epithet and the associations with dilettantism and preciosity that the period still retains.

To the first issue Davidson contributed a pair of impressionistic poems, "London" [67] and "Down-a-down," [68] which he labeled simply "Two Songs." The former and better suggests the impressionism in verse of Symons and Le Gallienne. Its first stanza reads:

> Athwart the sky a lowly sigh
>   From west to east the sweet wind carried;
> The sun stood still on Primrose Hill;
>   His light in all the city tarried:
> The clouds on viewless columns bloomed
> Like smouldering lilies unconsumed.

But the poet's interests were not restricted to this attenuated and overdelicate description. He offered in the second issue of the *Yellow Book* a poem contrasting sharply with the previous contributions. Written partly in Limehouse vernacular, "Thirty Bob a Week" [69] expresses the laborer's unsniveling acceptance of the harsh realities of life and demonstrates that Davidson could compose with even greater success in the masculine vein of the activists, Henley and Kipling.

"The Ballad of a Nun," [70] his next contribution, struck many readers as distinctly new and original—those that it did not offend or mystify. In actuality he had merely refined Swinburne's ironic blasphemy and combined it with the dramatic objectivity of the literary ballad. Davidson's poem is the swiftly sketched story of a sister of charity who abandons her order for carnal pleasure; on her return to the abbey she is welcomed by the Holy Virgin who has miraculously replaced her in her absence and who forthwith congratulates her:

> You are sister to the mountains now,
>   And sister to the day and night;
>   Sister to God. . . .

The poem had a career no less wandering than its subject.
Frank Harris recalls that, as the editor of the *Fortnightly
Review*, he was obliged to reject the poem because Frederick Chapman, managing director of the review, objected to
it as disgustingly licentious.[71] And Henry Harland is reported to have sneered at the manuscript upon first seeing
it.[72] In spite of these misadventures it appeared in the
third issue of the *Yellow Book* and soon became notorious.

Perhaps no poem of the decade attracted more attention
at the time of its appearance than this amoral ballad. Certainly no single work of Davidson's created a wider sensation. When he disappeared fifteen years later, the *Manchester Guardian* recalled its reception as an outstanding
event in the poet's career:

> . . . the appearance of "A Ballad of a Nun" in the
> "Yellow Book"—then in the full notoriety of its brief
> but fantastic course—brought his name into some
> prominence. The poem showed vigour, imagination,
> and a rich command of words, though it is not the best
> of Davidson's ballads. A suspicion of impropriety at-
> tached to it, and this gained for it popularity which
> its literary merits might have missed. When, shortly
> afterwards, it was published with others, in a volume,
> the late Dean Farrar, who was then canon of West-
> minster, came across one or two of its stanzas quoted
> in a review. He jumped to the conclusion that the
> poem was of a religious cast, and declaimed these
> stanzas in his sermon at St. Margaret's the following
> Sunday. The public—which has a pleasing confidence
> in the literary taste of the clergy—proceeded, on this

THE *YELLOW BOOK*   175

recommendation, to buy the book, and Davidson believed himself a made man.[73]

Davidson himself always attributed the poem's fame to this instance of mistaken identity. Writing Edmund Gosse in 1900 he recalled bitterly the sequel to the poem's appearance:

> In this country a writer must misrepresent the world, or be understood to have done so, in order to make money. I learned this most saliently from the false vogue of a poem of mine, "A Ballad of a Nun," an entirely non-moral piece which was mistaken for an Anglican tract, and belauded for a month or two on that account. When the error was discovered the poem and the author were shortly dropped, and criticism generally has never forgiven me for its mistake.[74]

In his ballads of the nineties Davidson expressed with ironic or dramatic indirection ideas that in private he was already stating frankly.*

As Davidson's trademark "A Ballad of a Nun" received the highest tribute that can be paid to literary fame: It was universally parodied. Owen Seaman, the humorist for *Punch* and subsequently its editor, wrote the most popular of the parodies, "A Ballad of a Bun," at which, C. Lewis Hind recalls, all "inner literary London laughed,† and which may be said to have confirmed Owen Seaman's career as a parodist." [75] Of all the lines in Davidson's long ballad the following were most frequently praised by reviewers and parodied by humorists:

* See Appendix B.
† "Inner literary London" was at this time rife with feuds; Hind, editor of the ultraconservative *Academy*, seems to have harbored a grudge against Davidson.

High on a hill the convent hung,
  Across a duchy looking down,
Where everlasting mountains flung
  Their shadows over tower and town.

·   ·   ·   ·   ·

The adventurous sun took Heaven by storm;
  Clouds scattered largesses of rain;
The sounding cities, rich and warm,
  Smouldered and glittered in the plain.

Sometimes it was a wandering wind,
  Sometimes the fragrance of the pine,
Sometimes the thought how others sinned,
  That turned her sweet blood into wine.

Seaman travestied these impressionistic verses, making
sport of Davidson's slow recognition, his association with
the decadents, and the practice by Bodley Head poets of
scratching one another's back in critical reviews:

Across the sounding City's fogs
  There hurtled round her weary head
The thunder of the rolling logs;
  "The Critics' Carnival!" she said.

Immortal prigs took heaven by storm,
  Prigs scattered largesses of praise;
The work of both was rather warm;
  "This is," she said, "the thing that pays!"

Sharp envy turned her wine to blood—
  I mean it turned her blood to wine;
And this resolve came like a flood—
  The cake of knowledge must be mine! [76]

A thinly disguised Davidson, Seaman's nun attempts to
cater to the public taste for belletristic verse, only to find

after a brief triumph that public taste has shifted from "the seedy sex-impressionist" and Darwinian determinism to "songs and tales of pleasant cheer":

> "Alack!" she said, "I lost the art,
>   And left my womanhood foredone,
> When first I trafficked in the mart
>   All for a mess of Bodley bun.
>
> "I cannot cut my kin at will,
>   Or jilt the protoplastic germ;
> I am sister to the microbe still,
>   And second-cousin to the worm!"

It is the element of exaggerated truth which makes caricature successful. The mockery may have rankled in the side of Davidson, but that shrewd businessman Lane knew good advertising when he saw it; in due course he enlisted Seaman's professional services as court jester to his bards.

Among the literati "A Ballad of a Nun" was something of a byword: A parody of it or facetious allusion to it was instantly recognized.* The Bodley Head and its mannered poets became a natural butt for lampooners and cartoonists; humorists vied to outdo one another in ridiculing Lane's "nest of singing birds." [77] Most of these "ribald rhymes" were lame and ephemeral, but at least one parody

---

* W. Robertson Nicoll recalls a meeting of the Omar Khayyám Club in the summer of 1895 which was attended by Watts-Dunton, Gosse, Clement Shorter, H. W. Massingham, Gissing, and Edward Clodd, among others, and at which Meredith and Hardy were guests of honor: "Mr. Cust [H. J. C. Cust, editor of the *Pall Mall Gazette*] and Mr. Cook [Sir E. T. Cook, editor of the *Westminster Review*], who had been talking amicably all the evening, then spoke, and I remember Mr. Cust closed by parodying a verse of poor John Davidson's, closing with something about

> Maiden aunt to the North Pole,
> And mother-in-law to the Equator."

W. R. Nicoll, *A Bookman's Letters* (4th ed., London and New York, Hodder and Stoughton, 1913), pp. 7–8.

deserves preservation. Le Gallienne's prose fantasia, *The Quest of the Golden Girl* (1896), had created sufficient stir to prompt its own burlesque imitation, *The Quest of the Gilt-Edged Girl* (1897) by "Richard de Lyrienne," also published by Lane. Among its brighter moments is a "Sexagesimal Symposium," during which J. M. Barrie offers to give "a swatch o' ma freen' John Davidson's poem about that nun lassie" and recites the following version:

> Abune a brae the convent hung,
>   Oot ower a burnie lookin' doon;
> Whaur mony a michty mountain flung
>   Its shadows ower baith tower and toon.
>
> Within its wa's a lassie dwelt,
>   And oh, but she was wae, pair thing,
> Until one day she really felt
>   She maun be oot and hae a fling.
>
> "I carena though they don't aloo
>   Me oot," says she, "tae tell the truth;
> I'm sister tae the North Pole noo
>   And second cousin tae the Sooth." [78]

Apparently the pseudonymous author of this parody expected his readers to recall Davidson's minor lyric three years after it had originally appeared. The too earnest ballad was literally laughed to death, and for all its fame considerably damaged the poet's reputation as a lyricist.

As Davidson continued to appear in the *Yellow Book* and under the auspices of the Bodley Head, he was invariably linked with the aesthetes and decadents as a "sex-impressionist." The remaining Bodleians must always have regarded him as an outlaw, but he persisted in the uneasy relationship partly from an ungovernable inclination to imitate and thereby capture the literary market, partly

"SOME PERSONS OF 'THE NINETIES'"
Caricatures by Sir Max Beerbohm, 1925

2 Walter Sickert   3 George Moore   5 Oscar Wilde   6 W. B. Yeats   7 'Enoch Soames'
ichard Le Gallienne   4 John Davidson

9 Henry Harland   12 Max Beerbohm
rthur Symons   10 Charles Conder   13 Aubrey Beardsley
11 William Rothenstein

from an ingenuous notion that all rebels had the same aims as he. Remembering his self-preoccupation and tendency to jump at conclusions, one easily sees how he might have mistaken the sense impressionism and amorality of the aesthetes for his own more robust views. He sympathized wholeheartedly with their aim to extend experience and to divorce art from conventional beauty and morality. He sympathized briefly too with the political liberalism of several Bodleians, thinking it a necessary corollary to their liberation of art. Then he discovered that they did not share his worship of nature or intend to adopt his vulgar gospel of materialism. In his disenchantment he came to feel that they had betrayed themselves and him. Fundamentally sentimental, moralistic, and evangelical, Davidson had only a transient connection with these products of the universities and London, aristocrats of taste whose only law was art for the sake of art.

In Paternalian circles there had always been some question about Davidson's credentials. When the collected edition of his plays appeared in 1894, a number of critics protested against the impropriety of its frontispiece by Beardsley containing portrait caricatures of Sir Augustus Harris, Oscar Wilde, Genée, Mabel Beardsley, Richard Le Gallienne, and Henry Harland as characters from *Scaramouch in Naxos*.[79] This graphic tour de force, they felt, was not in keeping with the spirit of the volume's contents.* Their

* See John Lane, Introduction, Aubrey Beardsley, *Under the Hill and Other Essays in Prose and Verse* (London and New York, John Lane, The Bodley Head, 1921), pp. ix–x. Lane recalls that this was one of two occasions in which Beardsley replied to hostile criticism of his work in the press. The *Daily Chronicle* for 1 Mar. 1894 had declared that the frontispiece was "an error in taste which is to be regretted." Beardsley replied, flippantly admitting to two of the caricatures: "Sir,–In your review of Mr. Davidson's plays, I find myself convicted of an error in taste, for having introduced portraits into my frontispiece to that book. I cannot help feeling that your reviewer is unduly severe. One of the gentlemen who forms part of my decoration is surely beautiful enough

feelings were summed up by Quiller-Couch in the *Speaker:*
". . . admirer as I am of Mr. Aubrey Beardsley's work, I
must protest that the vilely sensual faces in his frontispiece
to these 'Plays' are miserably out of keeping with the sunny
paganism of 'Scaramouch in Naxos.' . . . There is nothing
Greek about Mr. Beardsley's figures; their only relationship
with the Olympians is derived through the goddess Asel-
geia." [80] Writing in his memoirs, Sir William Rothenstein
mentions this matter of Davidson's mistaken identification
with the Bodley group:

> For John Davidson I had a great respect; I liked his
> *Fleet Street Eclogues* and his *Ballad of a Nun,* and
> Beardsley particularly admired his play *Mr Smith, a
> Tragedy* [*sic*]. Perhaps we attributed qualities to Da-
> vidson which he did not possess; since Davidson cared
> not at all for the baroque fantasy which pleased Au-
> brey so much in his play. He was a serious-minded,
> straight-hitting Scot—the last man, I had thought, who
> would put an end to his life. But I never knew what a
> struggle he had. Though there was a vogue for minor
> poetry, there was also one for limited editions,* so
> poets themselves got little or nothing for their pains.[81]

And finally, to cite another authority, J. Lewis May, Lane's
biographer, who compares the Davidson of this period to
the Virgil of the Georgics, says much the same thing: "He
was out of the 'movement,'—that is to say, he was not one
of the Beardsley, Dowson, Wilde group, but he was, from
the mere fact of his being in such strong reaction to it, very
certainly a child of the age." [82] As so often happens, in

---

to stand the test even of portraiture, the other owes me half a crown."
Lane identifies the subjects as Wilde and Augustus Harris respectively.

* The first volume of *Fleet Street Ecologues* (1893) was limited to 300
copies; *A Random Itinerary* (1894), for which Davidson received only
£20 outright, to 600 copies; *Plays* (1894), on which Davidson received one
shilling per copy sold, to 500 copies.

FRONTISPIECE TO JOHN DAVIDSON'S *PLAYS*, 1894
by Aubrey Beardsley

striving to correct an error, these commentators have perpetrated another. It is true, as they observe, that Davidson's personality and outlook became more akin to the rugged activism and gospel of self-reliance preached by Henley, Stevenson, and Kipling than to the Gallicism and decadence of the prodigal sons of Pater. At the same time his sensitivity to the colors and sounds of the external world, his spontaneous lyricism, and his desire to re-invigorate poetic language before his writing became submerged in a clumsy, calloused virility—all inclined him to the aesthetes.

Because his natural ambivalence was developed to an abnormal degree, Davidson was able to participate in the phenomenon of *fin de siècle* decadence and simultaneously to view it with ironic detachment. This is nowhere more evident than in the "Proem to *The Wonderful Mission of Earl Lavender*" as well as in the novel which it introduces. This poem first saw print in the fourth volume of the *Yellow Book,* January 1895. In its treatment of the ennui, melancholy, and excesses of the decade it is both sympathetic and satirical:

> Though our eyes turn ever waveward,
>   Where our sun is well-nigh set;
> Though our Century totters graveward,
>   We may laugh a little yet.
>
> Oh! our age-end style perplexes
>   All our elders' time has tamed;
> On our sleeves we wear our sexes,
>   Our diseases, unashamed.
>
> Have we lost the mood romantic
>   That was once our right by birth?
> Lo! the greenest girl is frantic
>   With the woe of all the earth! [83]

In the same issue with this swan song of the decadents appeared Will Rothenstein's portrait sketch of Davidson as "Bodley Head No. 2." *

In April 1895, after losing a suit for slander against the Marquess of Queensberry, Oscar Wilde was arrested and brought to trial in a counteraction. The fifth number of the *Yellow Book* was scheduled to appear in the same month but was unaccountably delayed. When it did appear late in April it contained none of Aubrey Beardsley's work although he had prepared for it a cover, title page, and four designs.[84] Led by William Watson and Wilfrid Meynell, with the moral support of Mrs. Humphry Ward, six of the Bodley Head's outstanding authors had joined forces to demand that Wilde's books be dropped from Lane's catalogue and that Beardsley's work be suppressed in the forthcoming issue of the *Yellow Book*. Because of Beardsley's association as illustrator with Wilde in the cult of decadence, these conservative Bodleians feared that his inclusion would be heaping coals on the fire. Watson cabled Lane, who was absent in America throughout the crisis, to suppress Beardsley's designs or he would withdraw all his books from the Bodley Head. Lane, feeling that he had no choice, protested and capitulated. The ultimatum and Lane's capitulation were grossly unfair because Beardsley

---

* See Frontispiece. The original of the pastel portrait, executed in 1894, is in the Print Room of the British Museum; I am indebted to the Keeper for permission to reproduce it here. In connection with this portrait Rothenstein recalls, "For some reason I coupled Davidson with William Watson, perhaps because I often met them together at the Hogarth Club when Lane was entertaining his authors, and I wanted to draw them together. Davidson was willing, but William Watson preferred to sit alone. Looking at my drawing of Davidson, Max [Beerbohm] remarked on the subtle way in which I had managed his toupee; greatly to my surprise, for I had not noticed, to Max's amusement, that he wore one. How much more observant was Max than I! He told me that Davidson was far from wishing to look younger than in fact he was, but having to depend on journalism for a living, he feared a bald head would prejudice his chances." Rothenstein, *1*, 181.

was in no wise implicated in the Wilde scandal. Furthermore, as Lane very well knew, the artist had stipulated that
nothing of Wilde's should appear in the *Yellow Book* while
he was associated with it, a policy he later transferred with
his services to the *Savoy*. Beardsley's caricatures of Wilde
in his illustrations to *Salomé,* Davidson's *Plays,* and elsewhere convey the scorn which he felt for their model. Lane
has been frequently censured for betraying Beardsley, and
the ultimate responsibility was unquestionably his. In his
favor recent evidence indicates that he was not fully informed, that he acted on the advice of a nervous subordinate in London, and that he was under severe pressure
from a number of his most important and influential
writers.

As if to signal the victory of stalwart masculinity over
unhealthy decadence, the first item in the fifth issue of the
Yellow Book was William Watson's somber "Hymn to the
Sea." The last was a long patriotic eclogue, "St George's
Day," by Davidson. This was his final contribution to the
quarterly. Whether the editors, embarking on a new policy
of conservatism, decided that by reputation he was too
closely linked with the more daring and artificial element
or whether he voluntarily withdrew can only be guessed.
Certainly Lane continued to publish his volumes of poetry.
In all events, Watson's proved a hollow triumph. With the
resignation of Beardsley and his recruitment by Leonard
Smithers and Arthur Symons for the rival *Savoy,* the quality of the *Yellow Book* began almost imperceptibly to deteriorate. No longer was it a genuinely representative magazine dedicated to offering only the best of the old and the
new. The crisis over the fifth number, like the outcome of
the trial which precipitated it, marked a turning point in
the fortunes of the *Yellow Book* and an end to the heyday
of *fin de siècle* poetry and manners.

A bold individualist himself, Davidson's sympathies were

with Wilde. After sentence was imposed he wrote to Lane, taking an enlightened view of the penalty:

> At first I was sorry at the sentence on Oscar, but I have since come back to my original opinion that whether he is guilty of the actual crime—crime, so-called; what the law has to do with it as long as there is no rape I fail to see—or not, punishment is his only hope for the future: two years hard labour! it will surely purge him even in the sight of unintelligent England.[85]

Characteristically Davidson viewed Wilde's disgrace and punishment not with any real understanding of the condemned man's feelings or the public's but from his own hard-headed, amoral point of view. The new hedonism practiced by Wilde had been merely one expression of the revolt against established morality during the final quarter of the century. As an ethical and aesthetic theory it was perhaps no more dangerous than other manifestations of the revolt. Certainly there is nowhere a more terrifying moral warning than the conclusion of *The Picture of Dorian Gray,* a work which reveals the other face of Wilde's own cloven personality. During the nineties it was chic if not quite proper to discuss openly free love, divorce, the emancipated woman, and a single standard. Nevertheless even the advocates of a new morality were content for the most part to confine their advocacy to discussion or at the most to clandestine violations of the old morality. Those who, like Wilde, were encouraged by a relaxed and shifting moral climate to parade their dubious conduct were as always in the minority. In Wilde's case there probably must be added the rarer phenomenon of a man driven by a sense of personal and artistic inadequacy. Although drug addiction, alcoholism, neurasthenia, homosexuality, and suicide, like religious conversions, are associated in the popular mind with the nineties, there is no reason to believe that they occurred more frequently than, say, during that decorous age which gave the world Samuel Johnson, Boswell, Christopher Smart, Cowper, and Wilkes. On the other hand, intellectual agitation for a new morality at the end of the century undoubtedly strengthened prejudices or stimulated unhealthy proclivities that might have been indulged in any event.

Sympathetic with the revolt and celebrating uninhibited sexual activity as healthy and noble, Davidson did not lift the barrier between principle and practice. For a few years during his association with the Bodley Head poets he embraced, playfully in the novels, seriously in the lyrics, a sensationalism and naturalism not unlike the ideas to which Wilde, Beardsley, Dowson, and Symons subscribed. It is now clear, as it was not to his contemporaries, that Davidson's hedonism was of a sterner, more positive and vigorous mold and that it was of a different lineage from that of the decadents. Their guides were the *libertins* of the Continent, whereas Davidson's sources were chiefly Anglo-Saxon. In time, as disappointment reinforced the tougher side of his nature, he recognized that they worshiped other gods than his. As he became increasingly impatient with their artificiality, he set out, even before Wilde's public ruin, to erase the impression of his decadent sympathies. Henceforth he employed a more masculine, explicit style in which to state his message.

Through his connection with Lane's firm, Davidson met writers of widely different interests. He gradually grew away from the Rhymers and formed strong ties with other individuals representing ideas completely divorced from aestheticism and decadence. E. J. O'Brien has observed that Davidson is "the sole bridge that we have between the period of the *malade imaginaire* and the Kipling period that followed." [86] And Holbrook Jackson, the first literary historian of the nineties, noted that he was "both an expression of and a protest against the decadent movement." [87] It is more accurate to think of Davidson not as abruptly shifting his allegiance from one to the other but as a minor Colossus bestriding the twin movements of decadence and counterdecadence. He participated in the major literary movements of the day without at any time losing his strong individuality or integrity of purpose. More than any other figure, he demonstrates that the different factions so busy feuding with one another were unwitting allies in the larger cause of romanticism.

7

W. B. Yeats has described the social unrest at the end of the century upon which the Parnassians of the Cheshire Cheese and Vigo Street turned their fastidious backs:

> Occasionally at some evening party some young woman asked a poet what he thought of strikes, or declared that to paint pictures or write poetry at such a moment was to resemble the fiddler Nero, for great meetings of revolutionary Socialists were disturbing Trafalgar Square on Sunday afternoons; a young man known to most of us told some such party that he had stood before a desk in an office not far from Southampton Row resolved to protect it with his life because it contained documents that would hang William Morris, and wound up by promising a revolution in six months. Shelley must have had some such immediate circle when he wrote to friends urging them to withdraw their money from the Funds. We poets continued to write verse and read it out at "The Cheshire Cheese," convinced that to take part in such movements would be only less disgraceful than to write for the newspapers.[88]

There were other poets and writers who were deeply concerned with current issues—social, political, scientific, and religious—who made them the subject matter of their works and wrote for the newspapers when they were not busy writing to them. Among them were Grant Allen, Edward Clodd, and William Watson.

Charles Grant Blairfindie Allen (1848–99) was easily the most revolutionary and outspoken of the socially conscious poets; his influence on Davidson's thought after 1895 was considerable. A disciple of Darwin and Spencer, Allen employed verse and prose fiction to disseminate, now earnestly, now facetiously, the gospel of evolution. Like Davidson he accepted a mechanistic and atheistic universe. On social and political issues he outstrode all contemporary poets, inciting rebellion or advocating socialism. He thus is a link between William Morris and the young Fabians, G. B. Shaw and H. G. Wells.

Fearless and sympathetic, Allen was always ready to give public recognition to struggling younger poets whose work he respected. Writing Longmans, the publishers, he observed, "They say that I discover a new poet once a fortnight. If so, I must have begun six weeks ago, for my discoveries to date are Watson, Davidson, Le Gallienne, and to tell you the truth, I am not in the least ashamed of them." [89] When asked in March 1895 if anyone could claim the right to having discovered him, Davidson replied, "Well, no, I discovered myself; but I may say that I have never met a more sympathetic and appreciative man than Mr. Grant Allen. He has an open mind for everything new, and does not, like some critics, keep back his kind words till an author no longer requires them." [90]

John Lane had published Allen's collection of sensational poems, *The Lower Slopes,* in 1894, revealing on the one hand a clear, unimpassioned mind concerned with metaphysical matters and, on the other, a fervent idealist and humanitarian, espousing social reform or revolution. Allen was in every respect a liberal and the friend of all liberal movements. In no field was his liberalism more extreme or outspoken than in that of relations between the sexes. Like the Pre-Raphaelites and Swinburne he was the knight-errant of the fallen woman, but not like them out of sentimentality or anti-Grundyism or from a perverse theory of art like Wilde and the aesthetes. Since society by its false standards had created the woman-of-ill-repute, it had in Allen's opinion no right to judge her. By the mid-nineties it was no longer the prostitute—Jenny, Faustine, Dolores "the world's delight," and the occupants of Wilde's "The Harlot's House"—but the society woman with a past who had become the fashionable object of men's chivalry and sympathy. In a period when sensation was the stock in trade of the publisher, no work created a greater flurry than Grant Allen's now completely forgotten *The Woman Who Did,* which appeared in 1895 as No. VIII in "The Keynote Series" of the Bodley Head.

Allen's *roman à thèse* suffers artistically like any work consecrated to the vindication of a single idea. Le Gallienne, who shared Allen's revolutionary ideas, concluded his review of *The Woman Who Did:* "the failure of Mr. Allen as a novelist, on this occasion, is nothing against his philosophy." [91] Today the story appears melodramatic, the tone sentimental, the characters unreal, the dialogue artificial. Allen sacrifices literary value to air free love, socialism, world federation, and atheism. But the novel's sympathetic presentation of Herminia Barton, a "new woman" who bears an illegitimate child by the man she loves, only to be rejected by the child in later life, stirred up a storm of controversy at the time. What made Allen's heroine so daringly different from other fallen women in the problem literature of the day was that she deliberately chose to break with convention in order to advance the cause of feminine freedom and was not driven to it by circumstances or weakness of character.

Davidson's letter to Mrs. Allen, acknowledging the gift of this book, shows greater interest in causes and Allen's ideas than critical acumen:

> There is nothing I would dream of criticising: it is a book that comes straight from the life and heart of a man whose gifts and accomplishments one admires the more one thinks of them, and whose good will I for one am proud and happy to have acquired. I think "One Who Did" strikes *the* keynote on the subject; and it does more: it presents a full score of the theme as it is possible to take it, and its admirable reasonableness appears best in its ending upon an unresolved chord.[92]

At the conclusion of the letter, which is more personal than those he generally wrote, Davidson promised to visit the Allens. The frequently postponed visit was at last made to their picturesque cottage "Hilltop," at Hindhead, overlooking "the Devil's Punch-bowl." Margaret Davidson accompanied him, and Le Gallienne in his green velvet jacket was also present. Although it rained steadily, as it does on English holidays, and Davidson had to exchange his soaked trousers for a dry pair belonging to his long-legged host, it was a carefree interlude such as he seldom enjoyed.[93]

For evidence of a further relationship between these two late Victorian yea-sayers and nay-sayers, one must turn to Davidson's poetry where the soft, tender lyrical note of the impressionists grows fainter and a more muscular strain rises to a discordant crescendo. While Allen's example gave him the courage to express unequivocally in poetry his own controversial ideas, his was not a slavish imitation. By the time he met Allen he had found his own lyric idiom and did not attempt to reproduce Allen's style. Although he respected the courage and candor of his friend, their nonconformism led them ultimately in different directions, Allen to socialistic radicalism and Davidson to aristocratic radicalism. Apart from this, Davidson and Allen had several features in common: Both were amateur scientists and keen observers of nature, both had a highly developed sense of irony and whimsy, both had started out as schoolmasters and become rebel thinkers and atheists.[94] Allen was gregarious, gentle, and full of warm humor, as his work testifies; he may have strengthened the more sanguine side of his friend's character. His death in 1899 deprived Davidson of a valuable and much needed comrade.

If Davidson enjoyed the encouragement and patronage of several men of letters—Le Gallienne, Grant Allen, and later Gosse—he was not slow to befriend others. His correspondence shows that on several occasions he attempted to assist fellow writers: Gissing, whose somber interest in the lower classes he briefly shared; [95] the Canadian poet, Richard Hovey, "a most picturesque figure—like a man out of French Romanticism: he seems to have come straight from fighting over Hernani shoulder to shoulder with Gautier"; [96] and his countrymen, J. E. Barlas,* J. M. Barrie, and Harry Lauder.† Aloof, proud, reserved, he was never-

---

* John Evelyn Barlas (Evelyn Douglas), 1860-1914, Scottish poet and author of *Songs of a Bayadere and Troubadour* (1895), among other volumes of verse. His early volume, *Bird Notes* (1887), had been dedicated to Davidson. Barlas was an ardent socialist and revolutionary. In a letter to Victor Plarr, Dowson writes: "The latest Rhymer is one Barlas [he was probably introduced by Davidson], a charming poet and anarchist, who was lately run in for shooting the House of Commons" (Plarr, *Dowson*, p. 60). Davidson replied to an inquiry from Gosse, on 21 June 1898, "No; Barlas is not dead. When I last heard of him he was in Gartnavel Asylum, Glasgow. I am afraid there is little chance of his recovery. His face was very handsome, and he was physically strong; but his head was small, and nothing in it to outweigh insanity." A.L.S., undated, from Rayleigh House, Shoreham, Sussex, B.C.U.L.L.

† Menzies Davidson recalls that Barrie and Lauder visited his father's London flat and were befriended by him.

theless touchingly pleased at any notice or kindness. His strong friendships with William Canton,* Le Gallienne, and Grant Allen date from favorable notices which they gave him. For William Watson he seems to have preserved a strong respect.† Although Watson and he were poles apart in temperament, poetic style, and views, they shared many nineteenth-century traits: earnestness, fortitude, humanitarianism, and a sense of the poet's responsibility as social critic, leader, and prophet.

Friends, like holidays, were all too few. With a single-minded devotion to his profession as poet and his responsibility as breadwinner, Davidson little by little denied himself the one solace that might have saved him and his work. Trials, professional and private, multiplied rapidly. There had been the desperate and futile struggle to win a precarious toe hold in the journalistic trade. Repeatedly he devised journalistic projects in order to earn a little money. For a time he undertook a second series of thoughtful travel sketches modeled on *A Random Itinerary,* which he intended to publish individually in the *Glasgow Herald* and later as a collection. To be christened *Causeway and Forest,* the book died stillborn; but the walking tours upon which it was based produced at least two of his loveliest lyrics, "In Romney Marsh" and "A Cinque Port." Preferring to write poetry and obliged to rely on journalism, Davidson was unable to make a métier out of his art or an art out of his métier. Oddly enough, when the chips are down his prose writings, less known than his poetry and never properly collected, strike the modern reader as his most urbane,

---

* Canton may also have helped Davidson obtain a pass for the South-Eastern Railway when the latter was collecting material for travel sketches in the *Glasgow Herald.* A.L.S., dated 13 Feb. 1894, from Hornsey, Y.U.L.

† Personal association between the two poets may have been limited to the exchange of inscribed copies of their works, although Davidson wrote to Lane that Watson was "one of the men whom it is good to think of." A.Ls.S., dated 27 Dec. 1894, from Hornsey, P.U.L., and undated, from Rayleigh House, Shoreham, N.L.S.

polished, and stimulating work. Pride in being a poet and prophet prevented him from developing what might have proved a superior talent.

In spite of mounting desperation and the warnings of publishers he would not come down in the price for his poems. To Clement Shorter, the elder critic and editor of the *Illustrated London News* to which he had periodically contributed, he wrote that his price would stay at four guineas a poem; William Watson got five and was "just about a guinea in front of me in the matter of reputation." [97] Belligerence and resentment began to undermine the equanimity which he had preserved in more cheerful days by a highly developed sense of irony and a proud independence. Always a cleft personality, a delicate balance of the fierce and the gentle, the dour and the sanguine, Davidson showed symptoms of losing his equilibrium.

Meanwhile the burden of professional disappointments, not markedly lightened by periodic successes, grew heavier, then crushing with the addition of personal reverses. His poor health, always a nuisance, was now a serious handicap, as innumerable letters to Lane declining invitations testify. In London he suffered from chronic asthma and bronchitis, "a thing one can neither fight nor pay off in any way." [98] He found relief from these ailments, but never a permanent cure, in solitary vacations which he could ill afford and finally in permanent retirement to Cornwall. When he disappeared in March 1909 there was some speculation in the press that his attacks of influenza, his asthma, and the lifelong heart disease were, like the fear of cancer, largely imaginary, the consequence of a neurotic temperament.[99] Davidson probably was something of a hypochondriac; he himself noted that in the greatest men genius is accompanied by some corresponding physical handicap: a nervous disorder, consumption, venereal disease, or madness.[100] To argue that his frequent respiratory ailments resulted from hypochondria or an unfounded theory is in no way to deny that he was repeatedly incapacitated by them. A man racked by asthma or chronic bronchitis is not much comforted by the knowledge that his suffering is partly psychological in origin. Anxiety over financial difficulties may have made him more susceptible to minor illnesses. Hard pressed to pay his own rent, he was obliged after his father's death to pay that on the house in Edinburgh where his mother and sister let lodgings to students. He contributed to their support and also to that of his brother, who suffered from mental illness.*

One of his stanchest friends and benefactors in this London period was Edmund Gosse. Between the lines of his letters to Gosse and others during the winter of 1894–95, it is possible to read his increasing wretchedness, embarrassment, and withdrawal. Early in December 1894 he begged Gosse to excuse him from meeting Austin Dobson at that time, pleading drudgery and a severe cold among other setbacks. Hopeful for a later interview with Gosse, he continued:

> Shall we be able to talk of this subject? One can write and publish things one wouldn't say. I believe two men who have had the same experience might: they would not have to explain anything: they could talk in symbols. But it would have to be a "two-handed

* Davidson's only brother, a victim of alcoholism, became violent sometime before the end of 1893. As his mother's life was in danger and her lodgings had been emptied, Davidson placed his brother in an asylum. (A.MS. notes by Edmund Gosse, undated, B.C.U.L.L. On English Board of Trade stationery, these notes were evidently made at the time that Gosse was helping to negotiate a Civil List pension for Davidson. This information is confirmed by Menzies Davidson.) Although Davidson repeatedly introduced the theme of madness into his writings, I find no evidence of hereditary insanity in the family as Gertrud von Petzold assumes, apparently as the result of confusing the poet's father, Alexander, with a Rev. J. D. Davidson (*John Davidson, und sein geistiges Werden unter dem Einfluss Nietzsches*, Leipzig, B. Tauchnitz, 1928, p. 8, n. 2).

crack" as they say in Scotland—the two alone together.[101]

The delicate subject to which he reticently alludes may
have been their common rebellion against the orthodoxy of
their parents. Notable is the arbitrary division of his personality into a private self and a public self. By an attitude
of irony Davidson had heretofore attempted to evade conflicting loyalties and ultimate choices. Like others before
and after, he was coming to the fork in the road where he
must choose with the few or by electing a *via media* compromise with the many.

To salvage something of his pride, he still endeavored to
repay kindness with kindness. In the same letter to Gosse
he praised the latter's forthcoming volume of poems, *In
Russet and Silver,* and hoped that he would be successful
in his attempts to review it. Three days later he wrote to
Gosse again on this subject, confessing to a habit which
was more virtue than fault but which prevented him from
becoming a successful critic: "My own [review] is short; I
never have been allowed much space in the *Speaker,* being
apt to say my own things rather than editorially-minded
things; but it speaks out straight and claims you as one of
the very few of the less young men who have kept in sympathy with the rising generation—one, indeed, who is
likely to keep abreast with all the generations he may pass
through." * Then at the end, unaware in his self-absorption that Gosse might misapply his meaning, he wrote,
"I am driven with drudgery, Xmas books, etc.—I hope this
will be my last year of the mere scavenging part of reviewing." [102] Harsh in his judgment of poets no longer living
and outspoken in conversation about living poets, David-

---

* As Quiller-Couch had reviewed *In Russet and Silver* in the *Speaker*
for 1 Dec. 1894, Davidson's review was not accepted. In the same letter
he informed Gosse that he had also sent it to Clement Shorter of the
Illustrated London News, where it appeared 19 Jan. 1895, p. 87.

TIES WITH OTHER CAMPS

son was considerate, if seldom enthusiastic, in his reviews.

Of the poems in Gosse's slender collection Davidson singled out "Neurasthesia," a somewhat mawkish plea for
pity toward the "lost generation" of the nineties, as "a very
remarkable and powerful poem." It was, he wrote, "a
poignant criticism . . . of the new despair and sadness of
the world"; he thereupon quoted it in full. Davidson's own
lighthearted sallies at the decadents notwithstanding,
"Neurasthesia" reached a hurt with the probing that both
assuages and intensifies:

> And some, of sterner mould, set hard their hearts,
>   To act the dreadful comedy of life,
> And wearily grow perfect in their parts;—
>   But all are wretched and their years are strife.[103]

Adversity, like the symbols of Greek drama invented to
portray it, wears two faces. Davidson in these years chose to
smile at defeat, but the fixed grin does not conceal the an-
guish on the reverse side of the mask.

Sometime in June 1895 the poet and his wife left their
inconvenient suburban house in Hornsey and took a flat
at 18 Warrington Crescent, W., in the Maida Vale district,
off Edgeware Road and north of Paddington Station. Almost at once he felt that they had made a mistake and predicted that any day they might leave these dreary lodgings
in disgust.[104] For some time he gave his club as his only
address; and, inviting Gosse to dine at the Grosvenor to
meet Professor McCormick of St. Andrews, he attempted
to dismiss lightly his inability to entertain at home:

> We are practically in hiding here at the top of a big
> house. Having tired of Hornsey and of searching for a
> less unsuitable abode than the one we have chosen,
> we took it in despair, but are so unsatisfied with the
> change that we tell nobody where we are, and are not

supposed to have an address at all—unless it be Mahomet's affair. I have at least and at last an attic to
work in, and that too in the heart of the promised
land for it seems that Maiden Hill is also called Mount
Zion.[105]

The flat in Maida Vale may not have been so shaming as
Davidson imagined, for when his poverty was greatest he
could apologize to his publisher for not possessing a valet.

As it grew plain that he had neither the will nor the
way for potboiling, and that ballad making would not provide a sufficient income, Davidson turned again to the
theater. He first undertook an original play, presumably
Godfrida (1898), and with it began a new chapter in his
career. Although he continued to publish lyrics, it was less
and less often; in general, they are without originality.
With the passing of time and his failure to win success in
any field, he grew more despondent and unable to apply
himself. In July 1896 he wrote to Lane that he had completed his *New Ballads,* soliciting him to secrecy. He added
that he was now "in great pain and misery conceiving a
play," that he had an unquenchable lust for gold, and that
he intended to give it full swing.[106] The note of defiance in
his letters as in his works became more strident, as he gradually found solace in the delusion that he was being persecuted. He showed less inclination than ever to see or meet
people. "I cannot come in to town oftener than once a
month while I am writing this play," he wrote in irritation
to Lane. "My work gets on my nerves as it never used to
do: the work is none the worse for that; but I am." [107] On
the rare occasions that he did come to the office in Vigo
Street he refused to meet anyone, referring editors to his
agent with the remark, "It is my work, not myself, that I
wish to be known" [108] or "I do wish people would rest
content with my books: whatever else may be said about

them they are better than myself." [109] The wounded animal, when it does not make a stand, retreats to its lair. Up
to this time Davidson had made a truce, if not peace, between the two sides of his nature. Now he divided his life
sharply into opposite worlds, and the chasm separating the
two grew wider and wider. For his family and a few friends
he reserved the remnants of his gentleness, humor, and
kindness. Even here, the douce was yielding to the dour.
Gone were the days of the "Banbury Cross" jingles he invented endlessly to entertain the boys, the games to train
their memories, and the lessons he personally conducted.
Instead they were sent off to school and hushed up while
at home so that he might have the absolute quiet he needed
in order to work. During the winter of 1897–98 he went
alone to Shoreham, near Brighton, in Sussex to devote his
entire energies to writing. He did not return to London to
stay until the autumn of 1898. On the other side of the
chasm, his inflexible idealism and sense of dedication found
an outlet in quarrels with the critics and in the ever wilder
fantasies of his works.

6

THE PHOENIX IN THE AVIARY

Each of us is on a mission to
shape the earth.
Novalis

Among his contemporaries of the nine-
ties John Davidson was invariably associated with John
Lane's select "nest of singing birds." These self-consciously
independent poets were united only by a common purpose
to restore freedom, honesty, and beauty to poetry. Although Davidson's lyrics stood out for their rough vigor,
no one seemed to feel that an eagle or a falcon from the
Highlands had strayed into the canary cage. Such was the
deference paid to individuality. They were even further
from suspecting that they harbored a phoenix who would
build his pyre from his own works and those of other poets.
The burly Scot's reputation as a *fin de siècle* poet rested
largely on two volumes of remarkable eclogues in a modern
vein and a number of ballads and songs whose perplexing,
amoral message was made palatable by their modest, engaging lyricism. In all he produced eight volumes of lyrics,
beginning with *In a Music Hall and Other Poems* of his
second year in London and ending with *Fleet Street and
Other Poems,* published posthumously in 1909. Though

after the turn of the century he applied himself almost entirely to long philosophical poems and plays in blank verse, he continued to produce rhymed lyrics sporadically throughout his life.

From first to last Davidson was convinced of his higher vocation as a poet. Although he was never slow to state categorically what poetry should be, his literary principles take the form of nebulous generalization or impassioned, subjective pronouncement. Again like his metaphysical views, his ideas about poetry develop gradually and are constantly shifting. He is consistent, however, in stressing the role of the imagination. In an essay defining the poet he writes, "The body, the whole body, is also the soul. It is the nerves, the heart, the liver, the seed that apprehend and think and feel . . . Imagination gathers the flower of the whole anatomy." [1] Davidson therefore opposes the imagination to "stout thought" and "memory," as he opposes poetry, the product of the imagination or whole body, to metaphysics, the exercise merely of the power to reflect. Since it alone unites all man's faculties and functions, the imagination is "the joy of life" without which an individual or society degenerates. It is the imagination which in each age has devoured and digested the universe, transmuting it into the great mythological or scientific systems. In spite of these high-sounding phrases, the imagination for him comes close to meaning sense experience; that is, the perception and transmutation of pure sensation by exercising in concert the material powers of the body. This capacity for concerted sense experience is equivalent to "genius" or "an awakening of the whole nature" and is found only in the abnormal man, as pure instinct, to which it is related, is found only in brutes. Genius is invariably accompanied by physical or mental disease, symptoms of this rare balance of bodily forces in an imbalanced civilization.[2]

Given imagination as the distillation of raw experience, it follows that the immediate origin of poetry is physical: "The senses are the ducts of the feelings; imagination is the gulf and the retort that swallows and transmutes sight and sound, touch and taste, and all emotion, passion, thought, into beauty and delight, into power and achievement." [3] The poet is therefore "the Experiencer," and poetry an impassioned, amoral, subjective statement of the world as he perceives it without rehearsal or reflection.* Spontaneity, liberty of utterance, sincerity, intensity, ruggedness, artlessness, and passion are the earmarks of true poetry. Of these the pre-eminent is spontaneity: "To be spontaneous is the whole art of poetry, and especially distinguishes it from the artifice of poetry." [4] Elsewhere he states that spontaneity is "the vesture of poetry." [5] Note that there is no concern here with poetic form: Poetry is judged by its fidelity to the truth of experience, whether conscious or psychic; form is achieved instinctively and incidentally. A poet may, often does, sacrifice conscious craftsmanship to spontaneous intuition or emotion. Like warfare, poetry "is not always an army on parade; sometimes it is an army coming back from the wars, epaulettes and pipe-clay gone, shoeless, ragged, wounded, starved, but with victory on its brows." [6] Rhyme, rhythm, and special diction are sec-

---

* Compare Davidson's similarly romantic ideas about the role of the critic: "Poetry is the product of originality, of a first-hand experience and observation of life, of a direct communion with men and women, with the seasons of the year, with day and night. The critic will therefore be well advised, if he have the good fortune to find something that seems to him poetry, to lay it out in the daylight and the moonlight, to take it into the street and the fields, to set against it his own experience and observation of life, and, should he be a poet himself, to remember how it was that he wrote his own poetry. In this way I reduce culture, which is only experience at second-hand, to its proper place as the merest hand-maiden of criticism." "The Criticism of Poetry," *The Man Forbid,* pp. 65–71; reprinted from the *Speaker,* 4 Mar. 1899, p. 258.

ondary attributes that serve only to distinguish poetry from prose. With Milton long before him and the exponents of free verse after, Davidson comes to feel that rhyme in particular is a property of decadence, an exquisite but effeminate adornment "as rouge on the cheek and belladonna on the eye." Rhythm alone is sufficient. In time he believes that blank verse is immensely superior to rhymed verse, precisely because it is "nude poetry, barbarous and beautiful, or athletic and refined, but always naked and unashamed." [7]

The poet's business in sum is to state the world as it is, to exclude no point of view or subject, however ugly, indecent, or repellent by standard measurement. "Poetry is immoral," Davidson declares. "It will state any and every morality . . . There is no passion of man or passion of Matter outside its province . . . a great poet is very apt to be for his own age and time, a great immoralist." [8] But the poet not only states the world, he also fashions it with his superior will; he transforms the world that he may transcend it. Owing allegiance to no tradition, school, or technique, he stands alone and aloof, "the man forbid," the precursor of the Outsider. In this respect he is akin to other types of hero: the empire builder, the deliverer, the evolutionist, the proletarian, the vivisectionist, the artist. The poet is critical but not righteous, judicious but not vindictive, detached but not diffident, ironical but not cynical, immoral but not anarchic, divine but not spiritual. "That," says Davidson, "is the great poet, and his great poetry is the affirmation of the will to live, the affirmation of the will to power." [9]

Tracing the origins of this neoromantic theory of poetry, one finds that it begins with the view of the poet held by the Spasmodics who in turn derived their ideas from earlier romantic poets, especially Coleridge, from

neo-Kantian psychology, and from Carlyle's conception of
the poet as hero. Like the Spasmodics Davidson stresses the
divine authority of the poet, the validity of experience,
and its subjective, intuitive character. Like them he also
believes that art, deriving immediately from the apprehension of nature by the artist, is necessarily irregular and
uncouth. But the Spasmodics accepted the dualism of
matter and spirit so that Davidson was obliged to adapt
some of their theories to his scientific monism. For example, Dobell's conception of poetic metaphor as a correspondent fact essentially related to the abstract truth for
which it stands becomes in Davidson a simple equation of
metaphor and fact: They are identical and indistinguishable because there is no boundary between the realms of
poetry and science.[10] That is to say, the description of a
star or the evocation of love in a poem and the chemical
analysis of sugar are as statements identical in validity
and kind. Recognition of this implies recognition that
science will eventually absorb literature: "Romance must
just 'fettle' its fine points to the yoke of science, or betake
itself to a nunnery . . ." [11]

From the Spasmodic theory of art Davidson moved to a
temporary discipleship to Walter Pater. Associating with
the aesthetes and decadents, he could scarcely escape exposure to the intoxicating passages of the conclusion to
The Renaissance and of *Marius the Epicurean*. He shared
briefly their interest in preserving the isolated, momentary,
sensuous experience independent of all moral implica-
tion. But it was not within him to remain content for
very long with a conception of poetry as a mere record of
sense impressions. Even when he was writing impressionist
lyrics and prose sketches for the periodicals of the nineties,
his mind was on larger, more earnest issues. On the flyleaf
of a presentation copy of his prose idyl, *A Random Itinerary* (1894), he inscribed:

"The Megalomaniac"

"My thought sublimes
    A common deed:
In evil times,
    In utmost need,
My spirit climbs
    Where dragons breed." [12]

His final formula for poetry is a repudiation of the narrow, intellectual aestheticism of Pater, although it is not an illogical by-product of it.

Whatever poetry may have been for Davidson during the interval of his association with the Rhymers, he finally regarded it as neither aesthetic nor decadent but as vigorously purposeful. Its purpose is to state the present and mold the future by asserting that the universe is material, with all the implications for humanity which this holds. Only materialism explains and makes endurable the essential paradoxicality of the universe which he long contended it is the business of poetry to state: "And thus, if we must have a single phrase to denote the nature of great poetry, let us say that its inmost being is a 'transcendent mirth,' maternity that sings a song in the pangs of travail, life that will be life, and a radiant fighting welcome to the stroke of doom." [13] Having first expanded the theories of the Spasmodics and Pater into a romantic concept of poetry as ironical and "immoral," apart from yet embracing all creeds, he proceeded to his own inflexible creed by which poetry becomes a scientific, synthetic statement of a material universe.

All his denials to the contrary, Davidson undoubtedly crystallized his ideas on poetry under the stimulus of vitalist thought in England and Nietzsche's theory of art. Even so, Nietzsche's influence on these ideas has been exaggerated. The German philosopher-poet's concepts of *Immoralismus* and of art as the product of disease and suffering helped the English poet-philosopher to formulate his own ideas on art, without altering their essential character or predominantly native origin. Nowhere in theory or practice does Davidson subscribe to Nietzsche's definition of art as the triumph of the Apollonian or form-giving genius over the Dionysian or destructive fever. Neither does he distinguish, as Nietzsche does and Yeats, between the Socratic or rationalistic spirit and the unscientific spirit of art.[14] He assimilates from Nietzsche, as from numerous other sources, only those aesthetic ideas which complement or complete his own; the rest he rejects. Like any self-respecting artist or thinker, he steadfastly denies the influence of those to whom he is most indebted, precisely because the synthesis is his.

Davidson's poetry in its development follows much the same pattern as his aesthetic theory, which is often rationalization after the fact. It progresses from the highly romantic comedies and Spasmodic dramas of his Scottish period to the impressionistic lyrics of the early years in London, and thence to the late rhetorical, often strident poems in blank verse which celebrate the Olympian egoism of man. In their impatience with form and their glorification of nature and sense experience, the lyrics, like the early plays, announce the later prophet and his message.

2

Davidson's contribution to the English lyric lies more in what he attempted and anticipated than in what he actually achieved. He lacked craftsmanship commensurate with his poetic energy and powerful imagination. An innovator rather than a creator, he adapted familiar lyric forms and traditional myth to contemporary subject matter and a modern message. In his eclogues of the nineties the shepherds of pastoral tradition become Fleet Street hacks and the bucolic setting a London newspaper office.* Each of the eclogues celebrates a holiday rooted in English tradition—All Hallows' Eve, Lammas, Midsummer Day, May Day, St. George's Day, and so on—which gives the poem its title, initial topic, and framework. The "shepherds' " song-debates express in rhymed and blank verse, now rhetorical and melodic, now conversational and flat, their varied impressions of the city, the countryside, their profession, and current topics. By contrasting the views of his journalist-shepherds and by opposing the urban dungeons in which they work to the rural scenes which they nostalgically recall, the poet sustains a nice balance and a peculiarly modern irony. Satire, sentiment, melody, color, wit, description of nature, and discursive opinion are woven into an intricate counterpoint of sound and sense. In "New Year's Day," for example, the poet introduces in succession Brian's caustic denunciation of modern journalism, Sandy's defense of their vocation, and Basil's recollections of country life, developing these themes contrapuntally until they are finally resolved. Too often in these lyrics, however, the way is paved with good intentions that add up only to an affected whimsical style. If the achievement is seldom equal to the aim, it is almost always ingeniously and richly musical. Davidson's interest in adapting music to verse recalls Tennyson's, Poe's, and Swinburne's more assured efforts. One of the principal contributions of nineteenth-century poetry was this re-

* In an interview Davidson subsequently recalled the inception of his *Fleet Street Eclogues*. As a teacher in Scotland he had had the idea of writing a Teacher's Calendar on the plan of Spenser's *Shepherd's Calendar*. This project was never carried out, but when, on his father's death, he inherited a copy of Gibbon's *Decline and Fall*, the boyish mood revived and with it the forgotten eclogues. Accordingly he began the series, substituting journalists for teachers and Fleet Street for Crieff or Greenock, and reading a chapter of Gibbon every morning before he set to work. *Bookman* (New York), Mar. 1895, pp. 85–7.

discovery of its affinity to music. Davidson's pastoral fugues
and madrigals may not be uniformly successful, but they
must be reckoned with in any account of this re-alliance.
The early eclogues are interesting chiefly as a novel experiment in contrasting moods and rhythms.

The dramatic element in the eclogues and to a lesser
degree in the poet's ballads enables him to view the human scene from different vantage points and to indulge
with ironic detachment the diverse sides of his own nature.
A sense of ambiguity and paradox characterizes his poems
of this time as he embraces a universe governed by cosmic
irony. To link the separate eclogues in a kind of series he
reintroduces his journalists into each poem, giving them
consistent points of view. Brian, the presiding spirit, represents the cynical urbanite, Basil the lover of nature, and
Menzies the romantic malcontent. Together they represent a composite world outlook which their creator sought
to encompass in his personality and poetry. The method
is not unlike that of *The Tempest* and Shakespeare's other
late plays. But in spite of their pretense to ironic objectivity, the poems are often transparently personal and confessional, as the use of his sons' names for two of the journalists playfully symbolizes. Taken together, the several
Fleet Street swains furnish a composite self-portrait of a
cultured, sensitive, mildly cynical, aesthetic individual
with a nevertheless practical bent who finds himself
caught in a commercial, Philistine society.* The intent of

* While many critics overlooked Davidson's conscious ambivalence or
were mystified by it, more sympathetic readers readily recognized him
as an adept ironist. Le Gallienne had noted his "whimsical association
of incongruities" (*Retrospective Reviews*, 2, 115–16), and George Cotterell
observed that he captured the unending conflict of the ideal and reality
in the journalist's life (*Academy*, 8 July 1893, p. 24). Lionel Johnson also
found that he possessed a comprehensive view of life, "half-jesting and half-
despairing, yet defiant all the while" (*Academy*, 5 Jan. 1895, p. 7). Other
critics, failing to note that the renegade Calvinist was interested in the
dissonances of modern life, complained that he was obscure and incon-

these urbanized pastorals is therefore the same as that of Davidson's early plays, to give artistic order to the contradictions of his own nature, although their method is more sophisticated and original.

Having revived and modernized the pastoral eclogue, Davidson was unable to sustain performance. To enrich their imagery and spin new variations, he introduced into his later eclogues fragments of fairy lore, legend, animal fable, and parable. Suggestions for these came from Chaucer, the brothers Grimm, Hans Christian Andersen, and Andrew Lang, as well as from tales heard in the smoky inglenooks of his childhood. Designed to illustrate the stoic hedonism which underlies his poems and to bridge the worlds of commonplace reality and ideal fantasy, these literary montages venture too closely upon the tour de force. Reliance upon such contrivances is a violation of the poet's own solemn rule of spontaneity. When he recognized his mistake and in his final volume, *Fleet Street and Other Poems* (1909), attempted to recapture the buoyant artlessness of the early poems, he had lost the deft touch. He never managed in the eclogues, as in the best of the ballads and descriptive pieces, to achieve a middle way between the carefree and the contrived. The eclogues bestride somewhat clumsily and self-consciously the dramatic realism of Browning's reveries and the dramatic symbolism of Eliot's.

Davidson occasionally carries over into his ballads, a more mature medium for him, the dramatic interplay of personality and idea employed in the eclogues. More often he has recourse in them to another ironic device. Appropriating pagan myth, Christian legend, and conventional notions of courage, love, and piety—whatever traditional

sistent. It speaks for Davidson's resistance to classification as well as for his lack of absolute clarity that he was understood only by an *avant-garde* of fellow poets and critics.

material is at hand—he gives them a new moral interpretation in keeping with his naturalistic hedonism at this time. The ballads are turnabout tales in which a simple, frequently familiar legend or parable culminates in an unexpected moral. For instance he plays the stock reaction of his readers to the account of creation in Genesis or to the legends of King Arthur against the new meaning which he attaches to them. Again, in "A Ballad of Euthanasia" he reads an arresting lesson into the old tale of the phantom lover, which Bürger had treated and Scott adapted in "William and Helen." He does not undertake in these narrative poems to create a new body of myth so much as to construct disturbingly revolutionary pastiches from the detritus of the old. This refurbishing of traditional legendary material is another manifestation of the "new understanding" which Davidson had applied to the hackneyed conventions of romantic comedy and of the picaresque and sentimental novel. But the best of the ballads are serious, independent, artistically integrated works where the plays and novels, however entertaining, are imitative and posturing.

Already in the juvenile poems of *In a Music Hall and Other Poems* (1891), Davidson had employed the traditional ballad and the narrative romance as vehicles for revolutionary messages. "Alice," "The Queen of Thule," and "Anselm and Bianca" teach that love is pure, natural, and amoral no matter what the circumstances or consequences; that nature's laws supersede those of society; and that the life of passion and self-realization embracing even murder and suicide is the only true life. Strident melodrama and sentimentality mar these and other poems from the first volume. By the time of succeeding volumes, the immoralist had learned the value of understatement, delayed revelation, ironic objectivity, and the subordination of revolutionary message to dramatic interest and direct sensuous appeal.

Characteristic of the new twist which he gave to the familiar is "The Last Ballad," the title poem of a volume that appeared in 1898. In this poem Lancelot, after seeking escape from his consuming passion for Guinevere in great deeds, severe penance, and a sacred quest, first succumbs to delirium and madness and then retires to the atavistic life of a hermit. Suffering purges him of his unmerited sense of guilt so that he finally recognizes the superior claims of his passion:

> His love, in utter woe annealed,
>   Escaped the furnace, sweet and clear—
> His love that on the world had sealed
>   The look, the soul of Guinevere.[15]

Although fourteen years his junior, Davidson's Lancelot bears a striking resemblance to Angelus in *Diabolus Amans,* not to mention other Spasmodic heroes.* A similar departure from tradition occurs in "A New Ballad of Tannhäuser." When the legendary hero journeys to the pope's court in Rome to expiate his sinful love for Venus, he learns from a miracle there that God regards such love as natural and pure, whereupon he returns sanctified to the Venusberg:

* August J. App, inconsistently it would seem, finds Davidson's Lancelot consonant with Swinburne's hedonistic version in "Tristram of Lyonesse" and "The Tale of Balen," but later states that he is "a last and striking example of the prevailing characterization of Lancelot during the nineteenth century" as lonely, repentant, and finally driven to madness. (*Lancelot in English Literature,* Washington, Catholic University of America, 1929, pp. 208–10.) Unlike Swinburne, Davidson does not degrade the love of Lancelot and Guinevere by championing their immorality, nor does he condemn it on moral grounds as Tennyson does. He lifts their love above sin, guilt, and remorse by accepting it as a natural fact symbolizing the amorality of the universe.

And so they wait, while empires sprung
Of hatred thunder past above,
Deep in the earth for ever young,
Tannhäuser and the Queen of Love.

A note appended to *New Ballads* of 1896 in which this
poem appeared explains its message: "In reverting to a
simpler form I have endeavoured to present passion rather
than sentiment, and once more to bear a hand in laying
the ghost of an unwholesome idea that still haunts the
world,—the idea of the inherent impurity of nature." [16]
Davidson's treatment of this theme is still mild compared
to the explicit sexual symbolism of his later plays, which
coincide in date almost exactly with the early erotic verse
and fiction of D. H. Lawrence. Both writers sought to
exorcise the demons of chastity, repression, and guilt attendant upon the narrow evangelicalism of their childhood. But where Lawrence had Hardy and the older
Georgians for guiding stars, Davidson bobbed in the rhetorical backwash of the late Victorians.

The author of "A New Ballad of Tannhäuser" was not,
of course, the first nineteenth-century poet to play the
heretic with legends thought inviolable. Swinburne in
"Hertha," "Hymn of Man," and other early poems had
repudiated supernaturalism, but he had embodied his
nature worship in more receptive pagan myths. In "Laus
Veneris" of the first series of *Poems and Ballads* (1866),
however, the older poet had treated the Tannhäuser legend
frankly and sensationally, drawing the moral that carnal
love while sinful in the conventional sense was well worth
divine punishment and superior to divine grace. Davidson and Swinburne possessed very dissimilar temperaments
so that their lyrics resemble each other's only superficially.
More restrained, objective, and modest, Davidson's lyrics
rarely exhibit the pagan sensuality and blasphemous satan-

ism of Swinburne's. These qualities do not appear until much later in the materialist's works, and then they express a code much more forbidding than the hedonism of the "Fleshly School." As the Chiron of English erotic poets, Swinburne had spoken of sin in terms usually reserved by the nineteenth century for virtue:

> In a twilight where virtues are vices,
>   In thy chapels, unknown of the sun,
> To a tune that enthralls and entices,
>   They were wed, and the twain were as one,
> For the tune from thine altar hath sounded
>   Since God bade the world's work begin,
> And the fume of the thine incense abounded,
>   To sweeten the sin.[17]

This transposition of the conventional meanings of sin and virtue is in keeping with nineteenth-century romantic irony, but Swinburne for all his self-conscious daring does not renounce the dichotomy of good and evil.

When Davidson justifies a life of uninhibited passion in "A Ballad of a Nun" and "A New Ballad of Tannhäuser," he is perhaps reflecting Swinburne's ironic immorality but he is enlarging its implications. Irony for Swinburne is still largely verbal and metaphorical, a matter of witty or paradoxical transvaluation. Irony for Davidson becomes conceptual and metaphysical; a question not of rebelling against the established morality or of substituting new values for old but of accepting all values or none. Contrary to what one might expect, open defiance does not lead Swinburne to neglect technical skill and the reworking of myth for didactic assertion; nor does a total irony preserve Davidson from dogmatic argument. Temperament, whether artistic or philosophical, prevails. The style of Davidson's ballads, although not their modern, amoral message, is in the popular romantic tradition of Sir

Walter Scott and Robert Buchanan, Swinburne's nemesis. However related in theme, they owe nothing to the form of Swinburne's *ballades,* intricate, artificial, Continental. In spite of his perverse desire to shock, Swinburne was a conscientious craftsman, the reincarnation of Catullus and Ovid, to whom poets less impatient and independent than Davidson willingly went to school.

William Morris had also pointed the way to the heretical treatment of legend when in "The Defence of Guenevere" (1858) he had created a new heroine, a breathing, pulsating Pre-Raphaelite "stunner," passionately and unashamedly professing her love for Launcelot but denying the slanderous charges against her. The influence of Morris' narrative and dramatic poems, with their attention to psychology, human cruelty, and violent climax, is immediately evident in at least two of Davidson's, "The Last Ballad" and "The Ordeal." Once again, however, it is a question not so much of direct influence as of the development of an established trend and its absorption into his own synthetic view of the universe.

Davidson, in what Douglas Bush has called these "thesis poems," is as ingenious at inventing a parable as at adapting a familiar tale. "A Ballad of Heaven," "A Ballad of Hell," "A Ballad in Blank Verse of the Making of a Poet," and "A Ballad of the Exodus from Houndsditch" are strange, macabre, apocalyptic poems, powerful in their fantasy although more explicit and melodramatic than his reworkings of traditional myths. One of the more restrained parables, "A Song of the Road," tells of a pilgrim, a modern Everyman, who seeks salvation first along the thorny road to heaven and then along the primrose path to hell, only to return to the *via media* of the full, varied life:

> He went by bank and brae
>   Where fern and heather spread;

> Azure bells beset the way,
>   And blossoms gold and red;
> Below, the burn sang all the day;
>   The larks sang overhead.
>
>   .   .   .   .   .
>
> Soon he came where men abode
>   And loved, and wrought, and died;
> And straight the Broad and Narrow ways,
>   Heaven fair and Hell obscene,
> For ever vanished out of space,
>   Spectres that ne'er had been.[18]

Even these stanzas illustrate the intrusion of the sermonic upon the fanciful in the ironist's most detached lyrics. The first for its kind is flawless; the second is inept and trite.

Although he made from the grist of myth his own strong gruel, Davidson was by temperament and conviction unsympathetic to this use of fictions. His rearing in a pious, puritanical household had taught him a suspicion of all myth and its hold on the popular imagination. The introduction to *The Theatrocrat* (1905) explains his subsequent emancipation from myth:

> In my ballads I have employed this of God and Sin and Heaven and Hell as the warp of myth in the loom of my poetry, giving the myth also a new orientation as the weaver changes the pattern of his web—an orientation which I have carried to its utmost limit in the Judgment-day of the "Prime Minister"; but no individual mind and imagination, and no general mind and imagination of any class, mass, or mob of men can enter a fateful battle in the name of a metaphysic, can live highly and die serenely to the tune of a mere folklore.* [19]

* Compare an earlier statement in which he rejects enslavement to myth but accepts exploitation of it: "It is a little tedious, this dominion

By repudiating myth altogether, Davidson thought of himself as leading a final, victorious charge in the war against theism conducted by Fitzgerald, Swinburne, Meredith, and James Thomson. Like Nietzsche, whose lyrics also reveal a devotion to freedom and some capacity for invention, he was carried by his demonic energy toward vast oracular visions. Except for a comparatively brief, intensive lyric period, Davidson always belonged to Apollo rather than Orpheus. More than any other poet of his time he approached the vision of the pure mystic, in which symbol and reality, finite and infinite become one. The true mystic is almost never a poet, for he sees things solely in terms of their essential selves, whereas the poet sees things in terms of other things. Insofar as he was a visionary Davidson was unsympathetic to poetry and therefore to myth, the matrix of poetry. When he ultimately divorced himself from the imagery of myth and metaphor, in order to celebrate in vigorous, explicit language the facts of science (or what he took for science), he signed his death warrant as a poet and, it may have been, as a man.

For the time being, in the volumes of the nineties, he resolved to write a new kind of lyric poetry and displayed a versatility that at first seemed inexhaustible. In a review of Davidson's earlier work, dated June 1894, Richard Le Gallienne observed that "not one of our younger poets is so inclusive in power, has so many strings to his bow, as Mr. Davidson . . . he is easily 'head of all our quire.' " [20] Not content to rejuvenate lyric verse by reinterpreting familiar folk lore, he joined others to introduce new subject matter. With an approving nod at Thomas Hood, Walt Whitman, Robert Buchanan, and W. E. Henley,

---

of mythology over the imagination of the modern world. Observe, I say dominion. There is life in all legend; no story will ever die. But it is not sufficient to retell the old tales; they must be transvalued; the imagination of the poet must exercise dominion over his fable." "*Tête-à-Tête*. Lord Smith. Lord Tennyson," *Speaker*, 1 July 1899, p. 741.

Davidson was among the first to write of trains, telegraph wires, and highways; of London suburbs, railroad stations, and Sunday crowds. He accepted the clutter, refuse, and mechanization of modern life without apology or eulogy. Among the earliest poems devoted to the city worker is "Piper, Play!," a wry variation on Blake's Introduction to his *Songs of Innocence.* Juxtaposed so as to convey the essential ambiguity of man's condition are its merry, rustic dancing tune, its grim picture of foundry workers returning home at night which the poet carried in his memory from his Glasgow days, and its undersong of proud stoic acceptance that refuses to lament or to glorify one's lot:

> Now the furnaces are out,
>   And the aching anvils sleep;
> Down the road the grimy rout
>   Tramples homeward twenty deep.
>   Piper, play! Piper, play!
>   Though we be o'erlaboured men,
>   Ripe for rest, pipe your best!
>   Let us foot it once again! [21]

On the other side of the spectrum he could write with equal facility of the seasons, frosty mornings, the sea, apple trees in bloom, laburnum and lilac, and the birds and native plants he knew so well. Always sensitive to the contrarieties of life, he presents cheek by jowl in these early poems the ugly sights of the city and charming evocations of country scenes. If they contain little of the dedicated authenticity of the later Georgians—Ralph Hodgson's bull, Walter de la Mare's old men by the doorways, D. H. Lawrence's vernal seductions—these poems are fully as faithful to the rural landscape.

Characteristic of the attempt to introduce into poetry material heretofore unacceptable is the title series that introduces *In a Music Hall and Other Poems.* These quick portraits of acrobats, singers, dancers, and comedians, while not uniformly felicitous, attempt through sense impressions to re-create the tawdry, raucous atmosphere of the provincial variety. When he reviewed this youthful hodgepodge in the spring of 1892, Yeats recognized "that search for new subject-matter, new emotions, which so clearly marks the reaction from the search for new forms merely." Comparing Davidson to Arthur Symons, whose *croquis* in verse of cabaret life are better known, Yeats saw in both poets a departure from "the generation now going out—the Gosse, Lang, and Dobson school"; that is, the polite society and academy poets. "The typical young poet of our day," he continued, "is an aesthete with a surfeit, searching sadly for his lost Philistinism, his heart full of an unsatisfied hunger for the commonplace. He is an Alastor tired of his woods and longing for beer and skittles." [22] When it came to putting his own construction upon another's work, Yeats was almost a match for Davidson himself. However much he might have seemed to resemble the "typical young poet" of the day, by which Yeats meant the French-influenced decadent and realist, the young Scot bedeviled by poverty and young children was no stranger to the dubious attractions of Philistinism. He was rather a renegade from Scottish Philistinism looking briefly and somewhat self-consciously in the stews and pubs for the active, physical life. Elsewhere more accurate, Yeats objected to the new poet's frequent crudity of phrase and insufficient detachment from his subject. These flaws, forgivable in verse belonging to his sixteenth year, persisted in much of his later work. When he avoided personal reference and found external symbols for his unique statement of life, Davidson wrote a handful or more of as distinguished lyrics as the decade produced.

Until he began to water the syrup, variety and freshness

abounded in the successive volumes. Like Blake and Whitman he embraced the world and humanity in their manifold contradictions, urban and rural, patrician and plebeian, human and natural. His restless search for new ways in which to express the paradoxicality and diversity of life prompted him to combine a grave subject with a lighthearted verse form. One example of this is "Piper, Play!"; but there are as well realistic, melancholy verses on an impoverished laborer's wife and the end of the world to the music-hall tunes of "Ta-ra-ra-boom-de-ay" and "After the Ball." Neither is as technically skillful as Kipling's, Noyes', and Masefield's subsequent experiments with such rhythms, but they are significant innovations nonetheless. Other *jeux d'esprit* include a lament to middle age in the form of a rousing drinking song and unflinching battle songs in the delicate cobweb of the villanelle. No one seemed to recognize that these apparent five-finger exercises are in reality metaphors symbolizing the irony and paradoxicality of the universe. It is no mere accident that a few years earlier Oscar Wilde sought in the brilliant epigrams and paradoxes of *The Picture of Dorian Gray* and *The Importance of Being Earnest* a similarly romantic and artistic resolution of the painful antinomies of existence. In both Davidson and Wilde paradox is more than cleverness; it embraces a metaphysical view of life as personally experienced. Wilde, with the classical training in form and wit of the universities and salons, possessed artistic discipline to the same degree that he lacked its private counterpart. Davidson, whose personal life was disappointingly discreet, infrequently wrote lyrics in which thought and form meet in perfect fusion. As William Archer observed some fifty years ago while the poet was still actively writing, "He is too much absorbed in what he has to say to consider . . . curiously the manner of saying it." [23]

3

Refusing to become the slave of form yet seldom its complete master, Davidson neglected to substitute new rules
for those that he broke. He saw in freedom only the joy
of life, not its responsibility. The consequent abuses make
for an inconsistent, uncouth, yet robust style. Reviewing
Ballads and Songs for the *Academy* in January 1895, Lionel
Johnson, a fellow Rhymer and an exceptionally perceptive
critic, noted the volume's strength of passion, imagination, and thought but singled out concomitant defects:
"a certain feverishness at times, an unpruned wealth of
words, a rapidity which makes the verse pant for want of
breath. This poet's wine can be heady and rasping and
crude." He added, "Even in his finest work there is just
some lack of the *ultima manus,* with its perfecting and
rounding touch: just that serenity and grace are sometimes
absent which mark the assured triumph of the masterpiece.
'What verse he will be writing in ten years!' is the reader's
conviction, rather than a complete confidence in the virtue of the verse before him." [24]

If many of the barbarisms in Davidson's verse are the result of cultivated carelessness, an equal number are the
result of excessive care, a too earnest desire to create a
poetic idiom suited to his ironic vision. The carelessness
produces generosity of length and lapses of taste; the care
produces labored ingenuity and playfulness. Few poets
have risked bathos or contrived elaborateness as deliberately as Davidson, with the result that he often flats when
he should sharp. No *naïf* unconscious of the effects he is
creating, he courted bathos and struck "the wrong note"
to make his poetry echo the discordance of life with its
mixture of the commonplace and the extraordinary. He
scorned the Victorian practice of treating the commonplace as if it were somehow extraordinary. In spite of his

association with the belle-lettrists of Vigo Street, he increasingly avoided elegance for a rougher, "automatic" style.

Convenience and expediency take frequent precedence over convention and expectation in his verse. In the interest of meter, rhyme, or spontaneity he employs dissyllabics like "power," "heaven," and "stolen" as monosyllabics; having robbed Peter to pay Paul, he pronounces "world's," "bruit," and "burn" as if they had two syllables each. These and similar liberties can be justified in many instances as Scotticisms or accepted nineteenth-century poetic practice, but not in all. On other occasions he violently distorts syntax, again to preserve meter or achieve a rhyme without loss of creative momentum. Curiously enough, he takes few liberties with metrics in the lyrics of the nineties. Aside from the substitution of an irregular foot or variation of verse pattern within a single lyric, usually functional, he does not depart from the traditional patterns of English lyric and blank verse. One listens almost in vain in the earlier rhymed lyrics for the rhythmic invention and intricacy of Swinburne or, on the other side of the tracks, for Kipling's brilliant adaptations of vulgar speech rhythms. Novelty of subject matter precedes novelty of form as always in the Scot's verse.*

* Davidson had a sensitive ear, and his poetry may have greater metrical variety than his readers perceive. When William Archer objected to the monotony of this stanza from "A Ballad of a Nun,"

> Long ere she left her cloudy bed,
> Still dreaming in the orient land,
> On many a mountain's happy head
> Dawn lightly laid her rosy hand,

the poet replied: "The unpleasing monotony in the repeated stanza appears, now that you point it out; my way of reading the verse hid it from me: I always give as full a value as possible to latent syllables as in 'or-i-ent' 'man-y -a mountain,' and that secures variety—by a fiction perhaps. I've been going over that verse several times to myself just now, and I would suggest that your displeasure arises not so much, or not

Nevertheless his experiments in *Holiday and Other Poems* (1906) with lines of uneven length and highly ir-regular, repetitive rhymes are noteworthy if tardy. Al-though he seldom escapes altogether a marked, regular beat to write what approximates free verse, as Henley, William Sharp, and John Todhunter do, his later lyrics are interesting as gropings toward the broken cadences and speech rhythms of much modern poetry. "Yuletide" opens with a periodic verse paragraph which echoes the heavy, halting dissonance of the traffic it describes:

> Now wheel and hoof and horn
> In every street
> Stunned to its chimney-tops,
> In every murky street—
> Each lamp-lit gorge by traffic rent
> Asunder,
> Ravines of serried shops
> By business tempests torn—
> In every echoing street,
> From early morn
> Till jaded night falls dead,
> Wheel, hoof, and horn
> Tumultuous thunder
> Beat
> Under
> A noteless firmament
> Of lead.[25]

Still more successful are his efforts to restore flexibility to traditional lyric forms and English blank verse. To achieve

---

at all, from the dissyllabic epithets as from the repetition of the same vowel-sound in 'orient' and 'rosy.' Read 'lily' instead of 'rosy' and pay attention to the sound only and I think you'll find the monotony vanishes —always pronouncing 'orient' as a trisyllable, although of course in the time of a dissyllable." A.L.S., dated 23 Oct. 1894, from 20 Park Ridings, N., Add. MS. 45291, ff. 84–5, B.M.

a tension of rhythmic forces, after the example of the greatest English poets, he varies the length of line and imposes
upon the basic iambic beat his own accentual pattern. A
passage from "Apple-Trees" illustrates this use of melodic
counterpoint to enhance emotional response, which is his
chief contribution to the liberation of prosody that began
in the nineties; he describes the silent song of the trees
in bloom:

> Though merle and throstle were loud,
> Silent *their* passion in spring,
> A blush of blossom wild-scented;
> And now when no song-birds sing,
> They are heavy with apples and proud
> And supremely contented—
> All fertile and green and sappy,
> No wish denied,
> Exceedingly quiet and happy
> And satisfied! [26]

The irregular pauses and hesitant rhythm of these lines indicate exactly how they should be read.

At his best Davidson is adept at fitting metrical pattern
to content, as in "Holiday" where the trochaic measure
holds in firm control a complex allegorical content, or in
"Song of a Train" which with its short chugging lines and
long sentences reproduces the sound and motion of its
subject. "A Runnable Stag," probably his finest metrical
achievement, captures by alternating iambics and ana-
pests, alliteration, assonance, internal rhyme, repetition
and refrain the headlong rhythm of the hunt and the inexorable climax of death:

> When the pods went pop on the broom, green broom,
>   And apples began to be golden-skinned,
> We harboured a stag in the Priory coomb,
>   And we feathered his trail up-wind, up-wind,

We feathered his trail up-wind—
A stag of warrant, a stag, a stag,
A runnable stag, a kingly crop,
Brow, bay and tray and three on top,
A stag, a runnable stag.[27]

Identical rhymes and repeated phrases he adapted from
Poe and welcomed as "the exquisite invention of the most
original genius in words the world has known."[28] In a
poem like "A Runnable Stag" these inventions are so refined and muted that they perform their proper work of
reinforcing the theme. Having borrowed a device and
employed it artfully, Davidson never knew when to give it
back. The later eclogues also contained in *Holiday* introduce Poe's recurrent and identical rhymes mechanically for their own sake. The derivativeness and imperfections of Davidson's work should not obscure the fact that
he did produce unique gems. The minor poet is expected
for some reason to turn out work of consistent finish and
distinction, however slight, whereas a major poet is allowed occasionally to nod and smear the line.

Davidson's diction, like his metrics, is richly varied but
more anarchic. It is, as Archer noted, "copious, colourful,
vital"; it too often, as Archer further observed, "declines
upon a commonplace, stereotyped epithet, now and then
ventures a too daring colloquialism."[29] Elizabethanisms
and other archaic expressions, Scottish vernacular, cock-
ney slang, and coinages occur side by side, adding a bizarre-
ness which attracted the decadents but repelled more conventional readers. The first series of *Fleet Street Eclogues*
contains in profusion such words as "drumlie," "hipped,"
"perpend," "ope," "dup," "snell," and "stilly." Again, Davidson coins the word "logomachy" for logrolling interests;
he uses "regnant" where "reigning" would be more satisfactory; he introduces and stanchly defends in pedantic
footnotes archaisms like "berserkir," "stareabouts,"

"estopped," "gat," "targe," and "shoon"; he is fond of such recondite words as "apanages," "undern," "quidnuncs," "cramoisie," and "chrysoprase," not to mention all the other semiprecious stones that fascinated the decadents; and finally, repeating a sin of his earlier works, he uses one part of speech for another as in "bronzing" and to "uncupboard."

In his defense let it be said that this poetic Esperanto was a calculated symbolic device, although once more he practised it with more exuberance than restraint. Davidson shared with Whitman a suspicion and scorn of words in their accepted literary usage because of their association with creeds and intolerances which he wished to discredit. He too concocted, but the more conscientiously as he was more the metaphysician, a universal language befitting his iconoclastic message. Although his contemporaries sometimes confused this new idiom with the artificiality and perversity of the decadents, Davidson wished to describe not an autonomous world of private aesthetic or illicit experience but the ironic contradictions and dissonances of modern life. Poetic language had become stale, inelastic, imprecise, and in the narrowest sense contemporary, a public utility unrelated to the poet's private enterprise. In this crisis the poet's only recourse was to create, actually to improvise, a new, synthetic idiom from miscellaneous materials—to produce what the Dada artist and poet, Karl Schwitters, considerably later called a *Merz* literature. Only a polyglot language, assembled from the individual poet's peculiar resources, could free him from shackling clichés and enable him to state the multitudinous variety and infinite complexity of the world as he experienced it. The theory is ingenious and sound, one developed more inventively by Pound, Joyce, Eliot, and in France by Apollinaire and André Breton. With a man like Davidson, who lacked formal learning, who was not inexhaustibly inventive, and whose preoccupations were primarily ideological rather than aesthetic, there was the danger that the theory would lead to a mannered style or restore Babel.

As if aware of this danger Davidson in *New Ballads* (1896) and later volumes periodically discarded this rhetorical, synthetic language for a plain, bareboned style so stripped of metaphor as to be scarcely poetry. He was best known, however, for a daring and deliberate juxtaposition of the banal, flippant, and understated with the lyrical, decorative, and florid. Since Davidson's poems are of a piece and, like those of Cowper and much of Browning, do not lend themselves to quotation out of context, it is always difficult to find a satisfactory illustration. The opening of "St Swithin's Day" gives an idea of his whimsical, bittersweet blending of mockery and poignancy:

BASIL

We four—since Easter-time we have not met.

BRIAN

And now the Dog Days bake us in our rooms
Like heretics in Dis's lidded tombs.

SANDY

Oh, for a little wind, a little wet!

BRIAN

A little wet, but not from heaven, I pray!
Have you forgotten 'tis St Swithin's Day?

BASIL

Cast books aside, strew paper, drop the pen!
Bring ice, bring lemons, bring St Julien!

SANDY

Bring garlands!

BRIAN

With the laurel, lest it fade,
Let Bacchus twist vine-leaf and cabbage-blade!

BASIL

I would I lay beside a brook at morn,
And watched the shepherd's-clock declare the hours;
And heard the husky whisper of the corn,
Legions of bees in leagues of summer flowers.[30]

The masculine and feminine qualities of Davidson's verse
carry through into style the same sense of paradox already
observed in the diversified subject matter and points of
view of the ballads and eclogues. Like D. H. Lawrence,
Davidson finds this opposition of the masculine and feminine manifested everywhere, not least of all in himself.
Thus the manner of the lyrics no less than their content
illustrates a central assumption of his metaphysics, the bisexuality of all being. Less explicitly than the discursive
Testaments and tragedies to follow, the lyrics carry on the
same prolonged process of argument and self-rationaliza-
tion. As in Lawrence, the lyrics suffer only when this
exorcism of personal furies takes the form of obvious symbolism and blatant sermonizing.

In his efforts to devise a vital language that would reflect the ironic or bisexual order of nature, Davidson was
frequently betrayed into a trickiness that solicited merciless parody. Owen Seaman in "A Vigo-Street Eclogue"
burlesques the pastoralism, the quaint diction and col-
loquialisms, the pedantry, and rough heartiness of *Fleet
Street Eclogues:*

MAECENAS *

What ho! a merry Christmas! Pff!
Sharp blows the frosty blizzards whff!
Pile on more logs and let them roll,
And pass the humming wassail-bowl!

* Maecenas represents Lane; John, Davidson; Richard, Le Gallienne;
George, Egerton; Grant, Allen; and Arthur, Benson. Other allusions in
the passage are to logrolling by the Bodley Head poets and to Allen's
sensational novel, *The Woman Who Did.*

JOHN

The wassail bowl! the wind is snell!
Drinc hael! and warm the poet's pell!

MAECENAS

Richard! say something rustic.

RICHARD

Lo!
The customary mistletoe,
Prehensile on the apple-bough,
Invites the usual kiss.

GEORGE

And now
Cathartic hellebore should be
A cure for imbecility.

GRANT

And now holly-berries have begun
To blush for Women That Have Done.

ARTHUR

The farmer sticks his stuffy goose!

MAECENAS

Come, come, you grow a little loose;
That's Michaelmas; you must remember
That Michaelmas is in September.[31]

Seaman's parody closes with a "Ballad of Resurrection,"
lampooning the ballad which Davidson appended irrele-
vantly to the eclogue "Christmas Eve" and later published
separately as "A Ballad of Hell." Davidson's ballad, itself
a serious parody of the resurrection myth, tells the story of
a young maid who, after her faithless lover has betrayed
her into stabbing herself so that they may have a death
tryst in hell, is welcomed into heaven as a "soul that knew

not fear." Seaman's heroine is more ladylike and circum·
spect:

> She sought the chemist in his place;
>   He sampled her with searching eye;
> She looked him frankly in the face
>   And told a wicked, wicked lie.

> "My hen," she said, "—a bantam blend—
>   Has hatched a poor demented chick;
> To ease the gentle creature's end
>   I want a pint of arsenic." [32]

At times one must be grateful to Davidson for having inspired Seaman.

The writers of the nineties may have been given to affec-
tation, for one reason or another, but they could laugh at
their own extravagance. Few were as capable of holding a
cracked mirror up to their own nature as Davidson. In
the early plays and novels he had accepted with practical
cynicism the element of show business in writing for general approval. Although he is more serious and responsible in the lyrics, he now and then utters a Wildean aside.
Good-naturedly he derides his vacillation between simple and elaborate diction and his use of inverted syntax:

BRIAN
> I love not brilliance; give me words
>   Of meadow-growth and garden plot,
> Of larks and blackcaps; gaudy birds,
>   Gay flowers and jewels like me not.

BASIL
> The age-end journalist it seems
>   Can change his spots and turn his dress,
> For you are he whose copy teems
>   With paradox and preciousness.[33]

Elsewhere he warns with tongue in cheek against "belle-trist jargon" and "the rant / Of wanton art and proud philosophy." In spite of this self-mockery or because of it, he continued to sin in these respects with impudence if not impunity. Eventually as pride destroyed his equi-librium, he came to regard even his vices as virtues.

Poetry for the Rhymers, to give them their due, was ideally simple, lucid, unadorned—a direct but artful re-cording of isolated experience without moral or social ref-erence. Striving for these qualities, they sometimes achieved only a transparent artificiality. A favorite para-dox of the decade was that simplicity results from artifice, and artifice aims only at simplicity. Although Davidson could be as mannered as any of his fellow Rhymers, he was never as precious. No man of his day or since could write the English tongue with greater sympathy for its purity and clarity. These stanzas from "In Romney Marsh" need not blush to join company with any by Housman or Mase-field:

> As I went down to Dymchurch Wall,
>   I heard the South sing o'er the land;
> I saw the yellow sunlight fall
>   On knolls where Norman churches stand.
>
>   .   .   .   .   .
>
> Masts in the offing wagged their tops;
>   The swinging waves pealed on the shore;
> The saffron beach, all diamond drops
>   And beads of surge, prolonged the roar.
>
>   .   .   .   .   .
>
> Night sank: like flakes of silver fire
>   The stars in one great shower came down;
> Shrill blew the wind; and shrill the wire
>   Rang out from Hythe to Romney town.[34]

Mere artifice had always been abhorrent to Davidson, and he felt increasingly cramped by the conventions of the *fin de siècle* lyric. As popular misunderstanding of the intent of his poems, a sense of failure, and the growing importance to him of his message drove him to greater explicitness, he sought a freer, more fluent medium.

Although he never gave up writing rhymed lyrics, he early began to experiment with blank verse. He had employed dramatic blank verse from the very first, but he now set out to make it more flexible and to adapt it to lyric expression. He wanted a vehicle that he could call upon effortlessly to describe the rich diversity of life and to convey whatever he wished to say, one that would be by turns dramatic, descriptive, lyrical, or didactic. In his hands blank verse served admirably to describe a traditional harvest scene that might have come from a medieval Book of Hours:

> By a Kentish road,
> Across the down where poles in ricks repose,
> Delivered from the burden of the bines,
> And golden apples on their twisted boughs
> Illumine ancient orchards, I descend,
> Watching and wondering to the Medway's bank.
> The alder and the hazel dip their leaves;
> The grass-green willow shakes; the spiny thorn,
> Embossed and lustrous with its load of haws,
> Shines in the water like a burning bush;
> And broad and deep, muttering outlandish things,
> The heavy river rolls its umber flood.[35]

Although these lines retain an underlying five-stress beat, thought and emotion again dictate a counterrhythm that is highly irregular. Blank verse served him equally well to establish in everyday speech the atmosphere of city streets at evening:

Night came down.
The cries of children playing in the street
Suddenly rose more voluble and shrill;
Ceased, and broke out again; and ceased and broke
In eager prate; then dwindled and expired. . . .

The workingmen with heavy iron tread,
The thin-shod clerks, the shopmen neat and plump,
Home from the city came. On muddy beer
The melancholy mean suburban street
Grew maudlin for an hour; pianos waked
In dissonance from dreams of rusty peace,
And unpitched voices quavered tedious songs
Of sentiment infirm or nerveless mirth.[36]

The metrical latitude of this verse is surprisingly advanced for so conservative a metricist and now seems fully as forward-looking as the French verse forms imported by Swinburne, Symons, Henley, and even the early Pound.* In spite of periodic flirtations with these modish forms, Davidson, like Hardy, Housman, and the Georgians, preferred to exploit the forgotten resources of traditional English verse patterns.

The fact that in such blank-verse passages as these Davidson is frequently versifying with only slight changes in wording selections from his own prose writings is not as damaging as it at first appears. It was not always poverty of inspiration which prompted him to pirate himself. In his blank verse of this time he was looking for a primitive,

* When Archer censured the form of his blank verse Davidson wrote him "I am afflicted by your criticism of my form. . . . I use blank verse newly as Wagner did music. If you take a chromatic score of Wagner's and attempt to play it in common time in one key you will have a terrifying result. You can't sing-song my blank verse. But if you will do me the great kindness some day to take me through the passage you condemn I shall be very much your debtor." A.L.S., dated 29 Nov. 1895, from 9 Fairmile Ave., Streatham, S. W., Add. MS. 45291, ff. 114–15, B.M.

virtually automatic art form, a precursor of "action writing," that would have the emotional stimulus and ceremonial quality of formal verse without what appeared to him its restraints and distractions. Unwittingly he was preparing the way for his powerful but almost formless Testaments and tragedies. His vision of reality as at once paradoxical and ordered remained the poet's, but he gradually neglected to give his poetry either paradox or order. A fluent and effective solvent for his thought, the blank verse of the later poems comes perilously close to prose rhetoric. His reputation as a poet, although not as a prophet and mystic, still rests upon his lyrics of the nineties. While he wrote with the greatest ease and strength in blank verse, the discipline imposed by the conventions of the rhymed lyric helped him to achieve in these poems a sustained economy and coherence that are elsewhere lacking.

4

Of all the cults in poetry toward the end of the century, the most widely followed was impressionism. It cut across other styles and movements, so that aesthete and vitalist, realist and symbolist alike wrote impressionist verse. Since the various artistic movements of the eighties and nineties had begun as revolts against complacent middle-class standardization, it was possible for a complete iconoclast like Davidson to enlist successively in each one. During the last decade, however, he remained in style principally an impressionist. Aside from their ideas and autobiographical interest, his lyrics are primarily important for their contribution to *fin de siècle* impressionism.

As a label "impressionism" originated with a painting, *Impression: soleil levant*, exhibited by Claude Monet at the first impressionist salon of the Société Anonyme in Paris in 1874. In this accepted sense it refers to the painting of solid objects dissolved by natural, exterior light as found in certain luminous works by Manet, Monet, Sisley, and Pissarro, which art historians distinguish from the later neoimpressionist and postimpressionist work of Signac, Seurat, Cézanne, Van Gogh, and Dégas. Applied to English lyric poetry, impressionism has a different history. For its origins and theory, English literary impressionism turned to two distinct traditions. The first was native: the hedonism of Fitzgerald's *Rubáiyát,* the Pre-Raphaelites' insistence upon fidelity to nature, James Thomson's ("B.V.") somnambulistic explorations of the city's and the mind's nocturnal moods, and the aesthetic atomism of Walter Pater. The second tradition was Continental: the aestheticism of the French Parnassian poet, Gautier, and the symbolism of Baudelaire, Rimbaud, Verlaine, and Mallarmé, whose chief propagandist in England was Arthur Symons.

In practice, impressionism as a conscious movement in English poetry first appeared in Wilde's volume of 1881 and in Henley's vivid hospital sketches, *Old Infirmary,* written from an Edinburgh cot in 1872–75 but not published until 1888. To be sure, Shelley, Coleridge, Poe, and William Morris had introduced lyric and psychological impressionism into their verse but only to define the more intense, enduring world of the imagination or moral consciousness. It was James Thomson's *The City of Dreadful Night,* first published in the *National Reformer* in 1874, which climaxed this native romantic impressionism. Under the influence of Pater and the French symbolists, later poets—Oscar Wilde, Yeats, Sharp, and Symons—turned to an impersonal, analytic impressionism. Davidson's lyric verse reflects both kinds but is more closely related to the former.

Although association with other styles and ideals lent the impressionist movement variety, the theoretical aim of the later impressionist poets was to suggest the essence of a scene, character, or object by stressing certain striking, carefully isolated details of form, pattern, color, odor, and sound. As with the French impressionist artists who painted out of doors in preference to the studio, the impressionist poet drew directly from reality without rehearsal and, in principle, without the intervention of conscious memory or intellect. Suggestive patterns perceptible to the physical senses were his chief concern. His poetry was therefore largely descriptive, conveying a mood, a feeling, or merely a formal design that belonged, now to the poet or to the reader, now to the autonomous subject matter. Impressionist poetry aimed ideally at being sensuous, intuitive, immediate, and amoral; in this sense, it superseded reason and science. It is not far from the pure impressionism of the London poets to certain early poems of Pound, the doctrinaire imagism of Amy Lowell and "H.D.," and the "Preludes" of T. S. Eliot. This definition, however, is valid only for the most rigid practitioners of aesthetic and pure impressionism. Even Henley, Wilde, and the artist J. M. Whistler on occasion violated the canons of abstract, formalist art, while others submitted even less faithfully. Davidson, grotesque, violent, hallucinatory, was as often expressionist as impressionist.

It has been said that English impressionist verse appeals more to the visual sense and French to the auditory, yet certain English poets felt that poetry was inseparable from music. According to the French symbolist theory of *les correspondances* and psychology of synesthesia, the response of one sense to an intense stimulus was frequently accompanied by corresponding involuntary responses or images of other senses. Thus a measure from a suite by Claude Debussy, Maurice Ravel, or Erik Satie might evoke in the listener the color of purple, another measure green, still another crimson. This meant a breakdown of the old arbitrary barriers among the arts and the exploitation of one art medium by another: music by painting and both by poetry. The theory of synesthesia appealed greatly to the impressionist poets and painters, as it has to artists of the present century who have extended the license to include the most unlikely materials. Henley divided his "London Voluntaries" into movements: "Grave," "Andante con moto," "Scherzando," and so on; Oscar Wilde wrote "Symphony in Yellow," a pure impressionist word-painting; Arthur Symons entitled a series of poetic variations "Divisions on a Ground"; and Davidson composed pieces like "Michaelmas" in the first series of *Fleet Street Eclogues* that are exercises in verbal music.

At times Davidson's impressionism is wholly visual, at times wholly auditory. These lines from "Laburnum and Lilac," for example, appeal to the eye, although identical rhymes and other sound effects are subtly employed to stress color patterns:

> Like ostrich plumes
> The jolly donahs wear,
> Light-tressed or dark,
> The lilac blooms
> In every park and square
> And blooms in Finsbury Park;
> Or heliotrope or mauve,
> Snowy or dark,
> The lilac blooms
> In white and purple plumes.[37]

"Spring Song," on the other hand, appeals directly to the ear by subordinating visual imagery to a dirgelike use of assonance, consonance, and rhyme:

> The curlew calls me where the salt winds blow;
>   His troubled note dwells mournfully and dies;
>   Then the long echo cries
> Deep in my heart. Ah, surely I must go!

> For there the tides, moon-haunted, ebb and flow;
> And there the seaboard murmurs resonant;
>   The waves their interwoven fugue repeat
>   And brooding surges beat
> A slow, melodious, continual chant.[38]

Yeats in "The Lake Isle of Innisfree," limpid fairy songs, and other early verse had likewise used musical effects to evoke an elusive mood and to reinforce symbolic imagery. In some of the later eclogues and in the conclusion to "Laburnum and Lilac" Davidson strove with greater ambition but less success to appeal simultaneously to several senses and to find verbal equivalents for pure odor, movement, and sound. He lacked the discipline and perseverance for this kind of technical virtuosity. His best imagery is simple and pictorial. When Bernard Shaw over the sobriquet "Corno di Bassetto" was writing critical arias in praise of Wagner for the *World* and Aubrey Beardsley was sketching fashionably dressed "Wagnerians" for the *Yellow Book,* Davidson was haunting not the Royal Opera House but the National Gallery where by the hour he studied the water colors and oils of J. M. W. Turner.

5

In spite of their revolutionary treatment of landscape and the country scene, it was neither the city-born Turner nor the country-born Constable, both full Academicians, who blew the trumpet that finally shook if it did not bring down the walls of the Royal Academy. This dramatic role was reserved for the dandified, cosmopolitan *bête noire* of cloven hoof and cleft tongue, James Abbott McNeill Whistler. In 1877 John Ruskin, the admirer of Turner and self-appointed police officer for a morally responsible art, accused Whistler in his painting "The Falling Rocket," then on exhibition at the New Grosvenor Galleries, of "flinging

a pot of paint in the public's face." The charge precipitated
the famous libel action which brought Whistler a farthing's
damages and Ruskin that much closer to premature senil-
ity. Unable to pay the costs of the suit, Whistler in 1879
went into bankruptcy. The lawsuit, often as farcical as any
scene in *Trial by Jury,* did serve one useful purpose by
prompting the artist to state the pure impressionist's position:

> The vast majority of folk cannot and will not con-
> sider a picture as a picture, apart from any story which
> it may be supposed to tell. . . . As music is the poetry
> of sound, so is painting the poetry of sight, and the
> subject matter has nothing to do with harmony of
> sound and color.
>
> Take the picture of my mother, exhibited at the
> Royal Academy as an *Arrangement in Gray and Black.*
> Now that is what it is. To me it is interesting as a pic-
> ture of my mother; but what can or ought the public
> to care about the identity of the portrait? [39]

Setting an example for the impressionist poets, Whistler
accordingly called his paintings "Arrangements," "Har-
monies," or "Nocturnes."

The French artists of the *Salon des Refusés,* no less than
English painters, were familiar to advanced English writers. Although Monet, Renoir, Cézanne, and others did not
become generally known in England until Roger Fry later
defended them vigorously, George Moore as early as 1891
had praised Monet, Pissarro, and Dégas as well as Whistler
in his *Modern Painting.* Nevertheless, the two artists who
commanded the widest attention in England at this time
were Turner and Whistler. The first with Byronic feverishness had set the departure from academic landscape and
genre painting to romantic idealization and impressionism; the second, turning for inspiration to the naturalism

of Courbet and the formal stylization of Japanese print makers, had carried impressionism to the extreme of impersonal detachment and abstraction. Thanks partly to the publicity given by the irascible Ruskin and partly to an imminent showdown between a romantically responsible art and an aesthetically purist one, Turner and Whistler loomed large in the minds of English writers who were only indirectly involved.

An examination of romantic and aesthetic impressionism in the work of Turner and Whistler respectively reveals a striking difference that helps to define Davidson's impressionist style. Although the two artists, representing different generations, share an interest in abstract patterns of light, shade, and space unrestricted by external reference, they do not view the world in the same way. In Turner the essential element of light gushes from some intensely bright as if celestial source and spreads with increasing diffuseness until it seems to drench all creation. In Whistler light and dark emanate from the subject and belong to it. There is consequently an emotional spirituality in Turner's canvases that Whistler's lack. Again, in Turner man and his works are dwarfed by a grandiose and supreme nature; but in Whistler man, his works, and nature are of equal importance and beauty. This may explain why the older painter is primarily a colorist and landscapist, while the younger is best known for his monochromatic portraits and city scenes. We are still aware of the autonomy of the natural scene in Turner, as the artist merely observes and records his emotional response to patterns imposed by an extrahuman force. Whistler himself consciously selects and arranges the patterns of his works, although the illusion is that the patterns emerge objectively from the subject matter. The hand and the head are seen in Whistler, but not the heart as in Turner. For the earlier impressionist, art still copies nature; for the later, to give credit for an epigram where it is probably due, nature has begun to copy art. The work of the one is poetic, subjective, and religious; and of the other, wholly impersonal and secular. Endeavoring to be a pure impressionist, Whistler admitted no moral or spiritual content into his art, recognizing only the aesthetic values of form and design.

Although Davidson, unlike Wilde, Symons, and at times Henley, rarely attempted the pure aestheticism of Whistler, he warmly admired Turner. Calling Turner "a greater man than Wordsworth . . . the greatest man of his time in England," he said that he "often painted with torches instead of pencils, or if he used pencils they were of asbestos and dipped in wells of crimson fire and gold." The turbulence, fury of imagination, and experimental audacity of Turner's "darkling pictures" with their element of myth and allegory excited his own romantic imagination; but he found "all that early and late storm and stress is the thundering approach to the harmonious tune of pure colour which resolves all discord, as in the three dawns of Baiae, Lucerne, and Norham Castle." He writes of this last painting after scrutinizing it closely:

> These paintings were dipped out of wells of coloured fire, of prismatic light. They are sheer miracle. Examine at close quarters the sunrise over Norham Castle. The yellow light is scraped on like butter and spread out with a dirty thumb; a shapeless stain as of a faded ink-blot that had been hastily smudged off, and a dull smear of brownish red that might have been a drop of blood from a pricked finger, are also noted. Stepping backward you watch the thing change into a golden and opal dawn reflected in a wide shallow reach of a crystal river; the smear of red takes the definite shape

of a cow at its morning draught, and the faded inkstain becomes the ethereal blue of Norham Keep.

It was Turner's lyrical, unabashedly romantic landscapes, almost mystical in concept, and not Whistler's abstract arrangements that he sought to translate into poetry. But he feared that mere words could not do them justice, that only music might reproduce their effects: "Light is sound; the rainbow its diatonic scale. Every one seems to feel this unconsciously, to know it intuitively." [40]

In spite of such demurrals many of the landscapes in Davidson's lyrics are unmistakably Turneresque. The descriptive passages of "A Ballad of a Nun" attempt to reproduce Turner in words, as do "In Romney Marsh" and parts of "In the Isle of Dogs." Although "Lammas," one of the early eclogues in blank verse, is overwrought and melodramatic, Davidson never surpassed its impressionistic descriptions of the Medway, harvesters, the fog lifting from Edinburgh, and little fishing smacks bobbing on the tide. When Spasmodic euphoria is not vying with decadent enervation in this poem, imagery and myth furnish verbal equivalents for Turner's pigments:

> While the sun, shut within a donjon high
> Of massive cloud, through secret loopholes flings
> His moted beams that quiver visibly
> Broadcast; or seem ethereal lances, stacked
> By the celestial watchmen who patrol
> The world at night, and on their silent rounds
> Move to the ghostly music of the spheres.[41]

And in the same poem he sketches a small, quick Monet:

> Dimly seen
> Beyond the weathergleam a pennon'd mast,
> A drift of smoke, hover and disappear;

> And in the midst dark sails of mackerel boats
> Over a reach of water, brown as tan,
> Dance, deftly tripping the uneven waves.[42]

Other, literary influences blend with that of Turner in the earlier impressionistic lyrics, so that at times these echo-laden pieces seem to have been distilled from Palgrave's *Golden Treasury.* Shakespeare and Milton are heard in their rhythm and syntax, Wordsworth in their diction, and Keats in their imagery. As he became familiar with later developments in nineteenth-century poetry and more self-reliant, Davidson's descriptive verse gained in economy and individuality.

James Thomson has left his mark upon the early lyrics, especially upon their spectral fantasies and urban scenes. Thomson's atmospheric descriptions of London at night, notably in *The City of Dreadful Night,* established a model for the later London poets. Relying on the telling image to communicate a general mood, this poem's gloomy impressionism furnished a model for Henley's *London Voluntaries and Other Verses,* Symons' volumes of the nineties, Binyon's *London Visions,* and such poems of Davidson's as "The Exodus from Houndsditch," "A Northern Suburb," and "The Thames Embankment." A test of Thomson's pervasive influence might be to decide whether he or Davidson wrote each of the following excerpts:

> I sat forlornly by the river-side,
>   And watched the bridge-lamps glow
>   like golden stars
> Above the blackness of the swelling tide
>   Down which they struck rough gold
>   in ruddier bars.[43]
>
> .   .   .   .   .
>
> A vapour sank, ill-smelling and unclean,
>   Over the orient city; and writhed and curled

Up Houndsditch like a mist in a ravine,
    Of some fantastic world,

Where wild weeds, half-way down the frowning bank,
    Flutter like poor apparel stained and sere,
And lamplike flowers with hearts of flame their rank
    And baleful blossoms rear.[44]

A trace of decadence in the second gives it away perhaps
as later in date. That he was directly influenced by Thomson and not through Henley or Symons is almost too apparent to argue. From Thomson as well as from Coleridge
and Poe came an interest in dream fantasy. From Thomson
too came in part a fascination with cosmic phenomena and
certain rudiments of his naturalistic hedonism. At the same
time, Thomson by his example may have taught the later
poet that a negative, despairing vision cannot endure. Accepting his forerunner's scientific determinism, even his
bleak pessimism, Davidson undertook to transform them
into an affirmative view of the universe.

After he came to London in 1890 and almost certainly
not before, Davidson discovered Henley whose realistic,
lusty impressionism may have influenced him, for the
young Scot was an aeolian lyre who involuntarily vibrated
to the various strains in the wind. Henley's *The Song of
the Sword and Other Verses* appeared in 1892. Lane published Davidson's first volume of *Fleet Street Eclogues* in
1893. Both collections are in places consciously impressionistic. If Davidson's lyrics contain reflected images and verbal echoes which suggest an attentive reading of Henley's
symphonic descriptions of London, there is no evidence of
slavish imitation. Henley's poems are uninhibitedly robust,
shocking, exclamatory, and expansive; Davidson's of this
time aim at ironic detachment, urbanity, and terseness.
Section IV of the former's "London Voluntaries" offers
this graphic description of Death:

And Death the while—
Death with his well-worn, lean, professional smile,
Death in his threadbare working trim—
Comes to your bedside, unannounced and bland,
And with expert, inevitable hand
Feels at your windpipe, fingers you in the lung,
Or flicks the clot well into the labouring heart . . .[45]

In "Queen Elizabeth's Day" Davidson strikes off an arrestingly similar but more fanciful image:

A kraken of the skies! Its teeth
Are closing in my throat;
A lithe arm rummages
Each aching lung.[46]

Who is to say that one is an unmistakable echo of the other or which in its distinct way is superior? Furthermore, although Henley gave impetus to the introduction of the contemporary and unlovely into poetry, to muscular self-reliance and jingoism, these became almost immediately part of the public demesne.

Henley, Davidson, Binyon, and Symons—all wrote of the city impressionistically yet each in his own manner. Henley is the complete, comprehensive impressionist, exulting in the physical life and calling upon all the senses to celebrate it. Davidson, who seldom attempted pure impressionism, generally had a problem to propound, a parable with a clear message to tell, as well as a scene to depict or a mood to evoke. Laurence Binyon in his *First Book of London Visions* (1896) was less ardent and hearty than Henley, more given to sensitive reflection, but he went even further than Henley in endowing the city with a voice and personality. He seldom drew the scene for its own sake but for the humanity which it reflected.[47] Of all these poets Arthur Symons in his pastiches of city streets, the music-hall, café, and stage-door life of Bohemia was, like Walter Sickert in painting, the most thoroughgoing impressionist. With Wilde he was intellectual, aloof, sophisticated, and his impressionism was inseparable from his fastidious aestheticism. Whereas Davidson wrote in a tradition exclusively English, Symons' models like his subject matter were Parisian.* But, as Yeats subsequently recalled, there was something new in the air that became for a few years a contagion. With the London poets and painters Davidson must be credited with recognizing in the raw life of the industrialized city a new source of inspiration and imagery. His interest in the city was not confined to subject matter and technique, however. Like Henley he recruited the sights and sounds of Glasgow, Edinburgh, and London as part of a larger vision of life.

6

A philosophy of irony and an unquestioning acceptance of life had led Davidson to adopt the impressionist style because it embraced all sense experience. The same motive attracted him briefly to the vogue for realism. Whereas impressionism minimized the importance of subject matter and subordinated it to the appearance and arrangement of sense perceptions, realism conscientiously sought out the ugly, sordid, and violent which it treated with detachment and exactness. For a brief interval Davidson regarded realism as salutary precisely because it won sufferance for the sensational, the impoverished and disinherited, and the language of the streets. Realism often mixes in his verse, as in Henley's, with impressionism:

* Yeats perceived the essential difference between the early verse of Davidson and Symons. Symons, he wrote, was a "scholar of the music-hall"; Davidson "claims to have lived his verses. . . . One has more fire and enthusiasm, and the other more art and subtlety." *Letters to the New Island*, pp. 144–45.

And yesterday the black rain fell
In sheets from London's smoky sky,

Like water through a dirty sieve.[48]

But he employs this style no more than the impressionist
for its own sake; it always serves the larger purpose of his
ironic vision. In "A Woman and Her Son" a grim picture
of poverty and human wretchedness contrasts ironically
with nature's grandeur; "Holiday at Hampton Court"
describes a Sunday afternoon crowd of noisy sightseers in
order to place in novel relationship England's glorious past
and the vulgar present.

No well-informed Englishman of the nineties could be
unaware of this latest importation from the Continent or
indifferent to it. George Moore had discovered Zola in the
latter seventies during his Parisian residence and hastened
to apply the experimental method of the French naturalists
to English characters and settings in *A Mummer's Wife*
(1885) and *Esther Waters* (1894). Zola's novels were widely
available to the sensation-seeking public in cheap, somewhat expurgated translations. In 1893 Zola had visited
England; and by the time of *l'affaire Dreyfus* and the publication of "J'accuse" in January 1898, it was only logical
that he seek asylum in London. Davidson knew personally
another English realist, George Gissing, whose Edwin Reardon in *New Grub Street* has a tragic career as a writer that
is strikingly prophetic of Davidson's own. Furthermore,
the contributions of Ella d'Arcy, George Egerton, and Hubert Crackanthorpe to the early volumes of the *Yellow
Book* are full of the realistic method.

Almost as soon as the movement appeared, however,
Davidson with his insular suspicion and romantic proclivities began to divorce himself from absolute realism. In a
review of Swinburne's *A Study of Ben Jonson* he had distinguished between "true realism" which is complex, ar-

tistic, and derived from the imagination and intellect, and "unreal, inartistic realism" which is merely scientific, clinical, and melodramatic. The latter, he wrote, "knows only one devil in man, Belial, the least erected spirit that fell. Of Goethe's high-bred Mephisto, and Milton's archangel though in ruins, he has as little cognizance as he has of the aesthetic brains of Jonson's or Balzac's splendid villains." [49] Although he hailed Ibsen's realism as a necessary and healthy lesson for his time, he added, "But once is enough." Then, in a curious, rather disparaging prediction of his own future stand, he observed, "Neither is man, as was long ago remarked, a naked animal, nor is his soul unclothed: even those who strip it of religion and duty are ready with another garment, if it were only some fantastic new protestantism of Every Man His Own God." [50]

Davidson did not deny that Zola, the Goncourts, de Maupassant, Huysmans, and their English imitators were in dead earnest or that they had not served the useful purpose of purging literature "of some peccant humours that accumulate during periods of transition." But when realism in the name of naturalism endeavored to prolong its life by subjecting literature to a rigid dogma, he rejected it for the higher realism of romance. Literature quite simply could not "wrap its imagination in a napkin, bury it certain fathoms in the earth, and go about with a notebook painting its epoch. That could not last; that could not even get begun." Davidson perceived that naturalistic practice could not indefinitely adhere to the authoritarianism of naturalistic theory, that insofar as he was an artist the writer could not be the scientist. For all their pretension to the experimental method and mechanistic psychology, Zola's Rougon-Macquart novels are as romantic as anything in Victor Hugo. Their celebration of human vitality, their tremendous dynamic energy and panoramic sweep, and their preoccupation with humanitarian themes reassert

the romantic impulse in man. Armed though he was with
notebook and stylographic pen, the naturalist could not
escape from the other half of himself:

> The realist assiduously attempting to set down what-
> ever is commonplace, whatever is matter-of-fact, *en
> pleine platitude,* struggling to circumscribe his *sens du
> réel* by those things only which can be touched, tasted,
> smelt, found himself, to his amazement, haunted at
> every step by a ghost which would not be laid—Imag-
> ination, in all men, but most unescapably in himself.
> . . . There is no help for it, but to imagine.[51]

Taken literally, realism was as narrow as rationalism. The
one "stated the world as Stomach"; the other was an "evis-
cerated Life-in-Death." [52] In the literature of the second
half of the nineteenth century, realism or naturalism, as it
became known after it achieved the authority of a formulated, scientific discipline, and utopian idealism were far
from mutually exclusive. This explains why a romantic like
Davidson came closer perhaps to understanding the utopian character of the naturalistic novel than did the naturalists themselves.

At the same time that he includes the city and the
squalor of its working class as proper subjects in lyric
poetry, Davidson continues to sound the pipes of Pan.
Among the Chilterns, in Epping Forest, and along the
Medway; in Regents Park, Finsbury Park, and Russell
Square; or on the banks of the beloved Clyde still vividly
remembered—here is his natural haunt. The beauty and
order of nature complement in his poetry the ugliness and
turmoil of the city. He celebrates one no less than the
other:

I need

No world more spacious than the region here . . .
The sloping shores that fringe the velvet tides

With heavy bullion and with golden lace
Of restless pebble woven and fine spun sand;
The villages that sleep the winter through,
And, wakening with the spring, keep festival
All summer and all autumn: this grey town
That pipes the morning up before the lark
With shrieking steam, and from a hundred stalks
Lacquers the sooty sky; where hammers clang
On iron hulls, and cranes in harbours creak
Rattle and swing, whole cargoes on their necks . . .[53]

As he brings nature to the city, so he brings the nature-sick soul of the city prisoner to the country. Although his iron-ical universe obliges him to make impartial room for both, his lyrics indicate a private preference for the world of nature. Given all that the city affords, he turns most often to its parks. It is never the nature of the complete deter-minist that he portrays, nature mechanical, inhuman, brutish. It is rather nature alive, breathing, anthropomor-phic; nature by turns passionate, placid, enraged, gentle; nature seeing and feeling as well as seen and felt.

No one has written more convincingly of English birds and flowers. Their songs and colors are as familiar to him as our wardrobes to us, and he makes delicate music simply by cataloguing their names:

> White is the snow of the leafless sloe,
> The saxifrage by the sedge,
> And white the lady-smocks a-row
> And sauce-alone in the hedge.[54]

Again:

> Water-plantain, rosy vagrant,
> Flings his garland on the wave;
> Mint in midstream rises fragrant,
> Dressed in green and lilac brave;

And that spies may never harass
      In their baths
The shining naiads, purple arras
Of the loosestrife veils the paths.[55]

The attraction to native flora and fauna is probably as
Celtic as it is Georgian, for W. H. Davies, Edward Thomas,
and later Dylan Thomas were also to roll their tongues
fondly over sweet country names. In their pastoral authenticity as in their experiments with diction the Georgian
poets were to take up where the older poet had left off in
his lyrics two decades earlier. That Davidson is occasionally
inexact in his botany and ornithology, as has been charged,
is as immaterial as it is that certain Chinese paintings depict butterflies that cannot be found in the lepidopterist's
handbook.

Although the impressionism of *Fleet Street Eclogues,*
Ballads and Songs, and the succeeding volumes is mixed
with other strains and interests, Davidson did not belong
for nothing to the generation of Whistler, Wilde, and
Symons. Seldom a sustained impressionist and never a
mere devotee of art for art's sake, he shared for a time during the nineties the impressionist's interest in objective
patterns. In spite of this he belongs first and last to the
critical and affirmative tradition in nineteenth-century
poetry. His most impressionistic pastiches imply an underlying principle uniting the separate impressions, as the
poet debates some ideological question or adumbrates a
view of life less parochial, less analytic than that of the
pure impressionist. His later verse is invariably didactic
and metaphysical, qualities inadmissible to impressionistic
art. In this respect he is closer to Meredith, Hardy, and the
vitalist poets—Henley, Stevenson, and Kipling—than he
is to the aesthetes.

The division between the impressionists and the polem-

icists at the end of the century, however, is seldom sharp.
If Pater, Swinburne, and Wilde taught the *fin de siècle*
poets to value the isolated moment for its own sake, a
singlehearted dedication to aesthetic and impressionist
principles brought each disciple in turn to an awareness
of their inadequacy. Sooner or later they turned to other
gods, old and new, for a renewal of faith: Ernest Dowson,
Lionel Johnson, and Wilde himself to Roman Catholicism;
Henley, Kipling, and Stevenson to vitalism, a modified
Christianity, and imperialism; Yeats first to Irish nationalism and theosophy, then to art and ritual; and Davidson to
Matter. As long as impressionism had rested on the firm
premise that individual sense experience alone is valid,
Davidson cheerfully embraced the style for the sake of the
premise. When impressionism deteriorated into a fashionable style and, after the trial of Wilde, into an unfashion-
able one, he for the most part abandoned it. Like Yeats he
was always working toward a conception of the universe
as a coherent system, and of individual experience not as
isolated and momentary but as part of a larger order. Impatient with the static, inverted poetry of the aesthetes and
decadents, he leveled his sights beyond theirs to "a new
cosmogony" and "a new habitation for the imagination
of man." He increasingly subordinated concern with technique to this comprehensive vision. His poetry as a consequence suffered, but its ideas remain a challenging part of
our present intellectual and moral heritage.

7

Davidson's verse of the nineties contains a liberal sampling of the social, political, and more abstract issues that
glided like winged seeds through the air of the time. Only
the absolute aesthete turned his back on these questions to
advocate an art fully insulated against all reality external
to itself. In his earlier lyrics the poet from Greenock, fresh

on the London scene, seems to echo current ideas eagerly
and indiscriminately. Thus in one poem he appears in the
role of liberal reformer, in another a confirmed autocrat.
The inconsistency is more real than apparent. No writer of
the time, not even Yeats, was as sensitive to its many contradictions. Le Gallienne, the poet's stanchest supporter,
had excused earlier liberties and excesses in his verse as
part and parcel of the "boy's imagination," the "tremendous vital energy," the "liberal strength," and "the courage
to be imperfect" that "prophesy a world about to form." [56]
As time elapsed and these vices persisted, he sought a
further explanation of his friend's rough impatience with
craft: "His temperament is one that will always, I think,
respond sensitively to the last change in the intellectual
and spiritual atmosphere; and his art may suffer for this
characteristic to the end." [57]

These lapses notwithstanding, Davidson in the interval
between his arrival in London and the publication of *The
Last Ballad and Other Poems* in 1899 kept the philosopher,
social critic, and poet within him in relatively stable balance. His outlook during this period was conscientiously
ironical, detached, empirical. It was sufficient, he thought,
to accept life wholly and on its own terms. Nature and its
irresistible processes, the supremacy of love, the joy of
physical life—these alone mattered; the rest was relative
and transitory. To be sure, he had treated these themes in
the romantic comedies and melodramas, but his concern
with them now was less obviously urgent; in the lyrics he
had greater poise and confidence. Although he attached
himself to certain causes—labor reform, woman's suffrage,
sexual enlightenment, and imperial expansion—it was not
because they promised immediate, practical benefits but because they seemed to announce a millennium truer to the
democracy of being. Nowhere is his relativism of this inter-

mediate period more evident than in his attitude toward
Christianity.

The early plays had attacked Christian institutions
openly. For the young romantic Davidson, the Church was
a dragon standing between the poet-knight and the society-
maiden whom he sought to free from the enchantment of
an antiquated morality, religion, and art. The warfare continues in the lyrics, but the heavy barrage and the suicidal
charge are abandoned for more oblique tactics. The poet
seldom descends in the lyrics to the vehement agnosticism
and anti-Christian militancy of *Diabolus Amans, Smith,* or
the much later *Theatrocrat* and *Mammon* plays. Still the
enemy of decayed creeds, jargons, and panaceas, with which
he lumps the Christian faith, he prefers a dialectic of pit-
ting one spiritual discipline against another. In this way
he can expose the fallacies and folly of both. Under the
pretense of presenting the Mohammedan's conception of
Judgment Day and his certainty of exclusive salvation,
Davidson in the early poem "The Mahdi" levels his mockery at Calvinism and its doctrine of divine election. The
evangelist lingers in the ironist, however. So terrifyingly
real is the picture of the end of the world with which the
poem concludes that it almost defeats the poem's satiric
purpose:

> Then shall the great Archangel blow
> The trump of doom, and at the sound
> The shrivelled rivers cease to flow,
> And ocean's bed be naked ground.
>
> A second blast; and like a light
> Blown by a wind the sun shall stream
> And wither out; and in that night
> The heavens shall vanish as a dream.[58]

"A Ballad of an Artist's Wife" on the other hand enlists Christian myth to illustrate a Davidsonian concept, the sinlessness and sanctity of all men. At Judgment, according to this poem, all humanity enter into Paradise, but the outcasts of this world receive a special welcome. Davidson is not, of course, expressing belief here or elsewhere in an afterlife but mocking a Christian myth by using it to demonstrate an idea the opposite of its intention. His most ambitious lyric dealing with the atrophy of Christianity is "A Ballad of the Exodus from Houndsditch." A renegade preacher denounces modern Christianity in a fire-and-brimstone sermon and in a vision beholds the history of man's enslavement in "Houndsditch":

> The king o'erthrew the priest; the folk did tame
> The king; and, having nobly played the man,
> Bowed to the yoke again, while God became
> A sleek-haired Anglican.[59]

The scales are evened at the end of the poem when the fanatic preacher is exposed as an obtuse prig. Similarly "A Woman and Her Son" focuses the spotlight of irony on the conflict between Christian faith and atheism, dismissing both as unpardonable bigotries. Davidson in these poems is as hard on the determinist and positivist as on the Christian.

The purpose of these narrative and dramatic lyrics is to show the creeds of the world, but especially the Christian, for what they are, alike outmoded and untenable. Since to condemn is as much of a commitment as to accept, the lyrics steadfastly avoid taking sides and plead for a suspension of all belief. At the end of "A Ballad in Blank Verse of the Making of a Poet," a young poet, who has gone through the successive stages of apostasy, recantation, and renewed apostasy and whose irresponsible shilly-shallying has understandably driven his pious parents to early graves, declares his emancipation from all creeds, including that of man's divinity. He resolves to preserve an open, ironic mind:

> No creed for me! I am a man apart:
> A mouthpiece for the creeds of all the world;
> A soulless life that angels may possess
> Or demons haunt, wherein the foulest things
> May loll at ease beside the loveliest;
> A martyr for all mundane moods to tear;
> The slave of every passion; and the slave
> Of heat and cold, of darkness and of light;
> A trembling lyre for every wind to sound.
> I am a man set by to overhear
> The inner harmony, the very tune
> Of Nature's heart; to be a thoroughfare
> For all the pageantry of Time . . .[60]

The thought of these lines may be that of *Childe Harold* and *Leaves of Grass,* but the manner is that of Hyde Park Corner. The strident posturing speaks for a resurgence of Spasmodic hysteria and Protestant evangelicalism in Davidson's work, although he makes a strenuous effort to remain apart from the poem and its attitudes. This pretense to neutrality is a departure from the frank self-expression and partisanship of the earlier dramas. Where they were lyrical and rhapsodic, the lyrics pretend to a dramatic objectivity. The objectivity is somewhat specious, and no one is deceived by it. In spite of its ironic pose and dramatic framework, "A Ballad in Blank Verse of the Making of a Poet" is as subjective as *Smith.* Only in the more descriptive, impressionistic poems does the mask of irony not slip askew.

This ironic pose is an important intermediate stage in the development of Davidson's ideas. It disposed him to an impressionist technique during the interlude of the nineties. Adopted only halfheartedly in the Scottish works, irony became the foundation on which he built the best of his lyrics. According to this doctrine of universal acceptance, every truth is accompanied by its own contradiction. Beyond all allegiance, commitment, and morality, the ironist is indifferent to the conventions of the past and present. In the early decades of the present century thinkers in rebellion against the positivism of science and the dogmatism of faith turned to irony and relativism. The result was a series of European movements, all of them romantic, antiauthoritarian, nihilistic in varying degrees. In many respects Davidson's ideas anticipate these movements, suggesting that his ideas were more advanced and international than those of most of his contemporaries.* Never permanently satisfying, philosophical irony is only a stopgap, the postlude to rebellion and the prelude to a new dogmatism.

From January to May 1899 Davidson conducted in the columns of the *Speaker* a warm controversy with A. T. Quiller-Couch, its assistant editor. As champion of a conservative and aesthetic art, "Q" argued that the poet should choose to deal only with the beautiful and uplifting. Davidson undertook to define and defend the eclectic principle of irony underlying all things including art. He called for a new "realism" or "Pre-Shakespearianism" that

* Although it is impossible to trace direct connections, Davidson's thought prefigures several modern movements. He anticipates the rejection of antiquity and celebration of physical energy and mechanistic movement by the Italian futurists; the absolute nihilism of Dada; the automatic symbols and distortions of the surrealists; the apotheosis of light, sun power, and "vision as comprehension" by the French Orphist, Delaunay; and the rhapsodic sun worship of the playboy-eccentric of the twenties Harry Crosby—among numerous other manifestations of cataclysmic romanticism in the twentieth century. See Georgine Oeri, "Delaunay in Search of Himself," *Arts*, Mar. 1959, pp. 32–8, for a review of Robert Delaunay, *Du Cubisme à l'art abstrait*, Paris, 1957; Malcolm Cowley, *Exile's Return; a Narrative of Ideas* (rev. ed., New York, W. W. Norton, 1951), ch. 8.

would reject nothing from its orbit. One of his letters to the *Speaker* explains the scientific foundation of this metaphysical and aesthetic principle:

> Behind phenomena I have found an inexorable irony. Phenomena themselves are often beautiful; but perhaps they are only accidentally connected with spiritual truth, skin-deep, the complexion of this irony. I may ultimately find that irony includes beauty, and is greater than beauty. If poetry, aided by science, should find that truth is ugly, poetry will say so; but, as nothing is ugly to science, perhaps poetry will learn a lesson.[61]

Davidson, himself a journalist, regarded the newspaper as one of the most potent forces in shaping this new realism because it taught the poet to find new subject matter in the "misery in which so many millions live." It was not, he insisted, a question of the photographic, pessimistic realism of the naturalist writers or of the evolutionary reforms of the ameliorists. An imperfect poet like Byron or Browning, he observed, might be a pessimist or optimist, but the perfect poet, Shakespeare, is above pessimism or optimism: ". . . Shakespeare, who was not a Shakespearian, represents the *Irony* which is the soul of things, and of which what are called Good and Evil, Beauty and Ugliness, are attributes." [62] Hence Davidson called his position "Pre-Shakespearianism," at once in deference and contradistinction to the Pre-Raphaelites, whose desire to rid literature of false convention in the name of a new realism had been commendable but had not gone far enough.

Although he stated that the purpose of the Pre-Shakespearian was not simply to record phenomena without discrimination but "to pierce to *what* may be behind phenomena," he repeatedly denied that he was the messiah of a new creed:

Irony is not a creed. The makers of creeds have always miscalled, denied some part of the world. Irony affirms and delights in the whole. Consciously, it is the deep complacence which contemplates with unalloyed satisfaction Love and Hate, the tiger and the nightingale, the horse and the blow-fly, Messalina and Galahad, the village natural and Napoleon. Unconsciously, it is the soul of the Universe. Steep Irony in Chaos, and the universe will string itself about it like crystals on a thread. Whence comes Chaos? Whence comes Irony? There is no reply. To believe that the universe was *made* is the essence of anthropomorphism. I would have no more interest in a made universe than in an eight-day clock or a suburban villa. Thought cannot conceive, nor fancy call by any name, the manner and agency of the becoming of the universe. But I perceive the universe as a golden bough of Irony, flowering with suns and systems.[63]

Prose passages like this are often more eloquent if less restrained than the lyrics which he wrote to illustrate the principle.

Insofar as it is the poet's business to see things in multiple perspective, to perceive analogies or distinctions where others have not seen them, Davidson is correct in calling him an ironist. But only the pure poet, if one could be found, is content indefinitely with the shifting kaleidoscope of undigested experience. Unless he relates these protean patterns to a spectrum from which they derive order and significance, the poet remains unsatisfied. Sooner or later he will find some body of thought or widely ramified myth to fill his mind and strengthen his individual insights. Davidson's difficulty was that he would be a thinker, and thought of itself and unadorned is death to poetry.

The principle of irony offered him a stay of sentence, but he could not remain long an ironist *in vacuo*. The bewilderment and misunderstanding with which readers of the *Speaker,* one of whom signed himself "Puzzled," replied to his open letters to Quiller-Couch may have persuaded him that, for all his aversion to creeds, he must abandon philosophy or work out a fully conceived intellectual system.

8

Meanwhile, until he arrived at a positive, scientific creed of materialism, the principle of irony served him well in the lyrics. It helped him avoid the dangers of introspection and self-awareness that lure every undeveloped writer. It provided, as in the early plays, a rationalization of his zest for life, his impatience with authority, and his uninhibited choice of subject matter. Irony enabled him to enter the laboratory, the pressroom, the slums, among other forbidden chambers, and to make poetry out of the materials of science and human misery. In the name of irony the raw facts of science and autobiographical experience were invested with romance, anonymity, and higher truth.

The worship of nature and the glorification of physical love, early themes reintroduced in the lyrics, are basic ingredients in the poet's emerging materialism. The juvenile poems of *In a Music-Hall* show his thought shaping from the pagan idealism of Shelley in "On a Hill-Top" to the pagan earth worship of Swinburne and Meredith, a rudimentary materialism, in "Kinnoul Hill" and "Thoreau." Although transcendental overtones can be heard in the earliest lyrics, they soon fade. Davidson's joy in nature owes more to nineteenth-century redactions of Lucretius than to Emerson. By the time of *Fleet Street Eclogues,* his next volume, the "second sight" of Wordsworth and the

mystic vision of Shelley disappear. Nature is offered for
her own sake or as an antidote to man's ills, particularly
end-of-the-century neurasthenia:

Ah! I know
How ill you are. You shall to-morrow do
What I now order you.
At early dawn through London you must go
Until you come where long black hedgerows grow,

With pink buds pearled, with here and there a tree,
And gates and stiles; and watch good country folk;
And scent the spicy smoke
Of withered weeds that burn where gardens be;
And in a ditch perhaps a primrose see.

The rooks shall stalk the plough, larks mount the skies,
Blackbirds and speckled thrushes sing aloud,
Hid in the warm white cloud
Mantling the thorn, and far away shall rise
The milky low of cows and farm yard cries.[64]

Implicit in Davidson's return to nature is his belief in its
harmonious relationship to man. His verse celebrating
this affinity alternates between the gently feminine, like
the passage just quoted, and the robustly masculine. The
hardy life of the ancient Viking as he stares into the moan-
ing storm, and of his descendant the gaunt harvester burnt
black by the sun, symbolizes the triumph of living at one
with the universe. Turning his back on pantheism as he
does on aestheticism, Davidson advocates a life of primitive simplicity and physical identification with nature:

No lofty Patron of Nature! No;
Nor a callous devotee of Art!
But the friend and the mate of the high and the low,
And the pal to take the vermin's part,

> Your inmost thought divinely wrought,
> In the grey earth of your brain aglow
> With the red earth burning in your heart.[65]

From Burns, Whitman, and, most directly, Grant Allen,* and not from Wordsworth's aloof, literary proletarianism, comes this hearty comradeship and "language such as men do use"; but the worship of the "red earth" in man looks forward to such later romantics as Lawrence, Robinson Jeffers, John Steinbeck, and Dylan Thomas.

Many of the later nature lyrics are concerned with still another theme borrowed from the early plays, nature's inexorable flux and the cycle of life and death. Even predominantly impressionistic pieces like "In Romney Marsh" and "A Cinque Port" link man and nature as subject to change. In the second of these, a gently elegiac poem, a former port stranded inland by a shifting shore line is the symbol for this process:

> Where argosies have wooed the breeze,
> The simple sheep are feeding now;
> And near and far across the bar
> The ploughman whistles at the plough;
> Where once the long waves washed the shore,
> Larks from their lowly lodgings soar.

---

* Compare Grant Allen's "A Cosmic Emotion":

> We stranded on the furthest sands of life,
>   Blood-brethren to the world, to sun and star,
>   To whatso moves on pinion, hoof, or fin,
> We raise above the clash of nature's strife
>   This mightier watchword, hymned through space afar,
>   "I am: whatever is, I count my kin."
>   (*Speaker,* 9 Feb. 1895, p. 160.)

But Davidson had already preached this message in "A Ballad of a Nun" and "A New Ballad of Tannhäuser," so that it may be a question not of an audible echo but of two poets again writing in a common tradition. Davidson entitled his poem quoted here "Earth to Earth" in mockery of the Christian burial service.

Below the down the stranded town
   Hears far away the rollers beat;
About the wall the seabirds call;
   The salt wind murmurs through the street;
Forlorn the sea's forsaken bride,
Awaits the end that shall betide.* [66]

Their absolute simplicity of phrasing and universal import save these verses from sentimentality.

In his last two volumes of lyrics (1898 and 1906) Davidson repeatedly employs symbols from nature to urge stoic resignation in the face of decay and death. From apple trees and summer rain man can learn the virtue of a serene acceptance of his natural lot:

No jealousy, anger, or fashion
Of strife
Perturbs in their stations
The apple-trees. Life
Is an effortless passion,
Fruit, bough, and stem,
A beautiful patience
For them. [67]

---

* The suggestion for this lyric may have come from Tennyson's *In Memoriam*, cxxiii:

There rolls the deep where grew the tree.
   O earth, what changes hast thou seen!
   There where the long street roars hath been
The stillness of the central sea.

                 .   .   .   .   .

But in my spirit will I dwell,
   And dream my dream, and hold it true;
   For tho' my lips may breathe adieu,
I cannot think the thing farewell.

(William J. Rolfe, ed., *The Poetic and Dramatic Works of Alfred Lord Tennyson*, Boston and New York, Houghton Mifflin Co., 1898, p. 194.) Davidson's borrowing, if conscious, is ironic as elsewhere since his Lucretian stoicism is a contradiction of Tennyson's spiritual comfort.

The tone in which this lesson is delivered becomes sterner and blunter, culminating in the villanelle of 1899, "The Price":

> Let Virtue play or Vice
> Beside his sombre firth
> Life is the lowest price
> Death wins with loaded dice.[68]

This late nineteenth-century Lucretianism rejects the classical concept of a hierarchical universe and the Christian view of man as fallen for an equation of man and nature. As yet in the lyrics Davidson's synthesis, combining the hedonist's celebration of nature, the stoic's self-reliance, and the scientist's denial of revelation, falls short of complete, explicit materialism.

Closely associated with nature in Davidson's mind is love. The earliest poems still describe love in the language of Plato and Shelley. But as nature in these poems is earthier than in Shelley's, so love in them is more physical and passionate. Davidson's lyrics, early and late, are intent upon restoring to man as to nature a capacity for love that is at once earthly and transcendent. All nature pulses with love and desire; even the blackbirds

> . . . with their oboe voices make
> The sweetest broken music all about
> The beauty of the day for beauty's sake . . .
> And all about the mates whose love they won,
> And all about the sunlight and the sun.[69]

The staying power of earthly love, not Christ's love and righteousness, redeems man and is proof against whatever adversity the world may present:

> They may doom till the moon forsakes
> Her dark, star-daisied lawn;
> They may doom till doomsday breaks

> With angels to trumpet the dawn;
> While love enchants the young,
> And the old have sorrow and care,
> No song shall be unsung,
> Unprayed no prayer.[70]

The solace of redemption and a spiritual afterworld give way to that of a vision in which Time is "one sweet bridal night" and Earth "One fragrant bridal bed." [71]

The fertility and vitality of nature are not new themes in Davidson's writing, for he sounds these strains boldly and triumphantly in his plays of the eighties. He never forgets, moreover, that love is a mixed blessing, that the price of life and love is death. The romantic comedies present the bright side of the moon; *Bruce, Diabolus Amans,* and *Smith,* the dark side. In keeping with his more consistently ironic view in the lyrics, he avoids oversimplification for a more muted, subtle, paradoxical treatment. Parable, allegory, and symbol now imply what in the dramas the spokesman-hero stepped to the front of the stage to preach. Furthermore, the joyful and somber moments of life occur simultaneously in the lyrics rather than alternately. Like Picasso in his split-vision paintings, Davidson presents the face of love simultaneously in profile and full view. Frequently he withholds this double exposure until the final, wry lines of the poem. "A Ballad of Euthanasia," for example, tells the familiar legend of a young maid who elopes with her spectral lover only to discover that she has chosen not death and damnation, as in previous versions, but the fulfillment of life:

> I find the sweetest kind
> Of Death is Love and Life.[72]

The moral of this and other hedonistic poems is that there is no life other than that of the present, that death is not the beginning of a new, spiritual life but a natural, in-

eluctable part of this, and that man achieves fulfillment
only through an unhesitant acceptance of love and its inevitable companion, death:

> Now I hear the deep
> Bourdon of the bee,
> Like a sound asleep
> Wandering o'er the lea;
> While the song-birds keep
> Urging nature's plea.
> Hark! the violets pray
> Swooning in the sun!
> Hush! the roses say
> Love and death are one! [73]

The vicissitudes and final disintegration of earthly existence, like its joys and victories, are part of the larger flux
of things. Love, physical, free, redemptive, yet carrying its
own death sting, alone resolves life's contradictions and
makes it endurable. Thus the paradoxes of traditional
Christianity are carried over into Davidson's evangelical
naturalism.

As earlier chapters have demonstrated, Davidson derived this frank paganism from Blake, Keats, the Spasmodics, Fitzgerald, the Pre-Raphaelites, and Swinburne.
It also owes a debt to James Thomson who in little-known,
cheerful poems like "The Naked Goddess," "Art," "Philosophy," and "Two Lovers" sang the praises of Aphrodite.
The relatively restrained eroticism of the Scottish poet's
lyrics belong also to what contemporary critics called, not
too accurately, the "new hedonism." * Davidson's close

---

* Novelty became the *dernier cri* of the nineties, with the result that
the most overworked adjective of the day was "new." For *l'art nouveau*,
the "new paganism," the "new voluptuousness," the "new spirit," the
"new humor," the "new realism," the "new unionism," etc., see Holbrook Jackson, *The Eighteen Nineties* (Harmondsworth, Penguin, 1939),
pp. 19–20.

friend, Grant Allen, had written in *The Lower Slopes*
(1894) lush, sensuous poems such as "The Return of
Aphrodite" and "The New Poetry" espousing a life of
hedonistic pleasure. Another exponent and friend was
Richard Le Gallienne, to whom Allen had dedicated "The
New Poetry." There is a clear line of development from
earlier romantics to the hedonists of the mid-century and
thence to these later poets. While the new hedonists' frank
preoccupation with earthly love paralleled that of the Pre-
Raphaelites and decadents, they differed from the first in
refusing to spiritualize love and from the second in seeing
love as a wholesome participation in life, not as an escape
through sensual pleasure from tawdry reality. Love for
the hedonist takes place out of doors under the sky and beside the sea; for the decadent, in a luxurious, orchidaceous
or sinister, opium-drenched interior. Davidson's contribution to the nineteenth-century treatment of love is that,
as much as Henley, he joins the so-called new hedonism to
the so-called new vitalism. In reality the only thing new
about either of these cults, which stretched their roots far
and deep into the century and before, is their assumption of
Darwinian science.

The concept of love as the pre-eminent creative and unifying force in nature inevitably informs Davidson's views
on women. These views, like those of Allen and Shaw, are
sexually revolutionary but unlike theirs are socially and
politically reactionary. As in so many nineteenth-century
men of letters—Schopenhauer, Butler, Nietzsche, Meredith, Conrad, Shaw, and Henry James come to mind—
Davidson's attitude toward sex rests on theory, ideal, or
personal preoccupation rather than on closely observed
fact. In Davidson's case it is not too ingenious to suggest
that through his pronouncements on women as well as
through his dramatic heroines he strove to place the feminine element in his artistic nature in proper relationship to

the masculine. Jean Cocteau has stated that these elements, of which we are all composed, are more exactly balanced in the artist. This balance results from a kind of spiritual incest or parthenogenesis, a "love of self for self," and results in the spiritual progeny of the work of art itself.[74] Davidson, for whom these elements exist in uneasy and imperfect balance, seeks in his writings more often a rational than an artistic reconciliation. As he came to stress the harshness of life, the supremacy of the will, and the superiority of robust thought to the gentler passions, he altered his style to one more rugged and increasingly stressed the subordinate role of woman. Strength in his heroes is indicated by domination over women and the feminine side of man's nature; weakness by subservience. The lyrics, much less explicitly than the plays, adumbrate this reassertion of masculinity. Although he recognized her as the biological means by which the world is to be made anew, Davidson advised the "new woman" not to take advantage of her recent gains but to face her splendid responsibility:

> Be bold and yet be bold,
> But be not overbold,
> Although the knell be toll'd
> Of the tyranny of old.
>
> And meet your splendid doom,
> On heaven-scaling wings,
> Women, from whose bright womb
> The radiant future springs!

It is the "new man" who with a freshly acquired self-reliance and sense of dedication must

> Heat the furnace hot:
> Smelt the things of thought
> Into dross and dew;
> Mould the world anew.[75]

Davidson did not always treat the new woman and "the
battle of the sexes" so humorlessly and unambiguously, as
his satiric novels testify. Shaw, Gilbert, and Beerbohm by
the survival of the wittiest have made us forget that the
majority did view these matters gravely.

9

A gospel of self-reliance and self-realization is oddly
enough no contradiction of a mechanistic universe. A
world of nature in keeping with Darwinian tenets, which
had driven Tennyson and Browning to a reassertion of
faith, Swinburne and Meredith to the comforts of a life
process and racial evolution, Thomson and Hardy to a
gloomy determinism, and Arnold and Yeats to the intellectual refuge of culture and tradition, was for the ironist
Davidson a thrilling challenge. He reasoned that man, the
highest form yet attained by matter and no mere by-blow of
blind evolution, could not be regarded as a slave to those
biological and chemical laws of which he was the purposeful expression.

Like Grant Allen, whose influence on the lyrics of this
time is discernible, Davidson eventually became a mecha-
nist without yielding to a despairing determinism. He recognized no dichotomy of man and matter or of the physical
universe and divine law. Allen, with his sturdy cheerfulness, could write jocose, irreverent verse on the popular
topics of evolution and progress:

> So the handsomest managed to wive,
>   While the ugliest went to the wall.[76]

In well-known lines of *In Memoriam* Tennyson had
vented his contempt for the theory of evolution by natural
selection:

> Let him, the wiser man who springs
>   Hereafter, up from childhood shape

> His action like the greater ape,
> But I was *born* to other things.*

Allen lightly replied:

> And surely such an ape as this
> May live a life not much amiss;
> May love the right, eschew the wrong;
> Defend the weaker from the strong;
> Teach other after apes to be
> Nobler and better far than he;
> In spite of calumny and scorn,
> Mould younger apes yet unborn
> To loftier thoughts and loftier still,
> Beyond all human hope or will;
> Yet act, himself, his little part
> On Nature's stage, with all his heart,
> And show that even an ape may be
> A credit to his ancestry.[77]

Allen, an evolutionist, a friend of Herbert Spencer, and an author of popular writings on science and religion, was more than a humorist. In serious but less engaging poems he attacked monopolistic interests, agitated for a people's revolution, espoused democracy and a federation of nations, and expressed interest in various metaphysical questions. A last bright flicker of the earlier revolutionary spirit, he is a significant if minor link between two generations of romantic liberals. His lucid, unimpassioned, skeptical mind, the mind of a thinker and a philosopher, had a stimulating and, while it lasted, beneficial effect on Davidson. The aftereffects may have been injurious, since he set the younger poet an example for poetry scarcely dis-

* *Poetic and Dramatic Works*, p. 194. At a public meeting Benjamin Disraeli similarly asked the rhetorical question "Is man an ape or an angel?" and, addressing the episcopal chairman, gave his dramatic reply, "My lord, I am on the side of the angels."

tinguishable from prose. When it came to treating the
new science in poetry, Davidson took up where Allen left
off. He determined to supply a detailed, scientific account
of the origin and destiny of the universe along evolutionary, materialistic lines. Where Allen had been whimsical
and sly, Davidson became dogmatic and ponderous. Yet
it is clear from the earlier lyrics that he too could discuss
serious subjects deftly, wittily, and melodiously. Until
philosophy and rancor made his poetry top-heavy, his muse
as often landed tails up as heads up.

Self-fulfillment through the exercise of individual responsibility and will is the dominant theme of the lyrics. It
begins to appear with the 1894 volume in such poems as
"The Vengeance of the Duchess," "A Ballad of Heaven,"
and "A Ballad in Blank Verse of the Making of a Poet."
"Thirty Bob a Week," also from this volume, finds in Darwinian evolution scientific basis for the doctrine of self-
fulfillment. The poem recommends in place of timorous
fatalism a proud acceptance of one's destiny as shaped
from the beginning of time by a nature self-willed and self-
ordained:

> And it's this way that I make it out to be:
>   No fathers, mothers, countries, climates—none;
> Nor Adam was responsible for me,
>   Nor society, nor systems, nary one:
> A little sleeping seed, I woke—I did, indeed—
>   A million years before the blooming sun.
>
> I woke because I thought the time had come;
>   Beyond my will there was no other cause;
> And everywhere I found myself at home,
>   Because I chose to be the thing I was;
> And in whatever shape of mollusc or of ape
>   I always went according to the laws.[78]

Far from being at tooth and claw, raw, ruthless nature and man are indissolubly partnered; each contains the other; they are alpha and omega. This is the germinal expression as found in the lyrics of Davidson's final metaphysical and ethical creed.

He offered the creed, although never as a creed, first tentatively and ironically, then affirmatively. From Saint-Simon to Taine scientific positivists had attributed man's actions to the deterministic influence of natural laws, race, and social environment. Without disavowing science, Davidson joined the romantic protest against positivism by reasserting man's supremacy of will and power to fashion his own destiny. "Lammas" describes the excruciating but glorious birth pangs of man as he produces out of himself a higher being, a god in a material universe. One of the journalists in this eclogue of 1896 delivers a bald sermon on self-determination:

> Live at speed;
> And call your least caprice the law of God;
> Disdain the shows of things, and every love
> Whose stamen is not hate; self-centred stand;
> Accept no second thought . . .
> You are your own birthright; let it serve you well:
> Be your own star, for strength is from within,
> And one against the world will always win! [79]

In much of its thought and its resumption of a rhetorical style "Lammas" recalls the Spasmodic melodramas of the Scottish years. The eclogue, the most prophetic of the earlier lyrics, also looks ahead to several themes which recur in the later works: euthanasia, eugenics, the philosophy of the ego and the superrace, and scientific materialism.

For a time, under the impact of Darwinism, Davidson was satisfied to regard man as evolving toward a higher

future state. By the late nineties he had worked out his
creed of egoism and supremacy of the will in much greater
detail and was ready to reject an outdated belief in further
evolutionary progress for the conviction that in man the
universe had achieved "the highest reach attainable by
Matter." Man, no longer becoming but become, is the
Man of Power or Man-God, equivalent to the Nietzschean
Übermensch. Although he had an early familiarity with
some of Nietzsche's ideas, he resisted for some time as alien
and unwholesome the influence of the German philosopher. The autobiographical hero of "A Ballad in Blank
Verse of the Making of a Poet" (1894), having adopted
ideas that are strikingly Nietzschean, renounces them as
another "new religion, bringing new offence, / Setting the
child against the father still." He thereupon declares his
independence from all thought except his own:

> Within my heart
> I'll gather all the universe, and sing
> As sweetly as the spheres; and I shall be
> The first of men to understand himself.[80]

In spite of this Promethean assertion, the doctrine of self-
realization which threads the lyrics of the nineties owes
much to native sources, if less to Nietzsche. It is closely allied to the gospel of action and self-reliance preached by
Carlyle, Morris, and Ruskin, which Davidson had already
incorporated into his youthful plays. Detaching this tradition from Victorian morality, he welded it to the activism
of Henley and Stevenson and then to his own brand of
materialism. This in turn he compounded, as a later
chapter will demonstrate, from the thought of Allen,
William Kingdon Clifford, and John Adam Cramb. When
applied to social questions and politics these ideas conducted him as it did others to autocracy, *Machtpolitik,*
and "the Ocean-State."

10

Stimulated by the current agitation for reform, he was briefly attracted to universal suffrage, trade unionism, and proportional representation. His first volume of lyrics attacked modern commercialism, condemning the "thankless upper ten" who prey upon "beasts of burden, mostly men." A vague humanitarianism and a Shelleyan vision of man's inheritance of a new earth had prompted him to make common cause with the contemporary liberals; the alliance was uneasy and short-lived. Although sincere in his sympathy with the worker's lot, which he deplored in several of the lyrics, he did not militate for reform or a general leveling of society but urged the common man to patient waiting, stoic fortitude, and pride in his harsh destiny. The laborer in "A Ballad of a Workman," like the god Sarmion in *Scaramouch in Naxos*, refuses the ancient gift of immortality and earthly riches for the superior gift of life as it is:

> I drop the dream of high renown,
> A nameless private in the strife:
> Life, take me; take me, clanging town;
> And death, the eager zest of life.
>
> The hammered anvils reel and chime;
> The breathless, belted wheels ring true;
> The workmen join the ends of time,
> And forge and mould the world anew.[81]

The workman has already become an anonymous pawn in the evolution of a stronger society, as the identity of the laborer is swallowed up in that of collective man. With an instinctive, crude vision of his humble role as an unknown soldier, he accepts cheerfully whatever sacrifices his destiny demands.

Such poems as "Thirty Bob a Week," "Northern Sub-urb," and "Piper, Play!" seemed to Davidson's contempo-raries to sound the note of social protest loud and clear. They won him a reputation as a liberal and socialist which he did not court and which he found embarrassing. Unlike William Morris and Grant Allen, he never agitated for popular revolution leading to a socialist democracy. On the contrary he repeatedly denounced socialism as part of "the debris and wreckage of Christendom," a stand which brought him into open opposition to both the revolutionary and Fabian socialists. His own position, to which readers and critics for a long time seemed curiously blind, was reactionary and autocratic. Written with de-liberate crudeness in the argot of the Limehouse worker and suggesting the humanitarianism of Grant Allen and George Gissing, "Thirty Bob a Week" offers the comfort of stoic resolution in place of social revolution:

> But I don't allow it's luck and all a toss;
> There's no such thing as being starred and crossed;
> It's just the power of some to be a boss,
> And the bally power of others to be bossed:
> I face the music, sir; you bet I ain't a cur;
> Strike me lucky if I don't believe I'm lost!

> . . . . .

> It's a naked child against a hungry wolf;
> It's playing bowls upon a splitting wreck;
> It's walking on a string across a gulf
> With millstones fore-and-aft about your neck;
> But the thing is daily done by many and many a one;
> And we fall, face forward, fighting, on the deck.[82]

Although Davidson continued to sing the potential might and glorious future of the worker, it was never as a self-governing or exclusive class. Through hard labor, endur-ance, and sacrifice beyond that to which he was already accustomed, the common man would achieve fulfillment as a superior laborer in a society governed by men of superior will and intellect: This is "the order of the universe." Neither the workers nor the decadent aristocracy would supply the leaders of the coming élite, but the professional middle class of scientists, industrialists, empire builders, artists, and intellectuals—the men of strength and action. From the fourth estate of the journalists comes the "true soldado" of the new Eldorado.

Not interested in social abuses themselves or in the abused, Davidson sees in man's inhumanity to man only an excuse for re-creating the world in the image of John Davidson:

> The Present is a dungeon dark
> Of social problems. Break the gaol!
> Get out into the splendid Past
> Or bid the splendid Future hail.[88]

While continuing to satirize the newly rich industrialist, he begins to admire him as a man of vitality, power, and self-realization. "The Feast of St Martha," one of his last eclogues published in 1906, presents a debate in which a pessimistic denunciation of material wealth and progress is set against an optimistic heralding of the future awaiting the man who exploits the weapons of capital, war, and imperialism. For such a man, driven by the will to happiness, the end justifies the means. The poet who had been regarded as a champion of the downtrodden and disinherited thus emerged as the demagogue of a ruthless if benevolent despotism. By a circuitous dialectical route that has become all too familiar, the arguments for social amelioration brought Davidson to a worship of individual power and a faith in the totalitarian state. Concurrently his thought, which had been ironical and ambivalent, petrified into a rigid, ugly system.

It would have been strange if the man who held these beliefs and who in several other respects belonged to the school of Henley and Kipling had not blown the trumpet of empire. With regard to the expansion of the empire by military force, Davidson was at first torn between innate aversion to suffering and sympathy with the oppressed on the one hand, and his conviction, on the other, that the strongest should rule. He therefore declined at first to condemn or praise an imperialist policy, contenting himself with a neutral role. Although the laureateship, unfilled from 1892 to 1895, and at the very least a knighthood awaited the poet who rattled his saber for the empire, Davidson was steadfastly devoted to his own principles and was never guilty of outright opportunism.* If he had expectations along these lines that were never realized, he might have been forgiven. His primary purpose was to incorporate into his own philosophical synthesis as many popular movements as were consonant with it. Imperialism fitted into it nicely.

England's destiny, as Davidson viewed it with unswerving idealism, was simply an extension of that of the superior individual who knows and fulfills himself. There was no doubt in the poet's mind that his country's mission was to lead the undeveloped peoples of the world to the fullest realization of their potentialities, just as Eng-

* It is interesting to note what Davidson's fellow poets thought of his qualifications for the laureateship. In 1895 the *Idler* invited twenty-two prominent writers to name their favorite candidates. When the results were in Swinburne received twelve votes as first choice; Kipling and Eric Mackay tagged behind with two votes each; William Morris, George Meredith, and William Watson each polled one vote; three abstained. Davidson, frequently coupled with Watson as the outstanding "romantic" and "classical" poets of the decade respectively, was mentioned only once and then as fourth choice. Swinburne received the majority as a "poet's poet," for his amorism and amorality disqualified him as much as did Davidson's iconoclasm and lack of tact. Alfred Austin, the queen's eventual choice in 1896, received no mention in the poll. *Idler*, Apr. 1895, pp. 400-19.

land by the sixteenth century had already realized hers. "St George's Day" makes a pretense of presenting impartially both sides of the imperialist question. Basil with his barker's spiel about "all good Englishmen" and "Greater England" is the thoroughgoing jingoist. The skeptical Menzies asks:

> Whence comes this patriotic craze?
> Spare us at least the hackneyed brag
> About the famous English flag.[84]

By the conclusion of the poem, however, Basil by superior fire power has reduced Menzies to helpless agreement, as all join in choric praise of England and the "English" spring. The argument on which Basil builds his case is that England's imperial destiny is the culmination of an evolutionary process and that the British Empire, unlike other empires, will not perish from the earth. For all its jingoism, so offensive and embarrassing today, the poem like Kipling's "Recessional" does not overlook the grave responsibility of being "the world's forlorn hope."

In the summer of 1899, four years after the fiasco of the Jameson Raid, the Boers, greatly provoked by the tactics of Cecil Rhodes, declared war on Great Britain. In the same year Davidson published his fifth volume of lyrics, *The Last Ballad and Other Poems*. Although it contains several blatantly chauvinistic poems, others reveal a troubled awareness of the horror of war or retreat into ironic neutrality. With "War Song" he has found the answer to his dilemma. War never ceases to be cruel and endless:

> In vain—always in vain,
> For war breeds war again!

Nevertheless, the poet justifies war by repudiating its old divine sanction and substituting that of power politics and imperial progress. Darwin and Rhodes join forces to demonstrate British fitness and to rationalize British self-aggrandizement:

> The shameful dream is past,
> The subtle maze untrod:
> We recognize at last
> That war is not of God.
> Wherefore we now uplift
> Our new unhallowed song:
> The race is to the swift,
> The battle to the strong.[85]

Opposed to war in practice, the idealist accepts it in principle as a necessary evil. Only by its means can England fulfill her sacred mission "to set the peoples free." As he continues to sing "God save the Queen" it is not the thought of empire or its fruits that appeal to Davidson so much as the empire builder, the individual who by taking his destiny into his own hands determines that of his myriad inferiors.

Davidson's complacent Anglophilia, vociferous imperialism, and mawkish hero worship, especially as they appear in the final eclogues of *Holiday and Other Poems* (1906), are more easily explained than excused. Their dangerous idealism and humorless naïveté today seem little short of appalling. To understand them one must remember the staggering death lists from South Africa, the sensationalistic journalism of W. T. Stead and Alfred Harmsworth, the contagious patriotism which reached an apotheosis of pride in the Jubilee of 1897, and later the rumblings of an approaching European war. One must remember too the compensation for unremitting failure and poverty which the embittered poet sought in these grandiose visions. Little by little his monomania metastasized until he saw in this widespread nationalism a popular endorsement of his personal ambition and hope for a world millennium. Finally one must remember that when his thinking was not subjective it was philosophical and utopian rather than practical. Abnormally sensitive to human suffering, he could not personally have condoned the barbarism and violence that appear so frequently in his later writings. In the child's world of his final poetry, myth and vision are inseparable from fact. The "Ode on the Coronation of Edward VII., of Britain, and of Greater Britain, King" (1902) furnishes a serious account of the origin of Earth out of Time and Matter, and the gradual evolution through strife and bloodshed of imperial Britain, the Ocean-State, as the supreme nation. Experience has only begun to teach us to expect not a more but often a less realistic, humane grasp of contemporary political events by the artist, whose fixation with an ideal may blind him to the hobbling resistance of human nature and circumstance.

11

As Davidson continued to suffer personal reverses, he clung stubbornly to the comforts of stoicism. It is his message to the end of the century and beyond. Sometimes he accepts man's fate with the courage of Roland at Roncesvalles. Sometimes he recommends the serene passivity of nature. More often he describes with deep sadness and resignation the loneliness of man's struggle:

> Why, he never can tell;
>   But, without a doubt,
> He knows very well
>   He must trample out
> Through forest and fell
>   The world about
> A way for himself,
> A way for himself.[86]

The noblest expression that Davidson gave to this theme
of persistence in the face of certain defeat is "A Runnable Stag." No mere hunting song, the poem pays tribute to the solitary, courageous spirit that would take its
own life rather than yield to its enemies:

> When he turned at bay in the leafy gloom,
>   In the emerald gloom where the brook ran deep,
> He heard in the distance the rollers boom,
>   And he saw in a vision of peaceful sleep,
>   In a wonderful vision of sleep,
>   A stag of warrant, a stag, a stag,
>   A runnable stag in a jewelled bed,
>   Under the sheltering ocean dead,
>   A stag, a runnable stag.[87]

The note of self-pity is not always absent from Davidson's
verse, but in the runnable stag he achieves a perfect ob-
jectification of his own sense of doom. His is never the
counsel of surrender or despair. If his poetry utters the
sentiments of hell, it is the voice of an indomitable Satan
one hears, not of the coward Belial or the opportunist
Beelzebub.

Closely related to the theme of stoic endurance is that
of pain. In a universe composed solely of sensory matter
and held together by precisely balanced contradictions,
pain is the necessary complement of pleasure. Almost as
if to make amends for having stressed the joy of life in his
youthful works, Davidson concentrates more and more
upon pain as "Love's needful shadow," "an undersong in
Love's refrain." Sensation, a rudimentary form of consciousness, is present throughout nature—in stones, trees,
and animals—but man alone knows that he suffers pain
and why. Sensation for Davidson forever oscillates between the two poles of pleasure and pain. Both are essential to knowledge; and self-fulfillment, the materialist's

substitute for salvation, is as attainable through suffering, sacrifice, and death as through happiness, love, and life. This is the moral of some of his most thoughtful poems: "A Ballad of an Artist's Wife," "A Ballad of Heaven," and "The Last Ballad." When he found that his dramatic ballads were often open to misinterpretation, he turned in other lyrics to symbolism and allegory. "Insomnia" published in 1899 states in somber, unmistakable terms that life is stretched between the poles of suffering and joy:

> The Seraph at his head was Agony;
>   Delight, more terrible, stood at his feet:
>   Their sixfold pinions beat
> The darkness, or were spread immovably,
>   Poising the rack, whose jewelled fabric meet
> To strain a god, did fitfully unmask
>   With olive light of chrysoprases dim
>   The smiling Seraphim
> Implacably intent upon their task.[88]

The grotesque imagery of this belongs still to decadence; the personification of pleasure and pain as fiendish seraphim is an ironic blasphemy that had been part of the stock in trade of earlier romantics. Here and generally hereafter Davidson forsakes the delicate irony and restraint of his earlier lyrics for melodramatic overstatement that at times reaches absurdity. More important for him now than poetic originality is the message that pain is knowledge and that in a materialistic universe suffering is the badge of superiority.

A corollary to this preoccupation with pain, one anticipated by the earliest plays and poems, is suicide and euthanasia. As stoic suffering testifies to the capacity of matter to endure its own nature, so suicide and euthanasia are the legitimate means by which matter triumphs over its limitations. Among man's inalienable rights as matter be-

come conscious and self-conscious is that of terminating
his own life and the lives of degenerate, useless inferiors.
Christian Science teaches that the mind, inspired by the
teachings of the Gospels, can dominate matter. Scientific
materialism, its exact opposite, teaches that matter must
slough off this and other spiritual fictions. Death, the natural outcome of life and the process by which it enters
merely another phase of material existence, holds no terror
for the materialist. Beauty is as present in death and dissolution as in young love.

"The Last Rose," one of the more successful lyrics in
which the poet subordinates personality and message, presents this theme through symbols that recall Yeats' early
verse. As the poem concludes, winter represents "the
traitor" Death and more specifically the end of the century and the world, while the rose is the supreme beauty
and vitality of life at the moment of extinction:

> In lee-valleys crowded,
> The sheep and the birds
> Were frozen and shrouded
> In flights and in herds.
> In highways
> And byways
> The young and the old
> Were tortured and maddened
> And killed by the cold.
> But many were gladdened
> By the beautiful last rose,
> The blossom of no name
> That came when the snow came,
> In darkness unfurled—
> The wonderful vast rose
> That filled all the world.[89]

Writing of Romeo's death speech, Davidson observes:

You are in the presence of the final triumph of the will to live, which every sane suicide must be; despair—really the highest power and sublimation of hope—choosing death rather than resignation; the will to live, the pride of life that *cannot* renounce, the beautiful, the transcendent passion whereby the world survives, destroying itself rather than want its will.[90]

Without specific reference to Nietzsche he clearly regards suicide as the ultimate expression of the individual's jubilant *Willzumacht*. He advocates for civilization the same solution as for the individual. To "weed" humanity and to create "a race of heroes in a golden age," he approves the "excellent expedient" of voluntary euthanasia and eugenic evolution.

The autobiographical and doctrinal elements that loom large in Davidson's writings raise psychological and aesthetic problems. "Lammas," for example, in a transparently confessional passage tells of the comfort that the poet has derived from the thought of suicide "at whichever pole of passion"—pleasure or pain—he chooses. Thereupon he announces that this "refuge of despair" is no longer open to him because other lives are dependent upon his. It is almost impossible to disengage these confessional statements from the contemporary intellectual environment which the poems also reflect. Most of Davidson's writing after 1895 is the product of a mind egocentric, hypersensitive, and easily unbalanced, intent upon the primary task of justifying a life of disappointment. At the same time, he identified himself intimately with many ideas of his age. Certain lyrics, notably "A Ballad of Heaven" and "A Ballad of an Artist's Wife," describe his personal struggle solely in terms of the new philosophy. Conversely in others he sees the new ideas solely in terms

of their relevance to his struggle. Like Hamlet, the prototype of all disenchanted idealists, he relates whatever he
experiences, from a rejected manuscript to a quasi-mystical
vision, to his own predicament. Butler and Shaw appealed
to the authority of Darwin to justify eugenic evolution,
socialism, and other pet theories, but never with such
obvious compulsion to justify themselves.

Davidson refashions current ideas to fit personal problems no less readily than he distorts facts in his own life
to document these ideas. His references to family religious
disputes, insanity, penury, and starvation have already
been found highly exaggerated. On rare occasions, when
less self-preoccupied, he draws skillfully upon his boyhood in Scotland, as in this picture of a nonconformist
communion service:

> The stealthy elders creaked about the floor,
> Guiding the cup and platter; looking down,
> The children in the gallery smirked and watched
> Who took the deepest draught; and ancient dames
> Crumpled their folded handkerchiefs, and pressed
> With knuckly fingers sprays of southernwood.[91]

To invest his remembrance of things past with the intense
importance that it held for him, he called upon every
rhetorical device learned from the evangelical pulpit. The
melodrama, fustian, blatant symbolism, parable, and dogmatic assertion of the later lyrics and blank-verse poems
are calculated to convince himself as well as his readers.
The use of its own weapons to destroy Protestant Christianity did not strike him as an inconsistency but as
another instance of life's irony.

It cannot be said too often that poetry has nothing to do
with assertion, scientific fact, or intellectual synthesis, although it is sometimes found in their company. A poem

seeks only to express concretely and memorably what at any given moment may be. As John B. Yeats, the artist, once said, the poet should feel free to say in the morning that he believes in marriage and in the evening that he no longer believes in it. As long as he adhered to the doctrine of universal irony and described the paradoxicality of life as he experienced it, Davidson belonged with the very best of the minor poets. When he abandoned this for a vast monistic system, he became a dynamic, more significant figure, a man of ideas, as some have thought a genius, but he was no longer the poet. The poet will remain a poet in spite of his creed, whatever it may be, not because of it.

The earth-born Titans, having captured Olympus and Helicon, were quite properly thrown out; they had no business there. Davidson in keeping with his rejection of myth defied this warning to announce his own deification:

> From the mountain's burning crest
>   Like a god I come again,
> And with an immortal zest
>   Challenge Fate to throw the main.[92]

In spite of almost continuous, desperate experimentation with intricate rhyme and metrical patterns, he failed in his later verse to reconcile the demands of poetry and those of propaganda. "New Year's Day," the concluding poem in *Holiday and Other Poems* (1906), the final volume of lyrics published during his lifetime, contains his farewell to pure lyricism:

> 'Tis not enough to mount and ride,
>   No saddle, bridle, whip, nor spur;
> To take the chance of time and tide,
>   And follow fame without demur.

I want some reason with my rhyme,
    A fateful purpose when I ride;
I want to tame the steeds of Time,
    To harness and command the tide:

I want a whip whose braided lash
    Can echo like the crack of doom;
I want an iron mace to smash
    The world and give the peoples room.[93]

Once again myth had the last word—it and the critics.

Only a small clique of friends and followers—Le Gallienne, George Cotterell, William Canton, Lionel Johnson, and later Filson Young and James Douglas—heaped great praise on the poet. The critics, with a few exceptions, regarded his work more objectively and fairly, although panegyrics like Le Gallienne's prompted some to balance the scales with severer opinions than they might have otherwise delivered. After the first two volumes of lyrics appeared, virtually all the reputable reviews conceded that Davidson exhibited unusual originality and power. They agreed that he was among the three or four most promising of the "younger poets," but that he had yet to achieve that perfection of form and fusion with sense which distinguish the outstanding poet.* As fresh

---

* In a review of *Ballads and Songs* the critic for the *Athenaeum* stated: "Of the many young men who today look up from the foot of Parnassus, Mr. John Davidson is the most original, and, to us, the most interesting." (*Athenaeum*, 26 Jan. 1895, p. 110.) H. D. Traill, comparing William Watson and Davidson, stated that there was no doubt that both were major poets, "easily ahead of the main body of their strictly contemporary competitors." Between the two it was a choice of greater mastery of form or greater imagination and poetic vision. (*Fortnightly Review*, 1 Mar. 1895, pp. 393–407.) C. Lewis Hind, on the other hand, in a series of articles on the younger poets observed that Davidson lacked finish and "fundamental brainwork," that his social fervor was vague and rhetorical, and that in lieu of a philosophy he had "emotions and instincts." "Some Younger Reputations," *Academy*, 4 Dec. 1897, pp. 489–90.

volumes marred by the same excesses came out, the re-
viewers became increasingly impatient and censorious.
The appearance of *New Ballads* in 1896 * prompted the
Athenaeum to state what had become a majority opinion:

> There was a time when we expected great things of
> him—when he seemed to have greater possibilities
> than, perhaps, any of the younger verse-writers. In
> book after book he is rebuking our confidence in him.
> What appeared to be minor defects, which a little
> care and labour would chasten, are growing into
> salient qualities, for which he has not merely indul-
> gence, but it would seem a sort of admiration. He is
> building the fabric of his art without design and with
> cheap materials.[94]

That there were personal factors which explained the
solidification of Davidson's nimble, ironic view into a
ponderous pedantry did not concern the critics. The poet
was frantically overwriting in an attempt to keep from
starving. Moreover, the early emotional need for a trans-
figuring synthesis had increased as the mediocrity of much
of his work was brought home to him. It was enough for
the reviewer that a refreshing style had deteriorated into
an offensive obsession.

Another, more fundamental reason explains the growing alienation of Davidson and his critics whom he had
always left to some degree baffled and disappointed. Bo-
tanic classification is the critic's trade, and Davidson would
not be classified. In rejecting the present and immediate
past, in embracing all that was revolutionary, he was the
most comprehensive romantic of his day. In him were reflected all the strains of the nineties which his fellow
writers, among them his harshest critics, represented

* *New Balads* is dated 1897 but was copyrighted, released, and reviewed
in the fall of 1896.

singly. He was, to sum up, the nimble prose satirist mocking everything except the authority of nature and common sense. He was in the same breath a decadent and counter-decadent, a friend of the aesthetes and writer of impressionist verse but also a dabbler in the Kiplingesque idiom and a Henleyan activist in love with the physical life. Associated with the innovators in verse and the extreme liberals in politics, he at the same time helped to keep alive traditional verse forms and anticipated the reactionary principles of twentieth-century totalitarianism. Reviewers debated whether his talent lay in the direction of pastoral and romantic song or of satire, social comment, and description of urban life. A divided yet single-minded personality with a larger purpose but with less formal order than any of his contemporaries, a poet-philosopher who was completely neither poet nor philosopher, none could wholly claim him or reject him.

7

IN AND OUT OF THE
LONDON THEATER,
1898-1904

And he who defends a pleasing dream is necessarily honoured amongst men more than a visionary whose course is towards the glacier heights and the icy solitudes of thought.

John Adam Cramb

Poetry is made to be known, loved, enjoyed, and the poetry which wins us with a tranquil and sure power is victorious in the end over that which thrills at first reading, and chills on the third or fourth.

Laurence Binyon

Along with sporadic efforts to recapture his fleeting popularity as a lyric poet, Davidson turned for a livelihood to the theater. He first tried adaptations of successful foreign plays for the celebrated performers Forbes Roberston, Beerbohm Tree, George Alexander, Lewis Waller, and Mrs. Patrick Campbell. In 1896, while the poet was still wearily occupied with ballads and eclogues, Forbes Robertson, attracted by his early plays, invited him to prepare an English version of François Coppée's *Pour la Couronne*. Although he had always regarded the drama as his true province, Davidson was greatly surprised by this proposal. During the five years that he had been in London he had been too busy and too poor to at-

tend the theater but once, he "had never dreamt of enter-
ing these regions under a foreign flag," and he did not
yet consider himself ready to resume his proper "calling
and election." [1] Penury left him no choice, but certain
parallels in Coppée's play to his own life and beliefs may
have made the task more inviting.

A romantic costume piece in the tradition of Victor
Hugo, *Pour la Couronne* portrays a fifteenth-century
Balkan patriot whose duty it is to kill his traitorous father,
a Bulgarian Macbeth, and then die in turn to save his
father's honor. Here in germinal form is the prevailing
theme of Davidson's works, the irreconcilable conflict of
father and son, parental authority and individual will. In
its original version entitled *Le Justicier,* the play had enjoyed an instantaneous and immense success in the winter
of 1894–95 at the Odéon in Paris and had been revived
in November of that year at the Théâtre Sarah Bernhardt.
Opening at the Lyceum Theater on February 27, 1896,
Davidson's adaptation, *For the Crown,* had Robertson and
Winifred Emery in the leading roles of the young patriot,
Constantine Brancomir, and his ruthless mother, Bazilde,
while Mrs. Patrick Campbell played a beautiful slave-
girl, Militza. Any playwright might have felt confident
with such a cast. Forbes Robertson at forty-three was beginning his first season as actor-manager of the Lyceum
and was shortly to achieve his greatest triumph as the
outstanding Hamlet of his generation. In Winifred Emery
he had a popular leading lady who had played with Henry
Irving at the Lyceum and accompanied that actor on two
American tours.

The real coup had been in obtaining the services of
"Mrs. Pat" in a relatively minor role. Only three years
earlier, after receiving notice at the Adelphi where she
had been acting in melodramas for the Gattis, she had become overnight a London sensation as Paula Tanqueray

in Arthur Wing Pinero's play. With her dark Italian beauty and rich, expressive voice she more than any other actress of the day created the vogue for the passionate, willful, complex heroine. When she revived the role of Paula in 1901, Davidson wrote to her:

> I had not seen Mrs. Tanqueray before.
>
> It was exceedingly beautiful and powerful, sometimes terrible, and of extraordinary sweetness wherever a tender note was struck.
>
> "Paula" is like an opal of many hues and lustres, with stains of life, and wounds of passion through which the disastrous fires glow that shatter it in the end.
>
> There are no words in which to thank so incomparable an artist.[2]

If, as Hamilton Fyfe suggests, Davidson here may be attributing greater merit to Pinero than to Mrs. Campbell, he knew from experience how dependent the playwright is upon the sensitivity and skill of the actor.[3] In their first collaboration the poet and the temperamental actress, both ungovernably romantic, respected each other's talents and struck up a warm friendship. They had private jokes during rehearsal, and the author allowed the star to recite a pretty little poem, "Butterflies," that he had meant to be sung, with an effect which they at least found pleasing. Mrs. Campbell over a quarter of a century later recollected, "It was a fine play and had a fine success. The little part, Militza, appealed to me, and I believe I played it well." [4] The heady glamour of the professional theater was a welcome distraction to Davidson in this interval and offered a temporary stay against approaching disaster.

On the opening night he watched the performance from the gallery, concealed and unrecognized. For all his contempt of the mob, he knew that it was in the "heavens" that the fate of his play would be determined. Not even Forbes Robertson was aware of the poet's presence in the theater until the audience called for him along with Coppée at the end. Writing from London on the following morning for the New York *Critic,* Arthur Waugh reported that the drama had held the audience spellbound from first to last and had received a tremendous demonstration at the close. "Everyone is glad of this," he commented, "because Mr. Davidson has now shown that he possesses a talent which may make him the one man needful to the English drama—a man-of-letters who is also a dramatist." [5] Praise from the critics and congratulations from a widening circle of friends were all too rare in the author's experience. Abruptly and capriciously the wheel of fortune had made its half turn.

The praise was well deserved, for by condensing and accelerating the action of the original play the "translator" had made it more acceptable to an English audience. He had retained little more than the plot and basic motivation of the French play and had discarded Coppée's alexandrines, tame and tedious to the English ear, for clipped, forceful blank verse and far stronger language. If Davidson's version made improvements, it also retained much of the rhetoric and romantic flummery of the original. There are bleak, flat stretches which must have called forth the utmost resources of Forbes Robertson and Mrs. Campbell, whose bewitching voice, the legend goes, once moved a house to tears with the line, "You brought me water, boy; I asked for beer."

In the mid-nineties public taste suddenly shifted from the new prose drama dedicated to the modern scene and modern social problems to shamelessly romantic pieces which gave the versifier, the designer, and the actor schooled in the grand style full swing for their exuberant

talents. Well-made, sophisticated comedies by Tom Robertson, Henry Arthur Jones, and Oscar Wilde and domestic
tragedies by Pinero were obliged to share if not to yield
the stage temporarily with historical extravaganza and romance. Audiences that had been filling the houses to see
George Alexander in *The Importance of Being Earnest*
and Mrs. Campbell in *The Second Mrs. Tanqueray* and
The Notorious Mrs. Ebbsmith now rushed to applaud
George du Maurier's *Trilby* with Beerbohm Tree as a
chilling Svengali; Anthony Hope's *The Prisoner of Zenda*,
complete with breath-taking adventure and love at high
voltage all in silk knee breeches; and Davidson's *For the
Crown,* which offered jaded appetites the illusion of witnessing heroic conflict and passionate jealousy in Bulgarian
palaces and mountain passes. And for a climactic spectacle,
at the Lyric Theater hero and heroine were being given
nightly to the lions in *The Sign of the Cross,* to the great
delight of the masses who had gone there on explicit
recommendations from the Sunday pulpits.[6]

It was not merely spectacle, derring-do, and erotic love
made respectable by a biblical setting and the triumph of
virtue which the audiences wanted, although these attractions were as powerful then as now. At the turn of the
century, however, they constituted the more vulgar manifestations of a middle-class desire for a restoration of the
poetic, ennobling, and moral to the theater. This demand
kept alive verse drama in spite of its general inferiority and
formidable competition from playwrights in prose. Davidson, Stephen Phillips, Maeterlinck, and Hofmannsthal offered the playgoer a world of elevated emotions and ideals
that served as an antidote to the worldly decadence of
Wilde's drawing rooms and the drabness of Shaw's and
Ibsen's bourgeois parlors.

Two motives prompted Davidson to exploit the vogue
for romantic claptrap, one practical, the other idealistic,

together reflecting his essential ambivalence. Although he would have taken umbrage at the charge of timeserving, he was not unwilling to peddle his wares in the market place, even if it meant using cheap, secondhand materials. It would give him the financial security necessary to produce his more important, original works. Moreover, rhetoric and unrestrained emotionalism came to him naturally as the Spasmodic plays and romantic comedies had shown. A second consideration was that a successful play, even one adapted from a foreign author, would secure him the ear of a new and considerable audience. He never attempted in his numerous adaptations to preserve the original play intact. The Spasmodic style of many passages, the pagan earth worship, the celebration of power and action, as well as the familiar lapses into bathos, discursive digression, and punning, brand *For the Crown* Davidson's play as much as Coppée's. Throughout there is a fundamental contradiction between the conventional heroic theme of love and duty of the French play and the splendid satanism of Davidson's Bazilde. His position as ironist at this time prevents him from choosing between these two moral codes of the old order and the new.

It is not difficult to pick out the passages of *For the Crown* which have been interpolated to strengthen and bring up to date its message. At one point, for example, the ambitious, unscrupulous Bazilde advises her son, who adheres to traditional notions of honor and duty to country:

> Be passionate!
> Cherish the highest hopes and follow them.
> Be passionate . . . Oh! this is to be great:
> To be impassioned always; sense and soul,
> Fibre and nerve, and blood and brain, one orb
> Of glowing power the fates themselves obey! [7]

Forbes Robertson's prompt copy of the English adaptation indicates that many passages were diluted or struck out in performance because of their alarming ardor. A comparison of the closing lines of the drama as found in Coppée's version, Davidson's, and the prompt copy reveals the middleman's only half successful efforts to superimpose his own ideas on the romantic formulas of the original. In this scene the young patriot Constantine has accepted the blame for having betrayed his country to the Turks, in order to conceal the fact that his father, whom he killed, had been the real traitor. He is bound to the statue of his father, who is now regarded as a national hero, and threatened with death. Rushing up to the prisoner, the slave-girl Militza embraces him, declares her secret love, stabs him and then herself. In the French play patricide has been atoned and the bishop-king of the Bulgars delivers a pious curtain speech: "Dieu seul fera justice à ce couple qui dort. / Prions pour son repos et respectons la mort." Davidson, who celebrated the final triumph of pagan love and the principle of an ironic order, assigned speeches to his Militza and bishop-king more in key with his philosophy:

> *Mil.* [*Stabbing herself.*] Oh, love and death are one!—that's—all—I—know!
> *Steph.* Shall not the Judge of all the earth do right?

To offset Davidson's deliberate ambiguity and restore the intent of the original, the prompt copy adds:

All Kneel.

> Respect the dead, and may the two sad souls
> Appearing now before the Judgement seat
> Find mercy there.[8]

Such an about-face could only exasperate both authors and
confuse the public.

If the critics were troubled by the play's inconsistency of
theme or even noted it, they did not say so. A. B. Walkley,
drama critic for the *Speaker,* may have been half conscious of the injection of new ideas when he observed
that Davidson had put "grit" and "bite" into Coppée's
wordy rhetoric. Judging romantic melodrama by its own
standards, he found *For the Crown* worthy of serious and
favorable attention.[9] The current fashion for historical
settings and operatic plots permitted the adapter a license
that he would not have enjoyed otherwise. When Walkley
reviewed *The Theatrocrat* nine years later, he pilloried
Davidson for writing a play with a modern setting and
theme in romantic blank verse.

More independent and forthright was the *Saturday Review*'s critic, G. B. Shaw, who declined to join in the general ovation accorded the play. Today his lone, scornful
voice can be heard clearly above the enthusiastic fanfare
of the other critics. As spokesman for the "new drama" he
exposed the fustian and melodrama of the piece and assigned it to those "later horrors of historical drama in five
acts and in blank verse which begins with Shakespeare."
Thanks to the Bard's unfortunate example, he snorted,
"every poor wretch with an excitable imagination, a command of literary bombast, and metric faculty enough to
march in step" had set out to emulate him with the result
that the announcement of a new historical play in verse
at a London theater produced an involuntary state of
panic among the critics. The one merit of *For the Crown,*
he allowed, was as a display of rhetoric for the sake of
rhetoric, "a form of entertainment which is chiefly interesting as the only known means by which an author or
speaker can make the public respect him for unmercifully
boring it." The initial responsibility had been Coppée's,

but in preparing an English version Davidson had compounded the felony. Since greater poets had caught the infection, he might be forgiven, "though only, I hope, on
the distinct understanding that it is not to occur again."
Noting the popular success of *For the Crown,* Shaw commented, "The public [rises] at it as Partridge rose at the
King in *Hamlet.*"

There was nothing personal in Shaw's animadversions
as he subsequently demonstrated in a material way. But
when it came to impassioned overstatement he was a
match for any blank-verse poet. His stinging review was
a minor skirmish in the battle then raging in the theater
and press between the advocates of a poetic and morally
uplifting drama dealing with heroic themes and those of
an emancipated drama in prose grappling realistically with
contemporary problems. It was partly in retaliation for
such plays as *For the Crown* and *The Only Way,* a popular dramatization by John Martin-Harvey of *A Tale of
Two Cities,* that Shaw wrote his antiromantic, antiheroic
comedies, *Arms and the Man* and *The Devil's Disciple.* In
retrospect Shaw seems on the side of the angels in his
contempt for this "Sahara of rhetorical blank verse," and
certainly his critical assaults upon it as well as those he
made in the theater make some of the best reading to
come out of the decade. Yet by his example, first as critic
and then as playwright, he encouraged others to forget
the important role of the poet in the theater and to dedicate themselves single-mindedly to the social-problem play.

There was one exception to the uniform mediocrity of
For the Crown which made the production for Shaw worth
attending. Although the cast had done as well as could
be expected from actors asked to portray "a pen-and-ink
monster" or "to fill a brainless void," the enchanting Mrs.
Pat alone had surpassed expectation. Admittedly she could
not act—who cared or wanted her to act? "Go and see her

move, stand, speak, look, kneel. Go and breathe the magic
atmosphere that is created by the grace of all these deeds;
and then talk to me about acting, forsooth!" Probing to
her strength as an artist, which was Davidson's weakness as a dramatist, he found her performance an embodied poem, lyric, not dramatic—and therefore so much
the worse for dramatic poetry.[10] Although the famous
friendship and the correspondence which produced it
were not to begin for another three years, it is evident
that the ardent Irishman was already half in love with
the personality if not the person of the young actress.
When she accused him some years later of having maligned
her repeatedly, he pointed to the evidence of his collected
reviews and protested, "Never did man paint his infatuation across the heavens as I painted mine for you, rap-
turously and shamelessly." Witness his review of For the
Crown: "Criticism? Just Gods! A mad rapture of adoration . . . I would not hear of your acting. 'On the highest plane one does not act, one is!' "[11] In this romantic
definition of the artist, Shaw comes close to Davidson's
own.

In spite of Shaw's drubbing, the play was assured of a
moderately good run. Its four extravagant sets, each by a
different designer, which even Shaw admired, contributed
to the box office appeal of romantic tragedy and a cast of
celebrities. The closing performance was on Saturday, May
30, bringing the total number to a little over a hundred.
During the nineties when theaters were fewer and reper-
tories larger, this was a satisfactory if far from sensational
showing.* Davidson's full share of the earnings was a mere
£200, but it was as large a windfall as he ever received

* An opera by Colin McAlpin, The Cross and the Crescent, based upon
For the Crown, was produced in 1903, and the play itself revived in 1905
after the original French version had been revived in the same year in
Paris. C. A. and H. W. Stonehill, Bibliographies of Modern Authors,
Second Series, p. 19.

from his writings. The production attracted notice to the adapter so that he received various proposals but always for adaptations. As he later recalled ruefully, he had succeeded or had seemed to succeed as an adapter; therefore from then on he was regarded exclusively as one. He began again upon a French play but exercised too much liberty in adapting it so that the production was abandoned.

2

Davidson's next venture in preparing foreign imports for domestic consumption was *The Children of the King, a Fairy Tale,* which opened at the Court Theater on October 16, 1897. Based upon a tale by Hans Andersen, the original German play, *Die Königskinder* by "Ernst Rosmer" (Elsa Bernstein) with musical accompaniment by Engelbert Humperdinck, had been first produced in Munich in January 1897 and then translated into English by the musical director, Carl Armbruster. Davidson revised this translation. Set in a fictitious German duchy of the sixteenth century, this reworking of the babes-in-the-wood story presents the adventures of a young Prince who goes to live incognito among his subjects for the purpose of learning their needs. He falls in love with a goose girl, whose parents are the daughter and the helper of the hangman. In the role of the Prince was John Martin-Harvey, young, boyishly handsome, and fresh from his triumph as Sidney Carton in *The Only Way*. Herbert Ross played a broom-binder, Isabel Bateman a witch, and Dion Boucicault the younger a minstrel, while the heroine was played by a vivacious young actress, popular in the music halls but as yet virtually unknown in the legitimate theater, Cissie Loftus. Harvey recalled that it was Boucicault who produced "the tender and charming play" and who had persuaded Arthur Chudleigh to finance it.[12]

In superficial respects *The Children of the King* does

not differ from the other masked balls which passed for
drama at the time. It has all the romantic passementerie
of the prince in disguise, the orphaned heroine, love at
first sight, magic spells, and delayed revelation. In addition, cloying sentimentality and trite symbolism clog the
action throughout. Davidson, however, meant his version
of the fairy tale to be something more than the usual
nursery pabulum. Bolder even than he had been in *For the
Crown,* he introduced wherever possible disturbingly
Davidsonian ideas. "To understand one must love—to love
one must suffer," the blind, aged Councillor tells the boy
king.[13] Elsewhere in the play the adapter found opportunity to instruct his audience that knowledge and power
derive from suffering. Not until he has bartered his
crown to buy a crust of bread for the cold and hungry
heroine and experienced the deprivations of his lowliest
subject, does the Prince earn the right to be king, "a
King whose royalty rooted in strength and wisdom, will
make his people strong and wise." Like the political
philosophy of Heine and other German romantics, Davidson's was a curious blend of the revolutionary and the
reactionary. In spite of the almost pious humanitarianism
of the play, it advocates not democracy or constitutional
monarchy but the stern, benevolent despotism of his other
writings. The unswerving devotion between the Prince
and the Goose Girl illustrates another favorite theme, that
only love is democratic—a theme carried over from Davidson's first play, *An Unhistorical Pastoral.* By assigning
titles rather than names to the characters of his dramatic
idyl, Davidson calls attention to its allegorical purpose.
In these borrowed plumes he employed fable and romance for the same purpose as in his original plays and
poems, to preach self-reliance, the sanctity of young physical love, and the supremacy of the will to power. It is little
wonder that the audience, made up for the most part of

children and their nurses, "sat in over-awed silence." [14]

Since he had to answer for his liberties to the original author, the actor-manager, and the audience, Davidson had somewhat sweetened and diluted the medicine. In spite of his concessions to popular taste the play did not prosper. Solemn preaching and the make-believe of fairy tale, whatever the proportion, do not mix. The production ran for only two weeks, closing on October 30 to make room at the Court for Louis Parker's *The Vagabond King* along similar but less didactic lines. Davidson's romantic comedy had attracted little notice. Although aware that the author had invested the fairy tale with a vague allegorical message of his own, the critic for the *Times* was disposed not to guess at the play's inner meaning but to accept it simply as "a play of strangely imaginative, poetic kind, albeit a little long-winded in effect." Its most interesting innovation, he found, was the technical one of orchestral accompaniment to spoken dialogue.[15] Apparently everyone conspired to ignore the somber lessons contributed by the adapter and to enjoy the production for Humperdinck's excellent score and the creditable performances by Harvey, Boucicault, and notably Cissie Loftus.

Whatever its shortcomings as drama, the play in the opinion of the management recommended itself as Christmas entertainment for young and old. On this assumption it was revived during December of the same year with the original cast, and everything was done to guarantee its acceptance as popular fare. To the *Times'* renewed regret, the liberties with the original text persisted, especially the happy ending, while Humperdinck's overture and much of his incidental music were omitted in favor of some songs "by another hand, according to the custom which prevails in the lower grades of comic opera." [16] These questionable improvements were not enough to preserve the production beyond the holidays, although it did not go entirely with-

out praise. J. W. Mackail wrote to Harvey that, thanks to
the exquisite performances by himself and Miss Loftus,
The Children of the King had given his household greater
pleasure than any other play for years past. Mrs. Mackail
went four times but after the fourth brought back the unhappy report "that the audience were as apathetic as ever."
Sympathizing with the task of having to play up against
"all this dull weight of stupidity," the Oxford don and
future professor commented, "There is a great deal in the
play that ought to be altered, and some bits that are tiresome and stupid, but that does not affect the absolute
beauty of the beautiful parts which are all that one remembers afterwards." *

Davidson had approached conscientiously the task of
adapting *Die Königskinder* but had made the grave mistake of using it as a vehicle for his own iconoclastic ideas.
Its revival therefore as part of the traditional Christmas
offering of pantomime, music-hall revue, and comic opera
was more of a mockery than a blessing. Although it was he
who had written the lyrics for the new interpolated songs,
he may have seen some virtue in the *Times'* opinion that it
would have been better to have left the original version
of the play alone, "even if the process consigned it to oblivion, than to present a finished and delicate work of art
in a form which is to some extent distorted." [17] Privately
he came to the conclusion that he had gone not so much
too far as not far enough in revising the play. When in

---

* There may have been an ulterior motive in Mackail's appreciation, for
at the end of his letter he mentions "another play, too, a modern one, in
which I would give a great deal to see you, Maeterlinck's 'Pelléas and
Mélisande.'" (Sir John Martin-Harvey, *The Book of Martin-Harvey*, London, H. Walker, Ltd., 1930, p. 154.) By a coincidence not so very odd,
Mrs. Patrick Campbell was taken by Alfred Sutro to see Harvey's performance in *The Children of the King*. She decided at once that only he
would do to play opposite her Mélisande in Forbes Robertson's forthcoming production of the Maeterlinck play. Mackail had made the English
translation. Martin-Harvey, *Autobiography*, p. 198.

1902 Martin-Harvey requested permission to revive his adaptation Davidson replied:

> I have no rights in "The Children of the King"—a business mistake on my part. I should, however, be very sorry to see the old version revived and would oppose such a revival if I had half an inch of ground to stand on. In my opinion it should be rewritten, mainly in blank verse, and the story developed: I remember proposing to do so; but the music presented.[*sic*] I should say also, then, that the music should be entirely subordinated to the play.

Characteristically Davidson shut his eyes to the folly of having tampered with *Die Königskinder* and insisted on removing from the work its one attraction to make further room for Davidsonian ideas. His letter to Martin-Harvey closes by postponing an appointment because of "a bad, bronchial cold which fastens me in my room" and suggesting, "Why not ask me for a version of 'Hernani'?" [18] The prophet of materialism by this time had put away childish things and turned entirely to blank verse setting forth his gospel without equivocation. Perceiving this, Martin-Harvey must have quickly demurred. Although the poet and he continued on friendly terms and occasionally corresponded about possible ventures, they never again collaborated.

3

After the failure of *The Children of the King,* further commissions to adapt plays were not immediately forthcoming. The disappointment had its solace, for Davidson could offer at best a watered version of his message in these foreign vessels. He welcomed the opportunity to speak his mind in his own words and, encouraged by a single theatrical success, ventured further where angels fear to tread. Once again he began to write original dramatic works. Between 1898 and 1900 he wrote or refurbished three romantic plays in alternating prose and blank verse: *Godfrida* (1898), *Self's the Man* (1901), and *The Knight of the Maypole* (1903).

The first of these, *Godfrida, a Play in Four Acts,* is set in the court of Provence around the middle of the fourteenth century. A study of passionate love, violent jealousy, and the conflict of strong wills, it has in ample measure all the faults of late nineteenth-century historic melodrama. The plot is artificial, relying on stale contrivance or arbitrary reversals of fortune to create suspense and achieve a denouement. While Isembert, the villain, may illustrate the author's philosophy of irony, his vacillation between satanic evil and selfless good strains credulity. Furthermore these quasi-allegorical figures who announce the author's ideas as if they wore sandwich boards are devoid of any originality. Siward and Godfrida, hero and heroine, are drawn partly after Chaucer's Troilus and Criseyde, partly after Othello and Desdemona; Jacobean drama affords numerous models for the antagonists, Isembert and Ermengarde. If the characters in *Godfrida* illustrated Davidson's message through consistent motivation and action rather than served as inconsistent mouthpieces for it, they might provide the excitement and violence of true romantic melodrama. Or if the conventions of the contemporary theater had permitted the playwright to invest his abstract principles with sufficient vitality, he might have written a powerful allegory. As it is, *Godfrida* flounders in some vague, unchartered morass between the two.

What militated against the new play's chances in its own day is the one thing that now recommends it for attention, its ideas. *Godfrida* seeks to prove that happiness and fulfillment can result only at the cost of an equal amount of suf-

fering for someone. It further demonstrates that in the
struggle of wills at the basis of all society, that will with
requited and unselfish love on its side prevails, whatever
the odds. Power and love when coupled are unassailable,
irresistible forces in human affairs. In an imaginary prose
colloquy between the Poet and the Interviewer which
serves the play as prologue, Davidson states his purpose,
with an eye to possible charges of obscurity by the critics.
Its lesson, the Poet points out, is stated in the play itself:

> . . . no felicity
> Can spring in men, except from barbèd roots
> Of discontent and envy, deeply struck
> In some sore heart that hoped to have the flower.[19]

Stung into defending the truth of these lines, Davidson
later wrote to the editor of the *Daily Chronicle,* "They
have perhaps no reference to lighter natures incapable of
staking their lives in the game of fate, or to philosophers
who only look on; but it seems to me true of those who
will win or lose it all. There can be no triumph without
defeat." This is "the order of the universe . . . victory
and defeat are one—the flower and the root." * [20] *Godfrida,* a transitional work, attempts to present in dramatic
terms the ironic vision which the poet had expressed
through narrative and nature imagery in his lyrics of the
nineties. More explicitly than in the lyrics, it also states

* Compare: "I ran through Wells's book [*The War of the Worlds*(?), 1898]
when it came out. The prophecy, the real meaning of the prophecy, was
right I thought: that the world will proceed to be under changing forms
just what it has been, or more intensely what it has been: comfort, pleasure, splendour for a few rooted in the misery, pain and degradation of the
mass; a garden carefully and inevitably kept exactly so by every religion
and every polity although the priests and the governors may honestly believe they are procuring radical reform: much admired by the optimist,
much abused by the pessimist: gravely stated as such and no other and
neither good nor bad, by me." A.L.S., to William Archer, dated 9 Mar.
1902, from 9 Fairmile Ave., Streatham, S. W., Add. MS. 45291, ff. 106–7, B.M.

in germinal form the morality of the later works, a morality reduced to strength of will, brains, and physical superiority. This morality finds its authority in nature, its driving and preserving force in sex, and its goal in power.

Still searching for a style in which to couch this message, the poet announces in the prologue to the play that he has cast his lot for romance rather than realism: "I mean by Romance the essence of reality. Romance does not give the bunches plucked from the stem: it offers the wine of life in chased goblets." The poet takes his characters from men and women as he knows them, "but that I myself may realise them, and make them more apparent and more engaging to an audience, I place them in an imaginary environment, and in the colour and vestments of another time." He has chosen the contemporary vogue for costume drama because he seeks to entertain and to give delight: "to give delight is to impart strength most directly, most permanently." But how does the artist give delight? What in his work imparts strength? Truth; and truth soon comes to mean for him, like the irony in which he previously found the cohesive principle of the universe, matter.[21] By a simple syllogism Davidson's aesthetics is inseparable from his metaphysics, just as his poetry gives way largely to philosophical assertion.

The plays of this period not only look ahead, they also look back. The style of *Godfrida* and of his next work, *Self's the Man,* like their message, recall the early Spasmodic dramas, *Diabolus Amans* and *Smith.* They preach the same romantic lesson of unfettered action and self-realization, and they preach it in the same way, through rhetoric and melodrama. Always latent in Davidson and suppressed only by conscious effort, the metaphysician springs fully grown in his work after 1900. As a result of this arrested birth and continued failure his poetic discipline and personality alike calcified.

Immediately upon completing *Godfrida* in March 1898, the author in a rare jubilant mood wrote to Lane from the Portland Hotel:

> I finished my play this morning, and went away on my bike to celebrate the event. When I returned at six I found your telegram; replied; and waited until 7:30 on a response. None arriving I came in to London on the chance of finding you at Portland Hotel. You had gone five minutes before my arrival. Being still in a celebrant mood—observe the celebrant blots —I went to the Café Royal; found two men, and celebrated; returned here: no Lane; celebrated and left, sorry, but celebrant.[22]

Like his other original plays from which he had hoped so much, this one proved a false dawn. Unlike the early ones, however, *Godfrida* did not have the excuse of being closet drama, since from the first Davidson had intended it for the legitimate stage. He read the play in succession to three managers who politely refused. Discouraged he wrote to Lane in April 1898, "I was forty-one yesterday, and I am eating my heart out to get my own things done in my own way. I have been attempting to write in periodicals again, but I am miles beyond that now. . . . Do help me by a speedy publication of *Godfrida*. It dangles about one like a thing born but unsevered. . . . This is no gross idle figure." [23] At any cost he must find some audience for his message of deliverance. In October of the same year Lane finally brought out the work in the uniform blue buckram binding of the volumes of lyrics, perhaps because he hoped that their reputation might sell this ugly duckling or because Davidson felt that this would symbolize the common message of all his works.

The reception of the book, whose weaknesses were all too apparent, was not one to gratify its author or pub-

lisher. Conscious of the need to entertain, Davidson was
never quite certain how to go about it or how to reconcile
entertainment with his real purpose of airing ideas. Since
the play is neither a sustained romantic tragicomedy nor
a symbolic drama of ideas, its thesis is nowhere convincingly demonstrated. The dean of late Victorian critics, William Archer, observed that *Godfrida* lacked both "the
depth of tragedy" and "the charm of comedy," that it was
"painful without being pathetic." [24] Another critic astutely
advised the poet to set his sights on Shakespeare, Browning, or Maeterlinck rather than on the Lyceum and St.
James's.[25] Still another, mocking the author's boast in the
prologue, commented, "You have indeed 'crushed wine
into your goblet'; but honestly, I think, the goblet is over-
chased, fantastical, and gilded rather than of gold." [26]

4

In September 1899 the poet-playwright completed a
second original drama in verse, *Self's the Man, a Tragicomedy*. It is a better play than *Godfrida* because it does
not cater so laboriously to the tasteless fashions of the day.
Still romantic and by present standards absurdly melodramatic, *Self's the Man* comes closer than its predecessor
to the frank purposefulness of the poet's final works. For
the first time since his Spasmodic dramas, Davidson does
not permit the play's rhetoric to interfere with a forthright, unprettified delivery of his unpopular message. Although he certainly intended the drama for the stage, he
also appealed to the reader's interest with extensive stage
directions and "chapter headings" in the manner of Shaw.
Whatever the author's intention, the work remains didactic closet drama along the lines of the later tragedies.

Set in the provincial court of Pavia during the middle
ages, *Self's the Man* concerns the efforts of a dissident
group of courtiers to depose Urban, an arrogant, auto-

cratic, but humorous king who has been elected by popular acclaim. Like *Godfrida* it is a play of intrigue, treach-
ery, and undying love. At the same time it is frankly a
thesis play, and its thesis is boldly announced in the epigraph which the author has chosen from his own eclogue,
"Lammas":

> Be your own star, for strength is from within,
> And one against the world will always win!

The minor characters who serve as foils and agents are no
more than stock figures, but the leading characters embody
fixed principles of conduct from which they derive their
vitality and interest. Of these Urban is the most important.

Urban, who combines the boyish charm and exuberance
of Prince Hal with the ruthless ambition of Marlowe's
Tamburlaine, is portrayed as a Renaissance Machiavellian
politician. In actuality he is a nineteenth-century man of
power. Davidson makes this clear in subsequent advertisements of the play:

> . . . it is a modern drama—a not altogether unsuit-
> able sub-title might be "New Wine in an Old Bottle,"
> for some part of the comedy is a fermenting anachro-
> nism which bursts the wineskin. Counterparts of
> Urban, the protagonist, may be found in Napo-
> leon III, Dom Pedro, Amadeus of Spain, Alexander
> of Bulgaria, Milan of Servia, poets, students, or pleas-
> ure-seekers attempting or half-attempting to act, and
> to be masters of men. Urban embodies the prevailing
> mood of the nineteenth century, which was, like most
> centuries, an age of dreamers and unrealized ideals;
> and he represents also the net result of the intellectual
> effort of the nineteenth century, viz., the conscious
> egoism which inevitably exalts the mind above the
> soul and the senses, and destroys the natural harmony
> of man. . . . Fate, such as may be found within the

covers of books, will not be detected anywhere in this
play; only character, and the want of it, and the use or
abuse the individual makes of the chances that occur.[27]

Urban's philosophy is that of the Henleyan activist grafted
to that of the Carlylean hero and the Nietzschean Overman. He is equally, however, the Spasmodic hero, motivated by self-love and exercising self-indulgence. When
his friend rebukes him for his ambition, he replies that
all men are consumed by their crowning passion:

> Oh, learn to love yourself!
> Consider how the silent sun is rapt
> In self-devotion! All things work for good
> To them that love themselves.[28]

There is no room in his egoistic code for remorse, pity, or
sentimental attachment to the past. "Power is my chosen
bride," he tells his discarded mistress, and he recognizes
the will to power as the guiding instinct in man. But it is
not enough for Urban to rule Lombardy. An imperialist
of the Cecil Rhodes—Robert Clive—Warren Hastings school, he seeks to conquer the world:

> My lords, it is with nations as with men:
> One must be first.[29]

In the paternalistic despot and the modern imperial state
Davidson has found substitutes for the parent and deity
in whom authority had traditionally been vested.

In willing his own destiny Urban has made one mistake.
He has renounced his love for the pagan slave-girl, Saturnia, in order to please the people by marrying Osmunda,
daughter of the leader of the opposition. Governed by intellectual principle and policy rather than by natural
impulse, he is as yet only the precursor of the Overman.
Great men should never compromise with their passions
and must learn to defy custom:

> To laugh at policy, to over-ride
> Wisdom, authority, experience,
> To break with the ragged past, and be
> The demiurge of order and a time
> Stamped with my own image—is to chafe
> Mankind, and mark my power and daring . . .
> Is to read triumph in a storm of hate.[30]

Because of his error Urban loses faith in his destiny, weakens, and repents. His downfall is followed Oedipus-fashion by prolonged exile and by death, but only after he has learned the last lesson of all, self-forgiveness and self-knowledge. "Though you were Judas, learn to forgive yourself," he says to Saturnia with whom he is symbolically reunited in a final death scene. The dignity and nobility of the tragic hero are at last his, but his ultimate vision is that of the man of power's supremacy in a godless universe, not the humble recognition of a higher order which traditionally concludes a tragedy. The capacity for redemption like the capacity for error is solely within Urban's own grasp. Davidson refused to call his play a tragedy, preferring to label it a tragicomedy, although he felt that "A farcical melodrama," "A Serio-comic Play," anything indicating "character" would have done as well.[31] By character he meant the role of paradox or irony in human destiny. In *Godfrida* Davidson had still compromised pretty much with the conventional dichotomy of good and evil by assigning each force to a single character, Siward the hero and Isembert the villain. The more complex Urban of *Self's the Man,* at once strong and weak, triumphant and defeated, like the later Mammon, embraces both roles. Ample precedent for this complexity of character exists in the protagonists of Kyd, Marlowe, and Shakespeare, whom Davidson certainly knew. But whereas the Elizabethan tragic hero reflects orthodox dualism and must ultimately resolve his divided nature by making a moral choice, Davidson's heroes recognize their ambivalence as part of the inevitable irony of the universe. Out of frailty, evil, and suffering, in oneself as well as in others, can come only good, the poet declares; and henceforth his amoral message will be:

> The complex heart of things
> Is never understood, till one is led
> To do wrong cheerfully that good may come.[32]

Irony strengthened by suffering has led him at last to a bleak, pitiless code.

Self's the Man had been commissioned by the actor-manager Beerbohm Tree who, Davidson remarked to Gosse, "with hardly a criticism, gave me carte-blanche to write it in my own way." [33] Commenting on this association the *Academy* queried, "Will it ever be enacted? Mr. Davidson is pathetically true to the 'poetic drama.' " [34] To this the author replied with simulated cheerfulness that *Godfrida* and *Self's the Man* would both be performed, if not immediately, then later. "It is only as always in matters of opinion, a question of the fulness of time," he explained. As for his other unacted plays, only *Scaramouch in Naxos* had any claim upon the stage, and this he would produce himself at Christmas time in his own theater, "with a new order of harlequinade to follow, as a holiday matinee entertainment." [35] This was whistling in the dark, for the *Academy* proved the more reliable prophet. The original title of the new work had been *King of the Lombards,* but on the publication in 1899 of Swinburne's *Rosamund, Queen of the Lombards,* Davidson changed his title to the unfortunate alternative, *Self's the Man, a Tragicomedy.* Quite understandably Tree regretted the carte blanche he had extended the author. Although an improvement over his previous plays and less sensational and strident than the later melodramas, the play's almost

pathological interest in torture, its occasional bloodthirsti-
ness, its ideological nature, and its amoral message made
it unsuitable for production. The poet preferred defeat
to success on terms other than his own, and in time found
grim satisfaction in predictable failure.

With this work Davidson changed publisher. *Godfrida*
had not prospered as the collection of earlier plays had in
1894, and Lane was reluctant to invest more in a leaking,
perhaps sinking ship. In a showdown always the businessman, he may have taken alarm at the latest directions of
his eccentric protégé. Grant Richards recounts the way in
which his long association with Davidson began:

> I did not go hunting for Davidson. I had known
> him pretty well from his first arrival in London, but it
> was, I believe, John Lane who had introduced me to
> him and I looked on him as a Lane poet whom it
> wouldn't be decent to attempt to seduce from the
> Bodley Head list. But one day Davidson wrote offer-
> ing me his play *Self's the Man* and I was glad to re-
> spond to his approach. He asked twenty pounds on ac-
> count of royalties! I paid that small sum, but, may I
> add? the sale of the play did not justify even so small
> an advance.[36]

For his part the author felt that Richards generally bun-
gled their first venture together. When the announcement
in the *Westminster Gazette* stated that the new play was
similar to the poet's early work in verse, presumably al-
luding to the pastoral plays written in Scotland, Davidson complained that this was "entirely inaccurate, and
. . . sufficient to damage in some degree my book." Nothing could have been more calculated to arouse the ire of a
writer who was already conscious to the point of belligerence of stating a new message. "No man who really thinks
and imagines," he wrote to Richards, "can write or would
dream of writing on the lines of twelve years ago. A stag-

nant mind, a mind that takes the mould of a creed may
go on writing on the same lines; but never a living
mind." [37] Davidson's final period was one of self-enfran-
chisement as much as of self-fulfillment; he repeatedly
rebelled against publishers' attempts to reprint his earlier
novels and poems, as he also struck back when critics compared his later with his youthful writings.

If there were difficulties before publication, they were
multiplied several times once the book appeared. The author had urged his new publisher to arrange to have the
book reviewed on the day of issue, pointing out that this
had always been the practice with his books although editors had to be coerced into taking notice of authors who
were not well established:

> Please believe me that I do not expect highly
> laudatory or intelligent notices of "Self's the Man":
> two or three generations hence will be time enough
> for that; but in your interest as well as mine I did
> hope for prompt attention: a book of this kind is dead
> for its own time, unless it crows lustily when it is
> born: I am concerned now that you should not even
> get back your outlay.[38]

The appeal for publicity contrasts sharply with his former
avoidance of personal advertisement. Although he felt
that the advertising Davidson wanted was overadvertis-
ing and produced little, Richards promised to spend at
least ten pounds as agreed.[39] Davidson had also cautioned
Richards against publishing the book during the obsequies
of the Queen, who had died the week previously. His reasons for this request are not clear, but he may have
feared that the press and public would overlook the play
in the excitement. It is not likely that he would have been
deterred by the unseemliness of bringing out a "revolutionary" work so close upon the event. When his warning

went unheeded, he lamented to the sympathetic Gosse that Richards might as well have put the edition into the furnace: "I have telegraphed to try and stop it; but I am afraid the blunder is irretrievable." [40]

Whether they praised or damned it, thought it suitable for the stage or not, most of the critics agreed that with all its vigor and power *Self's the Man* had serious defects. The plot was mechanically contrived, the characterization shadowy and inconsistent, the humor grotesque, the dialogue crabbed and stilted, and the poetry at times uncouth. The reviewers, still troubled by the strange combination of originality and staleness in his plays, traced his derivation all the way from Massinger and Marston to Beddoes and Willis' *Men of Airlie.* This charge had not become blunt with repetition, and the wounded playwright protested that it was scarcely to the credit of contemporary reviewing that he should have to deny so many times the entirely unfounded accusation of imitativeness.[41] When Gosse in an otherwise laudatory review of *Godfrida* had heard similar echoes, Davidson had disavowed these literary creditors with more tact but equal firmness:

> I suggest that you bring a preconceived theory to my plays. For example I have never read Massinger, or Shirley or Beddoes. I once tried "A New Way to Pay Old Debts," but found it uninteresting, and could not get through the first act. My first published play "An Unhistorical Pastoral" was written before I knew any Jacobean writer except, of course, Shakespeare— Jacobean, by the time-illusion for a dozen years. It was my third attempt at a pastoral, its predecessors having been burnt; and it is out of my own writing that any development has come, my "looseness" and "dullness" being original and not the result of imitation.[42]

It was the alert and accurate critic of the *Athenaeum* who, groping for further analogues, saw in Davidson a striking similarity to the Spasmodic school of poetry. Comparing *Self's the Man* and Alexander Smith's *A Life-Drama,* he concluded that "the palm must be awarded to the earlier poet." [43]

Both the critics and Davidson were right, they in discovering a close resemblance to his romantic predecessors, he in denying a major or conscious debt to them. In various *obiter dicta* he showed or claimed knowledge of Marlowe, Chapman, Kyd, and Jonson, as well as Shakespeare; and his indebtedness to the Spasmodic school has already been documented. Like many undisciplined talents, Davidson's was instinctively imitative. He was attracted by the physical vitality and lyricism of the Elizabethans, although their influence in later years was largely filtered through his more immediate romantic progenitors, notably the Spasmodics and Swinburne. Conversely he was unsympathetic to the contemporary vogues for realism, aestheticism, and decadence, although he briefly succumbed to their lure. Marlovian and Spasmodic melodrama lent themselves more readily to his satanic message, one that was as backward-looking as it was forward. He therefore found convenient the device of pouring his own ideas, new and molten as he thought them, into the discarded molds of older authors. As his career developed, his attitude toward borrowed conventions shifted.

In early works and to some extent in the dramatic adaptations and *The Knight of the Maypole* of the present period, he was playfully apologetic or aggressively defiant in his use of romantic convention. With growing confidence and poise, however, he achieved in the best eclogues and ballads of the nineties a unique ironic style by playing off traditional lyric form and myth against his new ideas. Something like this he sought to accomplish by dra-

matic means in *Self's the Man* and other original plays
of this time, but the requirements of a popular theater
coupled with his own absorption in ideas and indifference
to dramatic form obscured his ironic purpose.* Unlike
Shaw and Wilde he was unable to spoof the conventions
of melodrama and romance at the same time that he used
them as vehicles for his ideas and wit. Coming into the
theater at a time when popular taste in romantic and poetic drama had plunged to unprecedented depths, he un-
critically subscribed to this taste instead of contriving a
new set of conventions. In the plays of his third and last
period he employed romantic melodrama with unabashed
seriousness for the single purpose of expounding his synthetic gospel. By then he had become too concerned with
preaching, too bitter and weary from battling mounting
odds, to elevate this overworked genre to a personal style.
It was enough for him that his intellectual vision was
original, honest, modern, and consistent.

5

"Being now under the lash of necessity, and not yet
ready to die, having my Testaments and Tragedies to
write," Davidson later recalled, "I accepted commissions
for adaptations, and in due course made versions of five
foreign dramatic pieces . . . besides writing, also upon
commission, but at my own urgency, two original plays." [44]
Since he does not specify these plays by title and since all
but three of them are apparently lost, it is difficult to identify them with certainty. The poet's will helps, for it mentions the following adaptations which he wished destroyed:
Queen Fiametta, The Children of the King, Fanny Le-

---

* One reviewer of *Self's the Man* puzzled, "It is not clear whether the
play is meant as satire on self . . . or an idealization of it." (*Bookman*
[London], Mar. 1901, pp. 197–8.) Davidson would have replied that it was
neither; it was a statement of self.

grand, The Game of Life, and "a one-act piece from the
French, the title of which I forget: it was produced at the
Court Theatre." [45] *Fanny Legrand: a Dramatic Comment
on Alphonse Daudet's Novel "Sapho,"* reached rehearsal
but was forestalled by Clyde Fitch's adaptation of the same
novel which opened at the Adelphi in May 1902.[46] The
other adaptations have been swallowed up by oblivion.

Having failed to reconcile the requirements of the contemporary London theater and his discordant ideas, Davidson returned in *The Knight of the Maypole, a Comedy in
Four Acts,* to the manner and themes of his early pastoral
comedies. The imitation is a pallid one, without the conviction and liveliness of *An Unhistorical Pastoral* and *A
Romantic Farce.* Its plot, a patchwork of situations from
Measure for Measure and Restoration comedy, could not
be more commonplace and belongs to the degeneration
and provincialism of native English comedy before its
resuscitation by Gilbert, Wilde, and Shaw. Laid in the dissolute days immediately following the return of Charles II
to the throne, the play presents the rivalry of two cousins,
Anthony and Gabriel Ashe, for the estate of their deceased
uncle and the hand of Agnes Grey, the mistress of Rich-
mond Court Palace. The setting may be musty and the
plot creaky, but the characters illustrate Davidsonian weakness and strength. Like Urban of *Self's the Man,* Anthony
is a prototype of the man of power and relentless will who,
by allowing his reason and baser passions to dominate his
natural impulses, destroys rather than fulfills himself.
Gabriel, another nineteenth-century type, is the grandson
of Childe Harold, noble, solitary, melancholy, indomitable.
He is the victim of his own turbulent passions as much as
of the vices and follies of others. Together the two cousins
symbolize the conflict of rationalism and romantic idealism in the nineteenth century and the general failure of the
century to recognize man's full, material being. Thus this

play extends and applies to history an earlier, personal theme, the clash of generations in parent and child. In *The Knight of the Maypole* Davidson does not fuse his type of hero with his type of villain as he does in *Self's the Man* and the *Mammon* plays, because he is describing within the conventions of native comedy traditional man rather than the more fully integrated man. Even the apocalyptic *Mammon* plays depict the violence and brutality of a modern world caught between two warring dispensations. The borrowed convention of the rival cousins in *The Knight of the Maypole* may also symbolize, however unconsciously, the essential ambiguity which Davidson finds in all being and which he sought to subsume in his gospel of scientific monism. Just as the principal male characters in this play look back to those of the pastoral comedies, so Agnes is indistinguishable from Davidson's earlier heroines, who combine gentle domesticity and tender devotion with proud chastity; she does not share the sexual candor and freedom of the later heroines.

For a play that aims at being lighthearted, *The Knight of the Maypole* is solemn fare. It teaches with renewed doggedness that integrity of spirit, no matter how persecuted, will triumph over avarice and cynical indifference. Throughout Gabriel is the conscientious spokesman for self-reliance, the purity and imperishability of love, the cosmic order underlying terrestrial flux, and the privilege of suicide. There is much of the prig in him, as the author's pagan hedonism sours into an ascetic search for suffering and atonement. Ideological and dramatic inconsistencies make the play's message less than convincing. Although Davidson clearly regards the Restoration as an age of carefree hedonism close to his own youthful vision of a happy, natural world, he makes Anthony and King Charles reckless, unscrupulous libertines. At the same time, in order that Gabriel may have his sweetheart and

property restored to him in a final scene, Charles im-
plausibly abandons his pursuit of the heroine.

It is not its ideas which detract from *The Knight of the
Maypole*. Amid the trite sentimentalizing, decrepit humor,
contrived incidents, and straining after quaintness, Davidson's nineteenth-century materialism strikes the reader as
still vigorous. It is rather the gross incongruity and in-
completeness, devoid of wit or persuasion, with which he
joins these ideas to the archaisms of pastoral romance.
Even Davidson came to recognize that somewhere along
the way he had lost faith in ironic neutrality and had
committed himself to arbitrary, final answers irreconcilable with the mirth in sadness of Elizabethan comedy.
Henceforth he turned unswervingly to tragedy and melodrama as more fitting receptacles for his somber view of
life.

The author tells the story of *The Knight of the Maypole,* not without prejudice, in a letter to Grant Richards:

> I wrote it upon my own scenario for Daniel Froh-
> man, in 1890. He wouldn't have it; but produced in
> 1891 "If I were King," following closely the skeleton
> of my play.* I have shown it to Alexander who, of
> course, is not responsible for the similarity which he
> admits. And that is all. I shall say on the fly-leaf of the
> book:
> "This play was written in 1900, and after various
> adventures is now published.
> "All rights, including acting rights, reserved." When
> will you get it out? [47]

* There is a confusion of dates in this letter. Frohman produced J. H.
M'Carthy's *If I Were King* at the Hollis Theater in Boston in Oct. 1901,
with Edward Sothern in the role of François Villon. The play ran in
New York and on tour for two seasons. The London run lasted from
31 Aug. 1902 until Mar. 1903, with George Alexander in the principal role.
In recounting the history of his own play, Davidson must have made the
easy error of writing 1890 and 1891 for 1900 and 1901.

Since *If I Were King,* a successful play by Justin Huntly M'Carthy, was based upon M'Carthy's own novel of the same title, it is highly doubtful that Frohman, however enterprising, was indebted to Davidson's manuscript. The only resemblance, the impersonation of a king by a vagabond, is a cliché of romantic drama that was shared by several other popular works of the time, including *The Prisoner of Zenda, The Mandarin,* and *The Tar and the Tartar.* Davidson found himself in the position of the vendor whose merchandise is for sale on every corner. He did not take the discovery cheerfully and sought comfort in maligning his competitors.

Something of his deep disappointment at the failure of his plays either to reach the Strand or to capture the notice of the reading public is seen from an unusually confiding letter which he had written to Gosse late in December 1900, after completing *The Knight of the Maypole:*

> It is more than kind of you to ask after my affairs. They are anything but flourishing, and will hardly bear speaking of. Since we last corresponded I have written two plays [*Self's the Man* and *The Knight of the Maypole*] and adapted a third—harder to do than the other two together—besides a lot of miscellaneous matter; but none of my hopes ripen—not even the play I wrote most submissively to what I understood to be the conditions of an individual theatre. . . . There is a terrible sentence in George Eliot—the only thing of hers I ever remember, and I do not remember *it* properly; but it means that there are people in whose expression you find it written "sold, but not paid for." With wrinkles of laughter, however, I can still dislimn such an expression. As for my third venture in plays it is a sort of comedy, or as I should like to call it a "serio-comic play"; but it was written when my mind was worn-out and I'm afraid. . . .

Meanwhile my boys are fourteen and twelve; my wife is broken-hearted; and I seem to be dying piece-meal of chagrin.[48]

The disappointment was only partly because of the un-produced plays. Already he had begun in pamphlet form his series of Testaments in blank verse setting forth a gos-pel of materialism and the will to power. *The Testament of a Vivisector* and *The Testament of a Man Forbid* ap-peared in 1901, *The Testament of an Empire-Builder* in 1902. At this time he was still realistic enough not to ex-pect his Testaments and projected tragedies to win him financial security. In a prefatory note to the first of these messianic poems, he had announced that the new statement of materialism which it contained was likely to offend both the religious and the irreligious mind and that it was there-fore addressed only to "those who are willing to place all ideas in the crucible, and who are not afraid to fathom what is subconscious in themselves and others." [49] He looked to his ventures in the commercial theater to pay the way for these unpleasant but remarkable jeremiads. Although the standards at the Lyceum and St. James's were anything but uniformly high, Davidson unfortunately for his own purposes was incapable of meeting the minimum requirements of a popular theater. He had no gift for pot-boiling, and his romantic melodramas, for all their pre-posterousness, are more ambitious and have more literary merit than the tarnished tinsel which they emulated. Fur-thermore he always allowed his eccentric personality and unwelcome ideas to intrude even upon his journeywork. Consequently his contribution to the commercial theater of the turn of the century is abortive and unremembered.

Anxious to finance *The Testament of a Prime Minister* (1904), the fourth in the series, and to abandon the econ-omy of their paper binding for cloth, Davidson proposed to Richards that he publish *The Knight of the Maypole* to produce the necessary money. He predicted that "in spite of its form this comedy has a better chance of selling than anything of mine you have yet published." [50] In view of his account to date, this was not a rash statement; the new play could scarcely do worse. Neither the tone of his letter nor the terms which he asked betrayed any diminution of his robust optimism. Richards' expectations on the other hand no longer rose with each new work, so that the poet was obliged to settle for less than he requested.* The publisher relates in his autobiography that only two of Davidson's books ever paid out-of-pocket expenses: *Fleet Street and Other Poems,* which netted around £15, and *Holiday and Other Poems,* £20. [51]

Published on January 14, 1903, over two years after it had been completed, *The Knight of the Maypole* received scant attention. Formerly critics, although they may have judged his books deficient in merit, had given Davidson serious and generous attention. Now he no longer seemed timely. The gist of the few routine, noncommittal comments which the play evoked was that its author remained one of the few living writers who could produce poetic drama of quality and that his latest work seemed more suited to the stage than his earlier. Since he had attempted without avail to peddle the play to the theater managers, this encouragement must have had for him a hollow ring. The critic for the *Academy* welcomed in the comedy a return to the author's former Elizabethan gaiety in place of the sterner, truculent note of the more recent Testa-

---

* Davidson asked for £25 to account on acceptance of the manuscript, a royalty of 12½%, and "a good plain cloth or buckram binding, white paper, clear bold type." (A.L.S., dated 28 Aug. 1902, from 9 Fairmile Ave., Streatham, P.U.L.) He accepted, however, a paper binding, a 10% royalty, and no advance, although Richards sent him £25 on account of future royalties if any. Typed L.S., from Richards to Davidson, dated 10 Sept. 1902, P.U.L.

ments.[52] For Davidson, to be praised faintly was to be damned indeed; to be congratulated for resuming his Elizabethan style was to have his liver devoured by vultures. Privately he resolved as soon as possible to dedicate himself to original plays in which the modern note and message would be unmistakable and thus to give the public no further occasion for condescending to him. Meanwhile in order to live he awaited still further commissions from the powerful actor-managers.

6

In the spring of 1901 Davidson had accepted from Lewis Waller, who had recently entered the management of the Lyceum Theater, a commission to adapt Hugo's romantic tragedy, *Ruy Blas*. To complete the adaptation as swiftly as possible and collect the fee which was the only incentive for this secondhand merchandising, Davidson allowed himself a busman's holiday in his native Scotland. The steady application and freedom from anxiety which this kind of work required were no longer possible at home. Early in April 1901 he left his family in Streatham, the London suburb in which they had resided since the autumn of 1898, and went to Blairlogie by Stirling in the heart of his beloved Ochils. From there on April 19 he wrote to Richards, "I am here at the foot of a hill called Dunningalt which I shall climb every day when I am not translating Ruy Blas or writing Testaments." [53]

When he returned to England with the finished play is not known, but in November of the following year he again wrote to Richards from Scotland that the production of *Ruy Blas* had been postponed indefinitely. The reason for the postponement was the tremendous success at the Comedy of *Monsieur Beaucaire* by W. E. Henley and R. L. Stevenson in which Waller had the title role.[54] The delay had made it necessary for Davidson to secure still another commission, this time from George Alexander, the actor-manager of St. James's Theater. Reluctantly putting aside his next Testament, that of the Prime Minister, he had hied off in November 1902 to Glenfaulds, Rothesay, where he remained until late the following January. The result of this commission was "Lancelot," an original play which its author always referred to as "my Arthurian play." Alexander rejected the finished work. Knowing Davidson's unconventional interpretation of Arthurian material in his ballads, one can safely guess that "Lancelot," which was never produced and has since disappeared, was not a timid play.

At least one clue remains to indicate why the succession of managers whom Davidson approached with the play declined the opportunity. Less than a year before he died he urged Martin-Harvey to produce "Lancelot," reassuring him and more probably himself, "I know it to be a great play and certain of success: it is easily the chance of your life up to this present. There is no Lancelot but mine." [55] When Harvey replied that he had already "schemed out" his own scenario on the theme and balked at the assumption in Davidson's play of adultery between Lancelot and Guinevere, the dramatist stuck by his guns. He cited the passage—"very detailed too and quite roguish"—in which Malory makes the adultery clear, and concluded with confidence, "No; Mallory [*sic*] leaves no doubt that the queen and Lancelot committed adultery: time, place and the event are precisely stated. But my play is before the event. I disagree with you entirely as to the world's wish in the matter, and am certain it would rejoice in my play." [56] As Harvey remained adamant on this point, negotiations collapsed.

To date the unfortunate playwright had written at least eight dramas for the Strand, four of them original, of which only two or three adaptations had seen production.

His next published work, which with tongue in cheek he irreverently called *A Rosary,* was little more than a strand of unmatched, bright beads for trading with the barbaric public. Designed to produce the funds by which he might write the tragedies and Testaments laboring to be born, *A Rosary* was a miscellany of "incident, fable, parable, re-mark, conversation, prose and poetry." He proposed to Richards that he publish it, asking £30 in advance and explaining that the £200 received from Waller as an ad-vance on *Ruy Blas* had been eaten up by the expenses of his stay in Scotland and by delays in production. The £30 would release him from worry and enable him to write his "Testament of a Prime Minister," still in incubation.[57] When Richards suggested a cheap edition and no advance, he reckoned without the wrath of a writer scorned. David-son protested that a pasteboard cover like that he had given *The Knight of the Maypole* was "immoral, inartistic, unbusiness-like, unsaleable and in every way undesirable, a piece of false economy," and added:

> I am not anxious to publish the book: I wanted money or I would not have thought of it. Since you did not think it worth an advance I honestly think now that the best plan would be to return it to me. Isn't there a business saying "cut losses"? You showed me an ac-count that wasn't pleasant. My "Testaments" are a dif-ferent matter of course; loss or no loss, they are worth any man's while to publish; but the only excuse for the publication of "A Rosary" is that it should sell: it is evident that you don't think it will, therefore I say don't publish.[58]

In spite of this magnanimous gesture, Richards even more magnanimously published *A Rosary* with a cloth binding in the autumn of 1903. Although one reviewer found it "thorough Davidson . . . strong, and perverse, and racy, and original, and combatant as an Irishman at Donnybrook Fair," [59] this collection of odds and ends of string from his journalistic output was scarcely more successful than its predecessor, *Sentences and Paragraphs* (1893), which had the worst reception and smallest sale of all his works.

September and October of 1903 found the struggling adapter once more "on holiday" at Blairlogie, this time making a version of Racine's *Phèdre* for Mrs. Patrick Campbell, who desired to emulate Sarah Bernhardt's historic performance of the title role in 1872. In her memoirs the actress explains that she never produced the play because of Davidson's wish, expressed in his will, that no dramatic work of his ever again be presented. Although she recalls, in the grand and gracious manner of a first lady, that Davidson and she were "very friendly" and that others did not realize his gifts as she did, she leaves unexplained her failure to produce the play during the author's lifetime.[60] His version of *Phèdre* has never been produced or published. If Davidson despised the business of adapting, he must have hoped all the more that a repetition of the commercial success of *For the Crown* would relieve him of this drudgery.

The effort and time wasted upon these abortive commissions for Alexander and Mrs. Campbell increased the poet's anxiety for the success of his *Ruy Blas* which, two years after it had been written, still waited in the wings. Writing Richards from Blairlogie on October 4, 1903, he cheerfully suggested that *Ruy Blas* be printed and copyrighted in America, "and when Waller plays it triumphantly throughout the States, there will be plenty of sale for it, if not before." Meanwhile the play was to appear at the Imperial, but *Beaucaire*, its inexorable nemesis, had preceded it there in early November and was again holding up production.[61] Rehearsals finally began in December 1903, and Davidson was elated that Mrs. Camp-

bell had been engaged to play the part of the queen, a
trump card calculatingly kept secret from the press, but
not for long.[62] Three weeks before opening night the
brokers had bought up £2,000 of tickets. The success of
For the Crown and the report that "the incomparable
Mrs. Pat" was to play a leading role undoubtedly spurred
the sale. For his part Davidson was eager that the publication of the book shortly after the opening night also
prosper. With unusual self-effacement he struck out the
main part of his introductory note in which he bragged
about his other plays, deciding that this was "too cock-
a-hoop." [63] And he cautioned Richards against sending review copies to the *Outlook,* the *Guardian,* and the *Saturday Review,* in the hope that this would avert the trounc-
ing that these periodicals had given his previous plays.[64]

About the middle of February 1904 the long postponed
production took place, with Davidson's version of Hugo's
play re-entitled *A Queen's Romance.* Mrs. Campbell remembered it, perhaps with a charity that began at home,
as "a fine translation" and "a generous production" but
also recollected that "the critics found it tedious." "This,"
she wrote, "was tragic for John Davidson, who had put
some of his best work into the play." It was the first time
that Mrs. Campbell had appeared with Lewis Waller, and
there was some severe criticism of their excellent but completely divergent styles of acting. The actress, not distinguished for her professional modesty, explained disarmingly, "The reason I would give is that Mr. Waller addressed his blank verse to the universe; I spoke my blank
verse to him." [65] If her accusation is true, Waller may have
taken his cue from the author himself.

Killed by the critics, the much touted play ran only a
fortnight in spite of its initial financial success and a favorable reception by the opening-night audience. Davidson received from the production no more than his £200

advance, which he had long since spent. It would be a pleasant act of mercy to attribute the failure of *A Queen's Romance* to the jealousy and lack of harmony between the two principals, but the trouble went deeper than this. By condensing the play from five acts to three, changing the motivation of the characters, and reversing the order of scenes, the adapter had tried with the best of intentions to make the piece less inflated and preposterous. This had been a serious mistake. Where the new version was shorter, simpler, less operatic, and in some ways less tedious, it lacked the grandeur and heroic nonsense of Hugo's romantic balderdash. In spite of his precaution in not sending the *Saturday Review* an advance copy, it was precisely this criticism of the adaptation which his fellow-Bodleian, Max Beerbohm, made of it in his refreshing column:

> But a dramatic romance by Victor Hugo, with sober blank verse instead of its own intoxicated alexandrines, and with a cast of mimes who (for the most part) have neither the training nor the innate sense for the art of declamation, or for those beautiful extravagances of port and gesture which are of the essence of romantic acting—ah, show me where, in the whole range of our depressing native drama, I need go in fear of a more depressing phenomenon than this! . . . It matters not at all whether Mr. John Davidson, adapting and abbreviating "Ruy Blas" for home consumption, have or have not made it less credible by this or that compression. The point is that he has transferred a wild and inflated lie from a plane where we could accept it and revel in it to a plane where we must needs reject it with a yawn. I do not say that he could have done his work better. I do say that he ought not to have done it at all.[66]

Betrayed by his insularity and predilection for propaganda, Davidson had ignored the dramatic tradition in which Hugo was writing.

William Archer, as defendant of a realistic prose drama, took a different tack, condeming Hugo's *Ruy Blas* as absurdly and dangerously romantic. Then, in a curious about-face, he castigated Davidson for taking excessive liberties with the original. The outraged Scot replied with an open letter:

> You begin with a general attack on *Ruy Blas* as a vicious production of French Romanticism; and with that I have no quarrel. I love the theme; but not Victor Hugo's play. . . . [a] huge amorphous medley . . . a monstrosity impossible in any theatre. . . . I have nothing to say in defence of *Ruy Blas*. When, however, you extend your attack to *A Queen's Romance,* I wish to record my opinion, that in my adaptation I have smelted out of the impossible *Ruy Blas* a possible English play.[67]

By this he meant that he had transformed Hugo's romantic hero into a passionate Davidsonian egoist, and Hugo's tragedy of miscarried love into a play with materialist overtones. This alien matter apparently irritated a number of playgoers. On the opening night when Mrs. Campbell as the queen addressed the image of the Virgin with the words, "Mother, which art in Heaven," several women in the gallery hissed. If there had been a less commanding actress on the stage, Davidson later recalled, "the whole gallery would have caught it up in a species of panic." [68] In endeavoring to make *Ruy Blas* plausible and significant to a contemporary British audience, Davidson had only made it literary and didactic, thereby pleasing no one. To be sure, eight years earlier he had treated Coppée's play in the same manner with some success, but this was because he had exercised far less freedom and trifled with

a minor rather than a major work of its kind. Ibsen and
Strindberg, among other Continental dramatists, had discovered that historic intrigue and Hugoesque romance
did not lend themselves to middle-class tragedy. Although
Davidson shared with these playwrights their frank subjectivism, poetic symbolism, and preocupation with the
conflict of wills, he lacked their capacity to experiment
with the new techniques of naturalism and expression-
ism and their readiness to explore the bourgeois mentality.

In public the disappointed playwright bore a stalwart
front, but his profound despondency over the failure of
Ruy Blas is revealed in a letter which he wrote at this time
to Mrs. Grant Richards, declining an invitation:

> I am more perplexed in many ways than I have ever
> been in my life.
>
> "If ever fate implacably decreed
> A man's destruction and eternal death
> That man am I and that lost soul is mine,"
>
> as Ruy Blas says.[69]

Davidson now gave up all hope of achieving financial security as an adapter in the London theater. When Waller
suggested some years later that they again collaborate in
a play, the poet wrote to Richards, "I shall have to if we
can agree; but what a task of Sisyphus I am set!" [70] Apparently they could not agree or Davidson's hatred of this
kind of potboiling got the better of him, because he never
again undertook adapting successful foreign plays and
only once more wrote an original drama intended for
production.

7

During these fruitless years of writing plays to order,
the poet was endeavoring to lead a double life. In a succession of long Testaments in blank verse he continued to

set forth his personal declaration of independence from
the past and his annunciation of a new millennial order
based on materialism. At the same time, to subsidize these
and other serious works he was expending most of his
energy on adaptations and original plays for which he had
little inclination or which resisted stubbornly his real purpose. It is doubtful if any serious writer can maintain for
long and at the same time two distinct identities. Davidson's personal evangel of self-reliance, heroic suffering, and
the purity of love had asserted itself from the first in his
commissioned plays. When it became evident that this
expedient served no purpose, he dropped the role of popular playwright for one more natural.

Still torn between the desire to state his message in un-
shackled blank verse and the necessity to earn his daily
bread, the poet in desperation had written to Richards in
April 1902 to tell him of another stratagem:

> I am full of blank verse. I want to write. I began
> writing blank verse out of sheer *ennui* on Sundays
> when I was twelve: I am now in the same instinctive
> mood, although not from ennui—"Matter knows!" as
> the Lion says.* Is there no editor of a daily who would
> give me two guineas a day for an actual poem—not
> on current topics: that is so stupid—but an actual
> poem in the only form in which actual poetry can be
> written, English blank verse; my own poetry, not the
> editor's poetry, nor the public's poetry, but my poetry.
> Twenty lines less or more, never *less* than the length
> of a sonnet, of magnificent blank verse every morn-
> ing with my signature, large type and well-spaced.
> . . . is there no editor with the courage, ambition
> and wisdom to try that for a year—or a quarter? [71]

---

* For the allusion to the Lion, see *The Testament of an Empire-Builder*
(London, Grant Richards, 1902), p. 39.

On the following day he had viewed the idea more objectively and expressed the grim doubt that any editor would entertain such a proposal from him. Why had he acted impulsively?

> The thing trickled off my pen yesterday morning in a fit [of] despondency. I was forty-five three days ago, and have lying by me four unpublished plays three of which are highly regarded by those they were written for, and their production promised and announced: yet there they are no nearer the footlights. There is no language for the intense chagrin of this.[72]

Although he did occasionally write blank-verse poems for the periodicals, he abandoned the project of a daily poem. He could not keep up a series of poems the content of which must please; he confessed furthermore to a consuming desire to state the evil of the world as well as the good and should need a free hand to do this. The *Chronicle,* it was true, had printed his chauvinistic "Ode on the Coronation of Edward VII," but only because the full meaning of that poem lay beneath the surface and had not been detected by the editor.[73]

Everything to which the poet had set his hand in order to earn a respectable living had failed. It was apparently with the intention of writing what he pleased, as he pleased, and for whom he pleased that he undertook a play on commission from Bernard Shaw. When it came to the test, the temptation to write once more something that might pay proved too strong. Long after Davidson's death Shaw recounted the circumstances to Grant Richards:

> He told me he could not afford to write the great drama he had in his head on this subject because it would make no money and he had to drudge at journalism to support himself and his people. I asked him

how long it would take him to write the poem, and
how much he could earn by journalism in that time.
He said six months and £250, to be repaid out of
half his royalties (if any) on the poem. He took the
money, and gratefully resolved that he would enrich
me for my generosity. So instead of writing the great
poem he wrote what he thought would be a popular
melodrama with millions in it. I believe I have a copy
of this abortion somewhere.[74]

Shaw states elsewhere that the poet wrote the play for him
"a few years before he died." In this letter he asserted with
egocentric disregard for facts that when Davidson discovered he had done neither Shaw nor himself any good,
he committed suicide.*

The playwright's curtain speech to the London stage is
his next drama, *The Theatrocrat, a Tragic Play of Church
and State,* which he began writing in 1904 and which was
published late in 1905. It contains his reply to the theater
managers, critics, and playgoers alike. Promising at the
outset a merciless attack upon the decadence and commercialism of the contemporary theater and English society, the dramatic parable soon degenerates into absurd
melodrama and personal diatribe. Through this work
Davidson does not so much dramatize the decay of Christian civilization as vent the frustrations, grudges, and defeats that made up his experience in the theater. At the
same time the ironist is careful to have his characters
speak with rapture of the intermittent joys, triumphs, and
professional dedication of the actor which symbolize those
of every man's life. In spite of an effort to constrain or
conceal the subjective element, *The Theatrocrat,* like the
early Spasmodic plays to which it is spiritually akin, is

* In reply to my inquiry addressed to Shaw in Dec. 1948, Dr. F. E.
Lowenstein, his amanuensis, wrote that he could find no copy of the commissioned play and repeated Shaw's account of its composition.

charged with a telltale animus. The central conflict of the play, the sexual alienation and estrangement of the actor-manager Sir Tristram Sumner and his wife, culminating in their divorce, has the insistent ring of personal relevance. This is not to say that the plot of *The Theatrocrat* alludes to specific marital difficulties in the author's life. For all the confessional strain in Davidson's writing, his circumspect nature obliged him, even when poetic impulse failed, to find more convincing camouflage for personal problems. It is far more likely that Sir Tristram's broken marriage, like his professional fiasco, projects the author's private sense of general failure as husband, playwright, and literary personality. Moreover, Sir Tristram's predicament has in Davidson's thought a universal relevance. Sexual triumph and defeat are for the poet turned philosopher more than dramatic symbols of some other triumph or defeat; success or failure in one sphere invariably accompanies success or failure in all other spheres. Sexual failure and professional failure are inseparable in *The Theatrocrat* as in life. The materialist no longer distinguishes clearly between his symbols and the ideas which they represent; for him they share the same reality. Like the monsters pictured on medieval maps of unexplored regions, the ugly, obscene episodes in Davidson's late works lose their significance as symbols of the spiritual and psychological trials that await the adventurous voyager and become themselves ultimate realities. In its imaginative method *The Theatrocrat* belongs with the perversely literal, primitive allegories of the poet's final period, with which it will be discussed further.

8

An incorrigibly romantic nature and personal bitterness had made Davidson insensitive to shifting tastes in drama as well as to the fundamental requirements of the theater.

Since the "cup and saucer" plays of Tom Robertson, English *avant-garde* playwrights had been turning to the contemporary scene, social problems, and realism. After the
introduction of Ibsen by Edmund Gosse in the seventies
and his popularization by Archer, Shaw, and others in the
eighties and nineties, the movement had gained impetus.[75]
The opening scenes of *The Theatrocrat* recall the method
and subject matter of Ibsen's early plays but achieve only
a muddy copy of his peculiar blend of symbolism and romantic melodrama.[76] There is nothing of Ibsen's later symbolic realism in Davidson's plays. In the prose prologue to
Godfrida the Scottish romantic had expressed his fear that
any step forward from Ibsen would only land him in some
mystical abyss or the slough of naturalism.[77] Exercising
more parochial bias than critical judgment, he clung to the
rhetorical, declamatory style of Byron, Shelley, Bulwer-
Lytton, Tennyson, and Swinburne. The outrages perpetrated in the name of Shakespeare by these poets turned
playwrights and their imitators have earned their dramatic
works a long and merciful oblivion.

If a revolution was taking place in the theater, it was an
English revolution, leisurely and relatively unbloody. A
glance at the successful runs of the turn of the century
reveals that the contest between the Ancients and Moderns
for possession of the theater was protracted and that for
some time the two sides appeared to be evenly matched.
During the middle nineties the great resurgence of romantic historical drama had brought it abreast of the new
middle-class problem plays. Henry Irving, who did little
or nothing for modern drama, won his greatest acclaim in
Tennyson's *Becket;* he was making a triumphal tour in a
revival of the play when he died in 1905. The reaction of
the middle class against the airing in public of its soiled,
cumbersome linen and the influence of the great actor-
managers prolonged beyond their natural span the three

THE ANCIENTS AND MODERNS 335

R's of nineteenth-century theater—rhetoric, romance, and ruins. Moreover, the sensational success of Stephen Phillips' poetic dramas, the innovations in stage design of Gordon Craig, and the twilight world of Maeterlinck and the Irish playwrights indicate that the spirit of poetic drama was still alive, as does the crude but virile symbolism of *The Theatrocrat* and the subsequent *Mammon* plays. Davidson was defeated as much by his persistence in using popular melodrama and historical romance as vehicles for his thorny ideas as by the fickle winds of dramatic fashion. In France, Germany, Scandinavia, or possibly at home in Scotland, he might have found an atmosphere more salutary to his thoughtful poetic symbolism and, prospering, have avoided the lure of worldly success and the cliffy refuge of ideas for the higher satisfaction of writing good works. In spite of a clinging provincialism, he has literary affinities and epic ambitions that place him in the company of Ibsen, Nietzsche, Georg Brandes, Stefan George, and René Ghil. But speculation is the biographer's own lure and refuge and is better avoided. This much may be said of Davidson's later plays: The importance and force of their ideas distinguish them from most romantic drama of the day and consign them to a special limbo, where they must await resurrection and final judgment when a poetic drama once more enters the popular theater.

The Scot's contentious personality had promised tragedy from the outset. It was not until the last half decade of his life, however, that he lost his resiliency and became haunted by failure. Out of regard for the needs of his family he had made valiant if futile efforts to meet popular demands in literature and the theater. What this cost his fierce pride and integrity can be measured by the belligerent individualism of his final works in which he dropped once and for all any pretense of supplying the market.

8

REBELLION AND
DEFEAT, 1901-06

It always creates the world in its own
image; it cannot do otherwise; philosophy
is this tyrannical impulse itself, the
most spiritual Will to Power, the will to
"creation of the world," the will to the
causa prima.

Friedrich Nietzsche

During the last decade of his life, from
1901 to 1909, Davidson wrote five Testaments and three
poetic tragedies. Each of these works states unequivocally,
repetitiously, and vituperatively his letter to the world.
The Testaments, long polemics in inflated blank verse
disguised as dramatic monologues, are *The Testament of
a Vivisector* (1901), *of a Man Forbid* (1901), *of an Empire-
Builder* (1902), *of a Prime Minister* (1904), and finally,
The Testament of John Davidson (1908). Thus, chrono-
logically four of the five Testaments dovetail with the
theatrical period just under discussion. Logically they
embody the spiritual rebellion and emancipation of the
final years. The three poetic dramas of this period are *The
Theatrocrat* (1905), *The Triumph of Mammon* (1907),
and *Mammon and His Message* (1908). All of these works
were published by Grant Richards. The two *Mammon*

plays were part of a projected trilogy, *God and Mammon,* which was to contain the full and final statement of the poet's philosophy but which he did not live to complete. In reality these plays add little to what he had already stated or implied in the Testaments and elsewhere, but they do formulate with lurid and tiresome explicitness his blasphemous gospel of sexuality, primitivism, science, and power—a perverted religion of humanity.

The first of the dramatic monologues, *The Testament of a Vivisector,* is a shocking, brutal poem in which a vivisector expounds his materialist doctrines. In gruesome detail the spokesman-scientist recounts how he dissected without anesthesia the spinal column of a dying hack in order to discover the secret of life. While this description has the horrible fascination and unreality of the Grand Guignol or the torture chambers of Mme. Tussaud's waxworks, it is the poem's message which is relentlessly haunting. The vivisector regards both himself and his tormented victim as necessary, involuntary instruments in the service of raw, unconscious matter. The driving impulse of matter is toward consciousness and self-consciousness at any cost. By self-consciousness Davidson means the conscious knowledge by the universe of its origin, nature, and destiny as monistic and material. Pain is an inseparable condition of this blind lust for self-knowledge. In the final analysis, the vivisector discovers, pain and pleasure "differ in function by a jot, perhaps." Although matter created human thought to achieve its will for higher consciousness, thought occasionally seeks escape from pain in the fictions of Christianity and other religions. Inevitably some reliant thinker, "hateful to God and to God's enemies," appears to lead thought back to the purpose of its creator.[1] Pity, usefulness, the relief of human suffering are irrelevant considerations in matter's groping for higher knowledge and organization.

Davidson had implied this principle of pain in lyrics going back six and seven years. What is new in this first Testament is the incorporation of ideas adopted earlier with his final materialist synthesis and a prosaic, explicit style.

No poet of the time was more unlike Davidson than Francis Thompson, yet no contemporary wrote about his work of this period with as much intelligence. Davidson often found the greatest understanding and tolerance of his views not among the freethinkers and avowed atheists, who distorted his position to fit their own, but among orthodox Christians, especially Catholic writers like Chesterton, Lionel Johnson, and Thompson. If their ideal was Christocentric rather than anthropocentric or simply egocentric, they shared their fellow poet's dogmatism and semimystic emotionality. Davidson's faith was little more than a traceable aberration from their own. Entitling his review of *The Testament of a Vivisector* "A Thesis in Verse," Thompson hailed its author as a true poet, powerful, resolutely himself, gifted at seizing the poetic element from the ugliness of modern life, but brightest and best when he concentrated upon country sights and sounds as he had in his lyrics and eclogues. Preoccupation with thought was endangering his poetry. Thompson with others found a comparison of the new poem with Browning's inescapable. If Browning's characters were heightened and oversubtle, they were at least thinkable; but Davidson's vivisector was beyond reason and imagination. Where Browning's verse in similar psychological portraits had been tough and sinewy, Davidson's possessed "a Tennysonian linearity and languor which, in conjunction with its purposed prosaic character, often begot a horrible semblance of journalese chopped in lengths, like treacly coffee or strings of molasses." Through sheer authenticity of emotion and vital adequacy the poet here and there, almost by accident, achieved distinguished utterance "without an image, without a phrase which you can pluck off and hold up for detached admiration as poetry." But no poet who was an artist externally and apart from inspiration would juxtapose elevated with commonplace speech, leaving the juxtaposition uncorrected as if unscious of it.[2] Overlooking the precedent of Whitman, Thompson in spite of his measured judgment had missed Davidson's naïve purpose. To capture the rawness and inconsistency of reality, the poet of the universe thought it sufficient to write rawly, inconsistently. Furthermore, in the interest of clarity and ease of composition he increasingly transposed his ideas from earlier versions in prose or from their rational formulation in his mind without subjecting them to poetic refinement and compression.[3]

The hero of the next Testament, that of *A Man Forbid*, also published in 1901, is for all his post-Darwinian jargon a superannuated Byronic rebel who urges the world to divorce itself from the philosophy, art, and religion of the past. Absurd as this figure is, he speaks his Lucretian message in a few passages of rapturous blank verse:

Undo the past!
The rainbow reaches Asgard now no more;
Olympus stands untenanted; the dead
Have their serene abode in earth itself,
Our womb, our nurture, and our sepulchre.
Expel the sweet imaginings, profound
Humanities and golden legends, forms
Heroic, beauties, tripping shades, embalmed
Through hallowed ages in the fragrant hearts
And generous blood of men; the climbing thoughts
Whose roots ethereal grope among the stars,
Whose passion-flowers perfume eternity,
Weed out and tear, scatter and tread them down;
Dismantle and dilapidate high heaven.[4]

Like others among Davidson's nihilistic heroes who seek
to convert the world, the man forbid is stoned and driven
out of society. Lapidation obsessed Davidson because of
its ironic association with Christian martyrdom and its
telluric symbolism: "earth to earth." The Testament concludes with a glorious hymn to the beauty and peace that
the martyr-hero finds in nature and with his vision of the
earth returning to the sun to be consumed in flames.

In briefer notices than usual the critics agreed that,
while it contained nothing so fine as the conclusion of the
Vivisector, the second Testament showed unmistakable
signs of improvement. In the opinion of one it was the
best thing that Davidson had done.[5] Another thought it
less involved and dialectical in argument than the first,
less turgid and violent in expression; in other words, it
was more genuinely dramatic and poetic. Nevertheless
this reviewer deplored the new speculative, strenuous
vein and called upon the poet to return to the lyric grace
of the ballads and eclogues.[6] To this Davidson might
have countered, as he had already implied in his works,
that he was an older man, that as with Wordsworth the
"aching joys" and "dizzy raptures" were now no more.*

* John A. Lester Jr., writing of Davidson's fear of encroaching inadequacy as a poet, finds that "chill despair first strikes" in the eclogue
"Lammas" (1895). ("Prose-Poetry Transmutation in John Davidson," p. 40.)
This may be the first instance in which the poet publicly recognizes that
the fear has become a reality, but he had been tormented by the prospect
of extinguished genius throughout his adult life. As early as *Smith,* written
in 1886, the poet Hallowes voices this anxiety:

> To sink to that inanity abhorred,
> The wretch whose early fervour, burnt away,
> Leaves him, for lack of ease to smite his thought
> To white-heat—since the brazier of youth,
> That needs no sweat, is cold. . . .
> Maybe to live on grudging charity
> Of friends estranged; sneered at by smug success;
> Called poetaster: such had been my life;
> But I have chosen death.
>
> *(Plays,* pp. 238–9.)

The delight in the sights and sounds of nature which had been the source of Wordsworth's pantheism also contributed to Davidson's naturalism and later to his materialism. It was not so much the message as the savage, bombastic manner in which it was delivered that revealed the Scottish poet's tormented, exhausted mind.

In 1902 Richards brought out the third in the series of dramatic reveries, *The Testament of an Empire-Builder.* Up to this point there had been considerable confusion in the minds of readers about Davidson's intention in these poems. Were they ironical satires upon advanced views of the day? Were they objective psychological studies? Or did they express seriously Davidson's personal creed? Among less alert critics there had been those who had mistaken the first Testament for antivivisectionist propaganda. James Douglas, writing in the sporting newspaper, the *Star,* had congratulated the poet for attacking "an infamy too gross for the common terms of scorn and contempt and abhorrence." [7] Others, equally puzzled but more cautious, had adopted a policy of watchful waiting in the hope that future Testaments would make the poet's purpose more clear. Such mystification obscured the issue, for Davidson was not primarily concerned with the ethics of vivisection, imperialism, and other fashionable causes. As in his novels and stories, he was exploiting their current *réclame* to make his own lofty commentary upon the nature of experience and the universe. Davidson was as mystified by the critics' confusion as they were by his Testaments. In reply to a puzzled inquiry from Archer, he wrote from Blairlogie:

You see I am out of humanity's reach. . . .

I have no idea where to begin or what to say as you state only a general difficulty. My notion of the Vivisector is an imaginative one although I had in

mind such Titans as Magendie, Bernard, Mantegazza.*
I do not concern myself with the ordinary Vivisector
who cuts up a dog or two in an underground room in
a College because he believes it to be the thing to do
just as the country curate will go to the *foyer* of the
Empire when he visits London because he thinks he
is "seeing life"; but the passionate, obsessed giant,
hating religion, despising the "humanities," searching into the secrets of Nature in his bloody way
with the patience, delight, and self-torture of the
artist, until the commonplace of the philosopher, that
pain is normal and pleasure little more than an
accident, flashes upon him with overwhelming meaning, and the whole Universe which he identifies with
Matter becomes to him a reservoir of pain—an universe [*sic*] blind, dumb, unconscious artist, seeking
for self-knowledge and expression at the cost of any
agony. The poem is artistic, i.e. it [is] a statement of
the Vivisector (the spin of a penny determined
whether I should call the poems statements or testaments) not a condemnation or a criticism of him,
but a dramatic account of him without any intention on the author's part to persuade the world for or
against.—But all this may be beside the mark. If you
were to ask me a question I would try to answer it.[8]

* François Magendie (1783–1855), French physiologist and professor of
pathology in the Collège de France; investigator of motor and sensory
functions of the spinal roots; teacher of Claude Bernard.

Claude Bernard (1813–78), French physiologist and first occupant of
chair of physiology at the Sorbonne, for whom Louis Napoleon built the
first experimental laboratory. His *Introduction à la medicine expérimentale*
(1865) profoundly influenced Taine, Zola, and the French naturalistic
novelists.

Paolo Mantegazza (1831–1900), Italian physiognomist, physiologist, an-
thropologist; founder in Florence of the first museum of anthropology in
Italy, the Italian Anthropological Society, and the *Archivo per l'Antropolo-
gia e l'Etnologia;* author of many treatises; deputy and senator in the
Italian Parliament, 1865–76.

With the *Empire-Builder* there could be no mistaking
his clearly stated position for a jest or psychological character study. The issue was now in the open, the challenge
could not be ignored: Was poetry so unmistakably sermonic really poetry? And was Davidson's scientific, amoral
monism an acceptable faith?

The Testament of an Empire-Builder consists in the
main of two dream visions, loosely related by their oc-
currence in the mind of the same person, an imperialist,
and by their common theme. This theme is the repudiation of established moral values and the advocacy of an im-
perialistic civilization based boldly upon a lust for power
instead of a sanctimonious pretension to benevolence. In
the first vision a convocation of beasts, free of human
prejudice and fear, discusses uninhibitedly the nature of
the gods, evolution, the extinction of species, and man's
convenient fictions of soul and conscience. The allegorical
poem thus has a place with Kipling's *Jungle Books,* Orwell's
Animal Farm, and Thurber's *Fables for Our Times* in the
history of the modern satiric animal fable. As in the fantasies of Swift and Orwell, Davidson's animals do not
represent the fixed types of human folly and vice found
in Aesop and La Fontaine but herald a civilization chastened by decay and death. In its comments on this civilization Davidson's menagerie implies that man by inventing
a tyrannical soul may come to share the animals' enslavement and extinction, but that, if he wishes, he can avoid
this fate. Unlike most Utopian literature, which in William
Morris, Samuel Butler, Shaw, Davidson, and James Barrie
enjoyed a modern revival, the *Empire-Builder* is neither
pessimistic nor hopeful; it accepts an ironic universe.

The empire-builder's second vision is one of a heaven
and hell in which the Christian notion of these places is
reversed. To carry the heresy further, the poem makes it
clear that these supposed afterworlds are no more than

fictions for physical and psychological states. In these respects it recalls the more familiar third act of Shaw's *Man and Superman,* which follows it in publication by a year. No writer of the time had a monopoly on the device of the ironic reversal, for its effectiveness had been demonstrated by writers ranging from Butler to Lewis Carroll. Davidson's heaven is a gathering place of all humanity but especially the vital, active, ruthless people. Hell is made up of the altruists, agnostics, dreamers, cripples, cowards,

> And all deniers of the will to live,
> And all who shunned the strife for wealth and power:
> For every soul that had been damned on earth
> Was damned in Hell . . .

As the poem concludes, the speaker with evangelical fervor applies his conception of heaven and hell to this life and to England's imperial destiny:

> The English Hell
> For ever crowds upon the English Heaven.
> Secure your birthright; set the world at naught;
> Confront your fate; regard the naked deed;
> Enlarge your Hell; preserve it in repair;
> Only a splendid Hell keeps Heaven fair.[9]

Again Davidson is doing no more than adapting the theme of such earlier lyrics as "A Ballad of Heaven," "A Ballad of a Nun," and "Lammas" to his fully emergent materialism and chauvinism. With the waning of his energies and inspiration, he turns increasingly to the poetry and prose of his more fertile years for subject matter and ideas with which to buttress his tower of Nineveh.

The third Testament in the series is striking for its adaptation of the medieval animal fable, debate, and dream

vision to an ultramodern message and for its apocalyptic
character. It also suggests some deference on the part of
the author to Dante's vivid picturemaking and Bunyan's
simplicity of phrase. The traditional hell for which the
protagonist searches is described so vividly as to give the
lie to Davidson's insistence that there is no such place:

> I looked,
> And looked again to see the City of Dis
> Where heretics their heresies regret,
> Or scorn eternal pain, regretting nought,
> Entombed in sepulchres of fire, unpaved
> Till judgment, to be sealed for ever then;
> Or the deep-sighing forest ominous
> Where suicides like thorns and briars grow,
> Uncouth and barren wildings, rookery
> Obscene of mongrel birds; or to o'erhear
> That storm instinct with lamentation shrill,
> Where souls of tender lovers whirled about
> In utter darkness on the unstable air,
> Uplift unhallowed voices loud against
> The withering blast and terror of their flight.[10]

The hell which the empire-builder does behold is less
Dantesque than decadent: a pulsating cliff made up tier
on tier of the bodies of the damned whose eyes glare and
whose distended mouths shriek in turn as a "celestial
figure" operates a torture instrument in the form of a huge,
jeweled keyboard. Mellowed by distance, the unspeakable
music which results is akin to the music of the spheres.
Both scenes reveal something of Davidson's original gift
for vivid description and powerful fantasy, but they have
nothing of the compression, formal ordering, and melodic
counterpoint which mark his best lyrics. They bespeak a
resurgence in the poet of the evangelical stridency and
looseness of line found in the Spasmodic plays.

The Testament of an Empire-Builder is prefaced by a
remarkably prophetic "Parable" in which the author replies to those very critics who wish him to return to the
manner and content of his early lyrics. The Protagonist
of the parable explains to an assembled multitude, "I am
dissatisfied with the old songs and wish to sing new ones":

> With that they held their peace and listened atten-
> tively, and often with approval, because the new songs,
> like the old, contained many expressions of delight
> and hope. Besides it was exactly the superficial com-
> plexion of things that this people, like most peoples,
> loved to contemplate. Wherefore when pain and ter-
> ror, which are the blood and nerve, the entrails and
> inmost complexion of the world, began more fully to
> inform the Protagonist's songs, the people bade him
> cease.
>
> "We want the old songs," they cried. "The old
> lullabies, the old flatteries; our hearts ache for these;
> we never tire of these."

Explaining that he has known the dark places of life with
their solitude, travail, and pain as well as the joyful,
sunny places, the Protagonist persists in singing his new
songs. He also announces his intention of telling even
more Testaments, of "the Harlot, the Artist, the Christian,
the Mendicant, the Criminal, the Millionaire, the Proletarian, the Convertite, the Evolutionist, the Deliverer,
and others that are eager to be told." This is too much;
the majority of his audience leave and those who remain
stone the speaker to death saying, "We are only trying to
make out your meaning," and blaming it on "the Nature
of Things." Immediately they regret his death and wonder
what the unfinished Testaments were to be about. An
ancient man, who had thrown the first stone, tells them

that the poems were part of one great song, that to hear its name is to desire to sing it, but that no man will be permitted to do so: This too is "the Nature of Things." [11]

The third Testament attracted greater notice than the two preceding. In spite of its excessive length and tendency to break up into unrelated parts, it was the most imaginative and compelling so far in the series. Moreover its stratagem was apparent to all and therefore invited comment. Discussion centered not on its merits as poetry but on the poem's sensational ideas and the poet's right to air them. A few, like the reviewer for the *Manchester Guardian,* applauded the poet for flushing the polite imperialist and found the empire-builder's rejection of the comfortable euphemisms about evolution and the white man's burden serious and arresting.[12] James Douglas again enthusiastically if ineptly hailed Davidson as "the first poet to digest the new wonders of science which have subtly changed the old cosmogony, and made the very foundations of existence crumble away." [13] Even William Archer, who was to condemn almost without reservation the poet's later plays, found the poem's concluding vision "a magnificent piece of imaginative writing." [14]

Others, more alarmed, detected for the first time traces of Nietzsche's influence in the Scot's thought. The *Athenaeum,* which found the style of the *Empire-Builder* a marked advance over that of the previous poems in this genre, had serious misgivings about its content. It balked at the consciously or unconsciously Nietzschean principles of the author's spokesman and once more hedged with those who would conclude that Davidson "must needs seem to speak in the most tremendous irony or to blaspheme." [15] The *Academy,* whose hostility grew with each new work by the materialist poet, stated even more emphatically its disapproval of the supposed influence on him

of the German antichrist. With Davidson's latest poem it
was now quite evident, this journal noted, that all the
Testaments were "parts of a new gospel or at least a gospel
new to poetry—which he is preaching to a reluctant and
uncomprehending world." That the supreme egoist should
purchase his power and exclusive happiness with the suffering of the weak and the altruistic was a terrible gospel:
"It is the gospel of Nietzsche . . . and it might be written,
'Nietzsche is great, and Davidson is his prophet.' " [16] At
last the poet had made his thunder heard, and the distress
signals were being hoisted throughout the conservative
press.

For years Davidson had vehemently denied that he had
written his early plays and songs under the influence of
Elizabethan drink; now he was to be accused of addiction
to Nietzsche. To demonstrate his originality and "to sig-
nify to those who may care to know that I am neither
'disciple' nor 'prophet of Nietzsche,' " he composed his
"Ode on the Coronation of Edward VII., of Britain, and
of Greater Britain, King." The ode joins in curious alliance
the nebular hypothesis, the chemical evolution of the universe, and the imperialist evangel then sweeping the country. Written in honor of the coronation of Edward in 1901,
the ode hails the imperial destiny of Britain as the supreme
achievement of matter in its progress toward higher organization and self-knowledge. Thus Davidson's political
faith derives not from Nietzsche but from Darwin or rather
his followers, notably the political evolutionist and de-
fender of British imperialism, John Adam Cramb. Telling
Richards of the poem's forthcoming publication in the
Daily Chronicle, the author pointed out that it was the
reverse to the obverse of his *Empire-Builder.* Then, check-
ing himself, he added, "But there is no use bothering you
with the kind of thing one has to say to unintelligence." [17]

Gifted with a prodigious memory, John Davidson composed even his longest poems in his mind, as he paced back and forth in the inviolable sanctum of his study, puffing furiously at his pipe. Only later did he sit down and write out the poem in longhand, after which it was sent to his typist. Sometimes months or years elapsed before he could commit the work to paper. He made few revisions except in the very last manuscripts, which are laboriously worked over. In practice as in principle poetry for him was not a craft, a conscious ordering of parts into a whole, a trial-and-error search for the missing piece of the jigsaw puzzle. Poetry was the consequence of a romantic-religious moment of vision, for which the felicitous expression would come if the vision were direct and honest enough. As with Wordsworth the poem might be written years after the original experience, but not necessarily "in tranquillity"; the poem would be tranquil or ecstatic as the emotions surrounding the moment of vision had been one or the other.

By mid-November 1902 the poet had written some one hundred lines of his new Testament but, as with earlier poems in the series, had been obliged to put it aside while he undertook plays on commission. Early in June 1903 *The Testament of a Prime Minister* was "all ready" and he needed only "freedom from worry" to set it down.[18] Returning from Scotland at the end of October in the same year, where he had completed his translation of *Phèdre,* he informed Richards that he had at last resumed the *Prime Minister:* ". . . it grows and grows and will be an actual book."[19] It was almost a year to the day before he could complete the poem and persuade Richards to publish it. The most important of the Testaments up to this time, it contained Davidson's whole philosophy in summary. On the first of October 1904 he sent to Edmund Gosse an advance copy of the new book, accompanying it with a letter in which he wrote:

On one side I am a man with a message. I
fought against it, because to deliver it may entail the
death by starvation of my family and myself, and it
is a question if the highest message is worth that. But
it is useless considering ways and means: a message
is an entity in itself and *will* be delivered. In "The
Prime-Minister," I get it said more powerfully, elabo-
rately, and directly too, than in my other Testaments.[20]

By this time he had become so dedicated to the propaga-
tion of his personal faith that he willingly sacrificed to it
all chance for popular fame, physical health, the welfare of
his family, and ultimately the stability of his mind and his
life.

In addition to summarizing the ideas expounded in the
preceding Testaments, the fourth in the series offers a
wholly materialist and physiological explanation of such
Christian "fallacies" as God, Heaven and Hell, and sin. It
is clear that the *Prime Minister,* to a greater degree than
its predecessors, is the testament of John Davidson. The
introduction of a dying statesman as spokesman is no more
than a transparent dramatic ruse. As he slowly succumbs
to an incurable and unnamed disease, the prime minister
is assailed by doubt, despair, and a reluctance to die. By
the end of the poem he has mastered if not completely
exorcised these furies. A series of vivid, grimly described
flashbacks and nightmarish visions recalls his spiritual
development from worldly cynicism to the ameliorist's
belief in an imminent millennium, thence to Christian humanitarianism, and finally to a fully formulated gospel of
scientific materialism. Designed to symbolize the evolution
of modern thought, the poem is at the same time a highly
personalized document, and with Browning's *Paracelsus,*
Carlyle's *Sartor Resartus,* and Newman's *Apologia* shares

the subjective, confessional strain found in the works of all great moral and religious reformers.*

The content of this apostolic creed is not all that is redundant about it. The *Prime Minister,* like the *Empire-Builder,* relies heavily upon the devices of parable and vision. Employing Christian myth once more to overthrow Christian morality, the poem presents still another blasphemous vision of Judgment Day in which God welcomes into Heaven the blessed,

> The rich, the proud, and all the lusty lives
> That took their power and pleasure in the world.

On the other hand, the "Son of Man and His elect,"

> Apostles, martyrs, votarists, virgins, saints,
> The poor in spirit, the mourners and the meek,
> And they that hungered after righteousness,

are sentenced to eternal fire for having made "My splendid world a charnel-house, and Me / A God of infelicity and woe." [21] The Testament closes with an unflinching description of the prime minister's death almost Jacobean in its fascination with the morbid. On his deathbed the protagonist has a "memory" of the nebular beginnings of the earth. The process by which he accomplishes this mnemonic feat corresponds in the materialist's experience to Yeats' mystic evocation of *Spiritus Mundi,* the world's collective spirit or memory.† *The Testament of a Prime*

---

* Alfred Kazin finds the same quality in D. H. Lawrence: "Lawrence is so naturally religious about experience, his motivating purpose is so naturally the Protestant's exultant identification of his single consciousness with life itself . . ." "Lady Chatterley in America," *Atlantic Monthly,* July 1959, p. 36.

† When Archer objected that he did not understand how the prime minister arrived at the nebular hypothesis from his fanciful "recollection" of an early Saxon battle, Davidson carefully explained in materialist terms this instance of the free association of thought and memory: "I believe there is a hiatus there, where you put your finger on it. If it is a fault

Minister, again like its predecessor, resembles closely the
visionary lyric, "A Ballad of the Exodus from Houndsditch," with this difference, that Davidson in substituting
the dramatic first person for the narrative third has
dropped the pretense of objectivity. He reverts in the
Testaments to a frankly Protestant, Spasmodic subjectivism. As he hammered out his message to an airy thin-
ness, he no longer troubled to use a new anvil.

Recognizing the old cry of "Wolf" and wary of the
deception, the critics remained in the valley. Davidson,
devoured by his chagrin, wrote to Richards that the poem
"hangs fire," that no notice had yet appeared anywhere,
and of the men he had written to about it only Wemyss
Reid and William Archer had replied. Archer, out of kindness or a tolerance of qualities in poetry that he abhorred
in drama, wrote vaguely that he was "greatly impressed
by the power and beauty of much of the writing" and

---

then it seems to me a fault inherent in poetry. The dying man has told
the actual and also the imaginative matter that destroyed his power of
action. Then being only skin and bone, the fancy takes him that his keen
memory, power of utterance, and strength of wing must be lodged in his
skeleton, the most permanent part of him, the most powerful and material
part of man; for he knows how worn his brain and heart are, and yet
nothing seems beyond his conception. That recalls at once the skulls in
the church in Hythe which he had examined during his residence in
Walmer Castle; but now his memory of what he had seen or seemed to
see in the skull is shot through with later thoughts and imaginings, and
when he has summoned up the legendary battle in the necromantic camera
of the skull (the guide books tell of this purely traditional battle) his
imagination having pierced back to the beginnings of history in these
islands, hops further back to the beginnings of the world, imagination
being a law to itself: that is to say he holds in his hand a skull, the empty
casket of thought, imagination, speech, hearing, sight, the highest thing
that matter becomes; and in two strokes of the wing, back to the battle,
where this skull was conscious, then to the nebula, he extracts this skull
from that nebula. Poetry is accountable to logic; but logic must allow it
special scope when it 'bodies forth the forms of things unknown' or tells
as I am doing in my Testaments 'things unrecorded yet.'" A.L.S., dated
22 Oct. 1904, from 9 Fairmile Ave., Streatham, S. W., Add. MS. 45291,
ff. 112–13, B.M.

promised to write of it somewhere. It was his fate, Davidson complained, that this critic was asked to review his
plays, which he disliked, and never his other works, which
he appreciated.[22] When Archer finally reviewed the work
Davidson thanked him "for the high-termed praise and
the tolerant criticism. Criticism so generally takes it for
granted that if all men are not alike they ought to be: you
allow, you wish a man, to be himself." [23] In plea after plea
he appealed to Richards to advertise the new work, not as
a personal favor but out of sound business practice. After
suggesting that "a purse of money [is] going a-begging
here," the idealist that invariably eclipsed the practical
Davidson emerged. "Frankly," he wrote, "I think also you
should be glad to let it be widely known that such a book
had been published by you." [24] If he as author could disregard pecuniary considerations, not to mention aesthetic
ones, Richards as publisher was morally bound to follow
suit. Hard pressed financially, Richards felt in no position
to be quixotic. Advertisements or not, the book, as its
author had predicted, sold few copies.

The failure of the critics to perceive his absolute singu-
larity and their reliance upon stale, derogatory labels
to describe his work vexed Davidson more than honest
criticism would have, however adverse. He found their
reviews "very unimaginative and therefore uncritical," and
insisted that he was not a preacher but a poet, not a revolutionary but a realist:

> I am not preaching any gospel: who reads my Para-
> ble will see that I am trying to state The Nature of
> Things, beginning without any theory or system, but
> with my own experience and an acquaintance with
> such facts as I have—both bases increasing as I go on.
> To call me a "perverted voluptuary"—I like to
> smoke and drink upon occasion and am extravagant

in the matter of hansoms—but to call me a "perverted voluptuary" who have been the husband of
one wife since I married in 1885 is to be disingenuous
and malicious if the writer knows me at all, and if he
does not know me!—but it is a waste of time and
emotion to think or feel about it at all.

I have a lofty and profound purpose in my Testaments, and I call always on the Earth, and the Universe to help me.[25]

In its review of the *Prime Minister* the *Times Literary
Supplement* had reflected a growing repugnance to the
shrill formlessness of Davidson's poetry and plays. Quoting
Landor's definition of the best poetry as that "which, by
its own powers, produces the greatest and most durable
emotion in generous, well-informed minds," the writer of
this review declared that Davidson's verse did not meet the
test. The special business of poetry, he persisted, was to
give form to the formless:

> Poetry may ride the whirlwind but it cannot live
> there permanently. It is the "Paradiso" and not the
> "Inferno" which is the last word of the "Divina
> Commedia." Even Hamlet's doubts and struggles end
> in accepted silence; even the great Epicurean who was
> the very incarnation of the spirit that denies presents
> himself to us as a deliverer and sets forth his message
> as a message of light.

In what had become another critical cliché this reviewer
compared the *Prime Minister* to the poet's earlier work
represented by his *Selected Poems* published in the same
year by John Lane: "There are not more than two or three
living writers of English verse out of whose poems so good
a selection could be made. . . . The old is better." [26]

Davidson did not see the review until it was too late

for him to take countermeasures, but his rebuttal is contained in a letter to Richards. He was offended not so much by the condescension or derision of his critics as by their "ignorance or dishonesty." As for Hamlet's "accepted silence" cited in the review, he queried parenthetically, "Macbeth? Timon?" And it was dishonest, he protested, to compare his unfinished work to Dante's completed poem as if he had not written previous Testaments and announced in the preface to the *Empire-Builder* his intention of writing "The Testament of a Deliverer" and many others. Then growing vituperative as he does in the poems themselves, he stormed:

> But the first note of the deliverance is in the "Prime-Minister" itself, if the reviewer had chosen to listen. Like the others, however, he wants to be told that the old lies are true: it sounds like Churton Collins: the kind of things unfortunate men have to babble in girls' schools: imagine teaching literature, a matter of sinew and sperm to girls: imagine teaching literature at all! It is more shameful than it would be to teach the art of copulation. Of course, neither is taught in schools.

Literature and physical love were, like religion, holy matters not to be found in the newspapers or grammar schools. In refutation of Landor's definition of poetry, the *magister dixit* upon which the article was based, Davidson wrote that it was not a definition of poetry, whose appeal is to the imagination and not the mind, but of prose. The most dishonest thing in the review for him was the insistence on the ugliness of the tragic episode, for "I have made one of the ugliest things that ever happened beautiful to all eternity." No, he would not be deterred from his purpose; only death by starvation would stop him now.[27]

2

After the publication of *Godfrida* and *Holiday* in 1898 Davidson had severed business relations with John Lane, but in the spring of 1904 he renewed the connection. He had ready or contemplated more books than Richards was prepared at the time to underwrite. He approached Lane asking him to publish five new works in editions of two thousand copies each, for which he requested an advance of only £50. When the publisher hesitated (he ultimately declined), Davidson, his back to the wall, snapped at the hand that once had fed him:

> You could not "sink" money to better account than on me and my writings. When all the others are forgotten, it will be remembered that you published my books—when nobody else would; and believed in them—when the world gladly believed that their day was past.
>
>   . . . You compel me to write thus when you complain of "sinking a further sum": I can assure you I need the money, or I would have made no such offer; but no price is too great for money when one really needs it.[28]

In a postscript, his humiliation already complete, he brusquely offered Lane for £25 his dramatic adaptation of Daudet's *Sapho;* again Lane refused.

Lane's ugly duckling had left the nest at the Bodley Head and was unable now to return for the same reason: The firm's head and he could not agree on the sort of writing that the poet should produce. Davidson wished to disavow altogether his early work and to write only blank-verse poems and plays with a materialistic thesis. Psychologically and morally he was incapable of resuming his limited, worn repertory as a lieder singer. The publisher, on the other hand, wanted more ballads, eclogues, and whimsical plays, on the grounds that what had once seemed to prosper might do so again. When Lane showed only a lukewarm interest in the American copyright edition of *The Testament of a Prime Minister,* the nettled author remarked to Richards that he would not give the Bodley Head impresario the opportunity to refuse outright: ". . . he would delight to do so, and to brag about it, being paltry." [29] He consoled himself with the thought that there was plenty of time to pick up the matter in America as he intended to write a score or two of Testaments.

For some years Lane had felt that a collected edition of Davidson's earlier works might revive his reputation and be commercially profitable. To the apostle of materialism the proposal was anathema. He pointed out to Lane that there were already thousands of copies of his books in stock and that a collected edition was not likely to sell these copies or itself: "Ten years hence, or better, when I am dead, it may be worthwhile." [30] As Lane continued to press him, he again rejected the idea as useless: "The public says . . . 'No: this is not the bait for us. We won't have your ballads and your eclogues and your plays. They . . . make us think, which we can't abide. The bait for us is lullabies and sweet old lies.' " [31] Evidently by 1904 he was in such desperate need of money that he conquered all scruples, for in that year Lane published under Davidson's supervision a volume of his lyrics, *Selected Poems.* In deference to the wishes of the poet, the volume contained as its last selection the entire text of *The Testament of a Man Forbid.*

The *Athenaeum* struck the keynote of general opinion in its review of the collection. Although grateful for the slender volume, it urged a complete edition of Davidson's lyrics—the very thing he opposed!—to show the volume and variety of his work and to secure for him fuller recognition. Noting that his genius was lyrical, the *Athenaeum* voiced the hope that he would renounce further Testaments with their metaphysical bent and Nietzschean gloom and "go on singing the splendour of the workaday world." [32] The appearance of a retrospective volume at this time and its favorable reception seemed to Davidson singularly inopportune. Nearly coinciding with the *Prime Minister* which came out shortly after under Richards' imprint, it invited odious comparison. Lane had stated in his advertisement of *Selected Poems* what was completely true, that the poet's earlier volumes of lyrics had remained his most popular works. This was the kiss of Judas. To offset the suggestion that he had reached his twilight and to draw attention to his later work, the emancipated lyricist frantically urged Richards to retaliate with a stout advertisement of the latest Testament made up of carefully edited excerpts from favorable notices.[33] His direst fear had been realized; the public had discovered that he was a writer divided against himself. By divorcing himself from his past and by refusing to make any distinction between his private identity and his public mission, Davidson set out to force his publishers to accept him on his own terms.

It speaks for the deep respect which first Lane and then Richards had for Davidson, as well as for his compelling personality, that they endured with patience his fretful and in later years extravagant demands. They continued to publish his works long after they had ceased to make or hoped to make expenses on them. In spite of differences and the accumulation of some bitterness, the fashionable West End publisher and his renegade Rhymer remained on amicable terms for the remainder of the latter's life. Sporadically they exchanged books, news, and courtesies. An occasional touchiness, as of grudging friendship, in some of the poet's later letters alone hints at a wound that never fully healed.

Richards deserves even more credit and sympathy for staying by Davidson to the end, after his more trying qualities had begun to govern his business relations. Although the ex-Rhymer came to realize that his works which he regarded as most important would not be widely read or understood by his contemporaries, he clung to the delusion that after his death he would be recognized for a great poet and seer. When Richards declined to publish one of his works, he replied simply, "Of course I accept your decision although it is very disappointing. No man ever needed, or I believe, deserved, more to be backed against the world than I do." [34] His confidence in his own powers increasingly took the form of megalomania, until he believed that he was conferring a great honor upon his publisher. In September of 1905 he wrote Richards that he had resumed writing eclogues and to his own surprise had begun "a new series of ballads of a new order: and all this an intermezzo among my Testaments and Tragedies." "Being a great poet," he continued, "I need a great publisher." [35] Unable to return to lyrics that were melodic and ironical, he used the eclogue and ballad as vehicles for hoarse rhetoric and the pseudoscientific tenets of materialism. The handful of later lyrics that escape these obsessions are among the best that he wrote, but they were insufficient to repair his reputation or compensate his publisher, both now bankrupt.

In spite of his eccentricities and unpopularity Davidson maintained an unbroken association with Richards from 1901 until his death in 1909, except for one brief interval. By the end of 1904 the firm of Grant Richards, 48 Leicester Square, had fallen on evil days and into the hands of Alexander Moring of the De La More Press. Richards was temporarily without a business and Davidson without a publisher. December found the stranded poet in a desperate state of mind; he appealed to Richards:

> I should like to see you. Who is to publish my plays and Testaments now? I shall have a play of church and state ready shortly in which I apply the matter of my Testaments more directly to life, and I do not know what to do with it. It is positive agony to me to form a new connection for any purpose now.[36]

Depression gave way to elation when in the following year Richards established a new firm and promptly brought out the play in question, *The Theatrocrat. Holiday and Other Poems,* Davidson's first volume of new lyrics in seven years, appeared under the same auspices in 1906. By the publication of these works, he wrote Richards, the house of E. Grant Richards at 7 Carlton Street had "become the premier firm of publishers in the world, and this great light must not be hid under a bushel—nor is it." [37] The curve of his ambitions following that of his revived hopes, he completed the letter with a hearty plea to advertise the man Davidson and his works.

3

The Theatrocrat marks the final turning point of Davidson's career. In this play which, as he wrote Archer, "I menaced the world with," [38] he no longer sought a truce with the public but declared open war on all representatives of a degenerate Christian civilization. There was nothing abrupt about this decision for he had been rounding the point since 1901 when he had begun the series of Testaments. Two additional volumes of lyrics and considerable journalistic work intervened, but they were the work of his left hand. Completely absorbed in his task of scourging the world, his letters begin to read like his prefaces. In October 1904 he wrote to Archer:

My purpose in these Testaments is to aid in the overthrow of the rotten financial investment called Christendom: I perceive that this can be done only by purging the world of everything that is meant by spirit, soul, "other" world, though all the literature and art and religion of the past should go with it. I would start the world over again from the only mystery, Matter.

All this clarifies in the play I am writing: it is terrible also: it half kills me to write it. Fiend! I will make you know I can write a play. It will be saturated with this Matter of mine, and therefore unlicensable, and I will take license further to get my Matter stated; but it will be a great drama also.[39]

The Theatrocrat was finished by late December 1904. Surprising and indicative of his loosening grasp on practical matters is his expectation that the defiant new play would accomplish what his more conscientious efforts to reconcile the popular theater and his own principles had not. In his self-delusion he pinned all his hopes on its success. It would relieve him of the onus of a monthly poem for the journals; it would open the eyes of the public to the stupidity of Christianity and the glories of materialism; it would make a temple of the theater instead of a music hall. Irritated by Richards' misgivings about this lurid work, he wrote that he had expected his publisher to bring it out without delay and was disappointed that the business had not already been arranged with his agent, A. P. Watt.[40] Not until late November 1904, after he had failed to find a producer, did he finally persuade Richards to publish the "Tragic Play of Church and State."

The Theatrocrat is prefaced by a brief dedication in heroic couplets and a prose introduction of seventy-nine closely printed pages. The dedication, addressed "To the Generation Knocking at the Door," is in the straightforward idiom of Kipling and Henley, but it carries their emphasis upon action beyond all bounds of authority and morality:

> Break—break it open; let the knocker rust:
> Consider no "shalt not," and no man's "must":
> And, being entered, promptly take the lead,
> Setting aside the tradition, custom, creed;
> Nor watch the balance of the huckster's beam;
> Declare your hardiest thought, your proudest dream:
> Await no summons; laugh at all rebuff;
> High hearts and youth are destiny enough. . . .
> For this alone, this always, will succeed,
> The miracle and magic of the deed.

Although they do little more than echo similar exhortations to self-reliance in "Lammas" and other lyrics, these verses by virtue of their direct, earnest simplicity are superior to most of the blank verse in the play that follows. Davidson's introduction contains no apology for the tragedy or exegesis of it, but he does furnish for the first time in prose a detailed outline of the philosophy of scientific materialism, in all its historical, ethical, and aesthetic ramifications, upon which the tragedy is based.

As if he half expected his readers not to trouble themselves with the play itself and only cared if they digested the prose introduction, Davidson's preface also provides a convenient synopsis of the drama's "simple" plot. The action concerns the efforts of a dissolute, fading actor-manager, Sir Tristram Sumner, to recoup his fortunes with a production of *Troilus and Cressida;* his betrayal in this enterprise by his neurotic, telepathic wife and her former lover, the drunken actor, Warwick Groom; Sumner's final attempt at a comeback with a production of a play by the Bishop of St. James's, his wife's cousin and a confirmed materialist; and the destruction of all their hopes and lives when the bishop is hissed off the stage before completing his blasphemous prologue. Reading like a chapter from the history of the Borgias, the play is a grotesque, sensational tissue of sensuality, drunkenness, adultery, suicide, heresy, and murder. Davidson employs personages of the contemporary theater and church to symbolize the degeneration of the human body, passions, and intellect when stifled by a Christian, commercialistic society. In this respect his theme is identical with that of Joyce in *Dubliners* and *A Portrait of the Artist as a Young Man,* Pound in *Hugh Selwyn Mauberley,* and Lawrence in *Lady Chatterley's Lover.* At the same time it is perfectly evident that the characters of Davidson's play, like those in these later works, are *personae* who project the author's own ambitions and deep-seated grievances. Intensely egocentric, he no longer distinguishes between his private consciousness and ultimate reality. He is writing not for the public but for himself:

> I should add that there is no key to "The Theatrocrat": all the people in it are made essentially out of the good and evil in myself. My statement of the world and of the Universe as the world can know it has offended and will offend; but I have no purpose of offence; nor am I concerned to please: my purpose is to say that which is, to speak for the Universe.[41]

This is a radical departure from the statement of his purpose in the prologue to *Godfrida*—"My object is to give delight"—and of the source of his characters—"I take men and women as I know them." Whatever his avowed intention, *The Theatrocrat* in its flamboyant rhetoric and its reliance upon intercepted messages, concealments, near discoveries, poisonings, the play within a play, and eruptions of violence bears a continued resemblance to end-of-the-century romantic melodrama. The presence of these clichés betrays a lingering contradiction of purpose. In spite of his protestations of indifference to the sensibilities of his public, the playwright was so intent upon converting it to his salvational creed that he could not resist the shoddiest tricks of the very theater he was deriding. The play's originality lies in its powerful, oracular vision for which later authors were to find a fresher, more suitable expression.

Crippled by a bronchial ailment that he could not shake off, Davidson worked anxiously to publicize the new work before and after its publication. It was to be his final challenge as gladiator in the public arena. Since he had reversed his previous tactics by launching an avowed frontal assault upon Christian theology and morality, he appealed to Richards for publicity on an unprecedented scale: "I have never had a book published: I should like to have this one published, made known to the public, if possible." [42] Henceforth he was to make a careful distinction between the mere issuing of a book and publishing it. Richards was apparently convinced that *The Theatrocrat* could hope to appeal only to an intelligentsia. In time Davidson also was to come around to the view that during his lifetime he must address himself to an aristocracy of emancipated intellects, but on this occasion he stoutly believed that the general public would buy if given the chance:

> I am certain you are wrong about those who would read my book. The reading public is mainly the middle and lower middle classes: it is they who support the theatres and the churches . . . and who would buy and read my *Theatrocrat* if it were put before them. I have in the meantime exhausted my power of publishing my book, and unless the interest

which I have myself aroused or extorted be supported by advertisement the book will fall dead. It is true that the money paid to the newspapers by publishers is blackmail. But what payment is not blackmail?

He continued with a partiality that had its practical side, "Books are a luxury, and therefore they compete with everything for which money is paid, with cigars and soap, whisky and Cook's tours, fur coats and kisses." He assured Richards that his new firm had been admirably launched with "the only two books that are talked of—one, a fine new novel and a new departure in fiction; the other, the most important book that has appeared in England." [43] The novel to which he referred was Filson Young's *The Sands of Pleasure.* Although he had objected strongly to the simultaneous publication of Young's novel and *The Theatrocrat,* he yielded with great good will when Richards persisted in bringing out the work of his newest discovery with that of one of his oldest. Upon the appearance of the two books he wrote a highly laudatory review of the novel for the *Daily Mail,* which, he remarked to the publisher, "should sell an edition of the book—an achievement which should be the aim of all reviews." [44]

With the hope of selling his own book and thereby drawing attention to its message of delivery, the poet-prophet had sent copies at his expense to the leading critics, even to those from whom he could not have expected favorable notices. Walkley, Archer, Israel Zangwill, W. T. Stead, Beerbohm, John Morley, Christie Murray, and Sir Oliver Lodge received advance copies. [45] To make an international event of his new play, he also ordered extra copies sent to Georg Brandes in Copenhagen, May Meyerfeld in Berlin, and Paul Fort and René Ghil * in Paris. [46] Of the English

---

* The Continent does not seem to have been deeply stirred by the "international event." René Ghil did respond but only to propose that Grant Richards publish in translation a book of his own doctrine and poetic technique. A review of *The Theatrocrat* appeared in "the moribund

critics only Stead replied that he had read it, with the reassuring report that he had devoured half of the prose introduction at once and was taking it to the country to read sympathetically. Requesting that Richards send a copy of the book to the editor of the *Morning Leader*, Davidson added, "I write him, however, and every editor I know: I am entitled to do so; and we must publish, publish, publish." [47] He did not look for even unfavorable attention from certain periodicals. The *Westminster Gazette* had "become snobbisher since it opened a weekly school of the Muses." As for *Punch* it had not condescended to acknowledge his existence since nine years ago when it applied to him the chestnut, *"poeta nascitur* but *non fit* for publication." [48] Anxious as he was to publicize the book, the poet stuck by his principles; nor did he altogether bury the hatchet. Nursing an old wound, he wrote to Richards, "In sending a copy to Bernard Shaw I wish you would say to him that when you suggested that *I* should send him one I declined on the ground that his mind lived in a different world from mine and that he would not be interested." [49]

A number of editors dismissed Davidson as an angry old man, once a minor poet of some interest, now a mere crackpot. To one who declined to review his book he wrote a letter which he recommended that Richards use for all recalcitrant editors:

My dear Sir,

Many thanks for your letter. It is not my "trouble that I do not write for the public." . . . It is, has

Ecrits pour l'Art," Davidson informed Richards and humorously quoted its editor's promise to write a note in the French journal's last number *"'pour saluer* my name, work and decisive thought,' and for to 'rejoice himself in my high sympathy and the air which I bring to the triumph, which will be slow but which is sure *de notre même volonté.'* " A.L.S., dated 26 Jan. 1906, from Corveau, St. Ives, Cornwall, P.U.L.

been, and will be my instinct and purpose to write
that which I wish to write and not that which the
public wishes to read. It is men like me the world
needs. I want to make a new public, and I want great
editors to help me.[50]

He coolly assured another editor that his new book said
"what the world has been waiting three hundred years to
hear." [51] It is not surprising that Richards, less confident
of the crusade in the name of "Immorality" and more
concerned with the sale of the book, grew alarmed at such
tactics. His protest met with a reply that could have done
little to quiet his unrest: "I am not afraid of doing an
'undermannish' thing; no overman ever is." [52]

These aggressive overtures bore fruit, much of it bitter.
The leading London critics gave the controversial new
drama generous space but were almost unanimous in rejecting its philosophy of life and the use of the legitimate
stage for such blatant propagandizing. Walter de la Mare
observed that the world of *The Theatrocrat* was inhabited
by mere automatons which Davidson, who was their "Fate,
indifferent, inapproachable," manipulated to expound his
thesis; this done, they were annihilated. He noted that the
author had poured his immense energies into the introduction rather than into the play; and although he found
its gospel of intellect—beautified materialism—"a forlorn
fire to warm one's bones at in this cold world," he proclaimed that the introduction cried aloud for readers.
"Why must Mr. Davidson ventriloquise?" he asked. " 'Message' and play had better have parted company. The benefit would have been mutual. Tragedy needs a prologue
less than good wine a bush." [53]

A. B. Walkley, among the more influential progressive
critics, regarded the tragedy with a facetiousness which
suggested that the obsequies of the old didactic drama

need not be conducted solemnly. He reported that for
him the result of reading the two-hundred-odd pages of
the volume was "sheer bewilderment." His first thought
had been that Davidson had written the play for fun or
on a wager or *pour épater les bourgeois,* but after searching in vain for a trace of the poet's former irony and sly-
ness, he had found him in deadly earnest. Messages went
out with Henry Arthur Jones when motorcars came in, he
quipped. Davidson's claim to individualizing was " 'all
werry capital for him.' But we feel it hard that he should
individualize at our expense, making us feel awkward and
foolish because we can't make head or tail of his performance." [54] Since Walkley had devoted a full double column
to the play, summarizing the plot and message with clarity,
his air of bewilderment was more mock than real.* Good-
natured enough to give the book some notoriety, he could
not take it seriously.

The author who could take it no other way was in turn
bewildered. With some justice he wrote to Richards, "Why
did Walkley write that article? It wasn't witty; it wasn't
interesting; it read like the ordinary mean attempt of a
trade rival to settle some one's hash." [55] Still troubled two
days later, he continued, "Don't you think it proceeds
from absence of temperament—indifference to whatever
is not on the surface?" [56] He sat down at once to reply to
Walkley in a letter to the editor of the *Times.* In spite
of his "desolate feeling" that it would be barred, it was
printed in the next issue of the *Supplement.*[57] Declining
to bandy trivialities, he wrote that the teller of a new
thing must expect contempt and ridicule because men are

---

* That critics were genuinely at a loss as to how to take Davidson's play
is evident from the titles of their reviews: "Stark Nonsense," The *Evening
Standard and St. James's Gazette,* 30 Nov.; "On the Side of the Angels,"
The *Referee,* 10 Dec.; "A Bard Who Bewilders," The *Record,* 29 Dec.;
"A Stage 'Shocker,' " The *Era,* 30 Dec. 1905; "Mid-Winter Madness," The
Sheffield Daily Telegraph, 24 Jan. 1906.

made so. One by one he answered Walkley's charges with an absence of humor which showed that his vision was already dimmed by a cataract of personal rancor. To Walkley's flippant objection to the presence of "message" in the play and the frequency with which the word appears, he replied that he was using it in no mystical or pretentious sense, that he had been advised against the use of the word, but that it was natural for him to do what others were afraid to do. As for the critic's complete mystification by the message, Davidson proceeded to enlighten him with a solemn précis of his introduction to the tragedy.[58]

For some weeks after the appearance of *The Theatrocrat* the beleaguered poet was kept busy with rebuttals to the critics. In an article for the *Daily Chronicle* William Archer, acknowledged leader of the pan-Ibsen movement, had described the drama as "a crude romance of sensuality" and therefore unworthy of the great task of delivering Davidson's philosophy. Archer, who in criticism and personal letters had expressed respect for Davidson's thought and poetic ability, was objecting not to the message or its presence but to the sensational treatment of it in drama. He had kinder words for the preface, which like de la Mare he found the best thing in the book and which he compared to those of Shaw.[59] To mention Shaw was to drag a red herring or rather to wave a red flag across the trail. A few days later the outraged playwright denied in the pages of the *Daily Chronicle* the charge of aping Shaw: "Were there no introductions before Mr. Shaw? . . . Mr. Shaw works his work shiningly in the sight of all men; and I work mine still unregarded; but it helps neither Mr. Shaw nor me, nor the public, to say that anything of mine is Shawlike. I suppose Mr. Shaw and I have not two ideas in common." [60]

Although Shaw was a Fabian socialist and Davidson a materialist who advocated a paternalistic despotism, they had in truth many ideas in common. It was their dissimilar temperaments and talents which directed their similar protestantism into different channels. The purpose of his reply, Davidson explained to his publisher, was "if possible to do away the effect of Archer's stupid, sulky twaddle." [61] It was not to cancel his more general reply which appeared three weeks later after a second review in the *Chronicle*. He introduced this counterblast with a statement of sublime confidence in his mission: "This is not an apologia. Every deed is its own defence. For example, I have written and published 'The Theatrocrat,' the most profound and original of English books, and the most helpful." [62] Although it recalls the naïve, lofty arrogance of Nietzsche, the statement is one that a Spasmodic might have made, or Davidson himself before he came to London. There is this difference, that it lacks the note of deliberate exaggeration and self-mockery associated with the Spasmodics and the younger Davidson. The author of the Testaments and tragedies had forsaken irony for misanthropy and titanic pride, what Professor Bush has called his "scientific *hybris*." [63] He did not, then, come full circle so much as he spiraled ever higher toward Icarian self-destruction.

In statements to the press the literary outcast preserved a conscious dignity designed to conceal his deep chagrin and resentment at the reception of *The Theatrocrat*. When the critic for the *Westminster Gazette* wrote of his "fantastical propagandism of a new religion," [64] he patiently reiterated his purpose in a letter to that journal's editor:

> All poets are fanatics. No poet ever wrote a line that lives who was not willing to die for his figure of speech, his melody, his vision. I am a propagandist. All poets worthy of the name are propagandists. . . . I dislike the phrase "new religion" . . . The religious mood is the highest mood of the imagination: it is

constant in the world; only that in which it clothes itself changes. It is a new poetry I bring, the vision of the Universe in which my mind and imagination live. The real poetries of the past lived in symbols of the Universe . . . The abode of my imagination is the Universe itself, and I would have it so for all men. . . . The world is sick of Christendom. We must come out of Christendom into the Universe.[65]

His real state of mind—his vacillation between hope and despair, his unpurged anger, and his sense of persecution— emerges from his private correspondence. "Who is X in the Westminster?" he asks Richards. "How mean and paltry under the guise of good will! And what an inferior brain! He excuses himself for a most inadequate review of *The Theatrocrat* by the fact that it gave him a headache: he'll never get better of that headache." The anonymous reviewer reminded him of Carlyle "who was the embodiment of mean jealousy." [66] Shifting abruptly to another mood, he regarded the same review as rather notable and tolerant "when you consider that the writer is clearly a Christian and a moralist . . . It being the habit of Christians to deny all merit to those who are not Christians." He compared the reviews of the "surprised and confused" critic for the *Gazette* and the "bewildered" Walkley with what the most eminent musical critics of the world had said of Wagner's Nibelung tetralogy, "the greatest achievement in music," long after the public had discovered its greatness.* Then with venomous rage he turned on the dramatic critic for the *Referee,* a "frowzy old man" who had taken the poet's "scabbard, bent it, scratched it, kicked it, spat upon it . . . and said 'behold Davidson's Damas-

* Yet when a Glasgow lecturer ventured to mention *The Theatrocrat* and the *Ring of the Nibelung* in the same breath, Davidson wrote sharply of his "astonishing ineptitude." A.L.S., to G. Richards, dated 1 Feb. 1907, from 9 Fairmile Ave., Streatham, P.U.L.

cus *blade.'* " When he wrote "a gallant letter" in protest
to the *Referee*'s editor the result was "again, all the edge
and glamour of my sword blunted and dulled in his hog-
wash." This too, he pointed out, from a man who was a
Scot but was now only a journalist. "Hell!" exclaimed
Davidson who was never idly profane but who could curse
with any enraged Scot.[67]

Almost more offensive to the poet at bay than these
hostile critics were those disposed to be friendly. With the
genial tolerance of the Catholic intellectual, G. K. Chesterton had congratulated him for refusing to accept any
compromise of science and religion and for insisting upon
being a "Major Prophet" rather than a "Minor Poet." He
welcomed the materialist thinker more as a worthy opponent than as an ally: "Neither Christianity nor Rationalism would surmount their present empty position of
compromise, until the half of mankind on both sides
became as vexatious and dogmatic as Mr. Davidson." [68]
Davidson, who despised rationalism as much as Christianity and who always felt that Chesterton had modeled his
ballads and fantastic stories upon his own, was scarcely
grateful for what seemed to him a misinformed, condescending review.* Another unsolicited champion, James
Douglas, extravagantly placed Davidson in the company
of Ibsen, Tolstoy, and Shaw as one of the "four great
anarchists in contemporary literature." [69] Only bronchitis
and asthma prevented the junior member of this quartet
from dining with Douglas a fortnight later for the express
purpose of explaining to his fellow Celt that he had nothing

---

* Although loath to reprint his early works which he regarded as colorful but fallen leaves, Davidson had written to Richards, "I think we ought
to reprint 'Baptist Lake' and 'Earl Lavender,' the books out of which Max
[Beerbohm] and Chesterton learnt their prose as the latter learnt his verse
from my ballads." A.L.S., dated 5 June 1904, from 9 Fairmile Ave.,
Streatham, P.U.L.

in common with these "three foreigners" and that they had nothing to say to England." * [70]

No event proved more crucial in Davidson's literary development than the publication of *The Theatrocrat*. The poet announced in the introduction to the work that he had composed the drama in the autumn of 1904 "as a fresco in the series of my Testaments, and in order to bring home the matter contained in them by a closer application to life than is possible in dramatic monologue, also desiring to extend the circle of my readers and the effect of my message." [71] Implied is the admission that *The Theatrocrat* was intended to remedy those defects which the critics had found in the dramatic monologues. These had been that the speakers in the poems were mere shadows and mouthpieces for an intolerable message, that the psychological situations presented were improbable, and that the poems were at best diluted Browning. When he came to write the tragedy, however, all the care and much of the energy went, as the critics noted, into the introduction. The faults which marred the Testaments were compounded in the play. As a realistic or even heightened representation of life it is absurd; as moral and spiritual allegory it is either obscure or transparent. Force and vividness are occasionally present, and the author's fierce conviction; but their presence only calls greater attention to the obvious symbolism, the coarse sexuality, bathos, and unrelieved hysteria that detract from the play's important

* When *Holiday and Other Poems* was published in 1906, Davidson instructed Richards to send a review copy to the editor of the *Athenaeum*, "and let Douglas review it promptly on the first page: three columns: no wasteful talk about me and my ballads and the failure of the public to appreciate: no tiresome tattle about Ibsen and Nietzsche: no nauseous reference to Watts and the babblement of the Renascence of Wonder; but a great review . . . of a great book . . . let us have creative criticism." A.L.S., dated 9 June 1906, from 9 Fairmile Ave., Streatham, P.U.L.

theme. One finds nowhere dramatic interest nor, except
for occasional lyric outbursts, the distillation peculiar to
poetry. The play demonstrates that there is nothing more
perishable than message, however courageous or thera-
peutic, unrefined by art.

The play was equally important to Davidson's personal
well-being. For months he had been limping along on book
reviews, occasional eclogues, prose sketches, and other
drudgery for the press. To relieve his financial distress and
retrieve something of his self-respect, he needed a success.
Hard pressed as he was, he steadfastly refused to yield an
inch of his position. When Filson Young, Richards, and
others urged him to republish *Perfervid* and *Baptist Lake,*
his whimsical novels of the nineties, he refused for a long
time. He explained to Richards that they belonged to a
thing far behind him:

> But why not welcome *The Theatrocrat* instead? All
> the detraction of the literary critics concerning *The
> Theatrocrat* which you repeated to me when I last
> saw you, attended the publication of *Perfervid*—the
> title, the so-called want of homogeneity, etc. Ten
> years hence when I have published something ten
> years further forward than *The Theatrocrat,* you or
> another publisher will say "This new book of yours
> is so-and-so, and so-and-so: why not give us something
> like *The Theatrocrat:* that was a book!"

He ended the letter, "Nothing has ever brought me nearer
despair than the failure of *The Theatrocrat.*" [72] A critic,
who appealed to him through Richards to reissue *Perfervid,* met with a similar refusal. Davidson stated that it
was precisely such books that appeal to "average minds,"
since "there is just a little genius in it: they feel it, they
can see it: it is only a rung or two above them on the
ladder." Let the critic read his *Testament of a Prime*

Minister and learn it by heart. It did not matter if "a crowd of paltry literary critics" would welcome the early books or if they would sell or not; he did not wish to think of them or anyone to know of them. The only works of his youth that he would possibly consider republishing at this time were a few poems from *In a Music-Hall* and "the two best short stories in the English language 'The School Boy's Tragedy' and 'The Interregnum in Faeryland.' " *
"I want a great critic to study my actual works of genius and point out their merit," he implored.[73] Blunt, ironic, practical, and surpassingly courageous, Davidson was prevented by a single fixation, the greatness of his message and himself, from applying these virtues to his own craft. He had elected a road from which there was no retreat, along which there was no comfort, and at the end of which there was but a poor salvation.

4

As he struggled for survival on his own terms, minor irritations and major disappointments loomed equally large in the poet's mind. Bent on making of his works an emancipation proclamation of the spirit, he was compelled by poverty to turn out piecework for the periodicals. Yet his journalistic output was sporadic and uncertain, varying from two contributions in 1900, the year of *The*

---

* The copyright to these stories, originally published by Ward & Downey in *The Great Men* (1891), had since passed through several hands and now belonged to a firm of binders, Madgewick, Houlston & Co., Ltd. To reissue them it was necessary for Davidson to regain possession of the copyright and to buy up the scattered stock. After exasperating negotiation Richards secured for ten guineas the copyright to this volume and that of *Earl Lavender, Perfervid,* and *Baptist Lake.* The stock of these books had been remaindered over a period of years, and the bookstalls were glutted with the original editions. It was therefore infeasible to publish new editions. A.Ls.S., from Davidson to Richards, dated 6 Nov. 1906 and 13 Mar. [1907], P.U.L.; and letter press copy of typescript L.S., from Richards to Davidson, dated 8 Oct. 1906, in the University of Illinois Library.

Knight of the Maypole, to forty-one, the largest number
for any one year, in 1905, the year of *The Theatrocrat*.[74]
Each time he performed these chores with greater resentment and difficulty. To the dismay of his editors he took
a perverse satisfaction in permitting his insidious message
to creep into these contributions. He regarded everything
to which he set his hand as a stone in his final monument.
Shortly after the publication of *The Theatrocrat* he
lamented to Richards:

> I have begun an eclogue for the only monthly cer-
> tainty I have—(if it is a certainty: Watt had to coerce
> them into publishing the last one)—and I don't know
> whether I can afford to interrupt it.* Sometimes I get
> no more than a single stanza a day. I shall see how
> the world looks tomorrow, Sunday. But to have to
> write eclogues and reviews when I want to write my
> Testaments and Tragedies! It is like asking a woman
> about to bring forth a lusty son to stop and produce
> a litter of puppies first. The miracle is that I can do
> it: "nine farrow of that sow" already: shall I manage
> a tenth and an eleventh and a twelfth.[75]

The general inferiority of these eclogues which he contributed to the *Outlook* in 1905 speaks for his declining
powers. As early as 1894, if Yeats' memory serves him
right, he had remarked to the Irish poet when they met in
the British Museum after a long interval, "The fires are
out, and I must hammer the cold iron." [76] Poverty, chronic
illness, hostile criticism, and prolonged controversies with
former publishers and their successors were not new

* The eclogue to which he refers is probably "New Year's Eve. A Fleet
Street Eclogue," which appeared in the *Outlook* for 30 Dec. 1905. It was
the tenth and last to appear in that journal. All were reprinted in *Holiday
and Other Poems* (1906). The *Outlook* carried only one further contribution by Davidson, "A Song of Triumph," on 6 Jan. 1906. See Lester, "John
Davidson, a Grub Street Bibliography," pp. 24–7.

trials to him. In reality his misfortunes, surpassed only by those of Old Testament worthies, had pursued him throughout his life; but they seemed to grow in number and intensity as he became less equipped to endure them. To some extent he had always been able to expel these devils by a cheerful irony and pride in his work; now the evil eye was less easily stared down.

A theme which runs through his writings from the beginning is that of poverty. The starving artist or poet of his ballads of the nineties may have been an imaginative exaggeration or premonition. The image is amply confirmed, however, by the letters which Davidson wrote to his few intimates: thanking Gosse for assistance when his back was against the wall, declining invitations from the Grant Allens or the Richardses because his wife and he must remain social outcasts, or asking his publisher to send a desperately needed check. Gosse recorded that the poet was unable to make more than £100 a year by writing,[77] and Davidson himself stated that he could with difficulty earn thirty-five shillings a week. In "A Ballad of an Artist's Wife" and "A Ballad of Heaven" he had made a virtue of necessity by accepting poverty and suffering as an essential part of an ironic universe. "Nothing is lost that's wrought with tears," God reassures the musician in the latter poem after his wife and son have starved to death and he has died of a broken heart. This sentimentalized stoicism did not prove of lasting comfort. Mammon, the hero of the last two plays, is less tolerant of poverty and disease. Ruthlessly dedicated to an ideal world in which such hardships do not exist, he would send all beggars and incurables to the gas chamber.

Perhaps the most painful episode of Davidson's later life, one which caused him great humiliation, was the protracted effort of a few benefactors, notably William Symington McCormick, Edmund Gosse, Lord Crewe, and

Mrs. Leo Hunter, the celebrated patroness, to obtain for
him a Civil List pension. Thanks to their intercession he
did receive in December 1898 assistance from an anonymous quarter. In a state almost of giddiness he wrote at
once to McCormick of "this very extraordinary event,
great jail-delivery of despair and temporary installation in
the seventh heavens":

> I am unable as yet to connect it with any name. It is
> the entirely magical operation of a great unknown
> and unknowable entity, a Fund. . . .
>
> It is quite true as I said before that we were slid-
> ing down an icefloe, tilted at an angle of forty five
> degrees, at a frightful rate of acceleration; the ice
> was catching fire with the friction and the gulf
> yawned and sucked its tongue and licked its boltered
> [*sic*] chops almost within snapping distance. Hey,
> presto! The Fund claps its fundament * on the other
> end of the floe; and we are hoisted to equilibrium,
> snatched up, and planted once more on *terra firma*,
> and we haven't found our feet or our heads yet.[78]

When he discovered several weeks later who had been the
principal agent in this rescue, he wrote to Gosse:

> I know that it was you who wrought the miracle—
> to me and mine, a miracle—whereby we have been
> lifted from the "fearful pit and from the mirey clay."
>
> The difference between one and one million is I
> suppose astonishing; but the difference between zero
> and one cannot be stated at all—except as life and
> death. . . . "The grace of God before, behind thee,
> and on every hand enwheel thee round." [79]

---

* Davidson had always found punning an irresistible outlet for his
ironic, inverted view of things. In later years the puns like the view
are clumsier, cruder, less expressive of a double vision. *The Theatrocrat*
contains two puns on "fundament."

Late in 1900 McCormick and Gosse again made strenuous efforts to have the poet placed on the Civil List. Davidson had expressed to Gosse his desire for financial independence so that he might write as he wished:

> McCormick with extraordinary goodwill, is trying to
> get me a pension, and I dare not do other than be-
> lieve that he will succeed. In this country a writer
> must misrepresent the world, or be understood to
> have done so, in order to make money. . . . Poetry
> is the product of the whole soul, mind, and body;
> and in maturity, and with a regard for the only thing
> one has any right to trust in, one's own experience,
> honest poetry, full-bodied, full-souled, and rightly
> intellectual, will not be the thing that the bulk of
> readers and reviewers expect—who indeed regard po-
> etry always from a juvenile, often an infantile stand-
> point. There will be little flattery of men and their
> ways and deeds: impartial, intelligent, neither moral
> nor immoral, it will appeal genuinely only to half a
> hundred people in a generation. It is this poetry that
> I could now write in various forms but not without
> more leisure and so I hope for a pension.[80]

His reputation for writing just this unorthodox poetry
was the chief obstacle in the way of his winning recognition from the Crown as it was in the way of his winning
the popular acclaim which invariably precedes official
honors. Even so, his influential friends might have succeeded in obtaining an annual pension for him if the
death of the Queen in January 1901 had not given
Balfour, First Lord of the Treasury, the excuse he
sought to delay and then to reject the application.
Through his secretary, Balfour wrote to Gosse that while
he had "great sympathy for Davidson's struggles" and
believed his work "in part vigorous and original," he

could not satisfy himself that "in point both of quality &
quantity,* it can be said sufficiently to 'merit the gracious
consideration of the Sovereign & the gratitude of the
Country' within the meaning of the Civil List Act." As a
mark of his sympathy Balfour expressed himself willing
to contribute the token sum of £250 (equivalent to
an annuity of £10 a year) from another fund if a subscription could be started for the purpose of providing
Davidson with permanent financial help.[81]

Balfour's antipathy to Davidson is not difficult to understand. A Tory minister with philosophical pretensions
who had repeatedly attacked scientific materialism and
free thought, he was not predisposed to assist a notorious
materialist and atheist. Of Balfour's *Defence of Philosophic Doubt* (1879), which turned the batteries of philosophic agnosticism against scientific rationalism, Davidson had stated that he found it "a very meager, miserable
production." [82] It would have been a singular mark of
impartiality if the First Lord of the Treasury had not possessed similar views of Davidson's works. Again Davidson's independence and lack of tact did not help his cause.
He peremptorily refused a token annuity of £50 as a
slight upon those who had acted in his behalf and a
mockery of his hopes:

> £50 a year carries no mark of honour: it would be
> recognised in every quarter as a grudging charity ex-
> torted by importunity and pauperising the recipient:
> it would be less disgraceful to retire into the work-
> house than to accept £50 a year; and there it would
> cost the ratepayers more to support my family and me.

---

* Ruling aside the quality of Davidson's work, he could hardly have
been disqualified for insufficient quantity. His published works number
some forty volumes. Lester's bibliography of his journalistic contributions,
of necessity incomplete, lists 296 separate items.

Observing that there was no record of a Tory or illiberal
government granting an honorable pension except to a
partisan, he expressed gratitude to Gosse and Lord Crewe
but intimated that they should let the matter drop.[83]

The suit apparently was abandoned for a number of
years. Not until 1906, after Balfour's ministry had fallen
and the Liberals were in power, did Davidson's friends
renew the application. There were the usual bureaucratic
delays until he was beside himself with anxiety and disappointment over "the putrescent business of the pension."
Others, unknown writers, received substantial annuities;
the matter had been aired with a bad smell in the press;
and then, after being assured of a pension, he had again
been put off. With an earnestness that was only partly
mock he threatened to buy a powerful air gun that could
be carried up the sleeve and to shoot off the members
of the government one by one.[84] Finally in 1906 the poet,
who was opposed to both democracy and socialism and
who in his writings celebrated rule by an aristocratic elite
headed by a supreme autocrat, received from a Liberal
government an annual pension of £100. The pension was
too small and came too late to postpone an end already
inevitable.

Not the least of Davidson's afflictions during these final
years was his prolonged, enervating war with editors and
critics. The disheartening reception of *The Theatrocrat*
had brought his simmering contempt for the press to a
full boil. After that episode his general suspicion and
hatred found an outlet in a series of blood vendettas with
William Archer, A. B. Walkley, E. V. Lucas, and Alfred
Douglas. He had never been the critics' darling, but as his
work became belligerently propagandistic he seemed determined to alienate them further. For several years he
made a practice of replying to every review of his works

that he thought unfair, in itself enough to occupy one
man full time. It was also his policy to reply on the spur
of the moment, while in the heat of anger. His wrath
aroused by an American critic, he wrote to Richards, "It is
hateful that such jargon as he writes should dog one
across the Atlantic. But should not the publishers take
some concerted action in the matter of the general incompetence and the twaddle of the purveyors of literary
news. They have the whip hand: let them boycott the
advertising columns." Then abruptly with characteristic
detachment he cited his own outburst as having "the very
sound of the gibberish they talk in the Authors' Club." [85]
More and more he grew angry in haste to repent at leisure.

Out of natural reticence and principle Davidson had
shrunk for many years from the role of public man. He
had resisted any form of personal advertisement, objecting
even to the universal custom of quoting excerpts from
favorable reviews in the back of his books. Each of his
works must be judged on its own merits without reference
to his other works or to himself. He granted few inter-
views and in those divulged little of his background. When
his publisher requested a photograph, he was obliged to
admit that he had not had one taken in many years, confessing "I hate every photograph of myself I have ever
seen." [86] Only as old photographs of him appeared in the
press did he consent to sit for a new one, which he did
not like any more than the others: "It reminds me of
Peace the murderer, who was also a man of genius, however." [87] Of Walter Sickert, the artist, the best that he
could say was, "I remember Sickert: I like him very well;
but not his picture of me." [88] In fairness to the subject it
should be said that Sickert's pen and ink sketch of Davidson is not among his best.

The misunderstanding and neglect of his works taught
Davidson the value of publicity. His sudden interest in

self-advertisement coincides with the appearance of the
Testaments and tragedies. Identifying himself inseparably
with their destiny, he consented eagerly to any device that
would win them a wider audience. He proposed to Richards that he now advertise the *man* more than his books, or
at least as much. Suddenly jealous of his new scheme, he
suggested that he have the exclusive advantage of it for a
while. "Others will imitate but not quickly, as it is so
egotistic a departure, so patently egotistic," he exulted
and submitted a "modest program" for advertising his
new books and himself: "The advertisement of *me* is
not very glaring here yet: this is only the thin end of the
wedge: I shall develop it more fully later on." [89] He now
craved public attention like the vainest matinee idol. His
most trivial output, the mere mention of his name, would
draw attention to him and therefore to his more indi-
gestible works. Whereas he had earlier repudiated his
ballads and eclogues, his novels and short stories, and his
journalistic ephemera, he now considered having them
reprinted as decoys to lure the public within range of his
diatribes and sermons.

This change in attitude is reflected in his disarmingly
detached comments upon Beerbohm's caricature of him
which appeared in the *Morning Chronicle* in January
1908:

> Curious that it should have selected my caricature for
> reproduction. It is, doubtless, one of the cleverest—
> a presentation of the terrible intellectual disease,
> swelled head. The face and skull are entirely dis-
> figured by the turgidity of the brain, of the thyroid
> gland, and of the pharyngeal organs; the eye crushed
> out of position; the nose is extended and spread like
> an inverted snout; the hat has to be carried in the
> hand as it is much too small for the head; the body

becomes stunted; the other extremities small in sympathy with the cranium; and a constant vertigo requires the assistance of a staff to maintain an erect posture.[90]

Beerbohm himself could not have analyzed his drawing more accurately. It speaks for Davidson's acute observation and talent for self-examination that he could read so much into the simple caricature. A desire for recognition, even of an adverse kind, is in moderation perfectly normal. In combining personal withdrawal and professional exhibitionism to such an advanced degree, Davidson displayed symptoms of malignant egoism. It may not be going too far to find evidence of a latent paranoia.* Although he nowhere explicitly admits to the fear of insanity, his almost uninterrupted preoccupation with the theme of madness and his eagerness to demonstrate its association with genius indicate that for many years the possibility may have lurked in the recesses of his mind. Aside from certain personal prejudices and idiosyncrasies, he appears to have confined his irrationality largely to his works and eruptions in the press.

That he suffered intermittently for years from bronchitis and asthma is a known fact. As he grew older he was less able to resist these ailments, so that during the winter months he was almost continuously ill. Eventually they forced him into involuntary exile from a beloved but

* Cornelius Weygandt, who has traced the theme of madness in Davidson's works, believes that from the beginning his mind showed signs of abnormality but that the condition became increasingly worse. He finds that Davidson's interest in cruelty and pain proceeds from humane sensitiveness through shuddering acceptance and ironic scrutiny to savage delight. The first signs of obsession and derangement, he notes, appear in the last two Testaments. (Weygandt, *The Time of Yeats*, pp. 60–1.) Lester mentions Davidson's fear "that he too might fall a prey to a tragic illness which had afflicted his family" but gives no evidence beyond that of the poet's works. Lester, "Friedrich Nietzsche and John Davidson," p. 419, n. 44.

"MR. JOHN DAVIDSON"
Caricature by Sir Max Beerbohm, 1907

miasmic London, first to Shoreham in Sussex and finally
to the remote end of Cornwall in 1907. One of his most
prolonged attacks occurred when he was bedeviled by
the failure of *The Theatrocrat* and the feuds to which it
gave rise. He frequently refused to give in, jesting that a
bronchial cold gave his voice a deep timbre, "a 'stiff
bourdon' as Chaucer says," and boasting that he kept
going "like a young one when most men would have been
in bed." Confined by one respiratory infection or another, he could still take facetious cheer in the theory that
asthma was supposed to immunize its victims against other
diseases, was "neither more nor less than the elixir of
life." [91] Writing Archer in the winter of 1899, he made a
grim Davidsonian joke of his recurrent attacks of influenza:

> This influenza is a very horrible thing. I always
> insist that it is one of the old plagues that has lin-
> gered on in an emasculated form, impotent compared
> with its uncut prime, but with the nasty malice of the
> eunuch well developed. I used to think I had it every
> winter until two years ago the "authentic" beast
> came padding my way. I hope it has been kinder to
> you than it was to me, or if I must curse you, I hope
> it has dealt with you as it did with me. It made a way
> for itself through every organ of my body, and a
> post-mortem would track its spoor from my kidneys to
> my *pia mater*. Chiefly it so munched my head that
> the jackal insomnia takes a snack whenever he likes.
> All day my brain seems to be naked and a mouthful
> bitten out at the back; and at night I get out of bed
> and do the other odd thing that suggests itself, as
> this.[92]

The removal to Penzance may have prolonged his life,
but even there he suffered periodically from asthma and
influenza. He discovered that he had felt almost better in

London where the fog had relieved the congestion in his
lungs.

These setbacks left their mark on his character as on
his writings. Although defeat strengthened the courage
and independence that he had always shown, it also nourished the more somber side of his personality. He became less flexible, more dogmatic and irascible in his
professional dealings. He had periods of great depression
which sapped his energy and will, preventing all work.
Upon reviving he would again dissipate his resources in
vain acts of defiance. There are signs of delusions of being
persecuted, for which he found release in a savage fury
toward not only critics and journalists but also laborers,
the poor, and the diseased whose sufferings he had once
sympathetically described. Even a postal clerk unable to
read his nearly illegible handwriting came in for abuse.
"The sublime humour of the sorting clerk who wrote
above 'Carlton Street,'—'Try Carlton Street,' is not to be
matched out of officialdom," he sputtered.[93] Such outbursts, however trifling or sporadic they may have been,
contrast with the supreme stoical indifference that he had
previously manifested. Together with the iconoclasm of
his works that follow they mirror a consuming hatred of
society and withdrawal from it.

5

For a year prior to the publication of *The Theatrocrat*
Davidson had been composing lyrics, chiefly for the *Outlook* and the *Pall Mall Magazine*. He had drawn the material for a number of these poems from earlier prose accounts of tramps in and around London, dating back to
1893 and 1894. The reception of the *Prime Minister* and
The Theatrocrat at last made clear to him what his publisher already knew, that these works would not pay for
themselves, much less additional Testaments and trage-

dies. Although it is difficult today to understand how they could have been so shortsighted, they took steps to restore the poet's solvency as a lyric singer. Early in June 1906, on the eve of the summer holidays, Richards brought out *Holiday and Other Poems* as tempting fare for the vacation reader. Considering Davidson's views on the decadence of rhymed poetry and his dedication to announcing a materialist millennium, this volume was an embarrassing moral retreat. It was no more satisfying financially.

Holiday is a collection of journeyman work. Since it was an act of neither defiance nor conformity, it enjoyed the disadvantages of both and the advantages of neither. The volume is marred by periodic irruptions of Poe's more obvious tricks of style, verbal repetition and recurrent rhyme. The eclogues, which comprise two-thirds of its contents, substitute metrical ingenuity for the fluent ease of the earlier lyrics. In spite of this the volume contains a half dozen of Davidson's most successful rhymed lyrics, notably, "Holiday," "A Runnable Stag," "Apple Trees," and "Yuletide." These poems fuse the melodic tenderness of his early verse and the stalwart masculinity of his later poetry to produce an arresting paradoxicality all too uncommon in his final work. Although a combination of lyricism and robustness was no novelty in English poetry of the period—Stevenson, Henley, Kipling, and later Masefield and Lawrence come immediately to mind—no one could be more spontaneously lyric or vigorously robust than Davidson.

As if to retract its lyric contents, the poet appended to the volume a "Note on Poetry" in which he made it clear that in returning to the lyric strain he had not struck his colors. This postscript explains carefully that rhymed verse represents a primitive form of artistic expression, that it is merely "the manure and root of a higher manifestation of that art," namely blank verse. Blank verse alone is superior and sublime. Here is the popular theory of evolution applied without proof to poetry. "I know of nothing so entertaining, so absorbing, so full of contentment, as the making of blank verse," he wrote; "it is a supreme relief of nervous tension, the fullest discharge of emotion, the greatest deliverance of energy; it satisfies the blood and the brain, the bones and the marrow." [94] With this pronouncement, which reads like those advertising the patent medicines he so cordially detested, Davidson had —as he very well knew—again thrown down the gauntlet. For one critic who welcomed in the lyrics the return to the "pure boyishness" of the modern age,[95] there were numerous others—guardians of established verse—who dismissed the poetry and leveled their sights on the challenging Note. The poet was accused of blaming rhyme for an artificiality and decadence that were really produced by his own love of tricky ornament.[96] To define poetry, as he had, as spontaneous and undisciplined was to define anarchy, he was told; all poetry was voluntary servitude, but good poets bore the servitude with such ease and grace that it looked like freedom and the natural state. The Note was the product of an "isolated, wilfully disconnected spirit, disporting itself in a vacuum apart from realities . . . we store up in our minds the memory of the brightness, but we continue to go on our own road." [97] Both Davidson in his prose appendix and the critics in their reviews made the mistake of confusing the poet's thesis with the examples of his own poetry which he used to defend it. This was to look at the horizon through a reading glass. Davidson's personal obsessions and the frequent incompetence of his work no longer obscure the timeliness of his terrible vision and warning. History has shown at an ineffable cost that this vision, and the romantic malady that produced it, was not so isolated from realities as the critics who scornfully dismissed it.

9

PENZANCE AGAIN,
1907-09

> He was a son of God—a phrase which,
> if it means anything, means just
> that—and he must be about His
> Father's business, the service of a
> vast, vulgar, and meretricious beauty.
> *F. Scott Fitzgerald*

Toward the end of January 1906 David-
son had gone to St. Ives in Cornwall, a fishing hamlet and
popular resort whose winters were reputed to be milder
than those of Rome. Wishing to escape the inclement
weather of Streatham and to write still another play in
prose for the stage, he continued there until March of that
year. The subject and fate of the play that he wrote remain
another mystery. Upon his return home he began a work
much closer to his heart, a new tragedy in blank verse
and the first part of a projected trilogy illustrating further
his philosophy. This was *The Triumph of Mammon*
which, in spite of recurrent attacks of bronchitis and
asthma during the following winter, he completed in
February 1907. Richards had agreed to publish the work.
In a note appended to the play Davidson informed his
readers, "This book is published on the 11th of April, 1907,
my fiftieth birthday. Nine-tenths of my time, and that

389

which is more precious, have been wasted in the endeavour
to earn a livelihood. In a world of my own making I should
have been writing only what should be written." [1]

This melodrama is a grotesque hodgepodge of pseudo-
Shakespearian blank verse; elaborate stage settings in the
tradition of nineteenth-century historical drama; preposterous situations and dialogue; indecorous scenes concerned with castration and the consummation of marriage;
symbolic action, characters, and names—Christian, Mammon, Magnus, Gottlieb; Whitmanesque or archaic diction; and stale imagery. Nevertheless it possesses the same
demonic strength and energy to which Davidson's readers
had become accustomed. Set in Christianstadt, mythical
capital of Thule, the play "occupies about twenty hours
of 1907, or any succeeding year for some time to come."
Davidson combines allegory, feudal trappings, and such
twentieth-century paraphernalia as slot machines, battle-
ships, and telegrams to suggest, like Shaw, a timeless setting.
In crude, protoartistic fashion the play fuses the rodo-
montade of Spasmodic and romantic drama with something of Ibsen's and Maeterlinck's symbolist method, the
expressionist techniques of August Strindberg and Gordon Craig, and the epic drama of Bertolt Brecht.

The plot, wholly implausible except as romantic allegory, treats the return of a renegade prince, Mammon, a
modern counterpart of the prodigal son, to the Christian
state of Thule. After murdering his brother Magnus, he
enters into an unsanctified marriage with Guendolen, his
former sweetheart and his brother's virgin wife. Later
when the king has his son bound to the altar of the cathedral and threatens to emasculate him if he does not recant,
Mammon outwits his father and slays him. King Christian
is an image of the traditional but invalid authority vested
in God and the father, Magnus represents spineless convention, and Abbot Gottlieb and others stand for still

further anachronistic loyalties preserved by a moribund
Christianity. In destroying these opponents Mammon
destroys the institutions which they symbolize and the
false dichotomies of spirit and flesh, father and son, virtue
and sin upon which society has been based. He represents the new will to power and synthesis; Guendolen,
also in the Spasmodic tradition, is natural chastity. In a
final blood bath Mammon destroys by machine gun such
unwholesome rival factions as the Christians, pagan atheists, Teutonic nationalists, and Marxian socialists. He
commits all these deeds in the name of a materialist universe, a master civilization, and his own glorified ego. The
play is thus a parable, a modern morality employing symbolic character and action to predict the overthrow of
Christianity and the advent of a new autocratic order.

A prose epilogue to the verse drama takes up at random
such topics as the history of English literature, Wordsworth and Shakespeare, Turner, the nebular hypothesis,
light and sound—all regarded from the materialist view-
point. Displaying his wounds like a modern Coriolanus,
Davidson discusses in his epilogue the public neglect of his
Testaments and tragedies, which he attributes to the commercialism, conventional morality, and triviality of the
London literary and theatrical world. He promises to go
on pointing out these conditions until the world takes
note of them and produces his plays.

With his usual concern for the success of his book he
promptly instructed his publisher to send an early
copy to W. L. Courtney, the well-disposed drama critic
of the *Daily Telegraph,* but none to the *Academy* "who
would come out immediately with some stale imperti-
nence," and none to Shaw "who hates all poetry." [2] These
and other precautions did not avert a cold welcome. The
critics complained that workmanship, taste, self-control,
and humility had been abandoned to railing, dramatic

absurdities, and an overmastering egoism; the artist had been swallowed up in the zealot and reformer. "The whole performance reminds one of a small boy in a passion shouting bad words at his nurse!" scolded the *Academy* which itself had adopted the role of nanny to the contemporary arts.[3] The more impartial *Times Literary Supplement* reported that the drama's message was nothing but warmed-over Lucretius and that only the poetry, when not riddled with neologisms, was "passably good, and sometimes more than that."[4] Acknowledging his complimentary copy, A. E. Housman expressed a similar view to Grant Richards:

> Thanks for the Triumph of Mammon which is much more interesting to read than the Theatrocrat; but as for his knowledge which is going to change the world, it is just like the doctrine of the Trinity: probably false, and quite unimportant if true. The five lines at the top of p. 17 are the sort of thing he does really well.*[5]

Few except the author seemed disposed to take the work's message seriously.

Although Davidson was reluctant to be drawn into further controversy, loyalty to his convictions would not permit him to let these gibes go unacknowledged. He wrote to Richards from Penzance, "As I wrote at large about *The Theatrocrat,* when the attack was much less venomous, it seemed wise to write at least one auspicious letter about *The Triumph of Mammon,* especially since it has

---

* The lines in question are:

> . . . or beauty breaks
> In blossoms and the sweet sex of the rose
> Perfumes the way, or when the crescent moon,
> Recut anew in pallid gold, adorns
> The saffron sunset, like an odour changed
> To purest chrysolite and hung in heaven . . .

been suggested that it should be withdrawn." The open letter, brief and dignified if a little pompous, was sent to the *Athenaeum* and the *Times* as "the principal literary and principal news sheet in the world." [6] In it he stated that he had refrained from replying to the attacks on his latest work as he had not to previous attacks "because what I could say with full purpose would be unsuitable for publication in any periodical." Questions concerning art could not at the beginning of the twentieth century in England be discussed anywhere in public. He would have to note the animadversions upon his works and consider them in the appendices of his future works. As for the mounting virulence of his enemies, he rejoiced in it more than in the good will of his friends because a man's character and greatness would be known fully not by the company he kept but by the enemies he made.[7] This new policy of aloofness may have disappointed his enemies and put his friends at ease, but it meant that he had determined to subordinate his personality to his published writings. Swallowing his pride, he reserved his remaining powers to hurl at the world a final sheaf of thunderbolts.

Tardily the *Athenaeum* came to Davidson's defense. Referring to the poet's statement in the epilogue of his latest play that the world was unfitted for him and that he was therefore destroying it, the review stated, "It is uncritical to dismiss this attitude of defiance as a symptom of morbid egoism, for we find it in many great poets who have forced the world to worship them. The reformers of one age are the classics of the next. Mr. Davidson is as true a poet as Blake, and his genius compels us to accord him a hearing." [8] After a lame attempt to justify *The Triumph of Mammon,* first as an allegory that substitutes the cosmogony of man and science for that of Christianity, and then as an imaginative work whose delight is "purely aesthetic," Davidson's anonymous apologist called him

by his right name, a prophet. Here at last was recognition
that he must be judged by standards peculiar to his own
anomalous writings or at least to those half-inspired, half-
mad ravings of the oracle.

2

Davidson had shown less sustained interest in the fate
of *The Triumph of Mammon* than in that of any of his
previous works. This was partly because he had made up
his mind to let his writings speak for themselves and him,
and partly because he had to turn to the immediate problem of making ends meet. Accordingly he set out in March
1907 for a two months' tour of the southwestern counties,
Hants, Devonshire, and Cornwall, in search of fresh material for still another collection of lyrics. He had to do the
trip in the cheapest way possible, unable even to put up
Richards during a weekend visit. Still, it afforded him
one more holiday from family and the daily struggle for
survival. From boyhood he had taken pleasure in these
rural walks, as if he found in nature the comradeship and
harmony that he could not find among society. A lively
letter full of regional chat about Lyndhurst, Hants, shows
that he had regained some of his early whimsicality. His
description of Lord Leighton's enormous fresco in Lyndhurst Church, however, is more typical of the coarse,
masculine, irreverent humor of his later years. "It illustrates the parable of the ten Virgins," he wrote. "It seems
to me very Jovelike. Had the whole ten of them come up
to scratch, it would have been necessary to paint a Her-
cules-Christ: Jove is bridegroom enough for five virgins." [9]
His principles had come to dominate his most trifling
chatter.

From the first week in April until early May 1907 he
remained in Devonshire, either at Totnes near Dartmoor

Forest and the shore or at Christchurch. He was far from idle. In addition to collecting material for proposed lyrics and sketches he was searching for a new place in which to live. On May 9 he reported to Richards from Penzance that he had taken a house there. "I hope ultimately to be all spring, summer and autumn in London," he stated optimistically, "but I must get out of it in the winter if I am to live." [10] Like many of his expectations the plan to divide the year between London and Cornwall proved an empty daydream. Early in June he moved with his family to 6 Coulson's Terrace, Penzance. The house which he leased was part of a terrace like those of Bath and Belgrave Square, once handsome and fashionable but by this time run-down and backing on a slum street where children played noisily all day. Except for brief, infrequent holidays in London he remained in Cornwall, lonely and homesick, until his death. His exile was not merely physical but intellectual and spiritual as well. The truth of the matter was that Davidson, although older by a number of years than most of his fellow writers of the nineties, had outlived all but a few of them. Stevenson, Henley, Wilde, Dowson, Johnson, Gissing, Sharp, and Thompson died before he did. Their flame may have been hard and gemlike but it did not survive the steadier light of Ruskin, Morris, Tennyson, Samuel Butler, Spencer, Tyndall, and Leslie Stephen, the older generation whose skepticism and willingness to compromise had added fuel to their revolt. Only Beerbohm, Le Gallienne, Shaw, and Yeats were still living, but they had either left England or in their thinking had kept more attuned to the temper of the times. Davidson wandered like the only living man in a country inhabited by ghosts or, more accurately, like an implacable ghost in the land of the living.

If he felt himself in the realm of the dead, the rugged

coast of Cornwall and the inland country pocketed with
abandoned mines and quarries were no fair Elysian fields.
He did not escape there the torments which had made a
purgatory of his life. A man who was always cheerful when
the sun shone, who worshiped it as the ultimate source of
life and strength, and who met death at sunset after a
clear day, he was bitterly disappointed in the overrated
virtues of the Cornish coast. For a year his health appeared
to improve, but in February 1908 and the following
spring he had severe attacks of asthma and influenza from
which he was twelve months in recovering. "Cornwall, I'm
certain I must have told you before," he wrote to a friend,
"is a scandalous invention of the Great Western Railway.
It is the most abominable climate I ever struck." [11]

To add to his burden, he was unable to find a publisher
for the works prepared during the three months' sojourn
in the southwestern counties: the new play in prose, the
lyrics, and the sizable collection of prose sketches entitled
"Causeway and Forest." This last, comprising semiauto-
biographic material, short notices of Wilde, Gissing, and
others, and miscellaneous contributions to the periodicals,
had been compiled for the sole purpose of gaining money.
Richards and he were unable to agree on terms, perhaps
because similar books of his had failed so dismally. No
more is heard of "Causeway and Forest," as of the play,
beyond Davidson's suggestion that the shelved book be
published and dedicated to the editor of the *Academy* "in
order to have the pleasure of gibbeting his reiterated
lie." [12]

The episode to which this refers typifies the almost constant harassment to which the poet was subjected during
the last two years of his life. In a recent note on the in-
decency of novels by women authors, the *Academy* had
misquoted Davidson as saying that "the more masculine
and less delicate minds among men dislike women except

in their sexual relations." * Moreover, it had objected to the inclusion in the pension list of an author who had presumed to write of "the stolid mind and defective imagination of Matthew Arnold," a man so greatly his superior.[13] Departing from his resolution to answer no more of these attacks, Davidson wrote a prompt, indignant reply. He addressed it not to the editor but to the proprietors of the *Academy,* to ensure its being published. He charged the editor with misquoting him "designedly and very meanly" and of perpetrating "the basest lie that has been acted in the name of literary criticism." The letter concluded with the recommendation that the editor resign to make room for some more honest man.[14] Many disputes over principles deteriorate into clashes of personality. With Davidson, who seldom distinguished between an individual and his principles, literary quarrels began where others ended. Characteristic of this fusion of his personal life and his literary career is his decision to leave a farewell note in the form of a literary preface.

For Lord Alfred Douglas, then closely associated with the *Academy* and in large part responsible for its editorial policy, and for Frank Harris, still on friendly if guarded terms with Douglas, Davidson had a long-standing aversion. His contempt was born of previous quarrels, hatred for dishonest and wanton injury, and distaste for the celebrated effeteness of the one and the swaggering immodesty of the other. "When did Alfred Douglas become editor of *The Academy?*" he asked Richards.† "Such a

* What Davidson had actually written was that "the more masculine, and therefore more delicate, minds among men dislike women except in their sexual relations, as mothers, wives, lovers, sisters." "As if any one could substitute 'less delicate' for 'more delicate' inadvertently," Davidson remonstrated to Richards. A.L.S., dated 27 July 1907, from 6 Coulson's Terrace, Penzance, P.U.L.

† Lord Alfred Bruce Douglas was editor of the *Academy* from 1907 to 1910. His control of the review was not officially and publicly announced

thing should have been published from the housetops. In
the name of the Universe what have we to do with such
filthy fellows! And Frank Harris will be in it also of
course; a man with a loud voice and a dull pen who knows
and understands nothing." [15] When *The Testament of
John Davidson* appeared in October 1908, the old feud
with the *Academy* flared up, precipitating a vitriolic correspondence in that review.

Difficulties were not confined to editors. Copyright reg-
ulations before the Copyright Act of 1911 were infamously
inadequate; like other authors Davidson was often at the
none too tender mercies of publishers and booksellers at
home and abroad. The most extended dispute was with
Alexander Moring of the De La More Press, who had
bought out Grant Richards' first business and therefore held
all the stock of Davidson's works published by that firm.
For nearly two years Richards and the poet's agent, A. P.
Watt, negotiated without success to repurchase this stock.
With a sense of impending doom Davidson in February
1908 wished to reissue the best of his early prose and his
later plays.[16] He wished also to bring out his four Testaments in a single edition to herald the forthcoming
"Testament of a Deliverer," ultimately published as *The
Testament of John Davidson*.[17] When the transaction
finally collapsed he wearily dismissed both projects from
his mind, "knowing by experience that the true business
value of my remainders will appear in a year or two, and
that I will then be able to burn them for a five pound
note." [18] Moring he also dismissed as "a human swamp"
and "a dog in the manger." [19] Davidson's eye must have
been glittering ever to have persuaded Richards to reissue
his earlier works, since both knew that they could not sell
any faster than his new ones. To the end he had the fer-

until the issue of 10 Oct. 1908, when his name was proclaimed in inch-
high letters from the masthead.

vent, contagious militancy of a knight marching on Constantinople or tilting at windmills.

3

In his first letter to Richards after he had moved his family to Penzance, Davidson announced that he had at last begun the second part of his trilogy and that he intended to give it the ironical title of "The World's Failure." [20] By the end of the year he had completed the verse drama but was keeping it beside him until he could write the introduction and a concluding essay. He seemed as anxious and jealous for the new work as if it had been his first. It was a foregone conclusion in his mind that the firm of Grant Richards would publish the remaining parts of the trilogy as it had the first. He expressed the hope that the play would appear in the same month as Filson Young's forthcoming article on him,[21] but he missed his opportunity when the article came out on January 1 in the *Fortnightly Review*. On the last day of the old year Davidson informed his publisher that he now intended to call the play *Mammon and His Message* and that it should be ready not later than February. Characteristically he diverted a New Year's greeting into a left-handed pat on his own back: "I wish you a very happy and prosperous new year in your business and in your art—my books being part of your art." Then he added wistfully, "I do long to see London again; and shall, I hope, soon, but circumstances are devils of fellows." [22]

After his early enthusiasm had waned, Davidson took for him few measures to launch *Mammon and His Message*. Certain steps and precautions, however, seemed appropriate. Late in April he suggested to Richards that they make the date of publication "The fifth: that's Ascension Day, when Christ 'opened the Kingdom of Heaven to all believers.' By all means let me, on the same day, throw

wide the gates of the Universe to all unbelievers." The
only literary people to whom he had sent inscribed copies
of *The Triumph of Mammon,* he recalled not altogether
accurately, had been William Archer, Max Beerbohm,
and the editor of the *Glasgow Herald.* On this occasion
he would eliminate Archer: ". . . he is at present wrapt
up in Ibsen, one of these foreign belittlers of men; and
when he is not revising his translation of Ibsen, he is
reading 'Wee Magregor' and eating 'taiblet.' * He has
no right to express an opinion of my writings at all: a
man who can write a book about 37 living poets understands nothing about poetry." He could find no room in
his heart to forgive Archer for "an unsigned snuffling condemnation of 'The Triumph of Mammon' " which he believed the critic had written. Beerbohm received a copy
of the book and a letter as well, for he was, Davidson confessed, "the only writing person in London out of all
the crowd whom I seem to care at all for." [23] It is remarkable, in view of the Scot's sensitivity and pride, that he retained for Max a lifelong regard. As his quarterly pension
check permitted, he entertained Beerbohm and Richards
in turn at the stylish Trocadero restaurant.[24] Having declared that he would write no letters of advance publicity
or injunction concerning *Mammon and His Message,* he
soon warmed to the task and wrote two. He asked Richards
to send them along with review copies unless he knew
"of some terrible impediment." [25] An unpracticed eye
might have read a danger sign in this vacillation between

* *Wee Macgregor* (1902) by John Joy Bell, about a boy who talks in
dialect; dramatized, 1912. "TABLET . . . *Sc.* (*taiblet*), hardbake or almond
toffy made in tablets. *c. 1900 Wee Macgregor* i, 2. I want taiblet. *Ibid.* 5."
(*N.E.D.,* Oxford, Clarendon Press, 1919, *9,* 11.) Compare: "I saw you had
found 'Wee Magregor' [*sic*]? It is indeed good Scotch porridge—too much
boiled perhaps. J.J.B.—John Joy Bell: I taught him in Crieff Academy;
parsing and analysis that is. Literature is unteachable." A.L.S., Davidson
to William Archer, 23 Jan. 1903, from 9 Fairmile Ave. Streatham, S.W.,
Add. MS. 45291, ff. 109–10, B.M.

anxiety and indifference to details. If Richards seems to
have been blind to it, one must remember that he had
been long accustomed to the poet's capricious ways, that
they were now prevented by distance from meeting to iron
out problems, and that Davidson in all matters not related to his works remained common sense itself.

The purpose of his dramatic trilogy, the author announces in a prefatory note to *Mammon and His Message*,
is to show in the first two parts that Mammon, inspired by
his great personal message, is able "to transcend all dis-
honour, all crime, the utmost evil that he could do"; and
in the third, "the utmost evil that could be done to
him." [26] It is Davidson's ironic conviction, as it is Mammon's, that the end always justifies the means. *Mammon
and His Message* therefore is given over almost entirely to
the hero's attempts to overcome resistance to his creed and
impose his will upon Thule. He undertakes this first by
demagogy and bribery, then by the basest, most inhuman
acts. In Mammon's dictatorial measures and their consequences Davidson's readers might have read a stern
warning of modern political conditions. The powers withdraw their representatives, the army is mobilized, there is
no communication across borders, and recourse is had to
torture and brainwashing.

The action of Part II follows that of *The Triumph of
Mammon* by one week. As the play opens, Guendolen,
Princess of the Isles, a neighboring country that suggests
England of the past as Mammon's Thule suggests England's future, has become the mistress of Mammon and a
convert to his gospel of materialism. Although his conquest of Guendolen has been virtually effortless, the king
faces stiffer problems as the new ruler of Thule. Oswald,
his friend, who is leader of the army and newly created
Duke of Christianstadt, wishes to return to the old ways
of Christianity. Various non-Christian sects—the Teu-

tonics (race worshipers), the Reformers of the Isles (Marxian socialists), and the Neo-Pagans (nature idolaters)—
join in an uneasy conspiracy to dethrone Mammon by
seizing the Bank of Thule. Anselm, the papal legate, and
Gottlieb, the Abbot of Christianstadt, remain as unwelcome representatives of a decadent Christianity which
Mammon feels compelled to eradicate. Finally he must
cope with poverty, disease, and prostitution, the vestigial
remnants of Christendom.

With each of his problems the arrogant tyrant deals as
his despotic principles dictate. He urges the conscience-
stricken Oswald to marry at once his betrothed, Inga the
Volsung, an imperious, passionate pagan woman who
appears in many of Davidson's plays. "Keep your soul
bright with sin," he instructs Oswald, glorifying the body's
excretal and reproductive powers as alike a renewal of
life. The earth-mother Inga is set off by the gentle,
more passive Guendolen as Oswald, a lackluster character,
represents Mammon's lingering conscience.[27] Thus Oswald
and Mammon are the reverse and obverse sides of Davidson's own divided nature and the divided nature he finds
in all men. As Mammon's alter ego, Oswald is a familiar
psychological device much used by the earlier romantics,
as well as by the Spasmodics and decadents. He corresponds in this play to Angelus' *Doppelgänger* in *Diabolus Amans* and to Hallowes, the poet-friend of the hero in
Smith. This device enables the romantic to convey the
ambiguity of love, the existence side by side of *eros* and
agape, sexual love and spiritual, profane and divine,
ephemeral and eternal.[28] Davidson's lyrics record tenderly
and poignantly man's dilemma in the face of this paradox,
as the poet embraces an ironic universe. In later writings
he departs from other romantic poets by refusing to sub-
mit to any form of dualism and by seeking a primarily
intellectual resolution. Eros is elevated and exalted, agape

is absorbed into eros, so that the renegade from evangelical Calvinism may enjoy the illusion of destroying the pietistic, penitential side of his own character and of asserting the natural and egoistic. This is the unconscious, deeply subjective motive behind the writing of the Mammon plays. Mammon symbolizes this synthesis of self by sublimation when he overwhelms Oswald through superior force of character, argument, and physical strength. To eliminate altogether the anachronisms of conscience and mercy embodied in Oswald, Mammon orders him to assist in torturing Gottlieb on the rack, which ironically has been preserved in the royal museum. Then in defiance of whatever gentle virtues are left unbroken, he shamelessly seduces Inga. He justifies this betrayal to the voluptuous Volsung, "My message is a deed, always a deed." For her to remain a barren virgin or to accept the unworthy Oswald is for the universe to remain unfulfilled. From her embrace he goes with the unwitting Oswald to the museum where he enlarges his experience and illustrates his message further by torturing Abbot Gottlieb.

The central scene in the play is that in which Mammon endeavors to convert the papal legate Anselm to his barbaric creed. Here Davidson's hero becomes a tremendous, satanic figure tempting the old Christian with the power and beauty of his superior vision. In long, discursive speeches the king gives a materialist interpretation to each of the central Christian doctrines. When Anselm resists, Mammon hurls the priest from him in violent contempt, killing him. From this point on the play is a Spasmodic orgy, a series of episodes, each more horrible than the preceding, designed to exhibit Mammon's power and to complete his self-fulfillment through conscienceless action. Twice he seems burdened by guilt as he sees, beside the corpse of Anselm, apparitions of his father's and brother's bodies with the gaping wounds he had given them. But

these hallucinations, he explains to Oswald, result from
the unexpectedness of the idea of crime and the material
fatigue accompanying it. When Guendolen protests against
his burning the magnificent abbey of Christianstadt,
Mammon impresses her with the necessity of annihilating
the past, "Books, buildings, pictures and the hearts of
men." Wonderingly she envisages the destruction of civilization and the end of all humanity. Her pride matches
the enormity of her consort's as she shares his vision of a
world begun again, "And you and I in Eden left alone!"

The play ends with Mammon, who has overcome all
opposition by sheer terrorism, comparing himself to
Zenghis, Tamerlane, Mahomet, and in a final triumphant
address to his followers, to the sun:

> Suns cannot wait: in your own orbits you
> And all men move containëdly; your years
> Are measured by the gamut of the seasons
> And ebon-ivory scale of day and night;
> But my adventurous path no orbital
> Appointment knows: onward I move; my year,
> Eternity; my high arena, space
> With stars like sands bestrewn: my journey's end
> Still unattained and unattainable.
> Yet all the while you glide along with me,
> Planets and asteroids and meteorites,
> Clear depths of crystal and wandering fires.[29]

Verse like this results when a dramatic poet forgets the
magic formula that transforms abstract ideas into human
character and speech: The wand is arrested in mid-arc and
creatures speaking the tongue of Caliban and Hecate are
misbegotten. Mammon's final message is that men possess
in equal measure the capacity for greatness, but that only
one man has yet achieved this greatness. Through his hero
Davidson himself addresses the world:

I'll carve the world
In my own image, I, the first of men
To comprehend the greatness of mankind;
I'll melt the earth and cast it in my mould,
The form and beauty of the universe.[30]

Mammon has demonstrated that man's natural impulses will ultimately destroy mechanized society, with its intellect and morality, by utilizing its own weapons of money, industry, and armaments. Yet Mammon's fate as this Armageddon looms remains uncertain. If at the end of Part II he is once again in the ascendancy, further trials and momentary defeats clearly await him in a hostile, uncomprehending world. Whatever befalls him in the next and final part of the trilogy, the hero who is an idealization of John Davidson cannot fall short of absolute greatness.

There are marked sexual overtones in *Mammon and His Message* as elsewhere in Davidson's works; in fact the play is centered on the vital role of sex in human affairs. An obsession with the erotic had already marked his early Spasmodic plays which place an exaggerated emphasis upon the male vigor and irresistible physical attractiveness of their heroes. In the novels and ballads of the London period it as often showed itself in the familiar decadent forms of sadism, algolagnia, and masochism. As with his other fixed ideas, Davidson's fascination with sex found expression in the vogue of the moment. The Testaments and tragedies of his final period return uninhibitedly to the Spasmodic stress upon Herculean virility, linking intellectual and political power with sexual energy and introducing boldly the themes of adultery, vivisection, and human torture.

Since this sexual fixation is present in his work continuously and from the outset, it cannot be attributed to a

passing literary influence or to any single personal experience. There is no evidence in Davidson's case, moreover, as there is with Whitman, Dostoevsky, Swinburne,
Carlyle, Ruskin, Henry James, and Wilde, of physical
disability, sexual aberration, or psychic abnormality.
Nevertheless some sexual conflict and obsession seem to
have been a part of the poet's nature from early manhood,
possibly earlier. Unfortunately those years are veiled in
shadow and reticence. His marriage by Victorian standards at least was a normal, happy one. Like the most
respectable paterfamilias of his day, he preserved an inviolable discretion regarding his domestic and personal
affairs. The modern imagination, liberated or reharnessed
by Freud and Kinsey, must guard against reading into
such secretiveness anything sinister or melodramatic.
Given Davidson's strong physical appetites and his insatiable vitality, which as so often were intensified by
chronic illness and neurasthenia, he may very well have
been physically and emotionally unsatisfied. Certainly
poverty, drudgery, and failure must have contributed to
a repression and sense of unfulfillment. It seems likely
that for him, as for many of his contemporaries, other
drives and frustrations and a romantic *mal de siècle* became partly focused in the sexual. This in turn sought in
his writings a release that was unobtainable in private life.

Neither the circumstances of his marriage, if known, nor
a desire to violate the conspiracy of silence contrived by
the Grundies in matters of sex is sufficient to explain fully
Davidson's militant frankness on the forbidden subject.
To account for a celebration of sexual power and prowess,
at times tenderly lyrical, at others belligerent to the point
of being offensive or ludicrous, it is necessary to look
more deeply into his personality. What had alienated him
in the religion of his childhood had not been so much its
emotional fervor and emphasis upon penitential suffer-

ing as its denial of the individual's supremacy and his essentially natural being. A fervent mystic as well as vitalist, he wished to escape the mundane and to satisfy his metaphysical yearning in a primitive creed of earth and body worship. This is the paradox of his creed, and it finds ample authority in the nineteenth century and after. But for Davidson as for D. H. Lawrence the sexual experience was not merely a symbol of man's highest fulfillment or part of some semi-Platonic ritual leading to this fulfillment; it was quite simply the fulfillment itself. The materialist recognizes no religious experience apart from the physical, no religious truth apart from chemical and biological fact. The body is a temple in the literal sense; the sexual act is one of worship and sacrifice; the way of pollution is the way to purification. Since it is the equivalent of the mystic's ecstatic vision and not as with earlier mystic poets a convenient image of that vision, the sexual union for Davidson is heroic and holy. It is subject to no laws and may express itself in any form that nature dictates, however cruel, criminal, or perverted by conventional standards.

Although this conception of sex is not explicit until the Mammon plays, the germ is seen growing vigorously in his earliest works, fertilized by Swinburne and through him undoubtedly by the "Divine Marquis," de Sade. If Davidson was directly influenced by the writings of de Sade, he carefully concealed the fact. His sadism is as firmly rooted in naturalistic philosophy, however, as de Sade's own and reflects no more than the revolutionary French aristocrat's a mere striving after salacious effect for its own sake. He had the further distinction of adding to the philosophic naturalism of the eighteenth century the sanction of nineteenth-century science and his own Protestant emotionality.

A corollary to the role of sex in Davidson's work is that

of pain. In the early story "The Schoolboy's Tragedy," in
the narrative poems "The Ordeal" and "The Vengeance
of the Duchess," in *The Testament of a Vivisector,* and
in other previous works, he had dealt frankly and often
brutally with the theme of pain. The apotheosis of pain
conveyed his resolute repudiation of Christian pity; it
conveyed equally an inverted, probably unconscious attraction to the physical suffering by which the Christian
martyr and mystic achieves the highest fulfillment of self.
To experience pain, both as victim and agent, especially
to inflict pain on one's self, is to exercise fully man's
powers and to achieve knowledge:

> Nothing is needless—nothing men can do.
> I mean to tap the reservoir of pain;
> I'll see this mystery through that once enthralled
> Religion;—and I'll make a law that men
> Who live too long shall die upon the rack!
> Thus I'll dislodge the rookeries and unearth
> The foul old lairs that nestle in the world's
> Intelligence and burrow in its heart! [31]

Shocking or preposterous as such lines are, the ideas
themselves cannot be dismissed as irrational or lunatic.
Subsequent writers have fully accustomed us to the notion of man's physicality. It is their crude, hysterical expression, their unspeakable illustration, and the dangerous application which others would give to these ideas
that are undoubtedly psychotic. Lacking in Davidson's
rage for order are humor, equilibrium of reason and
emotion, and a sense of artistic form.

Nietzsche may have taught Davidson to despise the
poor, depraved, and infirm as "the hatefullest legacy of
Christ" and to oppose all forms of state aid to the
weak and inefficient. Both reformers found in cruelty a
refuge from their intolerable compassion for man's suf-

fering. Mammon in a grimly humorous scene gives the
harlots of the city the choice of becoming honest women
and mothers or of leaving the country; he condemns the
beggars and criminals to euthanasia. Conversely he will
not tolerate the money-changers in his palace; he despises
money as "the viscera, the flesh of Christendom," which
does not prevent him from employing it for his own
purposes. Davidson's hatred of social refuse and gold is
more than a reflection of Nietzsche. It speaks for his own
love of youth, animal vigor, beauty, and sexual potency;
his horror of age, disease, impotence, and poverty, in society and above all, as he grew older and more infirm, in
himself. Physical pain and death in the hands of the enlightened despot become instruments for combating these
evils. Thus he again translates personal obsession into
materialist and vitalist terms, and into the Spasmodic
idiom.

Davidson denied employing symbolism and allegory
and was probably not conscious of doing so, because they
ran contrary to his concept of poetry. Yet the Mammon
plays like the Spasmodic melodramas from which they
derive rely heavily on these devices. The imagery of
jewels, gold, the stars and constellations, the burning of
the abbey and use of the torture rack, and the principal
episodes are charged with symbolic meaning. These plays
look forward to an ideal world, still only in the making, in
which the author can achieve the happiness, power, and
singleness of being denied him in this. To him this brave
new world is the only real world. The individual characters who inhabit the final plays not only symbolize social and political forces in ferment but also give body to
Davidson's conflicting states of mind. [32] Through them
he seeks a resolution for himself and for the world. The
poet's last works without exception possess the heightened, distorted quality of fantasy or dream usually found

in art which deals directly with psychological, moral, and spiritual experience. They find their nearest analogues in seventeenth-century literature, notably Bunyan; the work of Blake, "Monk" Lewis, and Thomas Lovell Beddoes; and most closely the Continental expressionist movement. Why is it, then, that the *Mammon* plays and the Testaments, with the possible exception of the last, are artistic failures? Seldom rising above the level of melodrama, diatribe, and swollen rhetoric, they are at best grotesque moralities or barbaric pageants parading wooden puppets. They never come alive or move as allegory. Their ideas are too forceful, too abstracted from human experience and needs, too uppermost as ideas to permit effective personification. Their sincerity too often takes the form of obscenity, coarseness, and hysteria. Their brutality and soullessness are too seldom redeemed by dramatic plausibility or imaginative splendor.

That Davidson continued to value the imagination is evident from the prose epilogue to *Mammon and His Message* in which he states, "It is by the imagination that religion or any cause lives and prospers." [33] He gives as curious examples of contemporary institutions which satisfy the imaginations of their adherents the Salvation Army and the annual carnival at West Penwith in Cornwall, whose local rivalry he describes with wit and a sharp eye. His own message, he maintains, is neither a new religion nor a new philosophy but "the beginning of a new poetry" designed to give the satisfaction no longer afforded the imaginations of men by the old, worn-out faiths.

For all his protestations it is doubtful that Davidson ever understood the imagination and how it functions in poetry. Herein lies his chief weakness as a poet. He reduced reality to the material and the imagination to the apprehension and assimilation of that which is perceptible to the senses. In the materialist canon this is the only definition possible, but it committed him to describing human experience and natural phenomena in terms of themselves instead of in terms of each other. Everything to the monist is of equal value and beauty because everything is equally material, whether stars, diamonds, loaves of bread, or human offal. *Mammon and His Message* treats with the same ingenuous reverence the sublimities of nature and contraception, love and excretion, jewels and food. Other poets have coupled images no less disparate, but in comparing evening to a nun breathless with adoration or to a patient etherized upon a table, they have insisted upon the metaphorical validity of their analogy to the same degree that they have been aware of its scientific fallacy. Precisely because irony is the central law governing the world of poetry, it cannot be made the law of the universe. For the metaphorical and ironic relationships that characterize, if not all poetry, at least the most exciting and memorable, the court poet of the universe substituted the jargon and elementary formulae of the Sunday scientist. When he is a poet in these final works, it is in spite of his doctrine and as if to spite himself. More often, to gain the rhapsodic effect, much of it wonderful of its kind, that he mistook for poetry, Davidson fell back upon the long-winded hyperboles, pedantic rant, and absurd histrionics of the Spasmodic. The result was not a new poetry, as he supposed, but an old dogma armed with the official credentials of the new science and the emotionalism of evangelical religion.

The amount of critical attention which *Mammon and His Message* received was equal to that given any of the poet's other works. Arguments both for and against adhered to the familiar patterns. Those who chose to defend the play concentrated for the most part on its message. In the opinion of one critic, it rang "the knell of the

merely abstract world of science and intellectual systems" by proclaiming a new faith. This champion, who
ignored Mammon to discuss his message, stated that in
attacking rationalism Davidson ranked himself with Swinburne and Nietzsche. In making clear that the conflict
was no longer between Christianity and the unbelieving
but between the Christian and some other faith, he belonged with Shaw and Mallock. "The conflict between
faith and faith will be deeper and more bitter, but more
wholesome and purifying than that between faith and
doubt," this reviewer predicted.* [34] While flattering, such
generalizations said very little. Other critics, also wel-
coming in the arena the presence of a new faith if unable
to accept it, noted Davidson's strong kinship with Christianity. Faith, action, earnestness, personality—the ingredients of the new gospel of materialism—were also the
ingredients of the old gospel.[35] Coming still closer to home,
the *Glasgow Herald* to which Davidson had contributed
frequently during his career, compared his energy to "that
of an orator carrying a countryside with him with an inexhaustible passion of rhetoric, or of a revivalist arguing,
pleading, preaching, with apparently miraculous renewal
of power and ever-recurring storms of emotion." [36] Davidson like Bunyan was close in spirit and purpose to the
itinerant evangelical preacher; he differed only in the
letter of his message. If his new message shared certain
qualities with the Christian, he left no doubt in the minds

* In spite of these comparisons Davidson was pleased with the review
and wrote to Richards: "I saw the *Athenaeum:* I fear I did misjudge
Rendall: I am glad he wasn't frightened after all. The review is by James
Douglas I understand. It is the civilest I have had; and sensible too, from
his point. The clear perception that the profound antithesis I insist on
exists, is further forward than any other published criticism has attained.
If Courtney would hasten out with his *Fortnightly* now!" (A.L.S., dated
24 Aug. 1908, 6 Coulson's Terrace, Penzance, P.U.L.) I find no other evidence that James Douglas, who wrote a less laudatory review for the *Star*,
is the author of this. Vernon Rendall was editor of the *Athenaeum*, 1901–
16; William L. Courtney, of the *Fortnightly Review*, from 1894.

of the most confused, said one reviewer, that his non-Christian creed led to an anti-Christian life.[37]

In opposition to those who found a new faith in *Mammon and His Message,* several objected that there was nothing at all new about the philosophy: "The non-moral superman, the need of self-realization, the glory of the body . . . and the old-fashioned *Uebermensch"* were very old hat. Thule was "a frank Cloud-cuckoo-land" while Mammon was a familiar bogeyman, "the superman turned bounder . . . a kind of provincial Nero" without Nero's redeeming artistic talent. Davidson himself had become a valetudinarian philosopher, prophet, and pedant. "Pedantry is the besetting danger of the superman," the *Times Literary Supplement* summed up, "prepossessed as he is with the fear of doing anything like other people." [38] But the most slashing review came from Walter de la Mare. Of the contemporary writers he was among those least likely to appreciate Davidson's later poetry, which was made of sterner stuff than his delicate spectral fantasies. De la Mare found even more offensive than the bestial, anarchical philosophy of the play its illustration in Mammon, "an epitome of the worst six Caesars—Suetonius condensed and distilled." "Around our bloated Gulliver revolves the Lilliput of Thule," he wrote. "It recalls a hundred dramas, unnumbered romances." Cleverness, egotism, and an effort to be shocking were poor exchange for the poet's earlier lyric gifts or for the sanity, lucidity, and restraint which the world and its art much needed.[39] It had always been easier to bury Davidson than to praise him, and the facetiousness with which de la Mare reviewed the play betrays an irritability and parochialism no more restrained than Davidson's own. The Gothic enormities perpetrated by Mammon had obscured for the younger Georgian the vital immediacy of Mammon's message.

The most consistent feature of the reviews which greeted

the controversial play was their inconsistency. For the
several defenders who praised the passionate energy and
virile strength of the verse, what they described as its
"tigerish" quality and "hot color," there were as many or
more who felt that these qualities had been wasted upon
a repellent subject matter and a turbulent, nonsensical
creed. For every defendant who hailed Davidson as a
spokesman of the coming dispensation, a twentieth-century
Lucretius, there were two detractors who found him a
stale, expendable reactionary. Unfortunately among critics
of any day there are fewer Solomons to say where truth
lies than there are Pilates who do not wait for an answer.
Davidson in retrospect stands out clearly as a Janus-like
figure, drawing his ideas from the century behind him and
molding them to personal needs and, as he supposed, the
needs of modern man. No other literary figure of his time
demonstrates more clearly that the political ideologies of
today are a corruption of the romantic ideals of yesterday.

4

Davidson's next and final work of consequence was *The
Testament of John Davidson,* the fifth in the series. It is
astonishing that he was able to write a poem of its length,
power, and imaginative sweep at this time. The new work
brimmed the edge of the poet's mind for several months
before it finally spilled over in unstanched flow. The idea
of a personal testament had been conceived in mid-January
1908, but by the end of the following April he had completed barely two hundred lines of the nearly twenty-five
hundred that make up the complete work.[40] On July 20
the minor epic was finished so that it must have been
written in less than three months, with interruptions from
other tasks. Richards published the poem in August, yielding in every particular to the poet's wishes "for this book,
which is my personal poem, which is me . . ." [41] Originally

called "The Testament of a Deliverer," the poem had later been given the title of "The Passionary of John Davidson." "I mean to create a legendary figure in my own name," the author had written to Richards, instructing him that " 'Passionary' is an old, almost unused, word for the history of a passion—any passion: the passion of Christ or of Sappho." [42] Subsequently he abandoned this title for the one finally chosen, after he had decided in a characteristic shift from quixoticism to practicality that there was no need to handicap the book with so unusual a word as "passionary." [43]

Concession and compromise seldom occur during these final years. A long, remarkably personal letter to Richards that stands out from the hundreds concerned with business matters reveals his increasing impatience with mundane intrusions and his withdrawal into a world of his own making. The letter begins with a description of a raucous tumult in the slum in front of "this delusive terrace" on which his house faced. At first supposing the hubbub "to be some temporary and accidental excrescence [*sic*] of sound, some flying disease of the air, such as breaks out at any moment in this irregular town," he discovers that it comes from street urchins at their springtime play. He resents the distraction because it prevents his working and introduces a jarring note into his private world:

> The bellowing continues in every note of discordance, and I find that this will go on till the first of May, as it has done for 2000 years and more. It is very coarse and horrible: it was once poetical and musical and full of divinity: now it has no meaning: —marbles are out, and horns are in; the week after it will be the spining [*sic*] of tops.

The letter, which may have been a sequel to a dinner party enjoyed on one of his infrequent trips to London,

continues with an account of a dream no more fantastic
than the daydreams he wove into *The Testament of John
Davidson:*

> Vermouth, chablis (of the Rhine), Leoville, port,
> Henessey, lined and laced my nerves and brain, and
> I saw half the night gigantic men and women whose
> flesh was not evolved out of carbon and nitrogen and
> oxygen and hydrogen; but out of fluorine, and iron
> and gold and silver, and yet of a fleshly consistence;
> their blood was of molten gold and their seed of the
> finest flower of flame; and I saw them in all their
> manners and customs, their social and individual af-
> fairs, in their natural functions, their arts and sciences:
> an astonishing people.[44]

On rare occasions he had written similar letters in which
he permitted fancy to take precedence over sobriety, but
in this the world of trivial, everyday affairs becomes almost
completely merged with that of his imagination and
writings. In the poem which he was writing at this time,
the personality of John Davidson is likewise swallowed up
in the single dimension of matter, transcending time and
space as in some fantasy by H. G. Wells.

The new volume contained, in addition to the blank
verse Testament, a dedicatory essay on contemporary political and social issues and a prologue and epilogue in rhymed
stanzas entitled "Honeymoon" and "The Last Journey."
The first of these poems, a sentimental, rather lush epitha-
lamion, alludes to a marriage that began in hope and
happiness but with the provision for joint suicide should
it be overtaken by sorrow and despair. The second lyric,
Davidson's best of this period, introduces the contrasting
themes of weariness, fortitude, and stoic acceptance. Together they represent the ironic extremes of man's existence as Davidson autobiographically views it. Referring
to these poems he wrote, "I place my Testament thus be-

tween the dawn and the close of life: my personal utterance as the Universe become conscious between the two most personal poems I have written as a *brother man*. . . . These additions will buoy the book." [45]

The dedicatory prose essay is addressed half mockingly "To the Peers Temporal of the United Kingdoms of Great Britain and Ireland," since as sharers with the Creator of the Universe of the common title of *"lord,"* they "will recognise integrity of thought and integrity of imagination, however unexpected the form and substance of these may be." [46] When Richards had expressed misgivings about Davidson's intention of addressing the essay to the peers of the realm, he had received a copy of the dedication with the calm assurance, "It might be to the village idiot, or the German Emperor, or to Jenny Willocks or to the Pope; it is my letter that matters, not the person addressed as I believe you will see." [47] On the book's publication the author instructed Richards to send copies to the Lord Chancellor, Lord Crewe, the Marquess of Lansdowne, and Lord Rosebery, adding, "The dedication of the book makes any inscription unnecessary." [48]

If the satiric dedication is whimsical in style, it is serious enough in purpose. Its impudence and ironic content bring to mind Shaw's preface to *Man and Superman* and *The Revolutionist's Handbook* which preceded it by five years. Davidson notes in his essay that the lords should be most familiar with the decadence of Christendom in England through the atrophy of their own function and prestige. To help them resume their former authority and once more rule as great men, he advises them how to cope with various contemporary problems and dissident groups. Tell the Irish, he urges, to forget what they require of England, to remember what England requires of them, and to get rid of their priests. Tell the workers to forget socialism, Nietzsche, and old-age pensions, to set to work, and to read Robert Burns. Tell the women of England to

forget the franchise, to assume their dependent role as
mothers in society, but to remember that with their superior intellects they indirectly and subtly rule the world.
Perceiving that society is on the verge of reverting to a
community of goods and women, he recommends as a
countermeasure that the franchise be extended only to
married men who are freeholders and to mothers of at least
three children. The preface is distinctly clever and startling, if the ideas are scarcely new, until the dedicator
abandons his impudence for a solemn account of the
creation of the universe according to the nebular hypothesis and the gospel of John Davidson. Dismissing the problems that he has been treating wittily as part of the debris
of Christendom, he reiterates tiresomely that he has "come
out of it all, and . . . found another abode for my mind
and imagination, not in any symbol of the Universe,
which Christendom was, but in the Universe itself." [49]
Davidson has forgotten that the cap and bells and not the
scourge become the reformer.

The Testament itself opens with the poet speaking in
his own person for the first time since his lyrics. He explains through symbolic language that, although materialism has furnished him a refuge from personal defeats,
he has left his celestial palace in the Milky Way and returned to earth to die by his own hand upon the mountain top of his choice. The poet-narrator proceeds to justify
suicide from the point of view of the heroic vitalist: "For
men must still descend to earth to die." By virtue of his
supreme will man is the only creature who chooses to
be born and to die:

"None should outlive his power," I said. "Who kills
Himself subdues the conqueror of kings:
Exempt from death is he who takes his life:
My time has come."

Strong as his death wish is, nature's instinctive will to life and knowledge is stronger; he must endure, "For when I die the Universe shall cease / To know itself." [50] The romantic setting, the outcast hero's solitude and preoccupation with death, his Hamletlike throes as he contemplates suicide belong to the romantic world of Beddoes and Hölderlin, of Childe Harold and Manfred, of James Thomson's *A City of Dreadful Night,* and in subject and theme at least to that of Arnold's *Empedocles on Etna.* The incoherence is unmistakably Spasmodic and the rhetoric Edwardian. Davidson pours into this assembled mold his own version of the neoromantic creed of self-determination and the will to supremacy.

The hero of the dramatic monologue has scarcely recovered from his first test when he beholds the goddess Diana approaching in her chariot. She has come, he perceives, to lure him in his weak condition to renewed worship of spirit, because it is he who in his prime had defied all gods. Gifted with human but supreme power, he pursues the goddess through a cavernous glen, whose description Chateaubriand and Bernadin de St.-Pierre might have envied. There he corners her and kills her dragon steed, in an encounter as richly and graphically narrated as any in Spenser whom Davidson is consciously emulating. Having introduced himself as the foe of the gods, the poet agrees to the goddess' request that he recount the tales of those who have dared like him to behold her: Orion, Actaeon, and Endymion. When she nearly expires at the tale of her beloved Endymion, he revives her with ambrosia and nectar after which he himself eats the celestial food. By this symbolic act, which at once parallels and parodies the Christian ritual of communion, the poet has blasphemed against his "high material nature" and succumbed to the allurements of the "Other World" of spirit. He may be a disgraced materialist, but it is as an arrogant,

irresistible Spasmodic, a worthy descendant of Goethe's
Faust and Bailey's Festus, that he sets out to seduce the
unwilling goddess. With this in view he leads her to his
secret grotto:

> My place of inspiration in my youth,
> My refuge, study, haunt and hermitage,
> The ground is hallowed, goddess: here can come
> No horror; only beauty and delight
> Inhabit mansions youth has sanctified.[51]

The grotto is not Olympus; even this refuge is haunted by
the poet's abhorrence of old age with its deterioration of
physical and material powers.

Diana employs all the delaying tactics she can muster to
avert a fate which for her is death. Although she acknowl-
edges a prophecy by Proteus that she should some day be
conquered by a man, she refuses to recognize in her ab-
ductor this destined lover and the slayer of Apollo, Aido-
neus, and Thor as he brags. To convince her, the poet
relates forcefully, often horribly, his destruction in turn
of each of these gods. The climax of the allegorical poem
is the long tale of his singing contest with Apollo: the final
struggle between man and the deities for the possession
of the universe. Apollo sang of the creation of the world
and of the Olympian gods as given in classical mythology;
the poet, of the material origin of the universe, the chemical evolution of earth, and man's fallacious invention of the
gods to explain material phenomena that stagger his imagination. Inasmuch as Davidson participates both as
principal in the contest and judge, the odds are decidedly
against Apollo. The palm was awarded to the poet in spite
of the reader's impression that Apollo emerged with more
points. Straightway the god died a hideous death.

Corrupted by the celestial food and reluctant to possess
the goddess against her will, the hero in a violation of his

material being swears that the gods exist. She then permits him to bring her to earth in more than one sense. Each pays the penalty for his crime, for materialism no less than other faiths punishes its apostates. Both lovers perish instantly, she because she has allowed her divine nature to be corrupted by union with man, he because in loving her he has committed the heresy of dualism.[52] They find themselves in the Hell of Deity, the last and most chilling of all hells, which Davidson has drawn out of the literature of decadence and Gothic fantasy. Diana is "impaled through all her sumptuous deity," strung on a stake next to Athene where she "Wriggled and yelled abominably hurt." For his quadruple crime against deity, the poet beholds himself crucified four times upon a wall of adamant:

> For I, as man, was guilty of the gods,
> Guilty of God; and in myself partook
> Uniquely of the nature of the gods,
> Having supped upon their food, and having loved
> A deity, and been by her belov'd.

In a supreme assertion of his humanity he frees himself and destroys this last of all hells with the blasphemous cry:

> Four persons in the Godhead—the Sire, the Son,
> The Holy Spirit, and the Evil One.

He has purged the universe of the last remnant of Other World, the hideous hell of the gods and virgin worship; and himself of God, "Pernicious slander of material truth." Once again the world is unified—reduced to a single essence, matter; to a single purpose, self-consciousness; and to a single principle, irony, by which all its contradictions are reconciled:

> And thus I made the world a fit abode
> For greatness and the men who yet may be;

And can myself with joy become again
The mountains and the ocean, the winds, the flowers,
And life and death, and fear and love and hope,
And tender sorrow and heavy grief, and all
Humanity, and all that thinks and is.[53]

The poem ends on a serene, Wordsworthian note as the poet renounces his intention of taking his life and accepts his unique mission to be the sight and hearing, the thought and imagination of the universe. He envisages the universe, resigned to attaining self-knowledge but once, destroying itself after his natural death and returning to its nebular origin.

In many respects *The Testament of John Davidson* is no more restrained than any of the poet's later messianic works; all his faults are there in autumnal abundance. The language is still marred by pedantic, pseudoscientific jargon and "poetic diction." On a page chosen at random occur "sidereal," "elixir," "affined," "febrilled," and "ganglioned"; on another, "pearly," "campaniles," and "groined embayment." The reader meets again the jarring juxtaposition of rhetoric and deliberate bathos, of the lapidary and the pedestrian. Digressions and parenthetical incursions, many of them interminable, interrupt the flow of narrative and thought. Something schoolboyish pervades the frankness of the erotic episodes and the coarse brutality of the scenes of physical violence.

Yet each of these faults, exasperating as it may be, has its compensating virtue. The intellectualized, polyglot diction reflects as before a sincere groping toward an anti-literary, synthetic language free of the hackneyed, tendentious meanings that words have accumulated through long usage.* The juxtaposition of the elevated and the

---

* Menzies Davidson recalls that his father, like Shaw, was also interested in phonetic spelling and that he corresponded with Theodore Roosevelt

commonplace continues to illustrate the paradoxicality inherent in all things. The digressions and parabolic structure of the poem, its interweaving of pagan and Christian myth, and its timeless, universal setting anticipate crudely the indivisible flux of consciousness and world memory associated with Henri Bergson and in literature with Joyce, Virginia Woolf, Gertrude Stein, and T. S. Eliot. The sexual candor and physical violence share the extravagant sensuality of adolescent dreams and the bravura of comic books depicting life in outer space rather than the sniggering, furtive lewdness of *graffiti* scratched in public toilets. Davidson's voice is the voice of youth everywhere not, as his contemporaries thought, of shrill dotage; a voice full of defiance, yearning, eagerness; at the same time exultant in the joy and challenge of life and desperate in the face of man's mortality. He felt himself a magus witnessing the birth of a vigorous, final civilization, and as gifts he wished to offer it not a gospel or creed but a new imagery and body of legend with which to clothe itself. Conscious of his epic purpose, he turned to the great poets, Spenser, Milton, and Wordsworth, for models of a versatile, vigorous style at which he aimed. He achieves, especially in the descriptive passages of his own Testament, effects that alternately terrify and delight. So staggering are they and so ambitious that the mind can scarcely retain an image or recall a line. Taken in its entirety *The Testament of John Davidson,* for all its faults, remains the most thoroughly conceived and imaginatively sustained of his late works.

The principal reason for the superiority of this final Testament is its incorporation of classic myth. Except in *Scaramouch in Naxos* and the ballads of the nineties the poet of materialism had heretofore scorned the use of this

---

on the subject of a new, phonetic dictionary. I have found no corroboration of this correspondence or project.

material. Although he takes extensive liberties with these myths, elaborating on them and molding them to fit his own philosophy, they impose upon his work an order, concreteness, substance, and human reference that it would otherwise lack. He is not completely successful, for the poem's symbolic import is sometimes lost in the graphic or dramatic immediacy of a particular scene. Except for an occasional maze the path through his enchanted wood is steady and direct; the sequence of events makes sense on both the narrative and allegorical levels. Douglas Bush says of the poem, ". . . the main ideas are unmistakable, though details of the mythological symbolism are not always clear or coherent. . . . Davidson was far too intent on his single-minded deliverance of a benighted world to be an artist, and in the *Testament* nothing does more to control his demonic energy and clarify his turbid imagination than such relics of old religion and the strangling past as classic myths." Davidson, in the opinion of this scholar, is "a real if ineffectual Titan," and the mythological passages of his final Testament "are written with a force and careless splendor which set them apart from most tame verse of the period." [54]

The publication of the poet's valedictory in early November 1908 precipitated the most bitter controversy of his career. For over a month the *Academy*—unquestionably in the person of Alfred Douglas or Frank Harris—attacked the work and its author in each of its issues. And each week the poet responded with equal virulence in a letter to the editor or, when he refused to print the replies, in the friendly columns of the *Star,* where they must have made curious reading for the habitués of the pubs and race tracks.[55] Seldom rising above the level of a fishwives' brawl, the feud illustrates the rabidly partisan nature of the criticism which Davidson's later works invited by their own belligerence and extremism. The *Academy* in its

decadence had dedicated itself to preserving the "old aristocracy." Socialism, free thought, materialism, the "new
drama" and the "new fiction" were grouped together in a
single conspiracy menacing the very existence of Tory
conservatism. Writers of the "new aristocracy"—Henley,
Kipling, Stevenson, William Watson—wished to preserve
the aristocratic ideal but to rejuvenate it by adapting it to
modern conditions. Frightened by the rough vitality, apparent crudeness, or moral earnestness of these intruders
upon their established world of privilege, the guardians
of the old order retreated into wit, asperity, and insult.

Had the *Academy* been prepared to discuss his philosophy seriously, Davidson undoubtedly would have welcomed the opportunity to air his views once more in
print. As it was he found himself lured into a contest in
name-calling from which he could hope to gain nothing.
Enervated by the fray and discouraged by the vulgar notoriety which his great personal Testament had provoked,
he sank into silent despair.* The book had received far
fewer notices than *Mammon and His Message,* and almost
all of these had been unsympathetic or openly hostile.
Committed beyond retreat to his message and unable to
cope with the larger objections to it, the poet could only
cavil at minor inaccuracies in the reviews. The unforgivable crime now was to link his name with earlier
nineteenth-century prophets, especially Carlyle, Nietzsche,
and Wagner. "I see some one speaks of the 'Twilight of
the Gods' and my 'Testament,'" he wrote to Richards.
"This is the kind of thing that makes me despair. I write

* The *Academy* was not content to let the quarrel rest. When Davidson's poem in blank verse, "The Wasp," appeared in the *Athenaeum* for
19 Dec. 1908, the *Academy* ridiculed it with withering sarcasm, dismissed
the poet as a "'tousey tike,'" and cited him ineptly as representative of the
modern poet no longer content with beer and skittles but insisting on
Heidsieck and after-theater supper parties. *Academy,* 26 Dec. 1908, pp.
603–4.

two thousand years after the 'Twilight of the Gods' which was the three hours' darkness at the crucifixion: that was the end of godhead. Nobody seems to understand anything at all about anything!" [56]

For the poet become prophet everything had lost its importance beside his message. "He lived and died singly for it, sacrificed everything to it," recalled his closest friend of these twilight years, Filson Young.[57] Although he is writing of Nietzsche and not Davidson, Eric Bentley describes exactly the latter's elected role as tragic scapegoat for his generation:

> More and more with the years, he felt himself to be a destiny, not a man but a symbol, not a teacher but a portent. He tried completely to identify himself with his message. He taught that the Christian epoch was disintegrating but that a new and glorious epoch would take its place. Therefore, he would himself enact the tragedy of the age in his own head and his own heart. He would disintegrate but he would preach faith and hope in a new gospel. He would be a Dionysos, torn to pieces that there might be more abundant life.[58]

More and more Davidson severed himself from the intellectual exchange, social intercourse, and strong family affections that normally would have nourished his powerful intellect and hungry emotions. "If I were rich," he told his wife, more in earnest than jest, shortly before he disappeared, "I would buy three houses—one for you, and one for me, and one for the boys." [59] All escape, all means of self-preservation he voluntarily cut off. Vanishing into the world of his Testaments and tragedies, he resolved upon suicide of the spirit.

5

Davidson had during the last six months of his life one remaining interest which revived much of his former enthusiasm and gave him the illusion of belonging still to the London literary world. As soon as it had become apparent several years before that his Testaments and tragedies "were not likely to be immediately remunerative (they will be a valuable property ultimately)," he had offered his services as literary adviser to Richards, by way of "indemnification for any temporary deficit." In this gratuitous capacity he had already made suggestions for publication ventures, but in the summer of 1907 during a holiday reunion at Ruan Minor he proposed to Richards that they make the position official. He offered to read manuscripts for £100 a year. The proposition hung fire for over a year until the hard-pressed exile wrote that he still waited for his reply "with the fiercest impatience." At the same time he urged the publisher to "begin at once a general library," reprints of the classics in the style of the "World's Classics," but without their extraneous editorial material:

> There are tens of thousands of readers who are irritated by introductions and by the mere name of an editor on the title page without knowing the source of their irritation: nothing and no one should come between the reader and a masterpiece. . . . all that introducing and annotating takes folk back into the schoolroom and the examination-hall, and the true purpose of literature as a means of entertainment, of solace, of stimulation, of the destruction of old ideas and values, and the creation of new ones becomes secondary.

In the series of " 'Masterpieces,' or whatever the library is
to be called," which he contemplated, an old book could
be read "even by a debauchee of letters as if it were a
new one." [60] On September 1, 1908, Richards agreed to
pay him £8 6s. 8d. a month for his services on the condition that the publisher might break off the arrangement
at a moment's notice without umbrage on Davidson's
part.[61]

The reports in which Richards' new adviser describes
his publication schemes would be of interest if only because they provide a catalogue of his favorite reading interspersed with his opinions, always arbitrary and almost always refreshing. Ideas tumbled from his brain, growing
and changing almost daily. The reprints of the classics
developed into a series of "Books of the World," which
he still later called "A Library of Books for Men and
Women." It was to include Rabelais' *Gargantua and Pan-
tagruel;* Voltaire's *Romances;* Goethe's *Whilhelm Meister*
[sic] in Carlyle's version, "the first original novel between
Cervantes and Stendhal"; Stendhal's *Convent of Parma*
[sic], "the greatest work of the most original French novelist"; and Balzac's *Physiology of Marriage,* "an enthrall-
ing book, that every wedded couple should read." *"Do*
give this idea every consideration," he wrote excitedly. "I
believe you could carry the *trade* with you; such splendid
new blood into the old anemic carcass of reprints—Cran-
ford, Walton's Lives, etc.! Think of it!" [62] He was evidently a great lover and reader of books, if not a deep one.
His personal library, which was strong in works about
Napoleon and by the French novelists, Hugo, the elder
and younger Dumas, de Maupassant, contained over five
hundred volumes—a large number for an impoverished
author who must have been often tempted to sell them for
a few pennies each. With Ernest Rhys and others, David-

son anticipated the widespread interest of the middle class in selected reading of the classics.

The fertility and scope of the ventures which he warmly urged upon Richards are amazing. His knowledge of literature may have been facile and inaccurate, but it rivaled in comprehensiveness that of an eighteenth-century encyclopedist. During a period of less than six months he offered sixty or seventy ideas, many of them outlined in painstaking detail. Further series which he envisaged included national libraries of English, Scotch, Irish, Welsh, American, Chinese, Russian, Basque, and other literatures; a library of anthologies to begin with Emerson's and to number also a "Miscellaneous Library"; a library of illustrated books illuminating different eras, such as Chaucer's *Tales,* Pepys' *Diary,* Hervey's letters and memoirs, and so on; a library of stories for children to include Malory, the Lambs' *Tales from Shakspere,* and Wagner stories; a "talk" series: "The Talk of Dr. Johnson," "of Wellington," "of Carlyle," "of Goethe," and other great talkers. Ideas for anthologies of threnodies and blank verse, for encyclopedias, even for a perpetual calendar or almanac came pouring out as if he foresaw some world holocaust and would collect in a time capsule only that moiety of culture which in his judgment was worth preservation.[63]

If this enthusiasm for literary classics seems hardly compatible with his strictures elsewhere against history, the culture of the past, and libraries, it can be explained as a vicarious outlet for the dynamic energy and zeal that had been dammed up by the failure of his own works. He did not, furthermore, divorce this editorial work from his principles. The "Library of Books for Men and Women" eventually developed with considerable additions into a plan for a series of limited editions—an "aristocratic" library for "Gentlemen and Ladies," to include Scott, Dick-

ens, Dante, Homer. One of his favorite ideas was a volume
to be entitled "Napoleon Speaks," culled from Napoleon's
exact words in memoirs and correspondences.* Apropos of
this project he recalled that "a number of years ago I made
a scenario for a Napoleon play (which I shall write some-
day), and it was then I saw that the life, deeds and drama
of Napoleon can be reëdified in a monologue spoken by
himself with occasional interruptions of interlocutors." [64]
Very close to his heart also was a Grant Richards or Chelsea
edition of the works of Thomas Carlyle in twelve volumes.
The prospectus for this edition shows his thorough reading
in Carlyle and, apart from differences in their views, a
great admiration: ". . . he is our greatest prose Man of
Letters. But he is not known. . . . He who knows Carlyle's 'Cromwell,' 'Frederick the Great,' and 'The French
Revolution' knows all that is worth knowing in the history
of Europe from 1600 A.D. to 1800 A.D." [65] Fancying himself
an elder statesman of letters, Davidson carried over into
his reader's reports and proposals the same blend of fanatic
idealism and practical shrewdness already displayed in the
promotion of his own writings. His zeal was tremendous
and would carry all obstacles before it. His ideas were
energetically and eloquently presented. If Richards had
had the capital and the vision to follow up some of them,

* Professor R. M. Johnston of Cambridge and Harvard Universities was
invited to edit the work, but Davidson and he clashed over their concepts
of its nature. Davidson wanted only Napoleon's extemporaneous sayings
with as little exposition as possible; Johnston wanted to draw from the
emperor's bulletins, addresses, etc. and to provide his own commentary.
Johnston also wanted his name connected with the book, which Davidson
adamantly opposed as an intrusion upon "the portrait of Napoleon which
will leap out of every page of our book with the very voice and glance
and gesture of Napoleon." (A.L.S., to G. Richards, dated 9 Mar. 1909,
from 6 Coulson's Terrace, P.U.L.) After Davidson's death Johnston
dropped out as editor, and Richards approached Temple Scott who agreed
to undertake the task and to adhere to Davidson's plan which he enthusiastically endorsed. A.L.S., to G. Richards, dated 31 July 1909, from Brentano's Publishing Dept.

he might have become one of the more prosperous and resourceful publishers of the new century. As it was, Davidson's publishing schemes were on the same vast scale as his other dreams.

The poet's own bitter experience crops out in one of the more quixotic, not to say megalomaniacal, recommendations. In February 1907, after writing an outspoken, humorous article on "Women's Rights" which he had difficulty in publishing,* he had proposed to Richards that he issue a series of "Present Day Pamphlets" to contain very short papers that no periodical would print and to sell for a penny.[66] As these pamphlets had not materialized, he now strongly urged Richards to publish a "Grant Richards' Magazine" modeled on *Blackwood's, Murray's,* and *Macmillan's.* He furnished a complete prospectus with suggestions as to format, price, and contents. It was to contain "no prizes, no fiction, no news, no poetry, no illustrations," but should be rather "a further evolution of the departmental idea rudimentary in England, more marked in America." There would be four principal departments: (1) "The Confessional," containing anonymous contributions devoted to "burdensome experiences, matters of conscience, narratives of wrong-doing, of injustice suffered, of terror, of passion, of madnesses—things the agents or undergoers dare not speak of to anyone"; (2) "The Court of Appeal," in which an author or other artist "aggrieved by wanton or malevolent criticism, or even want of recognition, could set forth his or her case without fear or favour"; (3) "The Clearing-House," to furnish "a judicial examination, with approval or reversal of the more important literary and dramatic criticism of the past month—impartial, trenchant, and anonymous, by several writers who could agree upon a general basis of opinion in order to

* Published as "Women's Rights in Realms Afar," *Fortnightly Review,* 2 Sept. 1907, pp. 417–22.

maintain homogeneity"; and (4) "an article on the principal topic of the month, the ablest available." The editor
of such a magazine must combine "the imperturbable
humour of Birrell" and "the inexhaustible sympathy with
the circumstances of life of Stead," someone adventurous
and in his prime.[67] At the top of the prospectus he wrote
and encircled, "Utopian? Not altogether." It speaks as
much for the vigorous union of letters and journalism at
the turn of the century as for Davidson's primary concern
with his own grievances that this idea for a Muses' court
of arbitration occurred to him. Richards, envisaging possibly an endless series of suits for libel, rejected the proposal
as "not practicable." [68]

In spite of his effort to keep in touch with the contemporary world of letters through his services to Richards,
Davidson more and more felt isolated from all reality except that of his personal vision. He had given up his club,
the Grosvenor, so that the dues of £8.8 could be applied
to the rent on his house. Unwilling that anyone know
where he was living after 1907, he gave 7 Carlton Street,
the location of Richards' firm, as his only address. It was
not merely social pride and seclusiveness that prompted
this evasion but also a last stubborn refusal to acknowledge
that he had ceased to exist in the only world that mattered,
London. The man who regarded his own writings as the
ultima res would rather be an editor of the works of others
than renounce his professional standing altogether. It was
a harsh penance. Writing Richards late in January 1909,
he thanked him for his monthly check and appealed to
him, "Let me earn it: it is half my income. I should have
satisfaction in reading a MS. a day—Sundays excepted."
"Sundays excepted" from the Savonarola of materialism!
To this he added fervently, "I wish I *could* see you—I
wish to the Universe we could sit down together in a club
or a restaurant with a bottle of claret and a dish of meat,

and eat and drink the stars! By Sirius and Aldebaran, and the star Groombridge that travels 250,000,000 miles a second!" Even his private jokes now found their origin in the cosmos. He announced with unfounded optimism that he would probably not leave Penzance until he left it for good to "go to high ground somewhere within the four mile radius [of London] for the rest of my time." [69]

Filson Young describes the wretchedness and loneliness of the poet's exiled life. Every morning he worked at his desk, reading manuscripts for Richards or attempting to write poetry, and "tortured by the clamour of children who were sent out to yell in the slums behind his house." In the afternoon he would take a walk alone "through the streets or roads of that Penzance which he loathed as his prison, and knew would be his grave." Later there would be a walk, perhaps with his wife, reading in one of the two available libraries, a meager supper, another lonely walk, and then bed. "He had no money to make excursions, and no humour to make acquaintances," recollects Young who with Richards was his only visitor. Clergymen, doctors, and other professional residents of Penzance, perceiving his loneliness, attempted for the most part unsuccessfully to make his acquaintance. The single luxury of entertaining a few friends at the Trocadero or Criterion restaurants ceased in the final year. Either out of economy or a desire for further austerity, he put aside the comfort of drink except on the rare visits of Young or Richards which became for him "a festival, almost a sacramental occasion." On these visits the friends would go for brisk walks, talk, laughing a great deal, or sit together silent. But always beneath the surface of his excellent talk lay bitterness, misery, and suffering, while "on the top was this pleasure in conversation, in congenial company, in laughter and momentary forgetting." [70]

Very occasionally there were gratifying signs that he had

not been altogether forgotten by the outside world. It was
always younger men, Filson Young, James Elroy Flecker,[71]
and Gordon Craig,* who sought him out. When Young
perceived that his friend was literally dying from want of
recognition, he wrote an article entitled "The New Poetry," one of the first to consider Davidson not so much
as a poet but as a metaphysician with a highly developed
religious sensitivity. Young had the greatest difficulty finding a publisher for the article until W. L. Courtney accepted it for the *Fortnightly Review* in January 1909.
Davidson was not slow to express his gratitude for this
tribute, which he described almost pathetically as "the
most generous gift that had ever been made to him." [72]
Although the article made an eloquent plea for greater
attention to the materialist's thought and place in literature, it represented a fair judgment of his work. Young
traced the poet's unpopularity to such obvious failings as
the regrettable fury and frenzy of his attacks upon "the old
spiritual rags," his obsession with pain, his lack of finish,
and especially his continual experimentation with words:

> He is continually brought up by words to which, in
> the absence of virgin words, words unsoiled by the
> association of an entirely different set of ideas, he
> is obliged to fit new meanings. . . . Is not Mr. David-
> son himself sometimes in danger of attacking unduly
> the names of things which, under different names, he
> is willing to accept himself? . . . In his anxiety to
> dissociate himself from Christendom, he is in danger
> of labouring at the destruction of much in existing

* "Gordon Craig has been writing me and sending me his *Mask*. He
carries a huge lateen sail in a very small and unbalasted [*sic*] xebec; but
he has read *The Theatrocrat,* and the iron has entered his hold. I want
him to have the 'Triumph of Mammon' and 'Mammon and His Message.'
I enclose a note which please forward with these two books." A.L.S., to
G. Richards, dated 14 May 1908, from 6 Coulson's Terrace, P.U.L.

human thought that is not Christian, but Universal, and which, therefore, on his own admission, cannot be destroyed; in danger of losing himself in the labyrinth of meanings that words can bear for different minds, and of falling away from the grand pursuit of his truth by following up and putting to death laggard ideas that are already spent or wounded mortally, and will perish of themselves.

Having made these reservations, Young hailed Davidson's definition of his task, "to destroy this unfit world, and make it over again in my own image," as "in some ways the bravest and sincerest piece of thought that has been uttered in literature for many a day." [73]

His works and his love of writing poetry failed to sustain Davidson as he confronted the Giant Despair. He announced ominously in February 1908, "I should like to leave my affairs in some shape behind me: I have had very distinct notice that I have barely a year or two to live in now." This is the first specific mention outside of his published writings that death was imminent. His conviction that he had cancer may date from about this time. Feverishly he attempted to throw himself into renewed creative activity as if he had barely enough time to put his literary affairs in order. In the same letter containing news of his death sentence he announced his intention to go on with the third part of the God and Mammon trilogy: "I have tried other things; but I find them impossible: that must be finished first." [74] Richards, to whom the letter was addressed, at once anxiously asked what it meant. Davidson replied, "It means dismay and despondence from prolonged insomnia such as I have not had for several years; and the hideous enfeeblement of asthma: these things set out a blank wall before me, and I require such great visions to be in health: indeed I now require to write

blank verse daily if I am not to die; it is physiological: one
could die of a constipated brain as well as—otherwise." As
soon as the second part of the trilogy was in print, he hoped
to begin the third and to finish it by Christmas. Veering
off on a more cheerful tack, he confided that he was beginning to be well again and to think in terms of "ten years
instead of one or two in which to be and do greatly." Then
he again hinted darkly, "Nevertheless there are things I
cannot write of. I shall tell you when I see you." Beneath
his signature came the poignant and by now automatic
request, "Can I have a cheque for January?" [75]

One of Davidson's last proposals to Richards was for an
anthology of blank verse with an introduction:

> As far as I know there is no study of English blank
> verse. English blank verse is the acme of poetry: a
> history and an examination, with copious illustrations
> of the infinite variety of manner and subject, would
> be a very important and a lasting book. Would Walter
> Raleigh care to make the selection and write of the
> form: its sudden, almost full-fledged birth; rapid de-
> velopment; splendid maturity; and sunset decadence
> in *Paradise Lost:* the long interval of formalists—
> Dryden, Thomson, Armstrong, Akenside; and then
> the new-birth with Blake and Wordsworth. A sub-
> ject for the most accomplished professor of litera-
> ture.[76]

He himself came to regard the writing of blank verse as
heroic exercise, joyful calisthenics of the mind and will.
During a long walk on one of Young's last visits to Cornwall, the poet had told his friend that no man could be
unhappy who could write blank verse, that to write blank
verse was "the sheerest, most intoxicating joy that he could
conceive." [77] There is no question of his sincerity, which
makes all the more pathetic his inability to write blank

verse with the ease and skill of the past. The unpublished volume of verse that he left behind makes clear that during the last year of his life his creative energies were played out, yet he strove to produce his daily output of lines almost up to the hour he died. With a touching pride he hoped that Elgar might be persuaded to set to music one of his last poems. On his writing table at the time he left Coulson's Terrace not to return lay three poems in manuscript, one complete, two incomplete.[78] Showing signs of anguished revision, these manuscripts bespeak a mind so overconscious of purging and purifying language that it has lost all feeling for the sound, meaning, and propriety of words. They spell out painfully the death throes of a poetic imagination, the last scene of a poet whose dream had been to create a new world divorced from the shame of the past and a new language with which to sing the splendor of this world.

The final months saw longer periods of deep, black depression and inanition punctuated by shorter periods of frantic, ineffectual activity. He clung with a pride born of desperation to the only identity he now acknowledged. When a sympathetic editor friend of Richards suggested through the publisher a solution to his difficulties, he wrote, "I am glad you explained to him why I don't write novels: the explanation is simple, I can't." He could no longer make the effort to please by imitation, be it imitation of himself, or to contemplate it. The righteous indignation that once had blazed furiously emitted only ephemeral sparks and a feeble glow. Yet he was never to know the serenity that comes with the humble acceptance of utter defeat. In the same letter, one of his last, he ridiculed "this cry for a Rabelais or a Shakespeare or a this or the other. No man worth a pinch of salt wants to be a Rabelais or Shakespeare but to be himself—I for example, to be the Davidson of my time and of all time." [79]

But the self-appointed spokesman for humanity no longer
spoke to men of what they recognized in a tongue that they
understood. He had built about himself stout prison walls
of exultant pride and that guilt which is an inverted form
of pride. Outside this solitary limbo of his own making he
had ceased to exist, and his last gesture was a full acceptance of this fact. His passion had reached its last station.

6

A rebel against the ignorant piety and self-renunciation
of his Scottish rearing, John Davidson committed early in
life the act of original sin. Eating of the tree of scientific
knowledge, he developed an incontinent appetite for its
fruit. Had he heeded the myths, both pagan and Christian,
which he relentlessly repudiated, he would have known
that this fruit invariably turns to ashes in the mouth.
Calvinism he had found degrading; evangelicalism offensive; the Church of Rome hollow and hypocritical; all
Christianity, he concluded, was decadent and corrupt. He
endeavored to substitute metaphysics for religion or, as
he put it, "theonomy for theosophy," man and science for
God and faith, the physical world for the spiritual. In his
very disbelief Davidson was continuously and passionately
religious. The consciousness of original sin, implicit but
unyielding, is seldom absent from his thought. Throughout his lifelong revolt he remained in essence a Calvinist,
an evangelical, and a nonconformist, daring to conduct
singlehandedly his private Reformation.

Others have observed in Davidson the persistence of
what they have variously called the Protestant, the Calvinist, the mystic, the ascetic, the Puritan, the religious,
and the metaphysical.[80] His celebration of the beauties and
joys of nature begins with a Wordsworthian pantheism
and culminates in a pagan naturalism as ardent as Burns'.
His cult of pain is that of the true penitent who accepts

gladly the privilege of disease, suffering, and martyrdom. For the Christian virtue of humility he substitutes the Promethean pride of the romantic egoist. But his glorification of man and of himself is, like that of Blake, Carlyle, and Nietzsche, no more than an inverted seeking for the divine. In Davidson the apotheosis of self is accompanied by an unremitting sense of inadequacy and sin which pursued him from the beginning. It is this which motivated his becoming a poet and which, according to Filson Young, ultimately turned him from poet to philosopher, "from song to tragic examination of the thing sung, and consequently to damnation of it." [81] Davidson begins and ends as a metaphysician, interrupting his chosen mission only long enough in a score of superior lyrics to state man's predicament rather than solve it. He emerges as a self-created symbol, the most memorable, heroic figure of his own writings, a figure out of myth and legend—an Icarus in his youth, an Oedipus in middle age, a Lear at last—the venturer into the unknown who in the face of certain destruction would divine the contents of the sealed casket, the treasure or horror behind the locked door, the answer to the fateful riddle. Driven like his legendary antecedents by the need to prove and justify himself, he sings the body divine and the supremacy of man. The price which he pays for his intellectual and spiritual pride would make anyone happy to give Olympus back to the gods.

As the poet grew older, the emphasis in his writings was increasingly upon the penalties rather than the rewards of being human, or upon the penalties as rewards. He may have completed with Burns and Carlyle a "triad of Presbyterian revolt against the world and Christianity"; [82] but he, no less than they, was conscious of the power and grandeur in men's lives of that which he was attacking, of a creed which at once attracted and repelled. Unable to worship Christ as the embodiment of God in man, he recognized in him, as Carlyle had, a figure of heroic dimensions. In declaring that God was modeled after Adam,[83] he was paying the deity the supreme compliment. Two months before Davidson's death Young wrote of him, "No poet, or man whose business was the expression of himself, who had been trained in youth upon the shorter Catechism, the Metrical Psalms, the Paraphrases, and the Bible of religious Scotland, could, having ceased to believe the gospel of his childhood, silently leave it alone. He must actually and aggressively disbelieve it; he must turn upon it and rend it, remembering its former power over him." [84] To this one might add that he must find or create its substitute, its exact equivalent, before he could fill the void which it had left and fully expiate his apostasy. In his irreverence Davidson was reverent; his most wicked and carnal blasphemies had the ring of fervent, devout prayers. If he did not quote Scripture, he ironically parodied it to his own purpose and made the blandishments of the devil sound like Scripture. His imaginative descriptions of the Christian heaven and hell, which he mockingly repudiated, are often more convincing than his materialist fantasies. Protestantism is a coin with two faces, heresy and grace; no matter how often it is tossed, how far it rolls, or what side comes up, no one can say with finality which is heads and which tails.

Since his search for a new religion originated in his own emotional and metaphysical needs, the subjective element in Davidson's works remains paramount. Deliberately he set out to make a fitter world for himself by asserting the demise of Christianity and refashioning the universe and the deity in his own image. There was nothing essentially new about this. Burns, Carlyle, Huxley, Tyndall, Wallace, and many other nineteenth-century intellectuals of middle-class or lower origins and aristocratic ideals had also set out to improve the existent world.[85] But where they had tinkered and mended and patched and striven to salvage, Davidson razed the structure to the ground. What he erected in its place was as much the product of the spade work of these and other nineteenth-century intellects— Meredith, W. K. Clifford, J. A. Cramb, Grant Allen—as of his own deeply emotional, dual personality. He retained much of their designs and materials, adapting them first to his desire for an Edenic joy and freedom and, when that was satisfied, to his equally compelling desire for a lost sense of sin and atonement.

If there is a solution to the mystery of a life that dictated its own end, it has come in the telling. In a very real sense Davidson in his life had conducted his own inquest. Every act he performed and every word he wrote now seem part of a predetermined doom. There can be little doubt of his suicide, if indeed there ever was any. All the familiar motives are there. In every sense except that of his own unpopular philosophy he was a failure, and he had been so for fifty-two years. He was in extremely poor health and at least in his morbid imagination was suffering from cancer. He was virtually destitute and had lost the capacity for earning enough to supplement his meager pension. He was physically and mentally exhausted. In another man any one of these might have been sufficient motivation for seeking escape. In Davidson, with his indomitable courage and capacity to endure defeat, they could well have furnished added inducement for living.

A further explanation is needed. Through his writings the renegade evangelical had made a pilgrimage that became a one-man crusade. Leaving behind the paternalistic religion of his forebears with its stress on self-denial and the humble acceptance of God's will, he accepted first a naturalistic hedonism with its uninhibited enjoyment of pleasure and stoic endurance of pain. From this he progressed to a creed that not only equated greatness and the ability to suffer pain but rationalized suicide as the highest form of self-realization. Although he had yet to write the third part of his trilogy and innumerable Testaments, there was more than one way to have the last word. His message was complete enough for posterity, and his own generation wanted no more of it. It is of course possible that what drove him to take his life was, as Heine wrote of the French-Swiss romantic artist, Leopold Robert, "the most terrible of emotions, when an artist discovers a disproportion between his desire to create and his ability to express it. This consciousness of inability is of itself half death, and the hand only helps to abridge the agony." [86] In the case of Davidson, the romantic ironist par excellence, it is more logical that he saw in self-inflicted death an opportunity to convert frustration into fulfillment, failure into triumph. The will to defeat and self-destruction is the will to power turned inside out; both are manifestations of romantic *hubris*.

His work was done; there remained only to demonstrate dramatically and incontrovertibly the culminating message of his life, the unique prerogative of suicide. What more plausible and fitting way to complete the Mammon cycle than to enact personally the end that in all probability he had reserved for his hero, a flamboyant self-portrait. His twisted imagination, which in later years had provided him with a series of delusions, came to his assistance. Inspired by a minor indisposition, he welcomed the idea of cancer. The utter deterioration of his material powers by a disease which others dreaded authorized on the moral plane of his philosophy the taking of his life. It also provided a dramatic and symbolic parallel in one realm of matter, the animal functions of the body, to the twilight of his intellectual powers in another. Finally, the act of suicide enabled the prophet of materialism and the high priest of self-determination to become a willing ally with nature in expediting the process whereby raw, unformed matter finally envelops us all.

The violent end also met, perhaps for the first time, the requirements of Davidson's contradictory and unresolved nature. It was at the same time an act of pity and cruelty, of humiliation and conquest, of expiation and impious defilement—the act of a romantic temperament whose ideals were drawn from science, of a poet who loved nature and humanity but not individuals and who was happy only in London, of a tenderhearted sentimentalist who was the greatest hater after Carlyle. In this single climactic gesture he had by the terms of his creed of irony concentrated all the contrarieties of his and man's existence. His last act as a courageous individual was also a powerful symbol and challenge to mankind. He had at the end confined "the paradox in the circle."

Viewed from another direction Davidson in his rebellion against the Christian God had been in tireless search for God's equivalent. His quest resembles that of numerous nineteenth- and twentieth-century heretics who have sought a substitute creator, father, savior, and source of vital, imperishable energy. He had found this divine principle in the abstract concept of irony, in an equally abstract concept of man, and in a deification of self. In man matter had achieved the self-knowledge, self-determination, and self-sufficiency of the Hebrew Jehovah. By the act of suicide Davidson appropriated the final and unique power of the Christian God, self-redemption and atonement. Like his hero Mammon he had assumed in person the attributes of both the deity and man, father and son, redeemer and sinner. Having denied God, he was compelled in behalf of himself and, more importantly, all men to re-enact God's great sacrifice of voluntary, salvational death.

10

HERESY AND THE
TRADITION

He said that new systems of nature
were but new fashions, which would
vary in every age; and even those who
pretend to demonstrate them from math-
ematical principles would flourish but
a short period of time, and be out of
vogue when that was determined.

Jonathan Swift

The philosophy of scientific materialism
which Davidson expounded tirelessly in his later works
took its special character from its origins. It was the product
of a rebellious but penitent personality and the coming
together in an assimilative mind of various nineteenth-
century doctrines. Heroic vitalism, naturalism, Darwinian
evolution, atheism, progress, imperialism, and hero worship were important ingredients in the recipe but not the
only ones. Although "the Don Quixote of materialism,"
as he has been called,[1] denied being a rationalist, an
atheist, a mystic, a metaphysician, a monist, a freethinker,
a Darwinian, an Ibsenite, a Nietzschean, a Wagnerian,
even a materialist—in short, everything which would have
belied his aggressive individualism—the fact remains that
to be a Davidsonian was to be all of these and more. The

444

origins of Davidson's synthesis do not become evident, however, until it has been broken down into its component parts.

For the cosmological basis of his system he turned to the nebular hypothesis. He accepted this hypothesis without qualification but contributed embellishments from nineteenth-century scientific investigation and his own amateurish dabblings in chemistry. Since he had in reality an unscientific, dogmatic mind, he never felt it his duty to explain how or why, to offer empirical proof for this assumption of the origin of the universe. He felt no more obliged to disprove other previously held physical and metaphysical systems.* By his boast as a poet he asserted or "stated" the universe,† employing the power of poetry to "certify the semi-certitudes of science" until science could learn the final answers and dismiss poetry forever. "Eternity: infinity:—only these are; and only these are conceivable," admitted Davidson the neophyte scientist. "But," added Davidson the unconscious mythmaker, "to conceive the limitless there must be limits, and by this contradiction we start eternity with a beginning and make of the infinite a womb called space." [2]

Filling this space in the beginning was the elastic, imponderable substance, ether, omnisolvent, omnicontinent, omnipresent, and omnipotent. Pure energy, ether still permeates more complex forms of matter—and all is matter—just as in the end all matter must devolve into this pristine

* "There are other hypotheses, but the nebular hypothesis in some form remains the most satisfying to the imagination. We cannot proceed a step without hypotheses. It is sometimes forgotten that God was only an hypothesis. Imagination transmutes hypothesis into poetry and religion." Epilogue, Mammon and His Message, p. 164.

† Davidson generally followed nineteenth-century practice by capitalizing such words as "universe," "matter," "ether," "energy," as well as "heaven," "hell," "other world," "sin." He may also have intended to stress their equivalence. In paraphrasing his thought I have used lower case for these words except where he intended a very special sense.

state: "ether to ether returneth." [3] From ether sprang lightning with its two poles or sexes and in its simplest state composed of electrons. Here in electricity imponderable matter first became ponderable. Forming groups, the electrons created the primal atom of hydrogen; or, as Davidson again blasphemes, "In the beginning was hydrogen." [4] Revolving by turn in gigantic swarms, the hydrogen atoms formed nebulae, and one of the smallest of many million, million nebulae broke off to form our solar system. From the hydrogen atom the atoms of other elements were evolved: first carbon, oxygen, and nitrogen, which are the basis of life; then additional elements by combinations of these atoms into molecules.

Life evolved through aeons of chemical selection until, after further geologic periods of natural selection, came man. Man represents the culmination of this evolutionary process, matter become fully conscious and self-conscious. Enshrining the two sexes of pure lightning and capable of the highest ecstasy and knowledge, man is the supreme ironic expression attainable by matter. "There *is* nothing anywhere higher than man," and evolution can produce nothing higher.[5] Thus the evolutionists and ameliorists who envisage a still higher species of man are wrong. Only man's social and political organization can be improved. This, announced Davidson, is the greatest message of all. What are its implications? It means the death of spirit, Christianity, and the afterlife; and conversely it means the glorification of man, self, and this life:

> Thus I break the world out of the imaginary chrysalis or cocoon of Other World in which it has slumbered so long; and man beholds himself, not now as that fabulous monster, half-god, half-devil, of the Christian era, but as Man, the very form and substance of the universe, the material of eternity, eternity itself . . .

It means an end of the strangling past; and end of our conceptions of humanity and divinity, of our ideas of good and evil, of our religion, our literature, our art, our polity; it means that which all men have desired in all ages, it means a new beginning; it means that the material forces of mind and imagination can now re-establish the world as if nothing had ever been thought or imagined before; it means that there is nothing greater than man anywhere; it means infinite terror, infinite greatness. And that is the meaning of me, and of my Testaments and Tragedies . . .[6]

Egoism and rhetorical eloquence are the ambrosia upon which Davidson's autointoxication feeds. He may be dogmatic, at times strident, but he is never petulant, never less than courageous, in his scientific humanism.

Since there was no room in the poet's system for any God, he scorned equally all mythologies. There was nothing new about recognizing the element of fiction in Genesis, but the Testaments and tragedies carried the higher criticism of the nineteenth century to its ultimate conclusion. Not only the Word but the Judaic-Christian conception of the universe, of which the Word was the mythical expression, must go. Theology must give way to theonomy as astrology had to astronomy. "The true theonomist finds the study of God to be a branch of mythology," Davidson declared.[7] He conceded that in times of great emotional stress even those who had rejected Christianity would, "without effort, become immortal soul, and clothe themselves as of old in God and Sin and Heaven and Hell." Compelling as it may be, Christianity is a putrescent anachronism and an evasion:

What we have to do is to leave it all; to cease being maggots in a corpse, and come out into the Universe. . . . The great poetries of the past lived in symbols

of the Universe—Olympus and Hades, Asgard and
Nifelheim, Heaven and Hell; but the abode of my
imagination is the Universe itself; and I would have
it so for all men.[8]

For myth Davidson would substitute scientific hypothesis
and terminology, and by the imagination transform them
into a new romance and poetry. In spite of his repudiation
of Christianity he adapted its configuration, many of its
myths, and often the phrasing of the Bible to his impious
message. Underlying his fiercest attacks upon Christian
dogma was an attraction to its spirit, its poetry, and the
personality of Christ.* His hatred was fed by love. Unable
to ignore the magnetic appeal of Christian belief, he offered naïve rationalizations of Christian myths from the
materialist point of view.

In the Davidsonian universe nothing is excluded or
morally condemned, not even error. The Christian concepts of heaven and hell, God and sin, are enormous fallacies, but as fallacies they are phenomena and must be
explained. Matter cannot belie itself; therefore no thought
of man, however fanciful, can be in essence an error; no
act, however base, a crime. Heaven and hell, for example,

* In a personal letter to George Foote, editor of the *Freethinker,* Davidson explained his view of Christ: "There are two Christs spoken of in
my writings: the Christ of the Christians whom I dislike, and a Christ
known to me out of the New Testament, as I know Hamlet or Don
Quixote: a most impressive person who went his own way and suffered
for it. His limitations, of course, are evident: he had no humor; he
would say a smart thing for the sake of the temporary triumph, as in the
quibbling repartee, 'Render unto Caesar the things that are Caesar's and
unto God the things that are God's'; and he was undeveloped on the
human side. If Christ had only had a wife and children! But he died too
soon. His early precocity was evidently followed by a long period of
hebetation; and at the end of his brilliant three years of publicity he
needed the wilderness instead of Jerusalem for further meditation and
development." Davidson seems totally unaware that he was also describing himself in this conception of Christ. In accordance with Davidson's
request the letter was published in the *Freethinker,* 22 Sept. 1907, p. 593.

are the conscious expression which man has given to his subconscious recollections of the peace of the raw ether, of the glory of the nebulae, and of the agony endured by matter when the solar system evolved spontaneously out of ether. Since man—body, mind, and soul—is composed entirely of matter, he creates a material heaven and hell. By the same token when man, failing to understand fully his own nature, wishes to designate the indestructibility of the matter that comprises his being, he calls it immortal soul. The raw ether of which man is made and to which he and the present solar system will ultimately devolve explain the Christian notion of God and the afterlife. "All the imaginings about the source of his being which man has maddened over, which he has clung to in good report and ill, which he has died for in battle and at the stake, have their roots in Material truth," Davidson explained.[9] Man's groping and stumbling after the truth through the mazes of error is part of the process whereby the universe attains complete self-consciousness. Once man realizes this, there is no longer need to substitute myth for fact.

Another source of man's notion of spiritual immortality is his and the universe's infinite capacity to reproduce. From this regenerative power comes also the idea of sin which, says the materialist, is "cognate and isomeric with the idea of God." [10] Sin is nothing more than the temporary exhaustion of the material forces of man. The discharge of this material energy may occur through acts of intense pleasure, moods of delight, trances of ecstasy; or it may be the consequence of a violent act such as murder, or the betrayal of a friend. By transferring the title of sin from its own physical impotence to the act in which the energy has been spent, enfeebled matter exacts "a species of vengeance." "It is the meanest, most cowardly thing man has done to call his courage Sin," Davidson protested.[11] In his tragedies and to some extent in his

Testaments, he dedicated himself to the rehabilitation of
that pride of spirit and its selfish acts which men had come
to regard as heinous.

By similar analogies Davidson found it a simple matter
to reconcile all man's cherished fallacies with material
truth. Some of his rationalizations are childlike in their
simplicity, but so is much of myth. The Christian concept of the Trinity, for instance, he reduced to the triple
form of the universe—ether, matter, and energy. The
Immaculate Conception, like the marriage of the sons of
God with the daughters of men, signifies that man pro-
creates something greater than man, namely, a conscious
and a self-conscious universe. What this poet of science
did not fully grasp, what perhaps no man of his generation could have fully grasped, was that in substituting
scientific hypothesis and unverified fact for traditional
myth he was substituting myth for myth.

Davidson's conception of the universe began as an
ironic one, like that of Yeats. The essential philosophic
difference between the two poets is that Yeats remained a
dualist, distinguishing sharply between the life of the
spirit and the life of the body, while Davidson became a
rigid monist. The latter's universe is one in which the
only common denominator is matter and the only constant element paradox or antithesis; it is a universe of
perpetual flux. Outside of material phenomena nothing
exists, no power for good or evil, no permanent abstract
values. No moral order has been or can be imposed upon
a godless, timeless, despiritualized universe. Without an
external authority there remains as in Nietzsche only
relative, subjective, man-made truth. What, then, gives
meaning and order to the universe? What prevents physical and social anarchy? Davidson's reply to this query
had originally been "Irony," a cosmic and moral tension
which he described variously and mysteriously as "inexo-

rable," "worshipful," "the soul of things," "the something behind phenomena," "the enigma within the enigma, the open secret, the only answer vouchsafed the eternal riddle." By irony he meant the underlying polarity of the universe:

> It is centric, the adamantine axis of the universe. At its poles are the illusions we call matter and spirit, day and night, pleasure and pain, beauty and ugliness. By it our enterprises are whirled away from our most resolved intentions. A playwright, wearing out his life in the abortive effort to found a county family, makes the literature of the world Shakespearian centuries after his death; the Pilgrim Fathers colonise America in the name of the Highest—that Tammany may flourish in New York; and out of the beautiful Shakespearianism may come evil; out of Tammany, good.[12]

After making this and similar pronouncements in the *Speaker*, he was accused in letters to the editor of offenses ranging from "vagueness" to "obscenity," by indignant readers ranging from Arthur Quiller-Couch to an indefatigable woman who coyly signed herself "Puzzled." [13]

As he became more of a metaphysician and less of a poet, Davidson concluded that the concept of irony was too loosely defined, too misleading, too closely associated with dualism. Above all, he wanted to avoid being mistaken for a dualist or the disciple of dualists. With latitudinarianism and other nineteenth-century compromises between rationalism and faith, he would have nothing to do. His controversies in the press with Quiller-Couch and others led him to adopt scientific materialism and then to formulate his own large, coherent statement of this position. Accordingly he substituted Nietzsche's term "Immorality" for that of "Irony," although he clearly meant to retain the earlier principle in the later. Immorality he defined in terms as old as Heraclitus and Lucretius:

> We know now that there is no moral order of the Universe, but that everything is constantly changing and becoming and returning to its first condition in a perpetual round of evolution and devolution; and this eternal tide of Matter, this restless ebb and flow I call Immorality. . . . The Universe is immoral, and no sooner has a morality of any order established itself than the Universe begins to undo it.[14]

His megalomaniacal involvement in this philosophy prevented him from heeding his own warning. To state the universe as he saw it, he concocted a ponderous new language of chemical terms, pedantic neologisms, and archaic expressions. Materialism enabled him to avoid identification with other beliefs and at the same time provided a concrete, scientific explanation of the abstract principle of irony. Since his philosophy reduces everything to matter, there can be no real contradiction in the universe. This simplification strengthened his philosophy but, as I have noted elsewhere, was death to his poetry.

From the celebration of man as the supreme achievement of a material universe followed the denial of all moral authority outside of the individual's private will. Although he nowhere went extensively into the problem of ethics, Davidson implied in his later works a social order which countenances unrestrained freedom and self-expression. He advocated a society controlled only by the mastery of the strongest will. His heroes are ruthless, unprincipled, single-purposed despots of unlimited ambition and cruelty, whose very supremacy assures an order, albeit a harsh one, and thereby staves off anarchy. These heroes are no more than abstract symbols of an as yet unattained ideal, unrelated to ordinary human needs or those of practical politics. Davidson in his lack of critical detachment and his preoccupation with ideas was indifferent to this limitation. In his blind, sadistic megalomania Mammon lacks the poise, humor, and dignity of Shaw's human and humane Caesar. He is an unintentional caricature of the "naturally great" man where Shaw's philosopher-emperor is a plausible dramatic embodiment. Yet Mammon and Caesar represent the same ideal, one based on the assumption that the man with the greatest will to power is also the wisest man. With Carlyle, Shaw, Henley, and Kipling, and other heroic vitalists, Davidson wanted strength and greatness in man:

> We must write greatly; we must be great: and I trust the famous writers of the day are as great as their reputations; the greater my contemporaries are the greater I am: we want men empowered to say that. I desire men to be great. I desire the meanest man to be great, and to feel great.[15]

So earnest was he in this ambition that he sacrificed artistry to the methods of propaganda in order to state it and overlooked that greatness is a relative quality which disappears when shared by all.

What precisely is greatness for Davidson? And what, if any, are the responsibilities and commitments of the great man? Neither in his prose works nor in his crude verse dramas and Testaments does he clearly define the great man. For Davidson as for Nietzsche and Carlyle, however, greatness is power; power alone justifies the great man and determines history. More often than not, his hero is presented negatively as an iconoclast, anarchist, and immoralist. He is the master destroyer rather than the master builder. The obsession of Davidson's heroes with punishment and cruelty undoubtedly takes its origin in the poet's desire to assert his own will by destroying within himself any inclination to Christian pity. The choice between reason and emotion is a dilemma common to the century. Frequently, as in Davidson, it resulted in the exchange of one dogma for another.

Almost without exception Davidson's later heroes are algolagnists, as to some extent was he.* In his illuminating study of the superman fixation in the nineteenth century, Eric Bentley explains the morbid fascination with pain among the heroic vitalists, particularly Carlyle and Nietzsche. He finds these two men "inverted Christians," a heretical sect that by the way included Davidson:

> Both were, by nature, highly passionate and, further, highly compassionate. Neither . . . could bear the thought of even an animal in pain, yet both are famous for the brutality of their political doctrine, their advocacy of slavery, and their admiration for bloody tyrants. . . . It is partly because Carlyle and Nietzsche were more highly sensitive and sympathetic than the rest of us, because, as the alienists have it, of their exaggerated algolagnic instincts, that they sensed the impotence of compassionate, modern man in the cruel processes which historical study was revealing, that they felt a need for personal renunciation and expiation, a need to be twice-born. . . . Since they were honest enough to accept the new world opened up by historical imagination, they must—even if it meant killing something inside them—adapt themselves, their weak, puritan, Protestant, Christian selves, to this world, though it would have been easier to shout an everlasting No or to rest at the center of indifference.[16]

---

* His obsession with physical pain was not confined to his writings. I am told by Menzies Davidson that on one occasion his father removed a sebaceous cyst from his scalp by applying nitric acid to it and sat all day without any anodyne while the acid gradually burned away the growth. The odor of burning tissue permeated the house.

Thus Davidson's Vivisector and his tyrant-hero Mammon torture not for the sake of sadistic pleasure or material knowledge but in order to purge their Christian and puritan selves which they know to be false, to prove themselves men dedicated to power and the new truth.

Closely allied to this interest in the infliction of pain is a concern with madness and suicide. A deeply subjective interest in these themes is imaginatively realized in the lyrics of the nineties. As he developed a metaphysical synthesis to include and reconcile the various elements in his thought, Davidson's concern with madness and suicide became that of the psychologist and philosopher. He was struck by the fact that genius in man, an atavistic marriage of intellect and brute instinct, is often accompanied by a handicap: a nervous disorder, consumption, venereal disease, or madness. It is chiefly the madman who sees behind the disorder and falseness of external appearances the inner coherence and meaning of the universe. His disability restores in him the delicate balance of material powers upset in the overintellectual modern man. Thus the madman alone is the fully natural human being.

Violence in human conduct is for Davidson a sign of personal power and therefore of wisdom and self-fulfillment. It is this aspect of suicide which absorbed his attention as early as *Smith* (1888) and *In a Music-Hall and Other Poems* (1891). The subject recurs frequently in successive works, but again the philosopher ultimately replaces the poet. When man's material powers begin to fail, Davidson reasoned, he is under obligation to destroy himself just as the man of power, the leader, is obligated to cull the derelicts and invalids from society. Each act is a form of purification and of obeisance to the supreme will of matter for self-consciousness. In *The Triumph of Mammon* the heroic protagonist approves highly of the pagan death of old Sweyn, who puts out to sea in a burn-

ing boat. Davidson reasserts man's power over personal
destiny, which inferior creeds have denied by refusing to
place final authority in the individual will.

The poet's political thinking is likewise dominated by
his consciousness of the supremacy of personal power. With
other heroic vitalists he is the apostle of an aristocratic
radicalism by which the autocrat or oligarch is the governing authority, answerable to no one beyond himself.
But here again he remains primarily the abstract theorist.
Unlike William Morris, Shaw, H. G. Wells, and other
contemporaries, he was rarely interested in practical reforms. He was allied with no political party or movement. Deeply sensitive, benevolent, humanitarian, he
nevertheless preserved for years an attitude of complete
ironic detachment toward current social and political
issues. While England and Ireland were being torn asun-
der by the struggle over home rule, he broached the topic
in *A Random Itinerary* for the sole purpose of drawing out
a farmer encountered in his country rambles. When he
recalled having seen Gladstone, he described in detail the
prime minister's physical appearance without a word for
his principles. When his contemporaries were being violently partisan over the question of free trade and the
war with South Africa, Davidson put the case for a vigorous imperialism in the manner of Meredith's Comic
Spirit: "The Emperor of Germany, as the French say, is
King of Kings; the King of Spain, King of men; the King
of France, King of asses; and the King of England, King
of devils; and he that is embarked with the devil must
make the passage along with him." [17] It was only after
1900 when he began to take himself and his message over-
earnestly that he forsook this Olympian irony for a factious
solemnity and brutality.

He departed still further from Shaw, Wells, and other
Fabians by his uncompromising rejection of socialism as

a solution to modern ills. He was neither revolutionist nor evolutionist:

> It is not a revolution I propose: revolution is nothing. . . . Were Socialism a realized ideal to-morrow there would be no actual change: only the dead corpse of Christendom floating up again upon the tide. Socialism, like Christianity, proceeds upon the assumption that men are not what they are. There is little difference between Feudalism and Socialism. Socialism would lay hands upon the earth and its products, upon man and his labour, not heroically, in arms, by superior craft and intellect, as Feudalism did, but unheroically by means of representative government (which is no government), by universal suffrage, bargains with the mob, and the prate of parliamentarians. Socialism is the decadence of Feudalism; that is to say, it is less than nothing. At its very utmost it is only a bad smell; rejoicing in itself very much at present, as bad smells are wont to do: Europe is noisome with it.[18]

Here as in similar late pronouncements Davidson may appear to echo Nietzsche's strictures against democracy, plutocracy, socialism, and all political dispensations except that of rule by a despot. In actuality he had despised socialism throughout his life. Moreover, political disillusionment and cynicism were in the air. One cannot help recalling Shaw's lighter deprecation of current political panaceas in the bandit gang of *Man and Superman*.

The most destructive spirit must have some constructive foundation, however vaguely delineated, upon which to base his attacks. Always prone to see in the current vogue, whether aesthetic, scientific, or political, a demonstration of his own principles, Davidson thumped vigorously on the Tories' imperialist drum. It was the Englishman who was destined to rule: "The Englishman is the Overman; and the history of England is the history of his evolution." [19] The British Empire or "Ocean-State" corresponds in the area of political action to the achievement in man of the highest form of matter. In his role as warrior the Davidsonian hero, like those of Carlyle and Nietzsche, fights for possession of the entire world. As the strongest he must rule; as the ruler he must be harsh, trust only himself, and divorce himself from deferential service to the masses. What is good for Mammon is good for Christianstadt.

Davidson's political development followed a pattern that has become almost commonplace. From an aesthetic and humane abhorrence of Philistinism and "the bitch goddess," he progressed to a deeply humanitarian and apparently democratic sympathy with the working masses, only to adopt finally a Nietzschean neofeudalism, based upon ability and power rather than birth or wealth, in which society is divided between the willing slaves and the ruling masters. Like Spengler, Carlyle, Nietzsche, and Herbert Spencer, he thought of history in evolutionary terms, as a continual flux in which one force is defeated and replaced by a stronger. And like the heroic vitalists he reduced history to personality. Christianity triumphed, he reasoned, when the pedantic eclecticism of Seneca went down before the inspiration of Saul of Tarsus and the sublime myth of a crucified God, embodied in the magnetic personality of Christ. Ironically Christianity died at the moment of its greatest triumph, on Calvary, and must be discarded. He had stated this anonymously in *Diabolus Amans* in 1885; he stated it openly in *A Random Itinerary* in 1894: "The whole world groans and travails with a new God. Wordsworth hints it; Tennyson and Carlyle hoped not; Swinburne sings it; Ibsen, that great Scotchman, says it. A new Heaven; a new Earth." [20] Believing it implicitly, he could do nothing but repeat the message in his many remaining works.

Although he shared their cyclical conception of history and repeatedly described the Christian era as decadent, Davidson was conscious of two fallacies committed by the historical evolutionists and heroic vitalists. He asserted in the first place that the millennium toward which the universe was supposed to be evolving had already arrived. He redefined in the second place cultural decadence. The idea of decadence, Bentley observes, has obsessed the historical mind since Nietzsche. It is a greatly overstated cliché used by Marx, Spengler, and Friedell among others to characterize the modern period. "It may be one of many aspects of an age," continues Bentley; ". . . it is not necessarily an adequate description of the whole culture, for autumn, to follow Spengler's metaphor, is also seed-time, and in so-called ages of decadence the seeds of the future are sown." [21] Kipling, whom Bentley mentions only as being non-Prussian, and Davidson, whom he does not mention at all, saw seeds of awakening and growth in the decadence of their time. Both noted that a new order, before it emerges, often expresses itself in the forms of the old. Davidson went so far as to concede, although he did not dwell on it, that the scientific theories on which he relied would themselves become outmoded and replaced. And he was conscious of championing scientific materialism and the pride of empire in a decadent form, that of rhymed verse:

> But all decadent forms can immediately become crescive . . . Literary criticism is in its infancy: the great crescive poem of Christendom, *The Divine Comedy,* took the decadent form of rhyme; the great decadent poem of Christendom, *Paradise Lost,* fell upon the ascendant form of blank verse.[22]

This is a curious but not unclear illustration of the fashionable theory that history is a continual, overlapping process of growth and decay.

The Scottish metaphysician was at no time a great or original political thinker. In theory heroic vitalism is positive as well as negative, constructive as well as destructive; but when applied to politics this is not often the case. It has its inception in rebellion and defiance and properly belongs to the negative phase of romanticism. Its idealism is so deeply rooted in disillusionment that it rarely has a chance to flower. Although he parted company with Carlyle and Nietzsche in stressing the greatness of the present rather than of the past or future, Davidson offered a program no more practical or clearly defined than they had. "It is Christendom that is the matter with the world," he cries. "The world is sick of Christendom." [23] But he never explains satisfactorily what he would create, as he does with great effectiveness what he would destroy. When he speaks of the past or the present the heroic vitalist employs argument and fact, if he is not above distortion or omission. When he speaks of the future he asserts wild generalities. This is largely true whether he be a socialist like Morris, Shaw, and Wells or an aristocratic radical like Carlyle, Nietzsche, and Davidson. The danger of heroic vitalism lies not in what it advocates but in what it fails to advocate. It is the vigorous clarity of the heroic vitalist's attack on democracy and Christianity and the obscurity of the panacea which he promises that made it possible for the Fascisti and Nazis to exploit his authority. This in turn has placed him under a popular stigma from which he has not recovered.*

* Crane Brinton with minor qualifications supports the view that National Socialism found its intellectual origin and justification in Nietzsche's thought. (Brinton, *Nietzsche*, Cambridge, Mass., 1948 [1941], pp. 200 ff.) Eric Bentley argues, convincingly to this reader, that the political policies

2

In principle and, when he could remember the principle or afford it, in practice Davidson resisted making critical pronouncements. He had a strong conviction that no art should be obliged to explain itself, and he was frequently reluctant to explain his. A writer who discussed works he had written or those of others was engaging in redundancy— a form of self-indulgence, it should be added, that he did not always resist. Although Archer, an incurable critic and theorist, repeatedly urged him to set down his principles of playwriting, Davidson as often declined:

> I wish I could say what I understand by drama; but I believe I shall never get it stated. Wagner could state his music in terms of letters, and Rossetti his letters in terms of colour and *vice versa;* but how to state literature in terms of literature? that was always my difficulty when I used to try to review. Browning once threatened to write the criticism as well as the poetry: my belief is that he couldn't have done it had he tried: I have seen some matter of his in the publications of the Browning Society, which is quite hopeless.
>
> A scientific treatment of literature, a phisology [*sic*] and pathology of literature seems to me the only possible form in which letters can be used in expounding letters.
>
> "But me no buts." Is it not the case that a profound and prolonged study of any art vitrifies, or is apt to vitrify vision into theory—they were once the same— so that instead of the critic's vision shifting with the individual play or picture or whatsoever, he sees

and practices of the fascists were a corruption and, in many instances, a violation of Nietzsche's positive principles. Bentley, *A Century of Hero-Worship,* pp. 150–1.

everything through the stained glass window of his
theory, and often can't see anything else? * [24]

To prove his point he needed to go no further than his
own reviews and essays where his comments on other
authors, which he was often lured into making, are bathed
in the spectrum of Davidsonian theory.

Davidson's critical opinions, like his other views, derive
about equally from his reading of other writers and his
experience as a poet. His aesthetic theories have been discussed elsewhere in this book, but not his controversial,
frequently inconsistent, but always independent judg-
ments of fellow writers. These opinions, of which there
are many, he drops seemingly at random in his prose
writings. Their purpose, however, even in commissioned
reviews, is to support his more abstruse philosophical pronouncements. As he justified his own poetry by purely
subjective standards, he appraised the work of other authors by the degree to which they could be made to con-
form to his philosophy. This bias leads him to impressionistic, sometimes preposterous observations, but it as
often results in startlingly clear insights.

The Victorian mandarins, Tennyson, Browning, and
Arnold, he either condemned without mercy or dismissed
with a patronizing acknowledgment of minor talent. Tennyson, admittedly "the master-artificer of our age," [25] was
not an artist but the author of diluted "confections of pas-

---

* Compare an earlier letter to Archer: "I expect you have forgotten
I had your copy of Pinero's 'Mrs. Tanqueray.' I never forgot, but kept
it by me, because I intended on returning it to examine briefly the whole
matter of dramatic art. I return it now with many thanks, and regret
having kept it so long, because I find it impossible to conduct that
magisterial enquiry: it seems to me that there is no such thing as dramatic art—no art at all, species or genus, that can be discussed: every
authentic person will do his own things in his own way, and no standard
can be applied to authentic productions except the law of their own being."
A.L.S., dated 8 Dec. 1899, from St. Winifred's, Fairmile Avenue, Streatham,
S.W., Add. MS. 45291, ff. 94–5, B.M.

sion for use in ladies' seminaries." Browning "with his frantic, terrified optimism, and the restless spinning jenny in his head," was not much more to his liking. He found them bourgeois to the core and associated them with the passing of the Reform Bills and the repeal of the Corn Law. It is significant that he assigned these views in an imaginary dialogue to Carlyle, an early idol whom he also subsequently repudiated.[26] Rejoicing in the woman in unwomanly rags of Thomas Hood's "Song of the Shirt," "in its place the most important English poem of the nineteenth century," he compared Tennyson and Browning to the Levite and the priest of the parable of the good Samaritan: They would have passed her on the other side. William Morris, he owned, stood by her side but he hardly saw her, nor could he have shown her as she is.[27] For Arnold with his clear, serene mind, his substitution of classicism and culture for the anarchy of dissent, evangelicalism, and Hebraism, Davidson could have no sympathy. He himself retained too much of the passionate obstinacy and subjectivism of the Hebraic mind to countenance the opposing qualities of the Hellenic. He commended the Pre-Raphaelites for their nonconformity but was suspicious of their decadence, romantic escapism, and lack of a strong moral core.

He turned instead to the earlier romantics, Blake, Burns, Keats, Shelley, but especially Wordsworth, for unconscious prophets of his new poetry. James Thomson, Laurence Binyon, Victor Plarr, and Selwyn Image he recognized as later, conscious exponents. Intimating that Wordsworth was his poetic and philosophic antecedent, Davidson found in such poems as "Lines Composed above Tintern Abbey" an unwitting anticipation, still couched in the old spiritual guise, of the gospel of materialism. Wordsworth's apocalyptic vision deteriorated into a pedantry which men rejected, because—and here he creates his

predecessor in his own image—Wordsworth lacked a great
audience and the world's applause. From a great immoralist and rebel, a pre-Davidsonian, the earlier romantic
sank therefore into a timeserver and a moralist.

In tracing his lineage to Wordsworth, the pantheist and
moralist, Davidson furnishes evidence that the apparent
conflicts underlying nineteenth-century thought—of science and religion, matter and spirit, romance and realism,
decadence and counterdecadence—were not so clear-cut
as has been believed. The bifurcation was horizontal as
well as vertical, dividing artists and intellectuals against
themselves as much as against each other, with the result
that by the end of the century the old dichotomies had
broken down or become realigned. It is this shifting of
values and meanings which enabled Davidson, the spokesman for science in poetry, to reject rationalism and its literary by-product, naturalism, for romance, which he
forced into a miscegenation with science. Such paradoxes
result as much from his incomplete awareness of his place
in the history of ideas as from his strange synthesis.

Davidson's literary criticism, which constitutes an important if not large part of his prose writing, has the merits
and shortcomings of all intuitive judgment. It abounds in
the witty paradoxes of the aesthetes, but out of reverence
for his own theories, not theirs. For example, the Eliza-
bethan-Jacobean age was a great period of drama and
poetry because "every aid to free and full utterance was
employed in the disdain of art." At the same time he
made keen individual observations as when he credited
Kyd with discovering a new function of the madman:
"Here was liberty at last; everything could be said; and
the kernel of the world appear through the rent in the
heart, the crack in the mind." [28] He recommended that
because of its seminal influence *The Spanish Tragedy* and
not *Edward III* be included in the appendix to all popular

editions of Shakespeare. Davidson yielded to none of the contemporary wits in striking off arresting aphorisms:

> . . . all contemporary poetry is minor poetry. . . . It is the centuries that give poetry its majority.

> . . . no man is a critic on his deathbed.

> If you praise a man you please only himself. In order to provide the greatest happiness for the greatest number, you must damn with faint praise, for then you please all a man's friends.

> We must carefully distinguish between the absence of tact and the presence of principle.[29]

Impulse and bias as often as considered appraisal dictated his critical exaggerations. He credited James Thomson with a passion and an intellect second only to Shakespeare's; he praised highly Meredith's "French Odes" because they "contain the first profound notes of the new epic—the epic of Democracy with Napoleon for hero"; and he admired Poe's intensity of mood and echoing rhymes, finding in his poems and not in Whitman's the seed of American literature.[30]

"Assertion is the alpha and omega of style," Shaw once stated. "He who has nothing to assert has not and can never have style." Davidson not only adopted this principle as a cornerstone for his own writing but applied it early in his judgment of other authors. He carefully distinguished between style, which is imperceptible, and stylism, which one notes at once. The latter is "the attempt to achieve style . . . the attempt of self-consciousness to be unconscious; the attempt to say something not in its own manner; but in a predetermined manner." By way of illustration, "Scott has style; Stevenson is a stylist." [31] For Davidson the ingredients of any style, whether in criticism or poetry, are uniform: spontaneity, originality, honesty, courage, and conviction:

> . . . spontaneity in criticism is the crowning glory of
> the student: in place of painful reference to notes and
> authorities he is enabled by perfect mastery to give
> an individual mind to the pleasure of composition
> . . . envy endows a forthright and splendid style
> with a prodigal portion of carelessness in matters of
> fact. Inaccuracy may be voluble, a lie may be glib; but
> neither can be spontaneous.[32]

Of all earlier critics he was most attracted to Hazlitt whom he found, if not the greatest critic, one of the greatest, and one whose greatness consisted in having "the courage to say as an author what he felt as a man." [33]

Shakespeare, Cromwell, Smollett, Blake, Napoleon, Hazlitt, Carlyle, Nietzsche—all strong-willed and outspoken, all with the itch of divine discontent—these were Davidson's heroes. Each was first a great man and then a master of language. In later life he disavowed the idols of his youth, but the mark of these personalities and of less known figures is on his misanthropy and many of his ideas. No man achieves a philosophic system unaided. Even the germinal metaphysics of his early verse is propped up by rotten lumber from a score of Elizabethan and earlier nineteenth-century poets. It is questionable that Davidson, before coming to London, was conscious of reconciling the contradictions of his age in a comprehensive monistic system. On the other hand, he was naturally disposed to this mission by the necessity to resolve an inner conflict, which made him abnormally sensitive to the contradictions around him. There is a messianic largeness of interest in the early plays and poems and the readiness of the ironist to distill, assimilate, and record all experience without moral judgment. But these elements are as yet raw and unformed. Just as his poetic talent was limited and frequently imitative, his philosophical bent took the direction of synthesis rather than creative thought. Personal desperation and powerful external agents were to catalyze this synthesis.

3

Davidson's consciousness of stating a new, superior vision and of the variability of truth shown by history prompted him to deny every influence. Eager to erase the past, he strove to sever ties with his teachers and actual allies. His creed, for instance, owed much to Darwinian thought, especially to its popular dissemination in Huxley, Spencer, Clifford, and others. To the concept of organic evolution he added those of vitalism, terminal evolution, and imperialism. His personal gospel of man's inheritance of the earth was reinforced with widely accepted scientific principles. Sensing that in time these would yield to newer principles, he was anxious that their repudiation not reflect on his gospel. Although he continued to the end to assert the validity of the nebular hypothesis, organic evolution, and related scientific postulates of the day, he privately admitted that they were questionable. Evolution, for one, lent itself too readily to determinism, which he detested, and overlooked the role of the human will in history. Future scientific discoveries were certain to replace Darwin's conclusions but, he predicted, would only confirm the essential truth of his message, the unique greatness of man. In a letter to Gosse he explained evolution as a useful but problematical hypothesis:

But I wish . . . to suggest that the evolutionary idea is even more misleading in Literature than in Science and Philosophy. Since the Ptolemaic System nothing more satisfactory to common sense has been offered in

any branch of knowledge than Evolution; but it is
now supposed that the sun does not go round the
earth, and it may very well be that the apparent
descent of Man is a sense-illusion too. I suggest that
English literature is a forest rather than a planta-
tion; that Evolution, applied to literature, reverses
the proverb, and cannot see the trees for the wood;
and that generalisation, admirable for classes, is mischievous in dealing with individuals. I mean that we
—that you and *I*, poets, thinkers, sinners, fortunate-
unfortunates, authentic persons, or whatever we may
call ourselves, or be called, must accept no creed; that
although Evolution is bound to rule the minds of
men for hundreds of years to come, the sinner—let us
use sinner; it is a modest term—the sinner knows it
will be dismissed in its turn as Creation is being dismissed now; and that although he may be compelled
to use the idea of Evolution in order to be understood of his contemporaries, he is unfettered by it, and
rejoices in his liberty.[34]

Lured by the specious security of suspended judgment,
Davidson forgot that the greatest bondage is freedom
without commitment. When the trap sprang he was left
with an untenable irony, misanthropy, and subjectivism.

Inevitably various radical groups, seeking prestige or
notoriety, attempted to enlist the intransigent materialist
in their cause. Having denied the "worship of matter"
and insisted that his purpose was not to create a new meta-
physic, philosophy, or theology but a new poetry, he rejected these overtures with honest indignation. When a
Nietzsche Society tried to inveigle him into contributing
a letter to their organ, *The Eagle and the Serpent,* with a
promise to reprint some of his writings, he refused, de-

scribing their tactics as "a modified form of bribery and corruption." He contrasted himself in this respect with Shaw, who "is different from me, because he has always been a publicist, which I never was." [35] After the society persisted, he viciously attacked it on the grounds that since Nietzsche "was the enemy of 'herds' " it was a *reductio ad absurdum;* that its journal was "an abominable trick-periodical"; and that its members, "these nauseous people," were "a small kind of petty devils bent on the degradation of everything better than they." "I had no idea they were so vile," he protested in innocence, as if they had willfully deceived him; "they advertise quack medicines, quack diet, and sexual condiments—in the name of Nietzsche and Emerson. Let us forget them." [36]

On another occasion the *New Age,* an advanced socialist organ, accepted one of his poems for publication. The poet accompanied his contribution with a letter in which he said that he had read the journal for some weeks with great pleasure and profit. Subsequently discovering its close affiliation with the socialist movement, he wrote another letter in a towering rage, withdrawing his endorsement. He objected in the strongest terms to the appearance of his poem under such a flag and declared that had he known the *New Age* supported "advanced" views nothing on earth would have induced him to write a line for it. His anger was not allayed when the editor gently hinted to him that he was in all probability the only man in Great Britain who could read the journal for weeks on end and not discover its political views.[37]

George Foote, champion of atheism and editor of the *Freethinker,* wrote several articles for that journal, defending Davidson's *The Theatrocrat* and impressing him into service, as he had already claimed Swinburne and Meredith.[38] The fact that Davidson had dismissed the

words "atheist" and "atheism" as misnomers and stated
that "you cannot disbelieve in what is not" did not dis-
courage Foote. Defining an atheist as "a person 'without
God,' " he argued. "Mr. Davidson is without God—therefore Mr. Davidson is an Atheist. It might almost be said
that he is *more* than an Atheist. He is a *dogmatic* Atheist . . ." [39] The unwilling recruit thanked his champion but declined to join any cause under the banner of
atheism. In a letter to the leader of free thought, which
he subsequently requested him to publish, he painstak-
ingly explained his position:

. . . Atheist, as Christian was at first, is a word of
contumely. If those who deny that God ever existed
(except in the mind of man as the most baleful delusion on record) accept this name, I would have them
note that the Christian precedent is full of omen. The
first Christians were in their day and way advanced
freethinkers. They gloried in their contumelious
nickname, with the result that their adoption of it
limited them, diverted them, spoiled their growth.
They could not grow except in depravity, and soon became the purple cancer of Christianity which we
know. If we accept the name of Atheist, we limit ourselves, we distort our growth; we will become depraved, we will develop a cancer or a wen. The power
of a name when the name stands for tenet is incal-
culable, and the effect of its adoption is always disastrous; because a name is adopted only when the
tenet is ripe and ready to decay. Consider, for example, Conservatism and Liberalism; the moment
they were named and known they began to putrefy. I
think the time has come for Freethinkers to rise above
theism and atheism, to come out of it altogether.
There is the word, Man, a virgin word, a zero. Let us

call ourselves Men, and begin all things over again as if the world had never dreamt of a drunken deity.

Davidson at this juncture wished only to assert the glory of the present; Foote, not to be put off by idle superstitions about names and institutions, urged the immediate task of destroying the past. In his reply he observed that theism still occupied the ground and possessed the weapons of wealth, prestige, and authority; it would be time enough to renounce the use of the militant word "atheism" and adopt "the Religion of Humanity" when the war against theism had been won. Davidson, he persisted, consciously or not, was "a brave soldier in the great war of the Liberation of Humanity." [40] In spite of his efforts to remain aloof Davidson found himself enmeshed in the contemporary conflict of belief and unbelief.

On similar grounds the poet of matter disclaimed affiliation at any time with one form of religion or another. An inquiry from A. S. Mories into his religious position elicited from him a stout denial that he had ever belonged to an evangelical sect or espoused atheism:

> Many thanks for your book, article, and letter. The idea of 'spirit,' 'spirituality,' becomes more and more hateful to me. There I am quite intolerant. There I would burn and slay. I am not a Monist—would call myself by no name; as soon as a thing is named after a tenet it begins to putrefy. I was never a Morisonian. The idea that men or boys are ever anything but themselves is a delusion. Men consist of carbon, oxygen, hydrogen, nitrogen, like the stars and the imponderable ether, and their souls are the manifold forces of the elements, of which they are (plus the omnipresent ether) the invisible elasticity, which is a solution of all the elements.
>
> No one ever understood this before me; all that was

ever meant by God, Spirit, other world, in any country, at any time, falls off the Universe like a dry scab,
the moment this is understood.[41]

Christianity, deism, rationalism—each, he implied, had
contributed to the evolution of his climactic message;
but they were no longer needed, indeed constituted a
threat, and must be sloughed off like a dead skin. To a
correspondent who was forming a large library he countered that this undertaking was in all likelihood heroic
but that his heroism took a different turn. With the exception of about a dozen books by two or three authors he
would gladly see destroyed the publications of the last
fifty years and the bulk of the literature of the past.[42]
Shaw's Caesar, when informed that the library at Alex-
andria is in flames, remarks indifferently that if immortal
books did not flatter mankind, the common executioner
would burn them. Whereupon he urges Ptolemy's tutor
and the custodian of Egyptian wisdom to build the future
upon the ruins of the past. There was no question in
Davidson's mind that that day of reckoning had arrived
and that his works, not the *Commentaries* on the Gallic
wars or *Three Plays for Puritans*, would be chosen to succeed the charred pile.

In April 1897 Cornelius Weygandt, then a young journalist preparing a series of articles on contemporary poets
for the Philadelphia *Evening Telegraph*, wrote to Davidson for information on his background. The poet wrote
back:

You ask regarding "educational influences" and
for "accurate information" of my "development." The
only education[al] influences I acknowledge are my
own passion, thought and experience. As for development, is it not the open secret of every poet's writing,
ready, indeed eager, to yield itself to the attentive

student? My readers must find my development in my books. An apple-tree produces apples, but you cannot expect it to pull, pare, core and serve its own fruit.[43]

Churlish as this reluctance to discuss his intellectual origins appears, it reflects a resolute wish to be self-sufficient and an embarrassed sense of owing much after all to others. Originality and sincerity of thought were for him the cardinal virtues. To confess the smallest debt was to set a shameful example and to destroy the efficacy of his message.

4

Of the foreign influences on Davidson the most probable are Goethe, Emerson, Whitman, Ibsen, and Nietzsche. Carlyle attracted the young poet's attention to Goethe, as he did that of many a Victorian. Goethe and Napoleon were the only great men within living memory according to Carlyle, an idolatry which Davidson shared. Although the German romanticist was for a long time a favorite author, his Scottish admirer knew him only in translation.[44] This was no handicap from Davidson's point of view since he respected Goethe primarily as a master spirit not unlike his own: "Goethe wasn't an artist; he was a great man, who found a way for himself in the endeavour of his art: and I should say that the born aesthete might find himself in the endeavour to be a great man." [45] In another mood, when he would brook no rivalry in greatness, he dismissed *Wilhelm Meister* as "a very overrated book" and accused its author of having made a fetish of himself, a "fetish and medicine-man in one." [46] Although they shared an indifference to artistic perfection and a faith in personality, few if any of Davidson's specific ideas owe their immediate origin to Goethe. Granting this, the German's preoccupation with the psychology, moral problems, and integrity of the individual and his romantic

Streben toward human fulfillment through action and
suffering—heroically expressed in Faust—are a seminal
form of the heroic vitalism found in Davidson. The relationship goes no deeper, for like Carlyle he was inspired
more by the legend of Goethe than by his writings.

Similarly the influence of Emerson and Whitman is only
of the most general kind. It may again have been Carlyle,
the friend and correspondent of the Concord transcendentalist, who introduced the young disciple to his writings.
Notwithstanding the debt of heroic vitalism to the doctrine of self-reliance, Emerson was too much the idealist
and mystic for one who stressed the overman in opposition to the oversoul. This reservation should not cloud a
fact already noted, that the distinction among the transcendentalism of Wordsworth and Emerson, the naturalism
of Swinburne and Meredith, and the materialism or determinism of Davidson and Hardy is largely one of degree
and terminology.* It was the perception that Wordsworth
and Carlyle, "the two potentates of English literature in
the nineteenth century," had the same aim as he, "to extend [their] self-consciousness into the self-consciousness of
the world," to substitute a Wordsworthdom and a Carlyle-
dom for Christendom, that prompted Davidson to acknowledge them as his proper ancestors.[47] Considerably
before Davidson, Whitman in *Leaves of Grass* had been a
trail blazer in showing that what once had been regarded
as ugly, sordid, and mean could be a proper subject for
poetry. Beyond this, the younger singer of the commonplace frequently aped the older's use of cataloguing and
slang. Attracted as he was to Whitman's glad acceptance of

---

* Joseph Warren Beach observes a natural and logical development from
transcendentalism to naturalism: "Human nature being what it is, transcendentalism was an absolutely necessary step in the transition from
supernaturalism to naturalism. . . . Under cover of transcendentalism
naturalism was enabled to make great advances." Beach, *Nature in
Nineteenth-Century Poetry*, p. 345.

life and "proletarian" style, the American laureate of man sang too often of the democratization of men to suit Davidson's aristocratic bias.

Because he owed little to the dramaturgy of Ibsen, Davidson willingly admitted his debt to the Norwegian's thought, adding hastily that no trace of Ibsen could be found in his work.[48] He made no attempt, as did Henry Arthur Jones, Arthur Wing Pinero, and Shaw, to imitate Ibsen or take up where Ibsen left off: "For me Ibsen is the end, not the beginning." [49] Davidson's symbolical dramas of conflict and self-assertion nevertheless strike the same note as Ibsen's great lyrical dramas, *Brand* and *Peer Gynt*. He could not conceal his admiration for many of the Norwegian dramatist's qualities which he shared: the savage exposure of Philistine hypocrisy and mediocrity; the championship of the individual spirit; the psychological probings and dissection; the obsession with the morbid, the socially and morally diseased, and the wretchedness of the world; and Ibsen's "vision of the joy of life," the dynamic, vital principle of energy which destroys man rather than be destroyed.[50] The recognition of a life force which knows no morality or scruple appealed to Davidson. Although these ideas were present in the works of his Scottish period before he could have been very familiar with Ibsen's plays, he had probably read Ibsen before he had Nietzsche and found in him a confirmation and crystallization of his own thoughts.[51]

The precise extent of Nietzsche's impress upon Davidson has been often weighed and debated. Certain scholars have found in addition to the evidence of his reading of Nietzsche a sufficient number of exact parallels to infer a strong, direct influence.[52] In the opposite camp are those who have minimized this influence or concluded that the truth lies somewhere between the two positions.[53] The most recent evidence indicates that Davidson encountered the German philosopher's ideas as early as November 1891 but that his own writings showed no traceable influence until the late 1890's.* The problem is complicated by the poet's reticence on the subject and the appearance in his early verse and plays, before he had any knowledge of Nietzsche's writings, of ideas that are strikingly similar to those of the German vitalist. By 1890 when he left Scotland for London, he had already written two dramas of revolt which adumbrate a theory of cosmic irony and immorality close to Nietzsche's concept of *Immoralismus*. *Smith* and, more outspokenly, *Diabolus Amans* repudiate the authority of literature, religion, and morality. These plays also celebrate the spirit of revolt and the right of the individual to complete self-determination, even to self-inflicted death—ideas that are again found not only in Nietzsche but elsewhere in the century.

Nietzsche was brought to public attention in Europe by the periodicals of the early nineties. After 1890 his reputation grew with rapid speed both in Germany and France, reaching its peak by 1900.[54] Ernst Elster introduced Nietzsche to his colleagues at the University of Glasgow as early as 1887, but it is unlikely that Davidson learned anything at that time beyond vague reports. Alexander Tille, "a furious Nietzschean" and later a well-known translator of his works into English, did not arrive in Glasgow until 1890 after Davidson had gone to London. Under Tille's influence Scotland became a center of Nietzsche study and

* See John A. Lester Jr., "Friedrich Nietzsche and John Davidson," pp. 411–29. Lester's research traces the influence of Nietzsche on Davidson through the latter's contributions to current periodicals as well as from the internal evidence of his writings. I would differ with Lester's conclusions only in his emphasis upon two sharply distinct periods of the Davidson-Nietzsche relationship, the first in 1891–93, the second in the late 1890's. From the gradual intrusion of dogmatism and virulent expression into the lyrics of the mid-nineties, it would seem that Nietzsche's influence asserted itself more gradually and imperceptibly, if only as a kindred voice heard in the memory.

propaganda.[55] Whereas the flow of French translations of the German's works began in 1892, the first major translations into English of his writings were those of Thomas Common and Tille in 1896, and of William A. Hausmann and John Gray in 1899.[56]

Early in November 1891 Davidson uncovered in a French periodical an article on Nietzsche by the Polish-born critic, Theodor de Wyzewa. Excited by his discovery he promptly translated large sections of de Wyzewa's article for an essay entitled "The New Sophist," which he contributed to the *Speaker* for November 28, 1891, and which, considerably revised, appeared as a column, headed "Frederick Nietzsche," in the *Glasgow Herald* for March 18, 1893. The selection of aphorisms from *Menschlich Allzumenschliches* in Davidson's *Sentences and Paragraphs,* published in November 1893, was culled from the *Speaker* essay.[57] So far as anyone has determined, these represent the first rendering of Nietzsche into English and are therefore of some historical importance. In spite of his eager introduction of Nietzsche to the English public, his first translator criticized the German for being a nihilist in philosophy.[58] There is scarcely any direct impact of Nietzsche's thought on Davidson's on this first encounter.

During the nineties, to which most of the lyrics belong, the poet was assimilating many ideas then in the air, including almost certainly Nietzsche's. The poems of this period reintroduce increasingly after a temporary lull the repudiation of Christianity, the conception of a higher type of man, a stress on the pride and strength of life, the rejection of the outmoded idea of the inherent impurity of nature, and an insistence upon the right to a life of sin. The fact that these ideas are found in Nietzsche does not necessarily prove that they owe their appearance at this time to his works. They can be found in equal measure if not in equal intensity in Shelley, Byron, Whitman, the

Spasmodics, Swinburne, and Henley. In their rudimentary form they are indigenous to English-speaking countries, although the vehemence and much of the terminology of their subsequent expression in Davidson is unmistakably Nietzschean. One can assume with safety only that the German prophet lent the weight of his authority, the force of his style, and the completeness of his formulation to ideas that were originally of German extraction but that had during the course of a century become international. Coleridge, Emerson, Carlyle, and Whitman renewed the contact with the parent country, thereby stimulating the growth of these ideas; but there is substantial evidence that the ideas developed more or less simultaneously and independently in the three countries. Nourished by Darwinism the transplanted seedlings flourished for a time in England. If Davidson lifted a page here and there from his compeer for his later tragedies and Testaments, it was to absorb them into his personalized system. The foundation of Davidson's structure is scientific materialism; to this Nietzsche contributed nothing.

In spite of his primary debt to ideas that by his time had become fully naturalized citizens, Davidson found support in Nietzsche for the misanthropy and antipathies that erupted in his final years. The winters of 1896–97 and 1897–98 saw him in the lonely Channel town of Shoreham, Sussex, where he had ample opportunity to nurse his grievances and read the new translations of Nietzsche that had begun to appear.[59] There is no reason to believe that his statement in an essay written in 1902 that "a year or two ago I knew by heart the three published volumes of the English translation of Nietzsche" is more than a slight exaggeration.[60] Evidence of a belated addiction to the intoxicating works of the writer whose ideas he had begun to discover early in the decade does not go much beyond this and the innumerable echoes and parallels found in the later plays and Testaments. As darkness descended upon the poet he must have turned more often to Nietzsche or to his example for a renewed affirmation of life.

It is logical that Davidson, more than any other of his countrymen, should have discovered an increasing kinship in the author of *Also Sprach Zarathustra* and *Zur Genealogie der Moral*. His despair and his expression of ideas common to many were more urgent, more in keeping with Nietzsche's own. Both hated nineteenth-century rationalism and determinism which they dismissed contemptuously as decadent. Along with rationalism they despised the assumptions and style of naturalism. Each reserved his greatest hatred, however, for Christianity and its priests, since the Christian religion by denying the freedom of the senses and hence of life itself had produced these later fallacies. Again, they attacked with equal vigor the classical education of the universities and intellectualism in general; they opposed equality of men and women; they believed in complete liberty of expression and action for the strongest willed; and they advocated government by a master or master class in place of a degenerate democracy or a vulgar socialism.

To Nietzsche Davidson was certainly indebted for the term and final conception of "immorality," although the Scottish materialist had arrived early at an elementary form of this concept in his notion of irony. His theory of the endless process whereby matter evolves and devolves may have owed something, if only a confirmation, to the German's idea of "eternal recurrence." But Davidson's version of this theory is a delimitation of the nebular hypothesis of Laplace and Tyndall and of Darwinian evolution, as it is implicit in the cosmology of Lucretius and Heraclitus. Once again an apparent debt probably boils down to an independent discovery of common property. Still other ideas which they shared were a distrust of nat-

ural selection,* a glorification of war as an expression of
the will to power, and a new asceticism which differed
from that of the puritan and evangelical in substituting
selfishness for sacrifice, acceptance for renunciation, affirmation for denial, and the body for the spirit.

The Anglo-Celtic differed from his opposite number
in Germany in one essential respect, on the strength of
which he denied all resemblance.† They did not agree on
the stage of evolution which man had reached. Dissatisfied with man's present degree of development, his abysmal
degeneration, Nietzsche anticipated the advent of the superman, an unscrupulous, pitiless demigod. Ridiculing
this invention Davidson celebrated modern man, notably
the Englishman of the turn of the century. At the same
time that he transposed to the present Nietzsche's optimism about the future and dismissed the overman as an
"absurd neologism," the so-called "English Nietzsche" did
not hesitate to borrow the distinguishing features of the
Übermensch for his own Mammon. The criteria of supremacy for both neoromantics were vitality, strength,
will, and brains. It was Davidson's fetish of originality and
his reservations about evolution which obliged him to reject the idea of a superman. The hero of *The Triumph
of Mammon* disclaims all allegiance to Nietzsche:

> He posed as Zoroaster, and led us back
> To Dionysos: not our mark at all;

---

* Nietzsche believed that Darwin was wrong, and that the overman
would evolve not by a process of natural selection but by the Dionysian
assertion of the will to power. (Brinton, *Nietzsche*, p. 81.) Nietzsche may
have encouraged Davidson to reject Darwinism, but skepticism about
science was in the air. See below, pp. 486–8.

† Shaw also asserted that "Davidson had nothing whatever to do with
Nietzsche or his philosophy. His specialty was an attempt to raise modern
materialism to the level of high poetry and eclipse Lucretius." (Richards,
Author Hunting, p. 224.) Shaw's assertions like Davidson's, while containing a hard kernel of truth, may be partly discounted as deliberate over-
statements.

The past is past. And, for his prophecy?—
Why, Florimond, this Nietzsche was a Christian . . .
His Antichrist is Christ, whose body and blood
And doctrine of miraculous rebirth,
Became the Overman: Back-of-beyond,
Or—what's the phrase?—Outside good-and-evil:
That's his millennium, and we'll none of it.[61]

This, if not shameless ingratitude, is gross misrepresentation. Davidson is rejecting Nietzsche's philosophy intact on the grounds that his overman is hand in glove with social evolution and progress, "bourgeois" concepts as alien to Nietzsche's vision as to Davidson's, or for that matter to Darwin's original findings from which they were erroneously derived. Summarily the creator of Mammon, a typical overman, renounced a kindred philosophy with which he was in agreement on most important issues.

Certain ideas which existed half-formed in the poet's mind undoubtedly owed their final shape to Nietzsche. Others he may have incorporated bodily under the desperate compulsion to devise a system of thought that would permit him at once to believe and disbelieve. But Nietzsche did not give Davidson his ideas so much as he encouraged the younger thinker to formulate these ideas and in certain instances provided the formula. In this capacity he acted more as a catalyst than an essential element in the younger man's work. For if Davidson borrowed individual ideas and phrases—to do the debtor justice, he was not always aware of the borrowing—his materialist synthesis was his own; and its central concepts were as much Anglo-Saxon in their immediate origin as Nietzschean, if not more. R. M. Wenley, more from hunch than marshaled evidence, put the case for Davidson neatly some years ago: "Possibly, when distance lends perspective, he may rank (in his final period) as an Anglo-Celtic

counterpart of Nietzsche in the neo-romantic renaissance.
In any case, lapse of time cannot put German spectacles
on him, much less expel his Scots Calvinism." [62] Nietzsche's personal example and soaring eloquence, together
with poverty and lack of public recognition, merely helped
to confirm the nascent metaphysician.

5

In the preface to *Major Barbara* Shaw protests against
the unpatriotic and misleading assumption by his critics
that, whenever his view strikes them as being outside the
range of an ordinary suburban churchwarden, he is echoing Schopenhauer, Nietzsche, Ibsen, Strindberg, Tolstoy,
or some other heresiarch of modern Europe. He denies this
stoutly and points to the relatively obscure but wholly
British sources of his ideas. [63] Too much has been written
about the influence of Emerson, Ibsen, Nietzsche, Tolstoy,
and other foreign thinkers upon English literature in the
nineteenth century and not enough upon the relationship
between intrinsically native thought and letters. To find
the major and most immediate sources of Davidson's synthesis it is necessary to search first in the garrets and out-
buildings of English intellectual history.

However much he may have asserted to the contrary,
Davidson lit his torch at the blaze of evolutionary optimism unconsciously kindled by Darwin and tenderly fed
by Tyndall, Spencer, and Huxley. In Davidson's hands it
became the gift of Prometheus, an instrument for the deification of man and particularly John Davidson, who disavowed the older Titans from whom he had received it. He
found Darwin and Darwin's popularizers too ready to
compromise, too disposed to tolerate religion or look the
other way. One figure who did carry the new science into
ethics and religion, which the more scientific-minded or
pusillanimous by-passed, was William Kingdon Clifford.

The essays and public lectures of this Cambridge mathematician and publicist of molecular science had been published in 1879, one year after his premature death at the age of thirty-three.[64] They were thus available to Davidson before his departure from Scotland, but there is no indication that he knew them until the nineties. Although Davidson lacks Clifford's orderliness and scientific caution, his clear, well-defined moral element, and his faith in the social amelioration promised by republicanism, his is nevertheless the strongest influence evident in the Scot's later thought or, in fact, in his entire intellectual development.

From Clifford he derived his conception of the origin and destiny of the universe in terms of the nebular hypothesis, originally formulated by Laplace and Tyndall. In Clifford he found also the corollaries to this postulate, the molecular theory of matter and the wave theory of light. The foremost explicator of Lucretian materialism in the nineteenth century, Clifford foresaw the gradual cooling of the sun and an end of life upon earth, a rudimentary expression of Davidson's conception of the recurrence of matter. Parallel to the evolution of matter but inseparable from it, Clifford explained, has been the evolution of consciousness or "mind-stuff." Consciousness is present in the lowest organisms and even inorganic substances, but it reaches its highest, most complex form in man. Moreover, since consciousness is only a more refined form of matter, the mind dies with the body; there is no immortality of the spirit, only dissolution into matter. The similarity of this materialism to Davidson's is so close that a direct influence cannot be denied, although the disciple took pains to cover the traces.

Clifford's frequent strictures against institutional Christianity read like Davidson's for which they must have served as a model. The mathematician's own religion was

a pagan glorification of man, a religion of the Prometheus
legend and the Wagnerian *Ring*.[65] The deposition of God
and the apotheosis of man follow logically once evolution
is applied to religion and ethics. The child of science,
Clifford's atheism like Davidson's is the stepchild of Calvinism and evangelicalism. In the interest of further socio-
logical evolution Clifford stressed man's supremacy and
freedom. At the same time, his ethical and political theories differed from Davidson's. Since he regarded man as a
social organism striving for higher and more complex
organization, the Cambridge radical concluded that all
men must contribute to the well-being of the tribe. Davidson, who went further in the direction of individualism,
did not recognize the subordination of the individual will
to the tribal will. Evolution led Clifford to advocate republicanism; conversely, the advocacy of autocratic despotism led Davidson to question evolution. Otherwise the
two materialists were in complete concert, even to their
rabid patriotism. With Davidson as with other late nineteenth-century thinkers, chauvinism took the form of devotion to the Empire. The general outline and many
details of his imperialism owe much to another, later dis-
seminator of current ideas, John Adam Cramb.

6

A fellow Scot and roughly Davidson's contemporary,
Cramb after a brilliant career at Glasgow University became lecturer, then professor of modern history, at Queen's
College, London. His *Origins and Destiny of Imperial
Britain,* which he had given from May to July 1900 as a
series of weekly lectures, appeared in the winter of that
year. A second edition was published in 1915 after the
outbreak of World War I when its thesis was again timely
and heartening. The book, which has been described as
"the most important phenomenon in the sphere of his-

JOHN ADAM CRAMB
485

torical pronouncement produced by the Boer War," [66] is
a defense of British imperialism along evolutionary lines.
Davidson was vastly impressed by it. In a letter to Edmund
Gosse which accompanied a gift of the book he praised it
as "the ablest, freshest, most imaginative and therefore
most intelligent statement of British imperialism, and a
revelation of the development and future of that idea only
possible to a man of genius." [67]

Written in a saber-rattling style, Cramb's book traces
the rise of imperial consciousness in the British people
from its first stirrings in Elizabethan England through
an unconscious evolution to its re-emergence in the nineteenth century as an ideal of imperial destiny. He justifies
this ideal by its dedication to justice and freedom for the
colonized races. War Cramb welcomes "as a phase in the
life-effort of the State towards complete self-fulfillment." [68]
The evolutionary conception of history in England found
its chief authorities in Carlyle and Spencer. During the
nineteenth century Continental historians gradually
shifted from a romantic emphasis upon the role of the
heroic individual to a deterministic emphasis upon that
of social and political forces, especially the masses. Strauss,
Renan, and Taine added the weight of their authority to
the new historicism; and in England Carlyle, Ruskin,
Froude, and Newman came to recognize that forces larger
than the individual govern the destiny of nations. Nevertheless, English historical thought remained for some time
firmly evolutionary, optimistic, and moral. Davidson, although he would have no part of the Darwinian cult and
predicted that the new philosophy would be neither evolutionary nor "synthetic," belongs in the main tradition
of English evolutionary thought. The influence on his
thought of Herbert Spencer, the founder of evolutionary
and synthetic philosophy, was lasting if general. When an
anonymous correspondent to the *Speaker* accused him of

espousing "Renan's Arch-Mocker under a new name," he
deftly turned the tables: "Worshipful Irony, the profound 'Irony of fate,' is doubtless responsible for Renan-
ism, and all 'isms, but is derived from none of them." [69]
His insistence upon the primacy of his principle is an unconscious acknowledgment that it is essentially native in
origin and character.

Darwinism, then, was equally behind the thinking of
Clifford, Cramb, and Davidson; it was the premise on
which all their conclusions were based; it was the scientific postulate which fostered their romantic ideal. It was
in brief the ladder that they kicked over once they had
arrived at their celebration of man's glorious present.
Nineteenth-century historiography uncovered one truth:
that every movement creates its own countermovement. At
the end of the century there arose the suspicion that the
principle of continuing evolution was defunct and had
ceased to operate in the natural and human world. Even
Spencer had to confess that "the Doctrine of Evolution
has not furnished guidance to the extent I had hoped."
Reflecting this trend, Cramb asserted that the philosophic
evolutionist's ideal of the infinite perfectibility of man
was, like dreams of lost Edens or heavens to come, a mere
illusion. All that existed for certain was the existentialist's
present: "Behold, the Eternal is now, and the Infinite is
here." [70] Davidson like Cramb mirrored the growing disillusionment with applied evolution. He cannot be said
to have derived this distrust entirely from Cramb, however, since in his satiric novel, Earl Lavender (1895), he
had treated the subject with ironic irreverence.

The completely ruthless expansionist policies of Joseph
Chamberlain, Cecil Rhodes, and Alfred Harmsworth,
epitomized in the orgy of Mafeking Night, did much to
discredit British imperialism and to invite re-examination

of evolutionary optimism. In the face of his own skepticism
Davidson clung to the ideal of racial supremacy. Writing
Gosse on the last day of the old century, he expressed
vigorous contempt for the false piety and sentimentality
of Anglo-Saxon literature:

> I share, with very limited knowledge, your
> equipped interest in the relations of literature to
> the life of the times. That the popular literature of
> England and America is false to the core I am very
> well persuaded: "Lest we Forget," so hungrily wel-
> comed on both sides of the Atlantic seems to me a
> paltry hymn—not nearly so good as some of Wesley's
> we used to sing in my father's church—a very antique
> quack poultice for an uneasy conscience, a pill against
> an earthquake. Lullaby, pill, poultice, or mild in-
> toxicant, that is the Anglo-American demand in lit-
> erature, a juggling demand which, if it be offered a
> sword can change it into a ladle, or the Sangreal to
> a spittoon and call it a cuspidor.
>
> But in action? Just because it is unintelligent, just
> because it is still the same blind force that conquered
> India at Agincourt 300 years before the event, it is
> still the first thing in the world this Anglo-Saxondom.
> And the *spirit* in it . . .

He closes the letter with a reference to Cramb as the interpreter of that spirit "and a great Herald of Hope." [71]
The idealist in Davidson deplored the decadence of Anglo-
Saxon literature and advocated a new literature fusing
poetry and science. The same optimism hailed in the
Anglo-Saxon race a vitality which could be harnessed to
deliver the world. Visionaries and inverted humanitarians
like Cramb and Davidson in their stopgap ideal of a benevolent, progressive "Ocean-state" sought to rehabilitate

the cause of empire and restore to it some of the moral righteousness and liberalism it had known under Gladstone.

Although Cramb is a spiritualist and an idealist, proclaiming the "unsubstantiality of substance" and the "immateriality of matter," he differs from Davidson only in the use of words. Both are Utopians and monists, viewing the universe essentially alike. In spite of remarkable parallels and unmistakable borrowings, it would be wrong to conclude that either Cramb or Clifford acted as a funnel through which applied and diluted Darwinism was poured into the bottles of Davidson's writings. Of the two Clifford had the greater influence on his thought. Cramb served only to show him how he could adopt imperialism as a corollary to the rest of his philosophy. But Davidson obtained his ideas and inspiration from many sources— from Wordsworth, Byron and Shelley, Carlyle, the Spasmodics, Swinburne and Meredith, Whitman and Emerson, Ibsen, Nietzsche, and in all probability "Novalis," and from Spencer and Grant Allen. The most apparent influence is still Nietzsche's, but only because his demonic ideas, forceful expression, and aphoristic gift would be heard clearly when echoed by any writer.

There is on the other hand strong internal evidence that it was chiefly Clifford and Cramb who helped the Scottish poet to assimilate the many ideas churning in his mind and shape them into something like a coherent philosophical system. Without forgetting that these ideas had their ultimate origin in the common headwaters of nineteenth-century European thought, one must conclude that Davidson's system belongs directly to the mainstream of English philosophical speculation. His Celtic perfervidness, pride, humor, and religiosity remain to be accounted for. These qualities he owed only to his Scottish ancestry, and they are the ingredients, more than his ideas, which make his work memorable.

7

Since his ideas and poetry are a *ne plus ultra* of their kind, Davidson has not had an extensive or clearly marked influence upon later writers. He failed to give his message the dramatic realization or poetic form that would have preserved his work once the message had lost its significance. No one now turns to him as to Shaw for his wit and comic skill or to Yeats for his ironic sense of history and lyric genius. The emphasis in modern poetry has been upon multiplicity of meaning through complex patterns of metaphor, upon formal order and ingenuity, or upon urbane circumspection. The best of poetry is intellectual, the worst intellectualized. It is therefore not surprising that a poet as romantic, didactic, formless, and intelligible as Davidson has gained almost no recognition. Yet the romantic spirit is hardy. Where it is found to a marked degree, there will be found also a close bond with that nineteenth-century romanticism which knew a brief but sensational climax in John Davidson.

Although forgotten today, the poet of materialism may have exerted a fleeting influence upon the generation that immediately followed him. Cornelius Weygandt, recalling his own youthful ardor for his works, concluded in sober middle age that he is a poet for youth alone.[72] Before Weygandt, James Elroy Flecker, while still a hot-headed, rebellious undergraduate at Oxford, took up the cudgels for his fellow iconoclast in a long essay which made willing allowance for Davidson's technical imperfections for the sake of his stirring message. "But he so far succeeds," Flecker loyally declared, "that his imperfections surpass the perfections of other men. So we must

490 HERESY AS TRADITION

deal with him as we would deal, say, with Keats, Shelley, or Tennyson." Maturity taught Flecker as it did Weygandt to qualify this view. In a later essay he wrote, "He was, after all, the greatest poet of his age; but it was not a glorious age." [73] Other writers whom Davidson may have influenced in their early works are G. K. Chesterton, James Stephens, and Roy Campbell.[74] Finally, his nature lyrics with their sharp eye for homely detail, unheightened recording of the country scene, and philosophic irony may have left their mark upon such Georgian "exurbanites" as Ralph Hodgson, Edward Thomas, and the young Robert Frost whom he anticipated by twenty years.

If Davidson's writings have suffered an eclipse, his total output embraces a philosophy of life which has endured in a distorted form up to the midpoint of the present century. Original or not, true or false, this philosophy received from him a more forceful expression in English and a larger hearing than it otherwise would have had.[75] D. H. Lawrence,* W. H. Hudson, Norman Douglas, Robinson Jeffers, and John Steinbeck, probably without being conscious of it, without having read much or any of his work, have echoed Davidson's pagan, primitive naturalism. Reading Jeffers, Douglas Bush is reminded of the earlier poet:

> For all Mr. Jeffers' massive earnestness, one cannot say that this "pagan" stoicism, this apotheosis of Life, goes much beyond such celebrations of the Man-God as *The Testament of John Davidson,* and his Prometheus has a large and sinister infusion of Woden and Nietzsche—an impression confirmed by the poet's more personal utterances.[76]

* Both Thouless and Bush stress the similarity of Davidson and Lawrence, notably in their common emphasis upon man's physical nature and their preoccupation with the father theme. Thouless, *Modern Poetic Drama,* pp. 113–14; Bush, *Mythology and the Romantic Tradition,* pp. 467–8.

There are also strong affinities between the spirit of Davidson's plays and the dramas of revolt by Elizabeth Baker, Stanley Houghton, and St. John Ervine, while his militant antinominism helped to clear the way for the more fertile experiments in language of Pound, Joyce, and Gertrude Stein. The temptation to trace direct influences must be resisted, for these apparent relationships can be attributed more surely to a common revolution. Heroic as Davidson is, the revolution is greater than he and has survived him in, among others, the howlers Allen Ginsberg and Gregory Corso.

There remains only to mention the Davidson legend. Those who remember him at all think of him as his own "man forbid," a defiant rebel and bitter image-smasher who destroyed himself rather than live in an indifferent and incorrigible world. The poet himself did much to foster this image, and it is perhaps the image which he would have liked preserved. It does not take into account the riant temperament, gentleness, underlying sympathy with humanity, and little vanities which completed his personality. The romantic conception of the Scottish misanthrope has been perpetuated periodically by poets who have "discovered" him. One of these, Ronald Campbell Macfie, apostrophized him in two elegies, both entitled "In Memoriam: John Davidson." The second concludes:

We blame thee not, thy failures we forget,
Forget the seeming-weak, the seeming-wrong;
But in our hearts there blooms and blossoms yet
The sweet, wild, poignant passion of thy song.[77]

A sonnet by Arthur H. Nethercot in the vein of E. A. Robinson, slightly more deserving as poetry, also recalled the poet as a writer of blasphemous lyrics, unfitted for this earth and punished by despair.[78] Davidson, who acknowledged no failure and who was nothing if not robust, would scarcely have been gratified by these cloying, condescending epitaphs.

The neglect and, what is more, the misconception of the poet of the universe since his death are not difficult to understand. How can one account for the totality of failure in his own time? He is at best an uneven poet, rough, somber, and often shallow, but other poets less original and less interesting succeeded where he did not. He is not a great thinker, neither profound nor truly creative, but he is extraordinarily vital, powerful, and significant. He is anything but a competent playwright nor did he regard himself highly in this capacity, yet his one professional success was as the adapter of a foreign play. The truth is that endowed with a small natural gift for lyric expression, he was unwilling to undergo that artistic discipline which would have enabled him to become a superior lyric poet like Yeats or Hopkins. With sufficient imagination and keenness of observation for two volumes of fresh, lively poems, he went on in a period that extorted a steady output from its poets to write five more. Having exhausted his inspiration and talent, he neglected to replenish them at the wellsprings of firsthand experience and observation of life.

Judged simply as a writer, Davidson's most deserving work is ironically his least known and enduring: certain of his stories, prose idyls, and novels and, above all, his prose contributions to the periodicals of the nineties. In this work that he took less seriously—and because he took it less seriously—his pawky wit, love of fantasy, and vigorous, spontaneous intellect enjoyed freer rein. His novels like *Laura Ruthven's Widowhood* and *Baptist Lake* are as full of provocative, prickly observations as the best familiar essays of the eighteenth century; his essays in the *Speaker*, the *Saturday Review*, and a host of forgotten journals are as inventive as any fiction. It may be that when the periodicals of the period are disinterred and combed, there will be found the major writing, among it some of Davidson's, of a period regarded up to now as minor.

Always more interested in ideas than in their literary realization, Davidson had found the lyric too confining for his nebulous, demonic visions. His medium, he thought, was blank verse, dramatic or descriptive; and in this he might have succeeded had he not withdrawn into himself and lost touch with humanity to whom and through whom a poet must communicate. He was the worse as a writer of blank verse for having failed as a lyric poet. In the preface to his last volume of poems, J. M. Synge, noting a trend in modern poetry, makes a relevant observation:

> The poetry of exaltation will be always the highest, but when men lose their poetic feeling for ordinary life, and cannot write poetry of ordinary things, their exalted poetry is likely to lose its strength of exaltation, in the way men cease to build beautiful churches when they have lost happiness in building shops.*

Never a poet of wide experience, Davidson gradually inhabited the shadowy, repetitious, incoherent world of private nightmare. His failure as a dramatist can be explained in the same way, that he cared nothing for his characters as human beings. He designed his plays as vehicles for leading actors, but he intended these actors to be vehicles for his leading ideas. Artistic quality was subordinated to this one obsessive purpose. Although he

---

* On the same occasion Synge recognized the need for the vigor and virility in modern poetry which is abundant in Davidson's work: "Even if we grant that exalted poetry can be kept successful, the strong things of life are needed in poetry also, to show that what is exalted or tender is not made by feeble blood. It may also be said that before verse can be human again it must learn to be brutal." John M. Synge, *Poems and Translations* (Churchtown, Dundrum, Cuala Press, 1919), pp. [1–2].

might, as William Archer intimated, have done for Scotland what Yeats and Synge did for Ireland, he early turned his back on the country of the Clyde to embrace the universe.

The final irony is that the materialist achieved in his own time no greater reputation as a man of ideas than he did as a poet or dramatist. In the same way that the public found his later verse turgid and strident where it had hailed his lyrics as refreshing and melodic, it saw in his deification of man as matter a stale, forbidding philosophy. Ideas which as late as 1895 had been shocking were by 1900 commonplace. To his younger contemporaries Davidson was beating a dead dog. Religion and science, faith and rationalism had struck a general truce; and people were concerned with more immediate issues of imperialist expansion, war, and reform. There was a leveling off, a period of prosperity and complacency which made the author of the unfinished Mammon trilogy and *The Testament of John Davidson* sound like an "Anarch old." Joseph Conrad in *The Secret Agent* (1907), a fictional study of the anarchist movement in England, portrays the nihilist agents as foolish and ineffectual, the police as vain and confident, and the London populace as supremely indifferent. On the Continent where there was more open revolutionary ferment Davidson's ideas might have achieved a greater fame, although there he would have been competing with the larger intellects of Nietzsche, Marx, and Engels. What is more, the Scottish materialist made the error of resting his ideas upon the earlier findings of the natural scientists. As the fame of these men yielded to that of younger pioneers in newer fields, James Frazer, Sigmund Freud, and Henri Bergson, Davidson's brand of Victorian radicalism seemed old-fashioned and unmarketable. If the younger D. H. Lawrence introduced into his verse and fiction ideas scarcely more advanced, he succeeded where Davidson failed because he was better informed in modern psychological and anthropological research, avoided bald, abstract statement, and drew upon immediate, recognizable experience for symbols in which to embody these ideas. Among Davidson's all too few readers the more perceptive condemned him for being out of date, others for being too advanced, whereas in reality his works represented a logical culmination of much nineteenth-century thought. For looking back when the order of nature is to face ahead, his public imposed upon him the saline penalty. Not until the deterioration of nineteenth-century aristocratic radicalism into twentieth-century totalitarianism has Davidson's message assumed a fresh historical importance.

Davidson's was the vain but courageous attempt of a man to fuse the disconnected, conflicting ideas of his age into an acceptable system, a man who lacked the educational equipment, artistic discipline, and emotional balance to achieve such a task. More importantly, he had the bad judgment to force an intellectual synthesis into the mold of poetry. Half recognizing its failure, he asserted its success by calling it a "new poetry." If his reach exceeded by too much his grasp, the poetry possesses a metaphysical scope and strength that almost justify it as philosophy, and his philosophy an imaginative sweep and vigor that almost transform it into poetry. No writer reflects so patently the dual impulse of the age to make a new statement of man in a new language. Was it worth the while of this abortive Mammon to state his abortive message? Was it worth the personal tragedy or, to be as uncharitable as his severest critic, was it worth the printer's ink? Herbert Spencer provides an appropriate apologia for the man of ideas:

It is not for nothing that he has in him these sympathies with some principles and repugnance to others.
He, with all his capacities, and aspirations, and beliefs,
is not an accident but a product of his time. He must
remember that while he is a descendant of the past,
he is a parent of the future; and that his thoughts
are as children born to him which he may not carelessly let die. . . . Not as adventitious therefore will
the wise man regard the faith which is in him. The
highest truth he sees he will fearlessly utter; knowing that, let what may come of it, he is thus playing
his right part in the world—knowing that if he can
effect the change he aims at—well: if not—well also;
though not *so* well.[79]

John Davidson, who rejected the past and with it his intellectual and literary forebears, now claims attention primarily as their prodigal heir.

APPENDIX A

As late as November 1899 Davidson, in a letter to William Archer that took the form of a mock centenary review, testified to the meager reception given his *Plays* and reasserted their originality:

I remember when you told me five years ago that you had reviewed my "Plays" in the *Westminster Gazette,* I replied that I did not know whether I should be able to forgive you or not. I have not forgiven you; and your remark in today's *Chronicle* rouses the old enmity. One reading of my "Plays" is not sufficient: I think indeed judging by this extract from the *Kioto Discriminator* of Nov 25, 1994 that many readings and generations may be necessary for their appreciation:—

"CENTENNIAL.

"We begin our diurnal centenary notices with the most famous English book of modern times, Davidson's 'Plays'—those five plays, of which the first collected edition appeared in 1894. It is to Japanese research and critical acumen that this work owes its long-delayed recognition: and it is therefore highly gratifying to us that we are able today to offer our readers two newly discovered details regarding its history.

"The indisputable fact which we now adduce

497

will demolish the contention of our too salient contemporary, the *Kioto Affirmer,* that this astonishing
book, although practically unread during the author's lifetime, enjoyed an intelligent reception at
the hands of contemporary critics. It has been discovered that although some notices of the book
appeared, only one critic gave it any attention, and
that only to damn it. And this critic—it is incredi-
ble but we have the initialled article before us—
this critic was no less a man than William Archer.
. . . Here it is sufficient to note—

1. That Archer failed to perceive the originality
and naturalness of the blank verse already apparent
in 'An Unhistorical Pastoral,' and developed immediately in 'A Romantic Farce.'

2. That he attacked what is the very breath of
these plays, their freedom from historical and geo-
graphical trammels, and the imaginative existence
of the characters and events.

3. That no idea of the book as a whole ever
crossed his mind.

"The second discovery is of great importance.
We have long held in contradiction to the general
opinion that 'An Unhistorical Pastoral,' although
written before the author's twenty-first year could
not possibly have been his first dramatic attempt.
A letter of Davidson's to the *Saturday Review* of
Nov 5. 1898 . . . gives the fullest confirmation of
our opinion, and proves conclusively that these five
plays—'three plays,' he says 'went to the making of
Bruce': '*Smith* had two still more abortive predecessors'—grew up in the author's mind, and are the essence of his experience thought and imagination
from boyhood to his thirty-first year. The five plays

are the acts of one play, and constitute a work in manner and substance unique in literature."
(A.L.S., dated 25 Nov. 1899, from St. Winifred's, Fairmile Ave., Streatham, S. W., Add. MS. 45291, ff. 90–3, B.M.)

APPENDIX B

When William Archer inquired as to his meaning in the conclusion to "A Ballad of a Nun" and questioned its propriety, Davidson replied in a letter that characteristically took the form of a blasphemous parable:

Accepting an idea of God the import is that God's sympathies were entirely with the nun: the Virgin on withdrawing tells her that not only has she made herself one with Nature by employing her body, however blindly, for its own appointed purpose, but has also made herself one with God while committing what she supposed to be deadly sin.

> "You are sister to the mountains now,
> And sister to the day and night,
> Sister to God."

Here is the comic version of it:

Scene Heaven: God, Christ, the Virgin.

GOD. It flabbergasts me quite! The intolerable mess these people make of every message given them. Look at all these lovely women and handsome fellows —made for each other!—shutting themselves up apart in order to save their souls. There again, now. Souls! What maggot has got into their heads I can't make out. I made them what they are—one and entire, and they go and divide themselves up into a trinity, and me too—mind, body, spirit. It's like my own grace, past finding out.

MARY. Yes, and not only do they misunderstand your message, but they misapply their own misunderstanding of it. Just look at all that Sodomy and Lesbianism and masturbation! My God! if there's a wrong way they find it out in their convents and monasteries.

CHRIST. Yes, and all this passion that is wasted in futile advocation of us—save the mark!—or poured out foully as mere excrement, could be so beautiful.

GOD. Look at marriage too. That's the very ugliest thing these men have invented. Imagine women with half a dozen or a dozen children, all by one man too; why it's loathsome in the last degree. That wasn't what I meant at all. I wonder why there is a sex question in the world.

MARY. Well you know I've got a notion that it's your own fault.

GOD. My fault! Lord bless me! Didn't I make them man and woman, for each other, without any question whatever?

MARY. Yes, but you're forgetting me.

GOD. You!

MARY. Yes. That miracle, you know. The immaculate business. If you'd gone about it in the ordinary way—it would have been more satisfactory for everybody concerned.

GOD. By Jove! I believe it would. We can do it that way yet.

CHRIST. Oh but that would be unfair to me!

Enter LUCIFER.

GOD. Well; what is it now?

LUCIFER. I want to tempt a nun down there. The abbess has just made her doorkeeper, and she'll hear and see things that'll make her an easy prey.

GOD. Go to it, old fellow.

Exit LUCIFER.

Now I'll tell you what I'll do. I'll give these people another chance. Lucifer—what an invaluable servant he is!—will succeed with the nun. And you, my dear, will go down and keep her place while she's enjoying herself with the boys. You'll tell her when she comes back, and get it made known, and if that doesn't open their eyes to my real sentiments then I'm a Dutchman.

(Scene closes)

But the author I imagine accepts no idea of God, and would use the most modern deity as he would Apollo or Oden. The whole idea of God the very word is obsolete: here is how he puts it in "A Ballad of the Making of a Poet":

"If it be terrible into the hands
   Of the living God to fall, how much more dire
   To sicken face to face, like our sad age,
   Chained to an icy corpse or deity,
   Decked though it be and painted and embalmed."

He doesn't mean any special idea, but the abstract idea, of God: he would suggest that we cease using the word God, just as we have ceased using the word codpiece: both will always be interesting in their spheres and degrees, but neither exist now, and will never be revived: the one is unscientific, the other indecent. (A.L.S., dated 26 Oct. 1894, from 20 Park Ridings, Hornsey, N., Add. MS. 45291, ff. 86–7, B.M.)

NOTES

The following abbreviations have been
used in the notes to conserve space:

B.C.U.L.L. The Brotherton Collection of the University of Leeds
            Library
B.M.   Department of Manuscripts, the British Museum
C.U.L.   The Libraries of Columbia University in the City of New
            York
H.E.H.L.   The Henry E. Huntington Library, San Marino, Cali-
            fornia
N.L.S.   Department of Manuscripts, the National Library of
            Scotland
P.U.L.   The Princeton University Library
Y.U.L.   The Yale University Library

CHAPTER 1

Penzance, 1909

1. Except where otherwise indicated, the information in this chapter is
drawn from the following sources: the *Times*, 27, 29, 30 Mar.; 1, 19, 24
Apr.; 20, 21, 22 Sept. 1909; *Cornishman*, 15 July 1949 (article by John
Penwith reprinted as "A Poet's End" in his *Leaves from a Cornish Notebook*, Penzance, The Cornish Library, undated); and personal conversa-
tions with the poet's son, Menzies Davidson.

2. The *Bristol Evening News*, 29 Mar. 1909, which professed to have
the story directly from Mrs. Davidson.

3. A.Ls.S., from Alexander Davidson to Grant Richards, dated 27 Mar.
and 1 Apr. 1909, from 6 Coulson's Terrace, Penzance, P.U.L.

4. From an original bill, P.U.L.

5. A.L.S., dated only "Saturday Night/ 10 P.M.," P.U.L. See also A.L.S.,
from Alexander Davidson to Richards, dated 11[4?] Apr. 1909, from
6 Coulson's Terrace, Penzance, P.U.L.

6. Ibid.

7. Ibid.

8. A.L.S., from Alexander Davidson to Richards, dated 10 Apr. 1909,
from London, P.U.L.

9. A.L.S., from Menzies Davidson to Richards, dated 15 Apr. 1909, from 6 Coulson's Terrace, P.U.L.

10. Typescript copy, P.U.L.

11. The autograph MSS. of this note and of the collection of poems it accompanied are in the P.U.L.

12. A.L.S., from Menzies Davidson to Richards, dated 15 Apr. 1909, P.U.L.

13. A.L.S., from Alexander Davidson to Richards, P.U.L. Written in Richards' hand on the letter is the date "7/3/09"; as 7 Mar. and 3 July are impossible dates, Richards must have intended to write "7/4/09" (7 Apr.).

14. A.L.S., dated only "Saturday Afternoon/ 5 P.M.," P.U.L.

15. Three telegrams, from Menzies Davidson to Richards, dated 17, 18 Apr. 1909, from Penzance, P.U.L.

16. A.L.S., dated 15 Aug. 1908, from 6 Coulson's Terrace, P.U.L.

17. Autograph MS. S. (Richards' copy), P.U.L. The will was published in its entirety in the *Times*, 19 Apr. 1909.

18. "The John Davidson Scandal," *Freethinker*, 3 Oct. 1909. For Foote's comments on Davidson's death, see the *Freethinker*, 22 Sept. 1909.

19. See Grant Richards, *Author Hunting* (London, H. Hamilton, 1934), p. 223.

20. The information in this paragraph is drawn mainly from a series of letters from Margaret and Alexander Davidson to Richards, dating from Mar. 1909 to Jan. 1910; P.U.L.

21. Four A.Ls.S., dated 13, 15, 19, 20 Apr. 1909, from Mason Croft, Stratford-on-Avon, P.U.L.

22. "The Tragedy of John Davidson," the *Times*, 26 Apr. 1909.

23. "A Last Word on John Davidson," the *Times*, 12 May 1909.

24. *Saturday Review*, 15 May 1909, pp. 623–5.

25. See the *Academy*, 24 Apr., 1 and 8 May 1909; pp. 28, 54–5, 77–8.

26. "Art and the Public," the *Times*, 8 May 1909.

27. The *Times*, 12 May 1909.

28. "The Revolt of the Poet," *Nation*, 24 Apr. 1909, pp. 118–20. Although unsigned, the article is believed to be by H. W. Massingham.

29. The *Times*, 19 Apr. 1909.

CHAPTER 2

Scotland, 1857–90

1. Except where otherwise noted, the strictly biographical information in this chapter is drawn from the following sources: *Bookman* (London), Nov. 1894, pp. 48–9 (unsigned article); Jane T. Stoddart, "An Interview with Mr. John Davidson," *Bookman* (New York), Mar. 1895, pp. 85–7; *Glasgow Herald*, 19, 24 Apr. 1909; *The Dictionary of National Biography*, Supplement: Jan. 1901–Dec. 1911 (3 vols., London, Oxford University Press, 1927 [1912]), *1*, 472–4 (article by Francis L. Bickley); and information given personally to the author by Menzies Davidson.

2. "A Ballad in Blank Verse of the Making of a Poet," *Ballads and Songs* (London, John Lane, The Bodley Head; Boston, Copeland & Day, 1894), p. 10.

3. "A Woman and Her Son," *New Ballads* (London and New York, John Lane, The Bodley Head, 1896), p. 29.

4. *A Rosary* (London, Grant Richards, 1903), pp. 99–101.

5. A.L.S., dated 20 Apr. 1905, from 9 Fairmile Ave., Streatham, P.U.L.

6. See John R. Fleming, *A History of the Church in Scotland, 1843–1874* (Edinburgh, T. & T. Clark, 1927), pp. 10–11. Dr. Morison was no mere agitator and controversialist. His commentaries upon the New Testament, far from being partisan interpretations, are among the best biblical exegeses that appeared in this period. See Fleming, pp. 96, 253; and William M. Taylor, *The Scottish Pulpit from the Reformation to the Present Day* (New York, Harper & Bros., 1887), pp. 38, 244.

7. David C. Somervell, *English Thought in the Nineteenth Century* (London, Methuen & Co., 1957), p. 117.

8. R. M. Wenley, ed., *Poems by John Davidson* (New York, Boni & Liveright, 1924), p. x.

9. Fleming, p. 49.

10. *A Second Series of Fleet Street Eclogues* (London, John Lane, The Bodley Head, 1895), p. 29.

11. *Ballads and Songs,* p. 29.

12. Robert Louis Stevenson, *Memories and Portraits* (London, Chatto & Windus, 1887), pp. 16–19. For further descriptions of Edinburgh University life about this time, see the contributions of Barrie, Stevenson, Lord Darling, and others to *The New Amphion* (Edinburgh, T. & A. Constable, 1886), published to help raise funds to found the Edinburgh University Students' Union.

13. Sir John A. Hammerton, *Barrie; the Story of a Genius* (London, Sampson, Low, Marston, 1929), p. 55.

14. See John Dickson Carr, *The Life of Sir Arthur Conan Doyle* (New York, Harper, 1949), p. 23.

15. For a series of quick, anecdotal profiles of Professors Masson, Blackie, Calderwood, Tait, Sellar, and others, as well as a very frank criticism of R. L. Stevenson by a former Edinburgh student, see James M. Barrie, *An Edinburgh Eleven* (London, Office of the *British Weekly*, 1889).

16. Ibid., p. 118.

17. "The Late Mr. John Davidson," *British Weekly,* 22 Apr. 1909. The article is signed "A Man of Kent," whom Grant Richards identified as the Rev. W. Robertson Nicoll.

18. See Wenley, *Poems by John Davidson,* p. xiii.

19. See William A. Knight, *Memoir of John Nichol* (Glasgow, J. MacLehose & Sons, 1896), p. xvi and chs. 2–5.

20. Ibid., p. xix.

21. Pp. xxiii–xxiv.

22. For the Nichols' views on politics and religion see ibid., pp. 121–2, 165, 215, 301.

23. Ibid., p. 163.

24. Sir Edmund W. Gosse, *The Life of Algernon Charles Swinburne* (New York, The Macmillan Co., 1917), pp. 243–4. For Swinburne's visit to Nichol in 1878, see also Georges Lafourcade, *Swinburne, a Literary Biography* (London, G. Bell & Sons, 1932), p. 221.

25. Knight, *John Nichol*, p. 204.

26. Gosse, *Swinburne*, pp. 243–4. Although Gosse's account of this meeting, which he purported to have directly from Davidson, may have been somewhat colored in the telling, Filson Young, the Scot's close friend in his final years, has confirmed its essential facts. (F. Young, "The Truth about John Davidson," *Saturday Review*, 15 May 1909, p. 624.)

27. Knight, p. 205.

28. Young, p. 624.

29. A.L.S., Ashley MS. A.560, B.M.

30. Excerpt from a letter, dated 10 May 1878, from Glasgow, *The Ashley Library, a Catalogue* (11 vols., London, privately printed, 1922), 2, 12. The British Museum reports that this letter is not among the papers from the Ashley Library now in its possession; its present location is unknown.

31. *Academy*, 23 Nov. 1889, pp. 331–2.

32. "Who Should Be Laureate?" *Idler*, Apr. 1895, p. 419.

33. From an undated clipping, P.U.L. On 22 June 1945 Sir John Hammerton wrote to Grant Richards, denying authorship of the article. A.L.S., P.U.L.

34. *In a Music Hall and Other Poems* (London, Ward & Downey, 1891), pp. 1–2.

35. "On Poetry," *Holiday and Other Poems* (London, E. Grant Richards, 1906), p. 147.

36. *The Cambridge Bibliography of English Literature* assigns this work to Davidson (New York, The Macmillan Co.; The Cambridge Univ. Press, 1941), *3*, 337. Charles A. Stonehill omits it from his bibliography of Davidson, *Bibliographies of Modern Authors*, Second Series (London, J. Castle, 1925). On 17 Nov. 1927, however, Stonehill in a letter to Frederick Coykendall, a collector of Davidsoniana, expressed his firm opinion that the work was by Davidson. He had seen a presentation copy of the work signed by this author. On 5 Oct. of the same year James F. Drake, the bookdealer, had written Coykendall to assure him of Davidson's authorship of the work. Drake himself had obtained a copy from a private collector in England who had stated that "a very limited edition only had been printed & nearly all destroyed." (A.Ls.S., C.U.L.) Aside from this considerable corroboration, it is reasonable to attribute authorship to Davidson on internal evidence.

37. Original autograph MS., entitled "After-Piece to 'Smith,'" P.U.L. In the Frederick Coykendall Collection at Columbia University is another

autograph version which Davidson sent to Lane a few days later, fearing that the original had "vanished into the welkin." (A.L.S., dated only "Monday," from 20 Park Ridings, Hornsey.) Both versions are substantially the same, but in the letter accompanying the second Davidson confessed that he could not recall whether the first edition of the play had consisted of 300 or 350 copies.

38. A.L.S., dated only "Thursday," P.U.L.

39. A.L.S., dated 21 Aug. 1889, N.L.S.

40. A.L.S., dated 27 Nov. 1889, from 12 Brisbane St, Greenock, N.L.S.

41. A.L.S., dated 28 Oct. 1889, from 12 Brisbane St., Greenock, H.E.H.L. Another presentation copy of Plays, inscribed by Davidson to William Michael Rossetti, is in the Coykendall Collection, C.U.L.

42. A.L.S., from Davidson to Bell, dated 5 Nov. 1889, from 12 Brisbane St., Greenock, H.E.H.L. In this letter Davidson writes, "Many thanks for obliging me in sending my book to Mr. Watts. I did not suppose him to be the editor, but somebody in London told me he had a responsible connection with the Athenaeum."

43. See the Athenaeum, 4 Sept. 1889, p. 314; Academy, 27 Aug. 1887, p. 132.

44. Academy, 19 Oct. 1889, p. 247.

45. A.L.S., undated, from 2 Alfred Terrace, Park Ridings, Hornsey, P.U.L.

46. Wenley, Poems by John Davidson, p. x.

47. A.L.S., dated 14 Nov. 1889, from 12 Brisbane St., Greenock, H.E.H.L.

48. British Weekly, 22 Apr. 1909.

49. A.L.S., to William Canton, dated only "Friday," from 2 Alfred Terrace, Park Ridings, Hornsey, N., P.U.L.

50. A.L.S., dated 26 Apr. 1909, from Devonshire Club, St. James's, Y.U.L.

51. Plays (London, Elkin Mathews & John Lane; Chicago, Stone & Kimball, 1894), pp. 223–4. Unless stated otherwise, all references to the early plays are to this edition.

CHAPTER 3

Something Old, Something New . . .

1. Plays, p. 78.

2. William Archer, Poets of the Younger Generation (London and New York, John Lane, The Bodley Head, 1902), pp. 122, 124.

3. Plays, p. 39.

4. Epilogue, The Triumph of Mammon (London, E. Grant Richards, 1907), p. 151.

5. Plays, pp. 117, 105, 99.

6. Ibid., p. 115.

7. Pp. 98–9, 97.

8. P. 123.

9. Pp. 121–2.

10. P. 119.

11. A.L.S., dated 6 May 1893, from 20 Park Ridings, Hornsey, N., P.U.L.

12. A.L.S., dated 8 Dec. 1893, from Hornsey, P.U.L.

13. William Ernest Henley, "Discharged," *In Hospital,* and "Out of the night that covers me," *Echoes,* in *Poems* (7 vols., London, David Nutt, 1908), *I*, 43–4, 125.

14. For a survey of this "literature of the will" see Jerome H. Buckley, *William Ernest Henley* (Princeton, 1945), ch. 1, *passim.*

15. Joseph Warren Beach, *The Concept of Nature in Nineteenth-Century English Poetry* (New York, The Macmillan Co., 1936), pp. 475–6.

16. William Blake, "Jerusalem," *The Prophetic Writings of William Blake,* D. J. Sloss and J. P. R. Wallis, eds. (2 vols., Oxford, The Clarendon Press, 1926), *I*, 460.

17. Archer, *Poets of the Younger Generation,* p. 128.

18. *Academy,* 27 Aug. 1887, p. 132.

19. *Plays,* pp. 147–8.

20. Ibid., pp. 210–11.

21. Archer, p. 130.

22. *Plays,* p. 251.

23. Ibid.

24. Archer, p. 135.

25. *Plays,* p. 274.

26. Ibid., pp. 258, 276.

27. Irving Babbitt, *Rousseau and Romanticism* (Boston and New York, Houghton Mifflin Co., 1919), p. 263.

28. *Plays,* pp. 266–7.

29. Ibid., p. 270.

30. Pp. 279–80.

31. A.L.S., dated 5 Nov. 1889, from 12 Brisbane St., H.E.H.L.

CHAPTER 4

The Devil's Disciple

1. *Diabolus Amans, a Dramatic Poem* (Glasgow, Wilson & McCormick, 1885), p. 11. Subsequent references to *Diabolus Amans* in this chapter are to this, the only, edition and are indicated by a page reference immediately following the quotation in the text.

2. See Theodore Martin, *Memoir of William Edmonstoune Aytoun* (Edinburgh and London, W. Blackwood & Sons, 1867), p. 148; and Jerome H. Buckley, *The Victorian Temper* (Harvard, 1951), pp. 57–60.

3. William Edmonstoune Aytoun, *Firmilian: or, the Student of Badajoz* (Edinburgh, W. Blackwood, 1854), pp. viii–ix.

4. Ibid., p. 164.

5. John Nichol, *Fragments of Criticism* (Edinburgh, James Nichol, 1860), pp. 89–91; reprinted from the *Oxford and Cambridge Magazine* (1856).

6. Martin, p. 146.

7. See Buckley, *Victorian Temper*, pp. 44, 52–3.

8. See Knight, *John Nichol*, pp. 205–6.

9. "On the Writing of Essays," *Dreamthorp with Selections from "Last Leaves" by Alexander Smith*, Hugh Walker, ed. (London, Oxford University Press [1914]), pp. 23, 25–6.

10. Nichol, p. 90.

11. Buckley, *Victorian Temper*, p. 55.

12. A.L.S., from Davidson to John Lane, dated only "Thursday," from Hornsey, P.U.L.; also advertisement in back of *The North Wall* (Glasgow, Wilson & McCormick, 1885).

13. *A Rosary*, p. 50; "On Poetry," *Holiday and Other Poems*, p. 156.

14. "Dolores," *Poems and Ballads, I*, in *The Complete Works of Algernon Charles Swinburne, 1*, 288.

15. "George Meredith's Odes," *The Man Forbid and Other Essays*, Edward J. O'Brien, ed. (Boston, Ball Publishing Co., 1910), p. 146. See also John Davidson, "Mr. Meredith's Nature Poems," *Daily Chronicle*, 18 Aug. 1898; "Another View of Mr. Meredith's Odes," *Saturday Review*, 19 Nov. 1898, pp. 664–5; "Another View of Mr. Meredith's Odes," *Saturday Reveiw*, 10 Dec. 1898, p. 786. Portions of the first two essays are reprinted in *A Rosary*, pp. 205–9; 203, 142.

16. George Meredith, "Modern Love," XLIII, *Poems* (2 vols., Westminster, Archibald Constable & Co., 1898), *1*, 45. For Swinburne's and Meredith's thought, I am indebted to Joseph Warren Beach, *The Concept of Nature in Nineteenth-Century English Poetry*, chs. 17–18.

17. "Mr. Meredith and Nature," *A Rosary*, pp. 205, 208–9.

18. Swinburne, "On the Downs," *Songs before Sunrise*, in *Complete Works, 2*, 256.

19. Swinburne, "Hymn of Man," ibid., *2*, 160–1.

20. *Plays*, p. 244. Subsequent references in this chapter to *Smith* are indicated by page reference to this edition immediately following the quotation in the text.

21. *Plays*, foreword.

22. Edmund Wilson, "Oscar Wilde: 'One Must Always Seek What Is Most Tragic,' " *Classics and Commercials* (New York, Farrar Straus & Co., 1950), *passim*.

23. "Crazy Jane Talks with the Bishop," *The Winding Stair and Other Poems*, in *The Variorum Edition of the Poems of W. B. Yeats*, Peter Allt and Russell K. Alspach, eds. (New York, The Macmillan Co., 1957), p. 513.

24. Babbitt, *Rousseau and Romanticism*, pp. 262–3.

25. Friedrich Schlegel, "Lyceumsfragment 108," *Friedrich Schlegel 1794–1802; seine prosaischen Jugendschriften*, J. Minor, ed. (2 vols., Vienna, C. Konegen, 1882), *2*, 198, 391; quoted by G. G. Sedgewick, *Of Irony: Especially in Drama* (2d ed., Univ. of Toronto, 1948), pp. 14–15.

CHAPTER 5

London 1890–98

1. Stoddart, "Interview with John Davidson," *Bookman* (New York), Mar. 1895, p. 87.

2. John A. Lester Jr., "Friedrich Nietzsche and John Davidson: A Study in Influence," *Journal of the History of Ideas*, June 1957, p. 416.

3. See Fred Brittain, *Arthur Quiller-Couch* (Cambridge Univ. Press, 1947), pp. 19–20.

4. See Buckley, *Henley*, pp. 154–61.

5. Stoddart, p. 87.

6. Victor F. Calverton, *Sex Expression in Literature* (New York, Boni & Liveright, 1926), p. 255.

7. A.L.S., dated "6 or 7 June" [1909], from London, P.U.L.

8. *Speaker*, 16 May 1891, p. 583; reprinted in *Sentences and Paragraphs* (London, Lawrence & Bullen, 1893), p. 119.

9. Ernest Rhys, *Letters from Limbo* (London, J. M. Dent & Sons, 1936), p. 90.

10. Ibid.

11. William Butler Yeats, "The Trembling of the Veil," *The Autobiography of William Butler Yeats* (New York, The Macmillan Co., 1938), p. 144. Victor Plarr, *Ernest Dowson, 1888–1897* (London, Elkin Mathews, 1914), p. 63; also the appended bibliography by Guy Harrison who quotes a list in Dr. Greene's handwriting of members and guests of the Rhymers' Club, p. 133.

12. Ernest Rhys, *Everyman Remembers* (London, J. M. Dent & Sons, 1931), p. 109.

13. Ibid., p. 106.

14. Yeats, pp. 257–8.

15. Mark Longaker, *Ernest Dowson* (Philadelphia and London, Univ. of Pennsylvania Press, 1944), p. 88.

16. Rhys, *Everyman Remembers*, p. 106.

17. Yeats, p. 270.

18. Ernest Dowson, "Non sum qualis eram bonae sub regno Cynarae," *The Poems of Ernest Dowson* (London and New York, John Lane, The Bodley Head, 1905), p. 28.

19. *Newspaper World*, 1 Jan. 1927, Grant Richards quoting from a letter of Robert H. Sherard, who stated that Davidson had made the remark in a review of one of Sherard's books.

20. Yeats, p. 270.

21. Morley Roberts, "The Rhymers' Club," *John o' London's Weekly*, 30 Sept. 1933, pp. 901–2.

22. Ibid., pp. 902, 908.

23. Rhys, *Everyman Remembers*, pp. 109–10; Frank Harris, *Contempo-*

rary Portraits, First Series (London, Methuen & Co., 1915), p. 124. Harris misquotes or lifts from context remarks made by Davidson in his published writings, repeating them as if they had been made to him in private conversation.

24. Rhys, ibid.; Richards, *Author Hunting,* p. 225.

25. Roberts, p. 902.

26. Yeats, p. 146.

27. Ibid., p. 145.

28. See Louis Macneice, *The Poetry of W. B. Yeats* (London and New York, Oxford University Press, 1941), pp. 31–3, 36.

29. Yeats, p. 146.

30. Ibid., p. 271.

31. Rhys, *Everyman Remembers,* p. 114.

32. Richard Le Gallienne, *The Romantic '90's* (London and New York, G. P. Putnam's Sons, 1926), p. 201.

33. A.L.S., dated 6 May 1893, from 20 Park Ridings, Hornsey, N., P.U.L.

34. Le Gallienne, p. 149.

35. Autograph reader's report by Le Gallienne, undated but stating at the head, "MS. returned Aug. 3, '93," P.U.L. For tepid reviews of *A Random Itinerary* by Le Gallienne and Grant Richards, see Richard Le Gallienne, *Retrospective Reviews* (2 vols., London, John Lane, The Bodley Head, 1896), 2, 34–9; and the *Academy,* 10 Mar. 1894, pp. 205–6.

36. Le Gallienne, *Retrospective Reviews, 2,* 112.

37. A.L.S., undated but written in 1894, from 20 Park Ridings, Hornsey, N., N.L.S.

38. See J. Lewis May, *John Lane and the Nineties* (London, John Lane, The Bodley Head, 1936), pp. 90–1, for the original version of the poem before the first line was altered and for the letter, written from Brentford, Nov. 1893, that accompanied it—both of which Le Gallienne sent to Lane.

39. *Ballads and Songs,* p. [130]. See Le Gallienne, *The Romantic '90's,* p. 152, for the complete autograph text of the poem reproduced in facsimile.

40. A.L.S., dated 16 Nov. 1894, from 20 Park Ridings, Hornsey, N., Add. MS. 45291, ff. 88–9, B.M.

41. "The 'New Hedonism,'" *Speaker,* 15 Dec. 1894, pp. 654–5.

42. The *Times,* 4–12 Dec. 1954.

43. "The 'New Hedonism,'" p. 655.

44. A.L.S., dated only "Wednesday," from 20 Park Ridings, Hornsey, N., P.U.L.

45. A.L.S., dated 16 Dec. 1894, from Hornsey, P.U.L.

46. See *The New Fiction and Other Papers* (London, Westminster Gazette Library, 1895), *3,* 25–73, for reprints of articles by "Philistine" in the *Westminster Gazette* attacking Le Gallienne and for the replies by Le Gallienne and others.

47. For the entire letter, dated 29 Jan. 1894, from 20 Park Ridings,

Hornsey, N., see Le Gallienne, *The Romantic '90's*, pp. 202–3. The letter did not appear in the *Westminster Gazette*.

48. Ibid., p. 198.

49. See May, pp. 30–41.

50. Ibid., p. 238.

51. A.L.S., undated but written between 1893 and 1895, from 20 Park Ridings, Hornsey, N., N.L.S.

52. Series of A.Ls.S., from Davidson to Lane, undated but written in late Sept. or early Oct. 1893, from Hornsey, P.U.L.

53. A.L.S., dated 29 Sept. 1893, P.U.L.

54. Autograph copy by Davidson of letter to him from Unwin, undated, C.U.L.

55. A.L.S., dated only "Sunday," from 20 Park Ridings, Hornsey, N., C.U.L.

56. Typescript L.S., from G. Herbert Thring, secretary of the Author's Society, to Davidson, dated 28 Sept. 1893, P.U.L.

57. Esmé Wingfield-Stratford, *The Victorian Sunset* (New York, W. Morrow & Co., 1932), pp. 323–4.

58. A.L.S., undated but written before June 1895, from 20 Park Ridings, Hornsey, N., N.L.S.

59. Rhys, *Everyman Remembers*, p. 166; compare Ernest Rhys, *Wales England Wed* (London, J. M. Dent & Sons, 1940), pp. 122–3.

60. Rhys, *Everyman Remembers*, pp. 251–7.

61. Harris, *Contemporary Portraits*, pp. 124–5. Harris' description is largely corroborated elsewhere.

62. A.L.S., dated 1 Jan. 1896, from 18 Warrington Crescent, W., N.L.S.

63. May, *John Lane*, p. 89.

64. A.L.S., undated but written before June 1895, from 20 Park Ridings, Hornsey, N., N.L.S.

65. See Patrick R. Chalmers, *Kenneth Grahame* (London, Methuen & Co., 1933), p. 64; May, pp. 71–4.

66. May, p. 73.

67. Reprinted in *Ballads and Songs*, pp. 86–7.

68. Incorporated as the third section of a longer poem, "Spring," *Ballads and Songs*, pp. 111–16.

69. Reprinted in *Ballads and Songs*, pp. 91–7.

70. Reprinted as "A Ballad of a Nun," *Ballads and Songs*, pp. 52–61.

71. Harris, pp. 127–9. Harris states that this occurred in 1890, an improbably early date for the poem.

72. Chalmers, pp. 65–6.

73. The *Manchester Guardian*, 19 Apr. 1909.

74. A.L.S., dated 28 Dec. 1900, from 9 Fairmile Ave., Streatham, B.C.U.L.L.

75. C. Lewis Hind, *More Authors and I* (New York, Dodd Mead & Co., 1922), p. 78.

76. Owen Seaman, *The Battle of the Bays* (9th ed., London and New York, John Lane, The Bodley Head, 1902), pp. 22 ff.

77. See May, *John Lane*, pp. 145–7, for a selection of these parodies directed at the Bodley Head poets, including Davidson.

78. Richard de Lyrienne, *The Quest of the Gilt-Edged Girl* (London and New York, John Lane, The Bodley Head, 1897), pp. 67–8. The author of this work is debated, and it has been variously attributed to Max Beerbohm and Hilaire Belloc, as well as to Le Gallienne himself. *Books of the "Nineties,"* Catalogue 42 (London, Elkin Mathews, Ltd., undated) ascribes it to David Hodge, a Glasgow journalist; Richard Whittington-Egan and Geoffrey Smerdon concur (*The Quest of the Golden Boy*, London, The Unicorn Press, 1960, p. 315).

79. See Aymer Vallance, comp., "List of Drawings by Aubrey Beardsley," in Robert Ross, *Aubrey Beardsley* (London and New York, John Lane, The Bodley Head, 1909), p. 90; also R. A. Walker, ed., *The Best of Beardsley* (London, John Lane, The Bodley Head, 1948), plate 16.

80. *Speaker*, 7 Apr. 1894, p. 393.

81. Sir William Rothenstein, *Men and Memories* (2 vols., New York, Coward-McCann, Inc., 1931), *1*, 181.

82. May, p. 98.

83. *A Full and True Account of the Wonderful Mission of Earl Lavender* (London, Ward & Downey, 1895), opposite title page.

84. See Osbert Burdett, *The Beardsley Period* (London, John Lane, The Bodley Head, 1925), p. 253; Wingfield-Stratford, *Victorian Sunset*, p. 325; May, pp. 90–1; and J. Benjamin Townsend, " 'The Yellow Book,' " *Princeton University Library Chronicle*, Winter 1955, pp. 101–3. The Princeton University Library possesses a unique dummy copy, formerly in the collection of Edmund Gosse, of the fifth number of the *Yellow Book* with the suppressed cover and plates by Beardsley.

85. A.L.S., dated 25 Mar. 1895, from 20 Park Ridings, Hornsey, N., P.U.L.

86. O'Brien, ed., *The Man Forbid*, p. 12.

87. Holbrook Jackson, *The Eighteen Nineties* (2d ed., Harmondsworth, Penguin Books, 1939), p. 178.

88. William Butler Yeats, ed., *Oxford Book of Modern Verse* (New York, Oxford Univ. Press, 1936), p. xi.

89. Edward Clodd, *Grant Allen, a Memoir* (London, Grant Richards, 1900), p. 203.

90. Stoddart, "Interview with John Davidson," p. 87.

91. Le Gallienne, *Retrospective Reviews*, 2, 225–31.

92. A.L.S., dated 22 Feb. 1895, from 20 Park Ridings, Hornsey, N., Y.U.L.

93. Davidson commemorated the occasion in some lame verses that he sent to Allen. A.MS.S., undated, Y.U.L.

94. See Clodd, pp. 8–9, 25, 32–3.

95. Two A.Ls.S., to John Lane, dated 17 Mar. 1894 and undated, from 20 Park Ridings, Hornsey, N., N.L.S.

96. A.L.S., to Edmund Gosse, dated 10 July 1894, from Hornsey, Ashley MS. B.571, B.M.

97. A.L.S., dated 9 Jan. 1895, from Hornsey, Ashley MS. A.557, B.M.

98. A.L.S., dated only "Sunday," from 9 Fairmile Ave., Streatham, S.W., N.L.S.

99. See the *Daily Chronicle*, 19 Apr.; *Vanity Fair*, 21 Apr. 1909.

100. Epilogue, *The Triumph of Mammon* (London, E. Grant Richards, 1907), pp. 168–9.

101. A.L.S., dated 4 Dec. 1894, from 20 Park Ridings, Hornsey, N., Ashley MS. B.561, B.M.

102. A.L.S., dated 7 Dec. 1894, from Hornsey, Ashley MS. B.565, B.M.

103. Edmund Gosse, *In Russet and Silver* (Chicago, Stone & Kimball, 1895), p. 53.

104. A.L.S., to Richards, dated 14 June 1895, from 18 Warrington Crescent, W., P.U.L.

105. A.L.S., dated 3 July 1895, from 18 Warrington Crescent, W., B.C.U.L.L.

106. A.L.S., dated 18 July 1896, from 18 Warrington Cresent, W., N.L.S.

107. A.L.S., dated 28 Aug. 1896, from 18 Warrington Crescent, W., P.U.L.

108. A.L.S., to Lane, dated 7 Feb. 1898, from Rayleigh House, Shoreham, Sussex, N.L.S.

109. A.L.S., to Lane, dated 4 Dec. 1898, from 18 Warrington Crescent, W., in the collection of Kenneth Hopkins.

CHAPTER 6

The Phoenix in the Aviary

1. *A Rosary*, pp. 209–10; reprinted in edited version from "The Criticism of Poetry," *Speaker*, 4 Mar. 1899, pp. 258–9.

2. Epilogue, *The Triumph of Mammon*, pp. 168–9.

3. Epilogue, *Mammon and His Message* (London, Grant Richards, 1908), p. 151.

4. "The Art of Poetry," *The Man Forbid*, p. 125; reprinted from the *Speaker*, 4 Feb. 1899, pp. 153–4.

5. *Academy*, 23 Nov. 1889, p. 331.

6. "The Criticism of Poetry," *The Man Forbid*, p. 71.

7. "On Poetry," *Holiday*, pp. 133, 151. Compare *The Man Forbid*, pp. 155–60; reprinted in part from "*Tête-à-Tête*. James Boswell. Dr. Johnson," *Speaker*, 6 May 1899, pp. 523–4.

8. Introduction, *The Theatrocrat, a Tragic Play of Church and State* (London, E. Grant Richards, 1905), p. 1.

9. *Holiday*, p. 143.

10. See Sydney Dobell, *Thoughts on Art, Philosophy, and Religion*, John Nichol, ed. (London, Elder & Co., 1876), pp. 17–20, 33, 51–3, 142. The aesthetic theories of the Spasmodics are summarized by Buckley, *The Victorian Temper*, pp. 44–5, 54–5.

11. *The Man Forbid,* p. 237; reprinted from "On Interviewing: Prose Eclogue," *Speaker,* 12 Jan. 1895, pp. 46–7.

12. Frederick Coykendall Collection, C.U.L.; published in the *Saturday Review,* 18 June 1898, p. 809, and reprinted in *The Last Ballad and Other Poems* (London and New York, John Lane, The Bodley Head, 1898), pp. 122–3.

13. *Holiday,* p. 149.

14. See Walter A. Kaufmann, *Nietzsche: Philosopher, Psychologist, Anti-Christ* (Princeton, 1950), pp. 105–10, 342–6.

15. *The Last Ballad,* p. 3.

16. *New Ballads,* pp. 114, 117; reprinted in edited version from the *Saturday Review,* 27 June 1896, pp. 642–4.

17. "Dolores," *The Complete Works of Algernon Charles Swinburne, 1,* 290.

18. *New Ballads,* pp. 47, 49.

19. *The Theatrocrat,* pp. 32–3.

20. Le Gallienne, *Retrospective Reviews,* 2, 118.

21. *New Ballads,* p. 96; reprinted from the *Daily Chronicle,* 18 Dec. 1895.

22. William Butler Yeats, "The Rhymers' Club," *Letters to the New Island* (Harvard Univ. Press, 1934), pp. 142, 146; reprinted from the *Boston Pilot,* 23 Apr. 1892.

23. Archer, *Poets of the Younger Generation,* p. 157.

24. Robert Shafer, ed., *Reviews and Critical Papers by Lionel Johnson* (London, Elkin Mathews, 1921), p. 46; reprinted from the *Academy,* 5 Jan. 1895, pp. 6–7.

25. *Holiday,* pp. 41–2; reprinted as excerpt from the *Pall Mall Magazine,* July–Dec. 1905, pp. 657–61.

26. Ibid., p. 30; reprinted from the *Pall Mall Magazine,* July–Dec. 1905, pp. 522–3.

27. P. 14; reprinted from "A Ballad of a Runnable Stag," *Pall Mall Magazine,* July–Dec. 1905, pp. 231–3.

28. P. 155.

29. Archer, p. 157.

30. *Fleet Street Eclogues* (London, Elkin Mathews & John Lane, 1893), pp. 43–4.

31. Owen Seaman, *The Battle of the Bays,* pp. 27–8.

32. Ibid., pp. 32–3.

33. "Good-Friday," *Fleet Street Eclogues,* pp. 32–3.

34. *Ballads and Songs,* pp. 107–8; reprinted from the *Speaker,* 17 Mar. 1894, p. 308.

35. "Lammas," *A Second Series of Fleet Street Eclogues,* p. 24.

36. "A Woman and Her Son," *New Ballads,* pp. 23–4.

37. *Holiday,* p. 26; reprinted in edited version from the *Pall Mall Magazine,* Jan.–June 1906, p. 436.

38. *New Ballads,* p. 19; reprinted from the *Daily Chronicle,* 8 Apr. 1896.

39. Quoted by Alfred H. Barr Jr., *What Is Modern Painting?* (New York, The Museum of Modern Art, 1943), p. 8.

40. *The Triumph of Mammon,* pp. 158–9.

41. *A Second Series of Fleet Street Eclogues,* p. 26.

42. Ibid., pp. 26–7.

43. James Thomson, *The City of Dreadful Night* (London, Reeves & Turner, 1880), p. 17.

44. "A Ballad of the Exodus from Houndsditch," *Ballads and Songs,* pp. 41–2.

45. William Ernest Henley, *The Song of the Sword and Other Verses* (London, David Nutt, 1892), pp. 30–1.

46. *Fleet Street Eclogues,* pp. 73–4.

47. Cornelius Weygandt, *The Time of Yeats* (New York and London, D. Appleton Century, 1937), p. 111.

48. "Good-Friday," *Fleet Street Eclogues,* p. 31.

49. *Academy,* 23 Nov. 1889, p. 331.

50. *Sentences and Paragraphs,* p. 16; reprinted in edited excerpt from "Mr. G. Bernard Shaw as Ibsen," *Speaker,* 31 Oct. 1891, pp. 538–9.

51. *The Man Forbid,* pp. 175–7; reprinted from *"Tête-à-Tête.* Froude. Carlyle," *Speaker,* 17 June 1899, pp. 689–90.

52. *Mammon and His Message,* p. 173.

53. "A Ballad in Blank Verse of the Making of a Poet," *Ballads and Songs,* pp. 8–9.

54. "St George's Day," *A Second Series of Fleet Street Eclogues,* p. 93; reprinted from the *Yellow Book,* Apr. 1895, pp. 299–317.

55. "Autumn," *Ballads and Songs,* pp. 122–3; reprinted from "Autumn Songs," *Speaker,* 25 Aug. 1894, p. 216.

56. Le Gallienne, *Retrospective Reviews,* 2, 113–14.

57. Ibid., p. 244.

58. *In a Music-Hall,* p. 96.

59. *Ballads and Songs,* p. 47.

60. Ibid., p. 34.

61. "Recent Views of Poetry," *Speaker,* 4 Mar. 1899, p. 260.

62. " 'Poetry and the Something Behind Phenomena,' " *Speaker,* 25 Mar. 1899, p. 346.

63. " 'Irony,' " *Speaker,* 6 May 1899, p. 523; reprinted in part in *The Man Forbid,* pp. 134–6.

64. "St Valentine's Eve," *Fleet Street Eclogues,* pp. 26–7.

65. *The Last Ballad,* pp. 112–13; reprinted in edited version from the *Speaker,* 27 Nov. 1897, p. 604.

66. *Ballads and Songs,* p. 110; reprinted from "Song of a Cinque Port," *Pall Mall Gazette,* 2 Mar. 1894, p. 2.

67. "Apple-Trees," *Holiday,* p. 30.

68. *The Last Ballad,* p. 143.

69."St Swithin's Day," *Fleet Street Eclogues,* p. 45; reprinted in edited version from "In the Hollow at Long Ditton," *Speaker,* 12 Dec. 1891, pp. 713-14.

70. "New Year's Day," ibid., p. 8.

71. "St Valentine's Eve," ibid., p. 25.

72. *New Ballads,* p. 54; reprinted with considerable revisions from "The King's Daughter of Norway: an Age-End Ballad of Euthanasia," *Speaker,* 8 Dec. 1894, p. 632.

73. "The Last Song," *Holiday,* pp. 11-12.

74. Jean Cocteau, *Opium,* Margaret Crosland and Sinclair Road, trans. (New York, Grove Press, 1958), p. 80.

75. "To the New Women" and "To the New Men," *Ballads and Songs,* pp. 4, 6.

76. Grant Allen, "A Ballade of Evolution," *The Lower Slopes* (London, Elkin Mathews & John Lane, 1894), p. 43.

77. "A Vindication," ibid., pp. 60-1.

78. *Ballads and Songs,* p. 96; reprinted from the *Yellow Book,* July 1894, pp. 99-102.

79. *A Second Series of Fleet Street Eclogues,* p. 38.

80. *Ballads and Songs,* pp. 33, 35.

81. *New Ballads,* p. 95; reprinted from the *Saturday Review,* 11 Jan. 1896, pp. 35-6.

82. *Ballads and Songs,* pp. 91-2, 97.

83. "St George's Day," *A Second Series of Fleet Street Eclogues,* p. 84.

84. Ibid., p. 97.

85. *The Last Ballad,* p. 105; reprinted from "War-Song for the Armies of Europe," *Saturday Review,* 9 Apr. 1898, p. 482.

86. "The Pioneer," ibid., p. 155; reprinted from the *Saturday Review,* 12 Feb. 1898, p. 197.

87. *Holiday,* p. 18.

88. *The Last Ballad,* pp. 134-5; reprinted from "Not Otherwise," *Saturday Review,* 4 June 1898, p. 745.

89. Ibid., pp. 138-9; reprinted from the *Speaker,* 30 Nov. 1895, p. 594.

90. *Holiday,* p. 144.

91. "A Ballad in Blank Verse," *Ballads and Songs,* p. 19.

92. "Holiday," *Holiday,* p. 8; reprinted with revisions from "Holiday. A Fleet Street Eclogue," *Outlook,* 23 Sept. 1905, p. 401.

93. Ibid., pp. 126-7; reprinted from "New Year's Eve. A Fleet Street Eclogue," *Outlook,* 30 Dec. 1905, p. 942.

94. *Athenaeum,* 12 Dec. 1896, p. 830.

CHAPTER 7

In and Out of the London Theater, 1898–1904

1. Introduction, *The Theatrocrat,* pp. 18–19.
2. Beatrice Stella (Mrs. Patrick) Campbell, *My Life and Some Letters* (New York, Dodd, Mead & Co., 1922), p. 102.
3. Henry Hamilton Fyfe, *Sir Arthur Wing Pinero's Plays and Players* (New York, Macmillan Co., 1930), p. 145.
4. Campbell, p. 102.
5. *Critic* (New York), 14 Mar. 1896, p. 187.
6. See Maurice W. Disher, *The Last Romantic; the Authorized Biography of Sir John Martin-Harvey* (London and New York, Hutchinson, 1948), p. 121.
7. *For the Crown, a Romantic Play, in Four Acts Done into English by John Davidson* (London, Nassau Press, 1896), p. 28.
8. François Coppée, *Pour la Couronne,* Henry Atwell, ed. (London, Hachette & Co., 1922), p. 120; *For the Crown,* p. 58; prompt copy with MS. revisions, P.U.L.
9. *Speaker,* 7 Mar. 1896, pp. 263–5.
10. "The Return of Mrs. Pat," *Saturday Review,* 7 Mar. 1896, pp. 248–50; reprinted in G. Bernard Shaw, *Dramatic Opinions and Essays* (2 vols., New York, Brentano's, 1906), *1,* 356–64.
11. Alan Dent, ed., *Bernard Shaw and Mrs. Patrick Campbell: Their Correspondence* (New York, Alfred Knopf, 1952), pp. 74–5.
12. Sir John Martin-Harvey, *The Autobiography of Sir John Martin-Harvey* (London, S. Low, Marston & Co., 1933), pp. 196–8; and Disher, pp. 122–3.
13. MS. prompt copy formerly in the possession of John Martin-Harvey, P.U.L. This may be a unique copy for the play was not published.
14. Disher, p. 123.
15. The *Times,* 14 Oct. 1897; see also the *Athenaeum,* 23 Oct. 1897, p. 568.
16. The *Times,* 6 Dec. 1897.
17. Ibid.
18. A.L.S., dated 15 Feb. 1902, from 9 Fairmile Ave., Streatham, P.U.L.
19. *Godfrida, a Play in Four Acts* (London and New York, John Lane, The Bodley Head, 1898), p. 4.
20. The *Daily Chronicle,* 19 Oct. 1898.
21. *Godfrida,* pp. 3–4.
22. A.L.S., undated, N.L.S.
23. *Books from the Library of John Lane, and Other Books of the Eighteen Nineties* (Dulau & Co., Ltd., 15 May 1929), Catalogue 165, item 221. The present location of this letter is unknown. It may have been destroyed with other items when Dulau & Co. was bombed out during World War II.

24. Archer, *Poets of the Younger Generation*, pp. 136–7.

25. *Academy*, 5 Nov. 1898, p. 192.

26. *Outlook*, 26 Nov. 1898, pp. 530–1.

27. Advertisement, in *The Knight of the Maypole, a Comedy in Four Acts* (London, Grant Richards, 1903).

28. *Self's the Man, a Tragi-comedy* (London, Grant Richards, 1901), p. 79.

29. Ibid., p. 136.

30. P. 177.

31. A.L.S., to Richards, dated 23 Jan. 1901, from 9 Fairmile Ave., Streatham, P.U.L.

32. *Self's the Man*, p. 142.

33. A.L.S., dated 29 Jan. 1899, from St. Winifred's, Fairmile Ave., Streatham, B.C.U.L.L.

34. *Academy*, 24 Nov. 1900, p. 484.

35. Ibid., 1 Dec. 1900, p. 523.

36. Richards, *Author Hunting*, p. 218.

37. A.L.S., undated, from 9 Fairmile Ave., Streatham, P.U.L.

38. A.L.S., dated 30 Jan. 1901, from 9 Fairmile Ave., Streatham, P.U.L.

39. Letter-press copy of a letter, from Richards to Davidson, dated 15 Apr. 1901, in the Library of the University of Illinois.

40. A.L.S., dated 29 Jan. 1901, from 9 Fairmile Ave., Streatham, B.C.U.L.L. Compare A.L.S., to William Archer, from 9 Fairmile Ave., Streatham, P.U.L., in which he makes the same complaint.

41. *Academy*, 16 Feb. 1901, pp. 140–1; 23 Feb. 1901, p. 171.

42. A.L.S., dated 29 Oct. 1898, from St. Winifred's, Fairmile Ave., Streatham, Ashley MS., B.572, B.M.

43. *Athenaeum*, 23 Mar. 1901, p. 379.

44. Introduction, *The Theatrocrat*, p. 20.

45. Autograph copy signed, P.U.L.

46. A.L.S., from Davidson to John Lane, dated 28 Mar. 1904, from 9 Fairmile Ave., Streatham, N.L.S.

47. A.L.S., dated 12 Oct. 1902, from 9 Fairmile Ave., Streatham, P.U.L.

48. A.L.S., dated 28 Dec. 1900, from 9 Fairmile Ave., Streatham, B.C.U.L.L.

49. *The Testament of a Vivisector* (London, Grant Richards, 1901), p. [5].

50. A.L.S., dated 28 Aug. 1902, from 9 Fairmile Ave., Streatham, P.U.L.

51. Richards, *Author Hunting*, p. 218.

52. See the *Academy*, 31 Jan. 1903, p. 102; *Spectator*, 7 Feb. 1903, p. 224.

53. A.L.S., from Struan House, Blairlogie by Stirling, P.U.L.

54. A.L.S., dated 16 Nov. 1902, from Glenfaulds, Rothesay, P.U.L.

55. A.L.S., dated 8 Apr. 1908, from 6 Coulson's Terrace, Penzance, P.U.L.

56. A.L.S., dated 23 Apr. 1908, from 6 Coulson's Terrace, Penzance, P.U.L.

57. A.L.S., dated 8 June 1903, from 9 Fairmile Ave., Streatham, P.U.L.

58. A.L.S., dated 29 June 1903, from 9 Fairmile Ave., Streatham, P.U.L.

59. *Academy*, 31 Oct. 1903, p. 467.

60. Campbell, *My Life and Some Letters*, p. 143. The typescripts with

autograph corrections of two versions of *Phèdre* which Davidson prepared for Mrs. Campbell are in the N.L.S.

61. A.L.S., P.U.L.

62. A.L.S., to Richards, dated 8 Dec. 1903, from 9 Fairmile Ave., Streatham, P.U.L.

63. A.L.S., to Richards, dated 22 Jan. 1904, from the Grosvenor Club, P.U.L.

64. A.L.S., dated 3 Feb. 1904, from the Grosvenor Club, P.U.L.

65. Campbell, pp. 237–8.

66. *Saturday Review*, 20 Feb. 1904, pp. 230–1; reprinted in Max Beerbohm, *Around Theatres* (2 vols., New York, Alfred Knopf, 1930), 2, 394–6.

67. Typescript copy, dated 17 Feb. 1904, P.U.L.

68. A.L.S., to Richards, undated but written in Dec. 1905, P.U.L. The letter written in defense of *The Theatrocrat* is a copy of one sent to the *Times* whose critic had objected to having the gallery in that play "hiss" instead of "boo." See the *Times Literary Supplement*, 15 Dec. 1905, p. 447.

69. A.L.S., dated 14 Feb. 1904, from 9 Fairmile Ave., Streatham, P.U.L.

70. A.L.S., undated, from 9 Fairmile Ave., Streatham, P.U.L.

71. A.L.S., dated 13 Apr. 1902, from 9 Fairmile Ave., Streatham, P.U.L.

72. A.L.S., dated 14 Apr. 1902, from 9 Fairmile Ave., Streatham, P.U.L.

73. A.L.S., to Richards, dated Jan. 1904, from 9 Fairmile Ave., Streatham, P.U.L.

74. Richards, *Author Hunting*, p. 224.

75. See Miriam A. Franc, *Ibsen in England* (Boston, Four Seas Co., 1919), especially chs. 1, 2.

76. Priscilla Thouless, *Modern Poetic Drama* (Oxford, Basil Blackford, 1934), p. 97.

77. *Godfrida*, p. 3.

CHAPTER 8

Rebellion and Defeat, 1901–06

1. *The Testament of a Vivisector*, pp. 10, 14–15.

2. The *Daily Chronicle*, 29 June 1901; reprinted in Francis Thompson, *Literary Criticisms*, the Rev. Terence L. Connolly, ed. (New York, E. P. Dutton, 1948), pp. 167–71.

3. See John A. Lester Jr., "Prose-Poetry Transmutation in the Poetry of John Davidson," *Modern Philology*, Aug. 1958, pp. 38–44.

4. *The Testament of a Man Forbid* (London, Grant Richards, 1901), pp. 11–12.

5. The *Pilot*; advertisement in *The Testament of an Empire-Builder* (London, Grant Richards, 1902), p. [3].

6. *Athenaeum*, 16 Nov. 1901, p. 659.

7. The *Star*, 4 June 1901.

8. A.L.S., dated 15 June 1901, from Blairlogie, Stirling, N.B., Add. MS. 45291, ff. 102–3, B.M.

9. *The Testament of an Empire-Builder*, pp. 77, 81.
10. Ibid., pp. 67–8.
11. Pp. 8, 10, 12–14.
12. The *Manchester Guardian*, 1 July 1902.
13. The *Star*, 22 May 1902.
14. The *Morning Leader*, 24 May 1902.
15. *Athenaeum*, 30 Aug. 1902, pp. 277–8.
16. *Academy*, 7 June 1902, p. 572.
17. A.L.S., dated 17 June 1902, from 9 Fairmile Ave., Streatham, S.W., N.L.S. The ode appeared in the *Daily Chronicle*, 9 Aug. 1902; it was reprinted in part and revised in *A Rosary*, pp. 6–11.
18. A.Ls.S., to Richards, dated 16 Nov. 1902, from Glenfaulds, Rothesay, N.B., and 8 June 1903, from 9 Fairmile Ave., Streatham, P.U.L.
19. A.L.S., dated 1 Nov. 1903, from the Grosvenor Club, P.U.L.
20. A.L.S., from 9 Fairmile Ave., Streatham, Y.U.L.
21. *The Testament of a Prime Minister* (London, Grant Richards, 1904), pp. 83, 85–6.
22. A.Ls.S., dated 8 Oct. 1904, from the Grosvenor Club, and 17 Oct. 1904, from 9 Fairmile Ave., Streatham, P.U.L.
23. A.L.S., dated 22 Oct. 1904, from 9 Fairmile Ave., Streatham, Add. MS. 45291, ff. 112–13, B.M.
24. A.L.S., dated 24 Oct. 1904, from 9 Fairmile Ave., Streatham, P.U.L.
25. A.L.S., to Archer, dated only "Thursday," from 9 Fairmile Ave., Streatham, Add. MS. 45291, ff. 116–17, B.M.
26. *Times Literary Supplement*, 28 Oct. 1904, p. 328.
27. A.L.S., dated only "Sunday," P.U.L.
28. A.L.S., dated 28 Mar. 1904, from 9 Fairmile Ave., Streatham, N.L.S.
29. A.L.S., undated but written in 1904, from 9 Fairmile Ave., Streatham, P.U.L.
30. A.L.S. [1901], from Stirling, quoted in *Books from the Library of John Lane*, item 235; present location unknown.
31. A.L.S. [1903], ibid., item 239; present location unknown.
32. *Athenaeum*, 18 Mar. 1905, pp. 329–30.
33. A.L.S., dated 18 Oct. 1904, from 9 Fairmile Ave., Streatham, P.U.L.
34. A.L.S., dated 25 Nov. 1903, from 9 Fairmile Ave., Streatham, P.U.L.
35. A.L.S., dated 5 Sept. 1905, from 9 Fairmile Ave., Streatham, P.U.L.
36. A.L.S., dated 6 Dec. 1904, from 9 Fairmile Ave., Streatham, P.U.L.
37. A.L.S., dated 23 Aug. 1906, from 9 Fairmile Ave., Streatham, P.U.L.
38. A.L.S., dated 28 Dec. 1904, from 9 Fairmile Ave., Streatham, Add. MS. 45291, f. 111, B.M.
39. A.L.S., dated 22 Oct. 1904, from 9 Fairmile Ave., Streatham, Add. MS. 45291, ff. 112–13, B.M.
40. A.L.S., dated 5 Sept. 1905, from 9 Fairmile Ave., Streatham, P.U.L.
41. *The Theatrocrat*, p. 24.
42. A.L.S., dated 13 Nov. 1905, from 9 Fairmile Ave., Streatham, P.U.L.
43. A.L.S., dated 3 Dec. 1905, from 9 Fairmile Ave., Streatham, P.U.L.

44. A.L.S., dated 18 Nov. 1905, from 9 Fairmile Ave., Streatham, P.U.L.
45. A.L.S., to Richards, dated 20 Nov. 1905, from 9 Fairmile Ave., Streatham, P.U.L.
46. A.L.S., to Richards, dated 22 Nov. 1905, from 9 Fairmile Ave., Streatham, P.U.L.
47. A.L.S., dated 18 Nov. 1905, from 9 Fairmile Ave., Streatham, P.U.L.
48. A.L.S., to Richards, dated 3 Dec. 1905, from 9 Fairmile Ave., Streatham, P.U.L.
49. A.L.S., dated 17 Nov. 1905 [probably by Richards on date of receipt], P.U.L.
50. A.L.S., dated 23 Nov. 1905, from 9 Fairmile Ave., Streatham, P.U.L.
51. A.L.S., to Richards, undated, P.U.L.
52. A.L.S., dated 21 Nov. 1905, from 9 Fairmile Ave., Streatham, P.U.L.
53. Bookman (London), Jan. 1906, pp. 178-9.
54. Times Literary Supplement, 8 Dec. 1905, p. 431.
55. A.L.S., dated 12 Dec. 1905, from 9 Fairmile Ave., Streatham, P.U.L.
56. A.L.S., dated 14 Dec. 1905, from 9 Fairmile Ave., Streatham, P.U.L.
57. A.L.S., to Richards, undated, P.U.L.
58. Times Literary Supplement, 15 Dec. 1905, p. 447.
59. The Daily Chronicle, 24 Nov. 1905.
60. "Theatrocratic," ibid., 28 Nov. 1905.
61. A.L.S., dated 28 Nov. 1905, from 9 Fairmile Ave., Streatham, P.U.L.
62. "At the Judgment–Seat," the Daily Chronicle, 20 Dec. 1905.
63. Douglas Bush, Mythology and the Romantic Tradition in English Poetry (Harvard Univ. Press, 1937), p. 522.
64. The Westminster Gazette, 9 Dec. 1905.
65. Ibid., 11 Dec. 1905; an autograph signed copy of this letter which Davidson sent to Richards is in the P.U.L.
66. A.L.S., dated only "Monday," from 9 Fairmile Ave., Streatham, P.U.L.
67. A.L.S., to Richards, dated only "Saturday" and "Sunday," P.U.L.
68. The Daily News, 21 Dec. 1905.
69. The Morning Leader, 24 Nov. 1905.
70. A.L.S., to Richards, dated 7 Dec. 1905, from 9 Fairmile Ave., Streatham, P.U.L.
71. The Theatrocrat, p. 17.
72. A.L.S., undated, from Corveau, St. Ives, Cornwall, P.U.L.
73. A.L.S., to Richards, dated 9 Oct. 1908, from 9 Fairmile Ave., Streatham, P.U.L.
74. See John A. Lester Jr., "John Davidson, a Grub Street Bibliography," Secretary's News Sheet, The Bibliographical Society of the University of Virginia, Sept. 1958. This very useful bibliography of Davidson's journalistic work is probably as complete as at present can be compiled.
75. A.L.S., dated only "Saturday" and "Sunday," P.U.L.
76. Yeats, "The Trembling of the Veil," p. 194.
77. A.MS., undated, B.C.U.L.L.

78. A.L.S., dated 18 Dec. 1898, from St. Winifred's, Fairmile Ave., Streatham, Ashley MS. B.574, B.M.

79. A.L.S., dated 29 Jan. 1899, from St. Winifred's, Fairmile Ave., Streatham, B.C.U.L.L.

80. A.L.S., dated 28 Dec. 1900, from 9 Fairmile Ave., Streatham, B.C.U.L.L.

81. A.L.S., from F. S. Parry, dated 7 Feb. 1901, from 10 Downing Street, B.C.U.L.L.

82. A.L.S., to Richards, dated 22 Sept. 1902, from 9 Fairmile Ave., Streatham, P.U.L.

83. A.L.S., to W. S. McCormick, dated 12 Feb. 1901, from 9 Fairmile Ave., Streatham, B.C.U.L.L.

84. A.Ls.S., to Richards, dated 21 and 24 June 1906, from 9 Fairmile Ave., Streatham, P.U.L.

85. A.L.S., dated 21 Nov. 1903, from 9 Fairmile Ave., Streatham, P.U.L.

86. A.L.S., dated 26 Aug. 1903, from 9 Fairmile Ave., Streatham, P.U.L.

87. A.L.S., to Richards, dated 11 Sept. 1904, from 9 Fairmile Ave., Streatham, P.U.L.

88. A.L.S., to Richards, dated 1 Jan. 1908, from 6 Coulson's Terrace, Penzance, P.U.L.

89. A.L.S., dated 23 Nov. 1903, from 9 Fairmile Ave., Streatham, P.U.L.

90. A.L.S., to Richards, dated 30 Jan. 1908, from 6 Coulson's Terrace, Penzance, P.U.L.

91. A.L.S., to Richards, dated 1 Feb. 1907, from 9 Fairmile Ave., Streatham, P.U.L.

92. A.L.S., dated 8 Dec. 1899, from St. Winifred's, Fairmile Ave., Streatham, Add. MS. 45291, ff. 94–5, B.M.

93. A.L.S., to Richards, dated 9 May 1906, from 9 Fairmile Ave., Streatham, P.U.L.

94. *Holiday and Other Poems*, p. 134.

95. *Athenaeum*, 11 Aug. 1906, p. 151.

96. *Academy*, 28 July 1906, pp. 77–8.

97. *Times Literary Supplement*, 17 Aug. 1906, p. 281.

CHAPTER 9

Penzance Again, 1907–09

1. *The Triumph of Mammon*, p. 151.

2. A.L.S., dated 4 Apr. 1907, P.U.L.

3. "The Tragedy of a Failure," *Academy*, 27 Apr. 1907, p. 408.

4. *Times Literary Supplement*, 19 Apr. 1907, p. 125.

5. Grant Richards, *Housman, 1897–1936* (New York, Oxford Univ. Press, 1942), p. 74.

6. A.L.S., dated 2 May 1907, from 3 Lannoweth Rd., Penzance, P.U.L.

7. *Athenaeum*, 4 May 1907, p. 540; *Times Literary Supplement*, 3 May 1907, p. 143.

8. *Athenaeum*, 15 June 1907, p. 723.

9. A.L.S., to Richards, dated 17 Mar. 1907, from Lyndhurst Villa, Lyndhurst, Hants, P.U.L.

10. A.L.S., written from Penzance but headed "9 Fairmile Avenue/ Streatham/ S.W.," P.U.L.

11. The *Daily Chronicle*, 19 Apr. 1909.

12. A.L.S., to Richards, dated 27 July 1907, from 6 Coulson's Terrace, Penzance, P.U.L.

13. *Academy*, 20 July 1907, p. 692.

14. *Academy*, 27 July 1907, p. 734. An autograph copy of the letter and a covering letter, both dated 21 July 1907, from 6 Coulson's Terrace, Penzance, are in the P.U.L.

15. A.L.S., dated 7 Aug. 1907, from 6 Coulson's Terrace, P.U.L.

16. A.L.S., to Richards, dated 17 Feb. 1908, from 6 Coulson's Terrace, P.U.L.

17. A.Ls.S., to Richards, dated 25 Jan. 1908 and undated, from 6 Coulson's Terrace, P.U.L.

18. A.L.S., to Richards, dated only "February," from 6 Coulson's Terrace, P.U.L.

19. A.Ls.S., to Richards, dated 3 June 1906, from 9 Fairmile Ave., Streatham; and 29 Jan. 1908, from 6 Coulson's Terrace, P.U.L.

20. A.L.S., dated 19 June 1907, from 6 Coulson's Terrace, P.U.L.

21. A.L.S., to Richards, dated 28 Dec. 1907, from 6 Coulson's Terrace, P.U.L.

22. A.L.S., dated 31 Dec. 1907, from 6 Coulson's Terrace, P.U.L.

23. A.L.S., to Richards, dated 28 Apr. 1908, from 6 Coulson's Terrace, P.U.L.

24. Richards, *Author Hunting*, pp. 221–2.

25. A.L.S., dated 28 Apr. 1908, from 6 Coulson's Terrace, P.U.L.

26. *Mammon and His Message*, p. xiii.

27. Priscilla Thouless, *Modern Poetic Drama*, p. 111.

28. Compare Eric Bentley on August Strindberg in *The Playwright as Thinker* (New York, Reynal & Hitchcock, 1946), p. 198.

29. *Mammon and His Message*, pp. 141–2.

30. Ibid., p. 57.

31. P. 89.

32. Thouless, p. 101.

33. *Mammon and His Message*, p. 152.

34. *Athenaeum*, 22 Aug. 1908, pp. 202–3.

35. The *Guardian* (London), 16 Sept. 1908.

36. The *Glasgow Herald*, 18 June 1908.

37. The *Guardian* (London), 16 Sept. 1908.

38. *Times Literary Supplement*, 14 May 1908, p. 156.

39. *Bookman* (London), July 1908, p. 151.

40. A.Ls.S., to Richards, dated 17, 25 Jan. and 24 Apr. 1908, from 6 Coulson's Terrace, P.U.L.

41. A.L.S., to Richards, dated 20 July 1908, from 6 Coulson's Terrace, P.U.L.

42. A.L.S., dated 24 Apr. 1908, from 6 Coulson's Terrace, P.U.L.

43. A.L.S., to Richards, dated 20 July 1908, from 6 Coulson's Terrace, P.U.L.

44. A.L.S., dated 24 Apr. 1908, from 6 Coulson's Terrace, P.U.L.

45. A.L.S., to Richards, dated 11 Aug. 1908, from 6 Coulson's Terrace, P.U.L.

46. *The Testament of John Davidson* (London, Grant Richards, 1908), p. 11.

47. A.L.S., dated only "Saturday," from 6 Coulson's Terrace, P.U.L.

48. A.L.S., dated 27 Oct. 1908, from 6 Coulson's Terrace, P.U.L.

49. *The Testament of John Davidson,* p. 28.

50. Ibid., pp. 46, 50.

51. P. 76.

52. See Bush, *Mythology and the Romantic Tradition,* pp. 465–8.

53. *The Testament of John Davidson,* pp. 139–41.

54. Bush, pp. 466, 468.

55. See the *Academy,* 7 Nov., pp. 439–40; 14 Nov., pp. 461–3; 21 Nov., pp. 490–1; 5 Dec., pp. 535–6; 12 Dec. 1908, p. 557; and the *Star,* 1 Dec. 1908.

56. A.L.S., dated 13 Nov. 1908, from 6 Coulson's Terrace, P.U.L.

57. *Saturday Review,* 15 May 1909, p. 623.

58. Eric Bentley, *A Century of Hero-Worship, a Study of the Idea of Heroism in Carlyle and Nietzsche* (Philadelphia and New York, J. B. Lippincott Co., 1944), p. 104.

59. The *Bristol Evening News,* 29 Mar. 1909.

60. A.L.S., to Richards, dated 17 Aug. 1908, from 6 Coulson's Terrace, P.U.L.

61. Letter-press copy of a letter, dated 1 Sept. 1908, in the Library of the University of Illinois.

62. A.MS.S., undated, P.U.L.

63. The information on Davidson's various publication proposals is drawn from a series of autograph manuscripts in the P.U.L.

64. A.MS., initialed, dated 12 Feb. 1909, P.U.L.

65. A.MS., initialed, undated, P.U.L.

66. A.L.S., dated 19 Feb. 1907, from 6 Coulson's Terrace, P.U.L.

67. A.MS., initialed, undated, P.U.L.

68. Letter-press copy of a letter, dated 16 Nov. 1908, in the Library of the University of Illinois.

69. A.L.S., dated 27 Jan. 1909, from 6 Coulson's Terrace, P.U.L.

70. *Saturday Review,* 15 May 1909, pp. 623–5.

71. See James Elroy Flecker, "John Davidson: Realist," *Monthly Review,* July 1905, pp. 36–49; reprinted in J. E. Flecker, *Collected Prose* (London, G. Bell & Sons, 1920), pp. 189–215.

72. *Saturday Review,* 15 May 1909, p. 624.

73. Filson Young, *Fortnightly Review,* 1 Jan. 1909, pp. 140–9.

74. A.L.S., to Richards, dated 17 Feb. 1908, from 6 Coulson's Terrace, P.U.L.

75. A.L.S., to Richards, dated 20 Feb. 1908, from 6 Coulson's Terrace, P.U.L.

76. A.MS., initialed, dated 18 Mar. 1909, P.U.L.

77. *Saturday Review*, 15 May 1909, p. 624.

78. The first, "Rain in the New Forest," appeared in the *Westminster Gazette*, 3 Apr. 1909, p. 3. The manuscripts of the unfinished poems, "Brockenhurst Station" and "III Southampton West," are in the P.U.L.

79. A.L.S., to Richards, dated 2 Mar. 1909, from 6 Coulson's Terrace, P.U.L.

80. See Young, *Fortnightly Review*, 1 Jan. 1909, pp. 136–52; A. S. Mories, "The Religious Significance of John Davidson," *Westminster Review*, July 1913, pp. 75–85; and Wenley, ed., *Poems by John Davidson*, pp. vii–xv.

81. Young, *Fortnightly Review*, 1 Jan. 1909, p. 139.

82. Ibid.

83. *A Random Itinerary* (London and Boston, Elkin Mathews & John Lane, 1893), p. 184.

84. Young, *Fortnightly Review*, 1 Jan. 1909, p. 140.

85. Ibid., p. 141.

86. Quoted by Alfred Werner, "The Author of the 'Lorelei' Speaks on Art," *Art News*, Sept. 1956, p. 53.

CHAPTER 10

Heresy and the Tradition

1. By Charles W. Bledsoe, "John Davidson: The Don Quixote of Materialism," unpublished Princeton University Senior Essay, 1934.

2. Epilogue, *Mammon and His Message*, pp. 173, 161.

3. Ibid., p. 161.

4. P. 164.

5. Introduction, *The Theatrocrat*, p. 76.

6. Dedication to the Peers Temporal, *The Testament of John Davidson*, p. 31.

7. *The Theatrocrat*, p. 32.

8. *Mammon and His Message*, p. 150.

9. *The Theatrocrat*, pp. 74–5.

10. Ibid., p. 77.

11. P. 67.

12. " 'Irony,' " *Speaker*, 22 Apr. 1899, p. 455; reprinted as "Thoughts on Irony," *The Man Forbid*, pp. 133–4.

13. For Davidson's original essay entitled "Pre-Shakespearianism," Q's "Literary Causeries" attacking Davidson's position, letters to the editor, and Davidson's replies to Q and others, see the *Speaker*: 28 Jan., pp. 107–8; 4 Feb., pp. 139–40, 153–4; 11 Feb., pp. 178–9; 18 Feb., pp. 206, 207–8; 25 Feb., pp. 232–3; 4 Mar., p. 260; 18 Mar., p. 316; 25 Mar., p. 346; 1 Apr., p. 371;

8 Apr., p. 398; 15 Apr., p. 426; 22 Apr., p. 455; 6 May 1899, p. 523. Edited portions of Davidson's essay are reprinted in *A Rosary*, pp. 35-9, and *The Man Forbid*, pp. 33-7; excerpts from his replies of 4 Mar. and 22 Apr., in *The Man Forbid*, pp. 133-4.

14. *The Theatrocrat*, pp. 25-6.

15. *Mammon and His Message*, p. 171.

16. Eric Bentley, *A Century of Hero-Worship*, p. 156.

17. "Knight-Errantry," *Speaker*, 19 Mar. 1898, pp. 359-60; edited version reprinted in *A Rosary*, pp. 102-11.

18. *Mammon and His Message*, p. 149.

19. *The Testament of John Davidson*, p. 18.

20. *A Random Itinerary*, pp. 185-6.

21. Bentley, p. 260.

22. "On Poetry," *Holiday and Other Poems*, p. 156.

23. *Mammon and His Message*, p. 150.

24. A.L.S., dated 23 Jan. 1903, from 9 Fairmile Ave., Streatham, Add. MS. 45291, ff. 109-10, B.M.

25. "The Art of Poetry," *Speaker*, 4 Feb. 1899, pp. 153-4; reprinted in *The Man Forbid*, pp. 125-30.

26. "*Tête-à-Tête*. Froude. Carlyle," *Speaker*, 17 June 1899, pp. 689-90; reprinted in *The Man Forbid*, pp. 169-80.

27. "Pre-Shakespearianism," *Speaker*, 28 Jan. 1899, pp. 107-8.

28. "The Art of Poetry," pp. 153-4.

29. "Another View of Mr. Meredith's Odes," *Saturday Review*, 19 Nov. 1898, pp. 664-5; *Sentences and Paragraphs*, pp. 115, 1, 13.

30. "*Tête-à-Tête*. Froude. Carlyle," pp. 689-90; *The Man Forbid*, p. 148; *Holiday*, p. 156.

31. "Style and Stylism," *A Rosary*, p. 25.

32. "A Study of Ben Jonson," *Academy*, 23 Nov. 1889, pp. 331-2.

33. "William Hazlitt, Essayist and Critic," *Academy*, 7 Sept. 1889, p. 146; edited excerpts reprinted in *Sentences and Paragraphs*, pp. 113-15.

34. A.L.S., dated 29 Oct. 1898, from St. Winifred's, Fairmile Ave., Streatham, Ashley MS. B.572, B.M.

35. A.L.S., to Richards, undated, from Glenfaulds, Rothesay, P.U.L.

36. A.Ls.S., to Richards, undated and dated 13 Dec. 1903, from Glenfaulds, Rothesay, P.U.L.

37. The *Manchester Courier*, 29 Mar. 1909.

38. See "Quackery," *Freethinker*, 11 Aug., p. 497; " 'What Price God?,' " 18 Aug., pp. 513-14; " 'What Price God?'—II," 25 Aug., pp. 529-30; "Mr. John Davidson's Position," 22 Sept. 1907, pp. 593-4.

39. *Freethinker*, 25 Aug. 1907, pp. 529-30.

40. *Freethinker*, 22 Sept. 1907, pp. 593-4.

41. Mories, "The Religious Significance of John Davidson," *Westminister Review*, July 1913, p. 83.

42. A.L.S., correspondent unknown, dated 28 Mar. 1904, from 9 Fairmile Ave., Streatham, P.U.L.

43. A.L.S., dated 27 Apr. 1897, from the Grosvenor Club, London; formerly in the possession of the late Mr. Weygandt, who quotes a shorter excerpt in his *The Time of Yeats*, p. 56. An enclosure accompanying the letter furnishes factual information about the early plays and poems but no personal revelations.

44. Stoddart, "Interview with John Davidson," *Bookman* (New York), Mar. 1895, pp. 85–7.

45. *A Rosary*, p. 163.

46. "*Tête-à-Tête*. Mrs. Scambler. Maud Emblem," *Speaker*, 19 Aug. 1899, p. 182; edited excerpts reprinted in *A Rosary*, pp. 113–17.

47. *The Theatrocrat*, pp. 13–14.

48. Stoddart, "Interview with John Davidson," p. 86.

49. Prologue, *Godfrida*, p. 3.

50. "Chanctonbury Ring," *Speaker* (Supp.), 30 Apr. 1898, pp. 553–4; excerpts reprinted in *A Rosary*, pp. 24, 164–7; and in its entirety in *The Man Forbid*, pp. 195–204. See also "Ibsen Himself," *Speaker*, 25 June 1898, pp. 790–1; edited excerpts reprinted in *A Rosary*, pp. 133–4, 167–74.

51. Weygandt, pp. 24, 27.

52. See Hayim Fineman, *John Davidson: A Study of the Relation of His Ideas to His Poetry* (Philadelphia, Univ. of Pennsylvania, 1916), *passim;* Gertrud von Petzold, *John Davidson, und sein geistiges Werden unter dem Einfluss Nietzsches, passim;* and E. J. O'Brien, ed., *The Man Forbid*, pp. 7, 15.

53. See R. M. Wenley, "Nietzsche—Traffics and Discoveries," *Monist*, Jan. 1921, pp. 133–49; Wenley, ed., *Poems by John Davidson*, pp. xviii–xix; Weygandt, *The Time of Yeats*, pp. 56–7; and B. Ifor Evans, *English Poetry in the Later Nineteenth Century* (London, Methuen & Co., 1933), p. 291.

54. See Geneviève Bianquis, *Nietzsche en France* (Paris, Universitaires de France, 1929), *passim;* and Brinton, *Nietzsche*, pp. 172–9.

55. Wenley, "Nietzsche—Traffics and Discoveries," pp. 135–6.

56. Lester, "Nietzsche and Davidson," *Journal of the History of Ideas*, June 1957, p. 420.

57. Ibid., pp. 416–18. For de Wyzewa's article, see "Littérature étrangère: Frédéric Nietsche, le dernier métaphysicien," *Revue Politique et Littéraire, Revue Bleue*, 7 Nov. 1891, pp. 586–92.

58. *Speaker*, 28 Nov. 1891, p. 641–2; edited excerpts reprinted in *Sentences and Paragraphs*, pp. 72–83.

59. Lester, "Nietzsche and Davidson," pp. 419–20.

60. "The Poetic Disciple of Nietzsche," the *Daily Chronicle*, 23 May 1902; compare Lester, p. 420.

61. *The Triumph of Mammon*, p. 103.

62. Wenley, *Poems by John Davidson*, p. xix.

63. George Bernard Shaw, *John Bull's Other Island and Major Barbara* (New York, Brentano's, 1918), p. 164.

64. William K. Clifford, *Lectures and Essays*, Leslie Stephen and Frederick Pollack, eds. (2 vols., London, Macmillan & Co., 1879).

65. Somervell, *English Thought in the Nineteenth Century*, p. 136.

66. Friedrich Brie, *Imperialistische Strömungen in der Englischen Literatur* (Halle, Saale, M. Niemeyer, 1928), p. 247.

67. A.L.S., dated 24 Dec. 1900, from 9 Fairmile Ave., Streatham, B.C.U.L.L.

68. John Adam Cramb, *The Origins and Destiny of Imperial Britain* (2d ed., London, John Murray, 1915), p. 91.

69. "Mr. Davidson and 'Irony,'" *Speaker*, 15 Apr. 1899, p. 426; "'Irony,'" *Speaker*, 22 Apr. 1899, p. 455.

70. Cramb, pp. 199, 209.

71. A.L.S., dated 31 Dec. 1900, from 9 Fairmile Ave., Streatham. B.C.U.L.L.

72. Weygandt, *The Time of Yeats*, pp. 54, 64.

73. Flecker, *Collected Prose*, pp. 190–1, 207.

74. See O'Brien, ed., *The Man Forbid*, p. 11; Weygandt, pp. 218, 426; Richards, *Author Hunting*, p. 73; Gilbert K. Chesterton, *The Autobiography of G. K. Chesterton* (New York, Sheed & Ward, 1936), pp. 91–2; and Herbert Palmer, *Post-Victorian Poetry* (London, J. M. Dent & Sons, 1938), pp. 61, 167–8.

75. O'Brien, p. 7.

76. Bush, *Mythology and the Romantic Tradition*, p. 524.

77. Ronald C. Macfie, *Odes and Other Poems* (London, John Murray, 1919), p. 105; reprinted from the *Poetry Review*, Stephen Phillips, ed., Mar. 1913, pp. 109–12.

78. "Sonnet of Heaven and Hell," *Literary Digest*, 27 July 1929, p. 33.

79. Herbert Spencer, *First Principles* (London, Williams & Norgate, 1862), p. 123.

INDEX

INDEX 535

Counterdecadence, 286, 464. *See also* Activists
Courbet, Gustave, 237
Courtney, William L., 391, 412 n., 434
Cowper, William, 185, 224
Crackanthorpe, Hubert, 172, 244
Craig, Gordon, 88, 335, 390, 434
Cramb, John Adam, 270, 287, 348, 441, 484–89; *Origins and Destiny of Imperial Britain*, 484
Crewe, Robert O. A. Milnes-, Marquess of, 377, 381, 417
Critic, 290
Crockett, Alexander (JD's grandfather), 30
Crockett, Helen. *See* Davidson, Helen Crockett
Cromwell, Oliver, 466
Crosby, Harry, 254
Cust, H. J. C., 177 n.

Dadaists, 106, 254 n.
Daily Chronicle, 4, 151, 179, 303, 331, 348, 369, 370; JD contributes to, 137
Daily Mail, 4, 22, 365
Daily News, JD employed by, 138
Daily Telegraph, 22, 391
Dante Alighieri, 345, 355, 430; *The Divine Comedy*, 459
D'Arcy, Ella, 244
Darwin, Charles, 27, 39, 64, 74, 187, 275, 282, 339, 348, 444, 467, 480, 482
Darwinism, 79, 122, 161, 177, 269, 478, 486. *See also* Evolution
Daudet, Alphonse, *Sapho*, 356
Davidson, Alexander (JD's father), 30, 33, 193 n.
Davidson, Alexander (JD's son), 4, 8, 18, 19, 52
Davidson, Euphemia (JD's sister), 30
Davidson, George (JD's brother), 30, 193 n.
Davidson, Helen Crockett (JD's mother), 30–32
Davidson, Rev. J. D., 193 n.
Davidson, John: at Penzance, 1–28, 389–443; disappearance and death, 1–28; evidence of suicide, 8–15; fear of cancer, 9, 12, 13; discovery of body, 15–17; burial, 17–19; disputes over reputation and treatment of JD, 23–28; birth, 29; in Scotland, 29–62; parents, 30–32; residence in Glasgow, 32–33; father, 32–34; in school, 35, 36; early jobs, 35–36; first writings, 35, 38; attends Edinburgh University, 38–42; teaches at Alexander's Charity, 42–50; friendship with Nichol, 42–50; meets Swinburne, 46; teaches at Perth Academy, 51; other teaching posts, 51, 53; clerkship in thread firm, 51, 52; marriage, 51–52; wife's family, 51–52; birth of children, 52; begins to publish poems and plays, 54–62; favorite reading, 63; the Spasmodics, 99–112; self-portrayal in *Smith*, 127–29; life in London, 135–97; arrival in the city, 136–40; the Rhymers, 140–46; hostility between Yeats and, 146–50; friendship with Le Gallienne, 150–59; pub-

546 INDEX

Lester, John A., Jr., 340 n., 384 n., 476 n.
Lewis, Matthew G. ("Monk"), 410
L'Isle-Adam, Villiers de, 148
Lister, Joseph, 39
Living Age, JD contributes to, 137
Lloyd's Weekly, 10
Loch Ling, 37
Locke, W. L., 21
Lodge, Sir Oliver, 365
Loftus, Cissie, 297, 299, 300
London poets, 240–43
Longmans, publishers, 187
Lowell, Amy, 233
Lowenstein, F. E., 332 n.
Lucas, E. V., 381
Lucretius, 131, 257, 260 n., 261, 339, 392, 452, 479, 480 n.
Luke, G. R., 44
Lyceum Theater, London, 288, 306, 320, 322
Lyly, John, 63
Lyric Theater, Hammersmith, 291

McAlpin, Colin, *The Cross and the Crescent,* 296 n.
MacArthur, John (JD's father-in-law), 52
MacArthur, Margaret Cameron. *See* Davidson, Margaret MacArthur
MacArthur, Menzies Cameron (JD's mother-in-law), 51–52
M'Carthy, Justin H., *If I Were King,* 318 n., 319
MacColl, D. S., 171
McCormick, Sir William Symington, 377, 378, 379; JD invites Gosse to meet, 195
Macdonald, George, *Within and Without,* 104
Macfie, Ronald Campbell, 491
Mackail, J. W., 300
Mackay, Eric, 274 n.
Maclean, Evan, 40 n.
MacLehose, James, 47
Macleod, Fiona. *See* Sharp, William
Macmillan's Magazine, 431
Macpherson, James, "Ossian" poems, 105
Macaulay, Thomas Babington, 1st Lord, 160 n.
Madgewick, Houlston, and Co., binders, 375 n.
Maeterlinck, Maurice, 88, 291, 306, 335, 390; *Pelléas and Mélisande,* 300 n.
Magendie, François, 342
Mallarmé, Stéphane, 232
Mallock, William Hurrell, 412
Malory, Sir Thomas, 429; *Morte d'Arthur,* 323

YALE STUDIES IN ENGLISH

This volume is the one hundred and forty-eighth of the Yale Studies in English, founded by Albert Stanburrough Cook in 1898 and edited by him until his death in 1927. Tucker Brooke succeeded him as editor, and served until 1941, when Benjamin C. Nangle succeeded him.

The following volumes are still in print. Orders should be addressed to YALE UNIVERSITY PRESS, New Haven, Connecticut.